The Medi
English Landscape,
1000–1540

GRAEME J. WHITE

B L O O M S B U R Y
LONDON · NEW DELHI · NEW YORK · SYDNEY

Bloomsbury Academic

An imprint of Bloomsbury Publishing Plc

50 Bedford Square
London
WC1B 3DP
UK

175 Fifth Avenue
New York
NY 10010
USA

www.bloomsbury.com

First published 2012

British Library Cataloguing-in-Publication Data
A catalogue record for this book is available from the British Library.

ISBN: HB: 978-1-4411-3506-3
PB: 978-1-4411-3525-4

Library of Congress Cataloging-in-Publication Data
A catalog record for this book is available from the Library of Congress.

Typeset by Fakenham Prepress Solutions, Fakenham, Norfolk NR21 8NN
Printed and bound in India

The Medieval English Landscape, 1000–1540

To my students, 1971–2010

Contents

List of figures

Note on measurements and other conventions

Measurements are normally given according to the metric scale (kilometres, hectares, etc.) but imperial equivalents are shown where these were historically significant. Decimal as well as pre-decimal monetary values are indicated where necessary. Places referred to in the text are normally located by county the first time they are mentioned, except for the most prominent towns including those from which the county name is derived. The 'historic' counties are used for this purpose, except where this would clearly be unhelpful: for example, to place Ely within the 'Isle of Ely' (which merged with Cambridgeshire in 1965) would be of little benefit to a reader seeking it on a map.

Abbreviations

AG. HIST. REV.:   *Agricultural History Review.*

EC. HIST. REV.:   *Economic History Review*, 2nd series.

EHD: *English Historical Documents* [I, c.500–1042
                          (1979) D. Whitelock ed., 2nd edn., London: Eyre
                          Methuen; II, 1042–1189 (1981), D. C. Douglas
                          and G. W. Greenway (eds), 2nd edn., London: Eyre
                          Methuen; III, 1189–1327 (1975), H. Rothwell ed.,
                          London: Eyre and Spottiswoode; IV, 1327–1485
                          (1969), A. R. Myers ed., London: Eyre and
                          Spottiswoode; V, 1485–1558 (1967), C. H. Williams
                          ed. London: Eyre and Spottiswoode].

ITINERARY OF LELAND: *Leland's Itinerary in England and Wales* (1907), L.
                          Toulmin-Smith ed., London: Bell.

PR: *Pipe Roll* [31 Hen.I (1833), J. Hunter ed., Record
                          Commission; 2–4 Hen.II (1844), J. Hunter ed.,
                          Record Commission; 5 Hen. II onwards (from
                          1884), Pipe Roll Society].

RRAN, III: *Regesta Regum Anglo-Normannorum*, III (1968–
                          69), H. A. Cronne and R. H. C. Davis (eds), Oxford:
                          Clarendon Press.

VCH: *Victoria History of the Counties of England* (1900–,
                          in progress), several editors and publishers.

Foreword

As a sub-discipline, 'landscape history' is often said to have been born with the publication of W. G. Hoskins's brilliantly-crafted *The Making of the English Landscape* in 1955. Although this famously railed against the 'England of the arterial by-pass, treeless and stinking of diesel oil' – along with much else belonging to the mid-twentieth century – the fact that national car ownership more than doubled during the 1950s made this a subject whose time had come. There was now an opportunity previously enjoyed only by a small minority for people to travel where and when they wanted in search of the legacies of the past – and no longer to be entirely dependent on what experts had decided should be presented to them as historically significant. The greatest appeal of landscape history is its accessibility to everyone and, accordingly, this book is the latest in a long line inspired by Hoskins which have sought to provide an historical context for features we live with every day.

While the subject can be defined as the history of people's impact on the physical landscape, there is some ambivalence over whether this should embrace features no longer apparent above ground or whether the focus should be on what can still be seen – in however modified a form – to this day. On the one hand there is a risk of making the subject too esoteric, the preserve of specialist investigators. On the other there is the danger of skewing the evidence according to the accidents of survival, so giving a misleading impression of our ancestors' experience. The approach taken here is to emphasize the surviving landscape as an historical source wherever possible, but not to ignore the fuller picture which can only be discerned through archaeological excavation or other advanced research. One of the joys of this subject is the encouragement it gives to the exercise of historical imagination: anyone whose local high street has a series of shops with narrow frontages – successors to burgage plots – or has to drive a car through a market place crowded with stallholders because the street pattern demands it, is experiencing something in common with our medieval forebears even if there is nothing obviously medieval on show. The experience is all the richer if there is also an understanding of what once graced the scene.

There are, of course, limits to the subject as well, quite apart from emphases within this book derived from the author's own interests. A study of the historic landscape focuses on the relationships between features made or modified by men and women – broadly interpreted but excluding the natural terrain. The focus is squarely on 'outdoors': the interiors of buildings figure only occasionally, usually to explain what can be seen from outside. As for the geographical coverage attempted in the pages which follow, it will not take any reader long to notice that certain parts of the country – Cheshire especially – receive more than their fair share of attention, both in the text and as illustrations. After 40 years pursuing this subject, I like to think that I have some familiarity with most corners of England, but there seems little point in neglecting what I know best. Despite the sterling efforts of several scholars based in the region, the north west in general, and Cheshire in particular, remain under-represented in surveys of the English landscape, so this attempt to redress the balance will, I hope, be forgiven.

It was an honour to be invited to write this book. The invitation came before the turn of the millennium but I was then heavily involved with the project whereby Chester College progressed to become the University of Chester. That goal having been achieved in 2005, further work for the University at a senior level prevented the book's completion until after my retirement. I must therefore express sincere gratitude to the publishers for their patience and forbearance. Over the years I have learned an enormous amount, and received much encouragement, from a succession of distinguished scholars, among whom I would single out Vivian Fisher and Otto Smail of a now-departed generation of medievalists, and more recently Christopher Taylor, Christopher Dyer and Edmund King. For their friendship and guidance over the years, and in most cases for advice on particular aspects of this book, I am very grateful to Paul Booth, John Doran, Diana Dunn, Peter Gaunt, Nick Higham, Philip Higson, Rob Liddiard, Rachel Swallow and Tom Driver, although it goes without saying that responsibility for any factual errors or for what might be considered misinterpretations is entirely my own. Thanks are also due to those who gave permission for the reproduction of illustrations to supplement those from my own collection, especially Mike Derbyshire who kindly supplied Figure 7; these are acknowledged at the appropriate points. Above all, I should like to thank my wife Heather for sharing my enthusiasm for landscape history and for her many insightful comments and suggestions; along with my daughter Elizabeth and son Benedict, she has been unfailingly supportive. However, my last words here must go to the members of the Chester Society for Landscape History, of which I am proud to be President, and to all the students whom it has been a privilege to teach, first in the Workers' Educational Association in Cambridgeshire from 1971 to 1977 and thereafter at Chester College, now the University of Chester. It has been a delight to share the subject with them, as a mutual learning experience, and if this book helps them, and others like them, to enjoy, explore and understand some aspects of the medieval English landscape, it will have succeeded in its purpose.

1

Continuity and change in the medieval English landscape

In the year 1000, England had been a united kingdom for less than a century. In 927, Athelstan king of Wessex and Mercia, the grandson of Alfred the Great, had conquered Northumbria, so extinguishing the last segment of independent Scandinavian rule. There had been periods after this when more than one king ruled in England, but they had not lasted long. By the turn of the millennium, the latest king of the Wessex line, Ethelred 'the Unready', was engaged in endless campaigning and diplomacy to preserve the frontiers of that kingdom and extend his influence over his neighbours. To the west lay the politically fragmented country of Wales, the border with which had been defined by the eighth-century linear earthwork Offa's Dyke from Basingwerk on the Dee to a point just east of the Wye estuary.[1] The northern end of this frontier would, however, be pushed eastwards by the close of the twelfth century, eventually to be fixed roughly as we know it today by Henry VIII's Act of Union with Wales in 1536. To the north, Scotland was also divided in 1000, both politically and in terms of the identity of its constituent peoples, although it was all to come under the control of Malcolm II – conventionally regarded as the first king of the whole of Scotland – within the following two decades. Here, an eastern frontier along the Tweed and a western one at the Solway Firth were not to be established – by force on both sides – until 1016 and 1092 respectively, and even then there could be no guarantee of their future stability.[2] As that pioneer of landscape history, W. G. Hoskins, put it, 'this border country belies its peaceful appearance today. Beneath its clouds are the scars of centuries of warfare and skirmishing.'[3]

England in 1000 was a country whose population had been growing steadily for several centuries but may still have been some way short of the level reached in Roman times. Only one person in ten lived in towns and there was a heavy preponderance towards the east and south of the country. Among the iconic structures associated with the medieval English landscape, castles had not yet arrived and monasteries were relatively few in number – although those which existed were exceptionally well-endowed, some with incomes which Domesday Book would later show to be comparable to the riches enjoyed by leading favourites of William the Conqueror.[4] Parish churches were, as yet, mostly small and timber-built but they were certainly proliferating, and those serving rural settlements were often witness to an important process of transition, as nucleated villages and open arable fields farmed in common were coming to replace dispersed hamlets with individually farmed enclosed fields: but this was a phenomenon which had neither run its full course by 1000, nor would ever characterize large parts of England.

If the year 1000 can be taken for convenience as a starting point for the period covered by this book, 1540 may fairly be treated as its end. All periodization is of course open to challenge,[5] but – collectively – the cultural changes associated with the Renaissance, seen for example in the development of new architectural styles, the religious changes initiated by the Reformation, the secularization of landownership following the dissolution of the monasteries, and the governmental changes occasioned by shifts in the balance of power between crown, council and House of Commons, all mark the years after 1540 as part of a new 'post-medieval' era which lies beyond our scope. In the momentous decade which had gone before, parliament had enacted Henry VIII's royal supremacy over the Church in England, had legislated for the suppression of the monasteries – by then numbering over 700 in England – and had formally united England and Wales. Open field farming – though still widespread – was in retreat, as arable fields were being enclosed and converted to permanent pasture, a process sometimes accompanied by the abandonment of their parent settlements. Castles had come and gone as major defensible structures, though several remained as gaols, hunting lodges and administrative centres, alongside the unfortified country houses which were coming to be built. Parish churches had become ubiquitous and in almost every case had grown grander in size and style as the middle ages had advanced: nearly all of them in stone and most towering above their local communities physically and psychologically. There were more bridges and better roads than at any time since the Roman occupation. Yet the total population was not dissimilar to that of 1000: having escalated until the early fourteenth century, it had then experienced a prolonged slump following the Black Death and seems once again to have been somewhere between 2 and 3 million – although 15% or more now lived in towns and London had witnessed extraordinary growth to at least 60,000, five or six times the number estimated for the period of the Norman Conquest.[6]

The political history of the intervening five centuries had revolved around two principal issues: first, the relationship between England and her neighbours, to north, west and south east, and second the extent to which power over the kingdom as a whole should be shared between the monarch and some form of 'representative assembly'. One potential issue which never became the force it might have done was the identity of England and 'the English'. The divisive legacy of 1066 – that of a Norman/French élite ruling over the subjugated English masses – eventually disappeared in the thirteenth century, following the loss of Normandy to France in 1204 and the triumph of the English language as the mother tongue even of the aristocracy.[7] As for a 'united kingdom of England', there were to be moments when it looked as if it might split into separate political units: in 1069, for example, when rebellion in the north prompted William the Conqueror's terrible 'Harrying' in reprisal, and again in 1149, when a country already divided by civil war faced invasion from the Scots.[8] As late as 1405, three rebels against Henry IV optimistically partitioned England and Wales between them in a 'Tripartite Indenture'. But these turned out to be fleeting affairs. Essentially, England retained its political cohesion throughout the period – troops and taxes could be raised in the south to assist in the defence of the north – despite there being some local adjustments to the frontiers from time to time and notwithstanding the existence of a few regions, notably Cheshire and Durham for much of the period, where the normal processes of royal government were modified so as to respect the privileges of a local potentate. Although the landscape of England was infinitely varied, politically the country was unified, in a way that medieval France, Germany, Spain and Italy were not. Local and regional affinities were certainly strong in medieval England, but there was general acceptance that these belonged within the context of one overarching kingdom. For the development of the English landscape, all this mattered. The king's journeys, the intermarriages between noble families, the selection of clergy for senior posts: all were conducted on a country-wide basis, contributing to a network of shared information about farming practices, building styles and skilled personnel across the country as a whole. Regional variations abounded, as anyone who crosses the country today through different terrain and geology can readily perceive, but so did connections between landscapes created in different parts of the kingdom.

But if England was formally united, it was hardly ever politically isolated. For most of the reign of Cnut (1016–35), the kingdom was part of a Scandinavian empire embracing Denmark and Norway. Had Cnut's dynasty become established long-term, these Scandinavian links might have significantly shaped England's political and cultural development, with manifestations in architecture, for example, which had more in common with Norway than with France. In the event, his line died out in 1042 and the next conqueror, William duke of Normandy, ruled kingdom and duchy together and went on to establish overlordship of Scotland and Wales. Through many vicissitudes, a political attachment to territory in France was to persist until Calais was eventually lost in 1558. Within the British Isles, Lordship of Ireland was added by Henry II in the 1170s, and although most of the country beyond what came to be known as the Pale (the area around the east coast ports) was subsequently left to its own devices, Wales and Scotland demanded more sustained attention; their bequests to the landscape include the fine series of castles built to secure Edward I's conquest of North Wales and the fortified pele towers which arose in the vulnerable northern shires after the Scots success at Bannockburn in 1314. Eventually, Wales would provide the base from which Henry VII launched his successful bid for the throne in 1485, the prelude to his son's Act of Union. In turn, a decisive English victory over the Scots at Flodden in 1513 would bring some peace for a generation, and a series of dynastic manoeuvres would unite the crowns of Scotland and England in the person of James VI and I in 1603.

The conduct of war and the question of how it should be paid for were issues which obliged medieval kings regularly to consult their subjects. The emergence of representative assemblies of 'the community of England' can be traced to a period well before *Magna Carta* in 1215, and by the late thirteenth century meetings of parliament – increasingly with members of the 'commons' (local communities) alongside individually summoned lords – had come to be accepted as a necessary part of the fabric of government. Edward I had the sense to use parliament constructively, encouraging the receipt of petitions from the Commons and the passing of legislation which dealt with social and economic issues. Some of this had direct relevance to the development of the landscape, such as the second Statute of Westminster in 1285, which allowed lords to erect a windmill and buildings for sheep and cattle on the common pasture, and provided for redress against those from neighbouring settlements who broke down enclosures made on the common. Parliament was to figure from hereon as an essential element in the government of England, to the point where, at the very end of our period, Henry VIII was careful to involve it in the establishment of his royal supremacy over the Church in England and in changes to the lawful succession to the throne.[9]

An unfolding political narrative, dominated by England's relations with her neighbours and by successive kings' dealings with lords and commons, forms the background to our story. But beyond these great events, what were the underlying forces which shaped the development of the English landscape in these five and a half centuries? Three themes stand out, and we shall encounter them repeatedly in the pages which follow. One is the impact of the rise and fall in population, which imposed pressures on resources differing in intensity from one century to another. In recent decades, some historians have argued that there has been too much emphasis on population trends as drivers of change, and have seen the commercialization of society, especially from the late twelfth century, as of at least comparable importance. But the proliferation of markets, the growth of towns, the increased activity in mining and manufacturing all took place in a context in which rising population provided a crucial stimulus to supply and demand. It is true that during the late-medieval slump in population commercial activity did not collapse; in some respects, it was energized by the better living standards many people now enjoyed. This is a warning against over-emphasizing the significance of population trends to the exclusion of other factors. But the fundamental relationship between size of population and the landscape which supported it remains very important. Alongside this theme is that of the imposition of power over the landscape, power exercised by different groups of people at different times but power to determine change – or lack of change – according to the interests of those in control. This is a story which involves not only the obviously powerful – kings, bishops, barons, abbots – but also the mass of the population acting both collectively to manage their surroundings and individually in the hope of improving their families' or their communities' fortunes. The third theme is the importance of technological progress. Our medieval forebears often displayed a healthy scepticism towards techno-logical advances, which for all their ingenuity could take decades, even centuries, to supplant traditional methods: spinning wheels, fulling mills, gunpowder all had their detractors, largely because their end-products were less consistently reliable than those generated by conventional means. But when and where they were eventually adopted, new technologies brought significant changes to the environment – in building, farming and industrial activity. It would of course be wrong to adopt a deterministic approach to any of these forces; essentially, they interplayed with each other to produce results which, at a local level, were unpredictable.[10] But they recur time and again, and it is appropriate here to give brief consideration to each of them in turn.

There is broad – though not complete – agreement among scholars over the trends in medieval population, but considerable disagreement over what the size of that population might have been. Archaeological evidence suggests that by the seventh century the population had begun to recover from a prolonged decline in the late-Roman and immediate post-Roman periods which had seen it fall to between 1 and 2 million by A.D. 500. Although England then suffered a visitation of bubonic plague in the 660s and again in the 680s, its impact seems to have been temporary, and freedom from plague for several centuries thereafter allowed a sustained period of population growth.[11] If growth continued from hereon until the Norman Conquest – as seems apparent from the evidence of more intensive farming and settlement, without any obvious catastrophic break – there is a problem in reconciling this with the figures suggested by the first useful document, Domesday Book of 1086: for here, too, the data has been taken to point to a population total somewhere around 2 million. Either the archaeologists' figure for 500 is too high or the historians' figure for 1086 is too low, but it is worth pausing to reflect upon the way in which the Domesday total is achieved. The total number of recorded individuals is 268,984 in the countryside, made up of 109,230 villeins, 81,849 bordars, 13,553 freemen, and so on, to which a figure which can only be estimated for boroughs has to be added. There are a host of problems with these figures: for a start, it is impossible to define what each category meant with any precision, and we can be sure that the Domesday investigators lacked consistency in their application of terms. On a literal reading of Domesday Book, there were only two mill-keepers, ten shepherds and 23 'men with gardens' in the whole of England, when in reality these people must normally have been counted in with one of the general groupings (usually as villeins).[12] A more serious issue, however, is the extent of under-recording in Domesday: not only the households of those who were entered (which probably demands a multiplier of five) but members of religious houses and those who lived in certain towns (notably London) and shires (in the north) which were omitted from the survey. Above all, it seems clear that, at least in some places, only a portion of the peasantry was actually counted. This is apparent, for example, from estate surveys of Burton Abbey about 1114 and 1126, covering various manors in Derbyshire and Staffordshire, which include numerous *censarii* (rent-paying peasants) omitted altogether from the equivalent Domesday entries. All this makes Domesday Book a very shaky foundation on which to rest statements of total population, but a figure somewhat in excess of the conventional 2 million seems plausible. If the real total was at least 2.5 million, possibly nearer 3 million, it would be easier to match this up with the archaeological evidence of a steady recovery in population from the sixth century onwards.[13]

Thereafter, estate surveys, rentals and the government enquiry which produced the Hundred Rolls of 1279 all demonstrate a burgeoning population. Cautious estimates of population totals for villages in Cambridgeshire, Essex, Leicestershire and west Yorkshire suggest a population density in 1300 very close to – sometimes greater than – that which pertained in the rural areas of these shires at the time of the 1801 census. If towns over 5,000 population are subtracted from the 1801 census total, we are left with an English rural population at that time of 6.3 million: a figure which may not be far from the mark for 1300 as well.[14] The twelfth and thirteenth centuries witnessed the intensification of farming and settlement, the expansion of cultivated areas, and the proliferation of new commercial centres – all tending to increase the incomes of lords able to spend on impressive domestic, fortified or ecclesiastical buildings. But this was achieved in circumstances of high birth and death rates; over the medieval period as a whole, only about half those born reached the age of 18 and only 10% passed 60. And it was not to last. On the Bishop of Winchester's extensive estates in southern England an appreciable rise in mortality is apparent from the number of heriots (inheritance fines) paid by peasants, which experienced notable peaks in 1272, 1289 and 1297.[15] This – together with a reduction in the amount of the bishop's land dedicated to producing food for the market – suggests that the population may have stopped growing in parts of this region before the thirteenth century was over. Thereafter, most of the country seems to have suffered from a series of catastrophes, including harvests ranging from poor to disastrous in seven of the 14 years between 1308 and 1321 and outbreaks of animal disease severely hitting stocks of sheep in 1313–17 and of cattle in 1319–21. Suffering was exacerbated by the very heavy tax burden imposed on the peasantry, particularly to pay for war against the Scots, and by the effects of that war on the northern shires in the shape of border raiding: factors which have contributed to debate over how far this was more than just a 'subsistence' crisis based on population outstripping resources. What is less controversial is its immediate impact: a dramatic increase in mortality – with heriots on the Winchester estates rocketing to over twice their normal level at times – and a fall in the total population of the country in the decade following 1314 of the order of 10%.[16]

The trend of population in the second quarter of the fourteenth century is by no means certain. There is evidence of abandoned land especially in the more arable south and east, to set against a continuing search for new farmland in the more pastoral north and west.[17] As magnets for those prepared to travel in search of new opportunities, urban centres appear to have been less affected than rural ones: by 1340 London had become one of the largest towns in Europe and was attracting immigrants from far and wide.[18] But nowhere escaped the Black Death, an epidemic of bubonic combined with pneumonic plague which reached England in the summer of 1348 via the port of Melcombe Regis near Weymouth and then spread rapidly to the whole of the country, before running its course early in 1350. Estimates of mortality vary, but the best modern opinion suggests somewhere between 40% and 50% over the two years from summer 1348.[19] Following such a catastrophic fall in population, one might expect substantial wage increases in response to a shortage of labour, a significant decline in rents and prices to reflect a slump in market-demand for land and goods, and easement of the terms of unfree peasant tenure because of difficulties in attracting tenants. All this came to pass, but not consistently so until there had been further serious visitations of the Black Death, especially in 1361 and 1375. Thereafter, the population remained in slump throughout the fifteenth century and by 1524–25, on the evidence of taxation data, stood at less than 2.5 million; an authoritative study, based on parish registers (which began in 1538) and back-projection from the 1871 census puts the population of England in 1541 slightly higher at 2.8 million. In a few places (such as Devon where tin working, cloth making and a long coastline offered a variety of employment opportunities) population may have begun to rise again from about 1480, but recent opinion is that on a national scale there was no sustained recovery before the 1530s. The reasons for this prolonged trough in the population graph remain controversial – probably a combination of high mortality (through endemic, and occasionally epidemic, disease) and low fertility (partly because more women entered the labour market) – but there is little doubt over its effects on the living standards of the majority, as real wages reached levels in the fifteenth century not seen again till late-Victorian times. Commentators bemoaned the fact that humble families were dressing as well as their social superiors and the consumption of meat, fuel and better-quality bread and ale all increased.[20] This is not of course the same as an improvement in the 'quality of life': bereavement remained a frequent experience and in many places it became a struggle to keep communal farming going, with too few people to till the land. But there can be no doubt that, in social and economic terms, the Black Death and its immediate aftermath must still be seen as one of the great 'turning points' in English history.

This applies to the landscape as well. The late fourteenth, fifteenth and early sixteenth centuries were a period of retreat from less favourable areas alongside depopulation and desertion of settlements even in long-cultivated lowlands. There was a widespread switch from arable to less labour-intensive pastoral farming – with sheep-rearing particularly significant – and the progressive enclosure of many open arable fields, as holdings became consolidated and landlords and tenants alike sought the opportunity to farm independently. In turn, some lords clearly suffered from the reduced incomes yielded by their estates, with predictable consequences for both secular and ecclesiastical building schemes. Yet through good luck, good management, enterprise or opportunism, there were always some individuals and corporate bodies capable of 'bucking the trend'. An episcopal visitation of Leicester Abbey in 1440, for example, noted that the monastic buildings had been extensively rebuilt, at a time when it is known that yearly income from sale of corn was falling from £573 (in 1341) to £240 (in 1477). One has only to look at the large number of parish churches in England which, in whole or in part, display the features of the late-medieval Perpendicular style to appreciate that there was still plenty of work to be had in the building trade.[21]

So the rise and fall in population, and the impact of these trends upon resources, is only part of the story. Much depended upon the response to changing circumstances by those with power over the landscape. Almost invariably, the answer to the question 'why is this here?' or 'why does it look like this?' is that 'someone decided it should be'. Why is the Sussex town of Battle on an awkward site on a ridge three kilometres off the main London to Hastings road? The answer lies in the power-politics of mid-eleventh century England and Normandy, in the decision of Harold Godwinson to pitch camp at Senlac and of William the Conqueror to attack him there, in William's determination to found an abbey on the site of his victory, and in the abbey's enterprise in laying out a planned town at its gates. As the Battle Abbey chronicler, displaying a good eye for landscape history, put it in the late twelfth century, 'the brethren who were in charge of the building began to apportion to individuals house-sites of definite dimensions [which] can be seen to have remained to this day, just as they were arranged'.[22] Why is there a magnificent cathedral at Peterborough but only a ruined gateway and a sixteenth-century house as the obvious reminders of the equally important medieval religious house at Ramsey, 16 kilometres to the south east? Both were the products of the Benedictine monastic revival under King Edgar, founded in the 960s and richly endowed with extensive tracts of fenland, to rank tenth and eleventh among all foundations in Domesday Book. But following the dissolution, Ramsey was granted to the Cromwell family, dismantled and rebuilt as a country mansion, while Peterborough was preserved through conversion to a cathedral serving an area carved out of the massive diocese of Lincoln: the fact that Peterborough had been chosen as the burial-place for Henry VIII's first wife Katherine of Aragon in 1536 was probably a major factor in the decision.[23] Ironically – but significantly because of what they tell us of their patrons' priorities – two of the greatest ecclesiastical buildings in the country, Westminster Abbey and King's College Chapel, Cambridge, owe their present grandeur largely to two kings conventionally regarded as 'failures', Henry III (remodelling the work of another 'failure' Edward the Confessor) and Henry VI respectively. 'Heroic' figures such as Richard I and Henry V, kings whose reputation rests mainly on their martial prowess, have no comparable legacy.

These are obvious examples, but it is important to stress that power over the landscape did not rest with the crown, the nobility and the ecclesiastical corporations alone, however adept they were at designing their own living spaces [24] as well as impacting upon everyone else's. In the broad curving ridge and furrow of former open field arable strips, now preserved in permanent pasture, in irregularly shaped fields near township boundaries, carved out of woodland or moorland to extend the bounds of cultivation, in green lanes or minor roads depressed below the surrounding land surface as 'hollow ways', we encounter the impact of generations of anonymous peasant-farmers, collectively shaping their environment in the everyday quest for survival. Similarly, in the provision and maintenance of churches and guild-halls, causeways and bridges, we can often discern communities rather than individuals acting in concert for the general good. This was collective, rather than individual, power, an expression of 'communal authority' embedded in the consciousness of townspeople and country dwellers and as potent, at its own level, as that which motivated those who combined to resist the crown during the political crises of the thirteenth century. But, to reinforce the earlier point about interconnecting factors, such initiatives arose in response to changing economic circumstances which affected the course of supply and demand and behind which, ultimately, lay shifts in the trend of population. They might also be encouraged by developments in technology, which improved agricultural productivity and offered new opportunities in building design.

Some advances are more obvious than others. Windmills, for example, first recorded in England in 1185, spread mainly in the midlands and east of England thereafter and their deliberately exposed locations (often in the midst of the arable fields) made them prominent features of their communities. In a military context, the evolution of weapons and artillery can be traced in the changing designs of castles, which though profoundly influenced by considerations of comfort and ostentatious display could not afford to neglect their role as defensible fortifications: from the restricted dimensions of most early motte-and-bailey castles within the 160-metre range of the shortbow depicted on the Bayeux Tapestry to the sophistication of the Edwardian castles of North Wales, designed not only to withstand the threat of fearsome new devices such as the trebuchet, but actively to combat them. Most famously, the design of churches and cathedrals benefited from the introduction early in the twelfth century of the pointed arch, allowing for a roof-span no longer constrained by the length of available timbers and for the thrust of the roof itself to be carried to ground level. This in turn allowed the walls to accommodate a greater expanse of windows, showing off the coloured glass increasingly seen in England thereafter.[25]

Other technological developments were more subtle. The introduction of a modern style of harness and of a stiff padded collar during the twelfth and thirteenth centuries paved the way for the progressive replacement of oxen by horses, first for haulage then for ploughing. The greater speed of horse-haulage (about twice that of oxen) contributed to a broadening of the area which could be served by individual market-centres, and hence to the quickening trade which helped to sustain the growth in population and the economy prior to 1300. It must also have been a factor in the building of new stone bridges, and the rebuilding in stone of earlier timber versions – wide enough to take horse-drawn carts – which characterized the twelfth, thirteenth and early fourteenth centuries and increasingly utilized the technology of pointed arches previously developed in an ecclesiastical context.[26] Beyond this, if 'technological improvement' is extended in meaning to embrace all innovation in agricultural practice, there is no doubt that there was plenty of dynamism in the face of changing pressures, whether in communally farmed or individually worked fields: witness, for example, the thirteenth- and early-fourteenth-century practice in eastern Norfolk of planting legumes (especially black peas) and manually spreading various forms of fertilizer in order to maintain the fertility of the soil, and the experimentation with cash-crops such as saffron in eastern England during the fifteenth century.[27] This was active engagement with the rural landscape rather than a passive response to force of circumstance.

Anyone who approaches the study of the medieval landscape has to accept that the limitations of evidence can be frustrating. There may sometimes be 'no more than a few smeared earthworks and an ambiguous mention in an old document', to quote one book which – despite these pessimistic comments – is in fact a very helpful guide to the interpretation of the historic landscape. It is right to be cautious in assessing the evidence: as the same author has written elsewhere, 'do not jump to conclusions; stalk them slowly'.[28] But in the early 1980s, a book with a similar title to this one warned of the threat to 'our medieval landscape heritage' from modern development[29] and few would argue that such a threat is any less potent today: so let us study, celebrate and do all we can to conserve this historic landscape as a precious resource for understanding the lives of previous generations. Our landscape links our present and our past and – now as in the medieval period – the relationship between population and resources, the individual and collective power to maintain continuity or to impose change, and the impact of progress in technology are dominant and enduring themes in the story. We shall encounter them repeatedly in the pages which follow.

2

The landscape of farming and hunting

When the twelfth-century writer Henry of Huntingdon, in conscious imitation of the Venerable Bede, produced a monumental *History of the English People*, he began by rejoicing in the diversity of the landscape: 'Britain … is the most blessed of islands, rich in crops and trees, with plentiful streams and woodland, delightful for its hunting-grounds of wildfowl and game, and teeming with many different kinds of land, sea and river birds'. Some of this was copied straight from Bede but it is still an interesting commentary upon the perceived productivity of the countryside, with pastoral farming and fishing singled out for special praise: 'like Ireland it is wonderful for feeding draught animals and cattle … so rich in grazing … remarkable too for its numerous springs and rivers that abound in fish'.[1] Convenient though it is to treat different forms of land use separately in the pages which follow, we do well to remember their interdependence and the fact that they were not always regarded as distinct: arable, pasture and meadow were managed together within communal farming regimes, fishing and fowling supplemented the diet of many a peasant farmer, and the privileged minority who spent their time hunting game – sometimes over farmland – relied for most of their incomes on the produce of their rural estates. An early-fourteenth century survey of Heaton Norris (Lancashire) hints at the dynamism of an agricultural economy which was prepared to put land to different uses at different times: 'certain acres of land and plats are of arable land, some of meadow land and some of pasture, and so meadow, arable and pasture cannot be separated because some are meadow and pasture and some arable land'.[2] And all who worked the land in the medieval period were aware of the risks inherent in allowing one resource to expand too far at the expense of others.

Arable

For the vast majority of the population, the success of the grain harvest was crucial. Within the ranks of the so-called peasantry of rural England there were many gradations, from substantial freemen with 40 acres or more of arable holdings who did not labour in person, made up local juries and are better described as 'freeholders'[3] to those whose unfree status tied them to their manors and to lives dominated by agricultural work for their own families' sustenance, and (if obligations were enforced) for their lords. Outright landless slavery – the condition of just over 10% of the recorded rural population in Domesday Book – disappeared in the wake of the Norman Conquest but many in the humbler ranks of society would have shared the sentiments of the late-tenth or early-eleventh century ploughman who was obliged to 'work so very hard' going out 'at dawn to drive the oxen to the field and yoke them to the plough' assisted by a 'boy who drives the oxen with a goad … hoarse from shouting and the cold'.[4]

Study of the land which they ploughed has long been dominated by a focus on great open arable fields, each typically extending to 50 hectares or more, divided into blocks called furlongs which were themselves composed of long narrow unenclosed strips. Two, three – occasionally four – of these fields were arranged around a nucleated settlement, the strips within them being dispersed among the farmers living in that settlement. There was communal regulation to control the rotation of crops between the fields, including provision for one field to be left fallow each year; livestock would also be released from the pastures at specific times to graze and manure the arable strips and meadows when their crops were not growing. In 1915 H. L. Gray coined the term 'midland system' to describe these arrangements, which he saw prevailing over 'at least half the soil of England' from County Durham through the midlands to the central southern counties, albeit with some exceptions inside this zone. An alternative estimate is that, at its maximum extent in the fourteenth century, between one-third and one-half of England's rural population lived in places where this system broadly operated.[5] In the sixteenth century this was described as 'champion' country, from the Latin *campus* used in medieval documents to refer to an open field. This is a preferable description of a type of landscape which prevailed far beyond the 'midlands' and witnessed some variation in the detailed working of the 'system': for example, 'wolds' regions with good pasture available (such as the Cotswolds themselves and the uplands of Lincolnshire, Leicestershire and Northamptonshire) typically favoured two-field open arable systems, while fertile lowland vales (characteristic of much of the south and midlands, especially the east midlands) sometimes developed three.[6] However, the overall picture painted a century ago has stood the test of time, this broad diagonal band featuring, for example, as the 'Central Province' in the influential *Atlas of Rural Settlement* published at the turn of the millennium and being reinforced by recent analysis of the references to 'champion' fields in John Leland's *Itinerary*, compiled either side of 1540.[7]

To west and east of this great 'champion' zone lay what the *Atlas* has defined as the 'Northern and Western' and 'South-Eastern Provinces'. Settlement here was more dispersed and field systems can broadly be described as embracing smaller pockets of unenclosed strips, with individuals' holdings distributed unevenly between them; 'closes' (enclosed fields) were encountered more often and these were mostly held 'in severalty' (that is separately, or individually). This led to a more hedged, wooded landscape as well as to considerable flexibility and variability in the communal regulation of cropping and pasturage. One of the Elizabethan commentators on all this, William Harrison rector of Radwinter and vicar of Wimbish in north-west Essex, lived on what has been identified as part of the frontier separating the 'Central' and 'South-Eastern' Provinces, and was therefore ideally placed to describe 'our soile' as 'being divided into champaign ground and woodland'.[8] Drawing lines on maps does of course imply sharp definition when realities on the ground are blurred. There were many places inside the 'champion' zone which did not have great open fields and others outside it which did. In south Cambridgeshire, where the River Cam has been taken as the boundary between the 'Central' and 'South-Eastern' Provinces, medieval fields apparently conforming to the 'midland system' have been found on both sides of the river, as have more irregular field patterns: but the 'midland' system does seem to have predominated to the west of the river rather than to the east, so the distinction holds good in general terms.[9] What is remarkable is not that settlements in several parts of the country chose not to conform to the highly regulated communal farming regime of the 'champion' zone, but that – in however limited a form, and with however many enclosed fields in amongst them – long narrow open arable strips, laid out so that adjacent strips belonged to different people, were to be found across the length and breadth of England, as they were over much of continental Europe, at some point during the middle ages.

There were exceptions, such as parts of the Weald in Kent, Sussex and Surrey, in southern Essex and in the Buckinghamshire Chilterns, where none of the arable seems ever to have been farmed other than in closes.[10] But given the widespread distribution of some form of open field farming in strips, from Cumberland to Cornwall to Kent, as well as within the 'champion' zone where it came to dominate the rural landscape, there were clearly powerful incentives to adopt this methodology for arable cultivation, at least in part.[11] There also seems to have been a widely held cultural expectation – rooted in that sense of 'community' touched upon in the previous chapter, with notions of fairness over the distribution of land of similar quality and a guarantee of a minimum stake therein – that some portion of the arable should be worked in open strips, alongside communal grazing rights in the accompanying pasture. All this would involve an element of land-sharing, even where a fully regulated 'system' was never adopted.

The earliest documentary reference to open field farming is usually taken to be a statement in the late-seventh-century *Laws of Ine*, King of Wessex, which required those who had 'common meadow or other land divided in shares' to compensate their neighbours if their failure to maintain fences led to cattle entering to 'eat up their common crops or grass'.[12] This says nothing about the circumstances in which such fields were created, but it is generally assumed that they developed as the population recovered from its post-Roman downturn and that various different processes were involved. Where there was a collective effort to clear woodland or drain marshland in order to win it for cultivation, this would tend towards a sharing out of the new resource, with the potential for expansion thereafter from the original nucleus of small open fields. From present-day field patterns, oval-shaped areas, probably the bounds of intakes from wood or marsh, are being identified in many parts of the country, often with evidence of open arable strips having been developed within them: examples range from Tunley (Lancashire) to Rashleigh (Devon) to Haslingfield (Cambridgeshire) and many more surely remain to be found.[13] Elsewhere, the original division of strips seems to have been in the context of an 'infield/outfield system', where the best arable land (the 'infield') was distributed among the farmers in strips and cropped every year, while the less fertile 'outfield' served as common pasture with portions being ploughed in rotation; all this might develop into more extensive and organized open field systems if rising population meant that the 'outfield' had to be brought into more frequent cultivation and – as pasture receded – the livestock had to be grazed over the fields as a whole. This is thought to have happened at some stage during the Anglo-Saxon period within – for example – the marshlands of the Severn estuary and also in settlements such as Comberton and Barton in the Bourn valley west of Cambridge.[14] Alongside this, there would have been many instances where open arable fields were created through the reorganization of an already-cleared and previously culti-vated landscape. Cases where open field strips appear to have respected ditches of Iron Age or Roman date – a phenomenon which has been found, for example, in parts of Cambridgeshire, Northamptonshire and Oxfordshire, where such ditches underlie the headlands defining the furlongs – may well illustrate this. So does the general alignment of fields to this day at Shapwick (Somerset), which can be traced back through eighteenth-century maps to the furlongs of medieval open fields and beyond them to boundaries of Roman or even earlier origin; this certainly suggests some continuity of previous territorial divisions when blocks of strips came to be laid out, continuity broadly maintained ever since.[15] It is of course possible that those plotting the new open fields merely re-used long abandoned field boundaries, but given the speed with which these can be obliterated by the regrowth of trees and shrubs this is improbable: the more likely hypothesis is that these ancient markers influenced the new arrangements because they were still functioning features in the landscape.[16]

Other than the cultural factors to which reference has already been made, one reason for ploughing in long narrow strips must have been the convenience of having plough teams tracking back and forth along roughly parallel lines. There is evidence from parts of Northamptonshire, Yorkshire and the silt fens of Lincolnshire, Norfolk and Cambridgeshire that early open strips were up to – sometimes in excess of – a kilometre in length, a circumstance which suggests replanning of the landscape on a grand scale.[17] But this was not the case everywhere and, in any event, these very long strips were normally subdivided later, so that a length of about 200 metres (or about 220 yards, our modern furlong) came to be widely adopted as a reasonable stretch for the teams to undertake before resting and turning around. Strips might be delineated one from another by stones or stakes at the ends or by nothing more than furrows or narrow balks of grass; the absence of more prominent barriers along and between them economised on land use and minimised the risk of obstruction and damage to the plough and its team. The practice of co-aration (whereby a number of peasant farmers each contributed one or more beasts to the plough team) encouraged the notion that working a field was an enterprise shared by all who had a stake in it, whether or not the livestock also pastured together in the arable fields when crops were not growing. Narrow strips also tended to result from the subdivision of holdings – whether through sales, leases, partible inheritance (where there was more than one heir, as was the widespread custom in East Anglia and the south east)[18] or the already-mentioned commitment to sharing out what had been cleared for cultivation by collective effort. None of this made the creation of open fields inevitable, but a combination of circumstances made them a reasonable answer to the question of how to arrange at least some of a community's stock of arable land: an answer which seems to have been reached over a remarkably large area of the country, notwithstanding differences of climate, soils and terrain, and whatever the local balance was between arable and other forms of land use, on the one hand, and between communal and individual farming on the other.

From these origins, open field farming developed in different ways in different places. Within the 'Central Province', the highly regulated communal farming regime we know as the 'midland system' became widespread

– fanning outwards, it has been argued, from an original heartland of 'the 'Cotswold Scarps and Vales, the Inner Midlands, the east Midlands and the Trent Valley' during the tenth, eleventh and twelfth centuries. Elsewhere, arable strips continued to be worked alongside enclosed fields, their farmers being only partially dependent upon a communal regime. Indeed, four main types of open field operation apart from the 'midland system' have been identified, with subtle sub-classes within them, ranging from those where strips were cropped and grazed separately – rather like a modern block of allotments – but with shared access to pasture beyond the designated arable area, as happened in the Lincolnshire Fens, to those in which there was communal regulation of cropping and grazing but in a context of many small open fields intermixed with closes.[19]

The factors which led to this divergence remain a matter for debate, since none of the pressures which might be thought to have encouraged rigorous communal regulation were peculiar to the 'Central Province'. It has been argued that rising population led to an extension of arable and consequent shortage of pasture, forcing communities to agree a tightly co-ordinated approach to the use of available land. Yet East Anglia, where a variety of less rigid 'systems' prevailed, had an appreciably higher density of population either side of the Norman Conquest than anywhere in the midlands. At a local level, the Domesday population density in mid-Devon around Exeter, an area of small enclosed fields, was appreciably higher than it was in 'champion' central and south-east Somerset.[20] Arguments can also be advanced that systematic, controlled use of great open fields and their associated pastures made for more efficient and productive farming, particularly as what have variously been called 'great', 'multiple' or 'federative' estates broke up into smaller units through portions being granted to religious institutions and members of the nobility: instead of individual settlements each contributing one specialist resource to a large and varied estate (which may sometimes be the origin of place names such as Haverhill (oats hill), or Barton (barley farm) the available land had to be put to multiple uses in order to make an all-round contribution to a smaller estate unit. But estate fragmentation was a widespread phenomenon not only in the midlands but also in East Anglia and the south east, and here it could lead to a landscape largely of enclosed rather than of open fields, as at the Rodings (Essex), where a large coherent estate later fragmented into 16 separate manors and eight ecclesiastical parishes.[21] Nor were great open fields onto which animals were admitted to graze after harvest the only way of making land work as both arable and pasture. There was an alternative, which had built-in flexibility to meet changes in circumstance, in the form of rotational 'convertible husbandry' in small enclosed fields. This involved grain being harvested for two to three years and closes being put to grass for the next six to eight (durations varying to allow for fluctuations in demand for grain), an approach to the mixed use of farmland in Devon which is known from documents by the mid-fourteenth century but seems apparent from pollen analysis by the end of the eighth. A similar system, on a cycle of about ten years, applied in parts of Cornwall, though here the rotation operated over blocks of open strips, like those which can still be seen at Forrabury, above Boscastle (Figure 1).[22] The contrasts in field patterns either side of the Quantock and Blackdown Hills in Somerset – great open fields to the east, more irregular patterns to the west – and a broadly similar divergence between north-west and south-east Suffolk, have been attributed not to soil or terrain but to distinct political and cultural experiences: in effect, to people in one region 'thinking differently' from those in the other.[23] Nothing in this paragraph invalidates an argument that in a particular place, population pressure, shortage of pasture, a perception that land could be managed more efficiently in communally regulated great open fields, might all have been factors in prompting the adoption of arrangements characteristic of 'champion' country, at any time between the late-Saxon period and the twelfth century. But none of these factors applied deterministically: there was always an alternative option.

Any decision to rearrange the farming landscape, including the replacement of a patchwork of intermingled strips and closes with carefully regulated great open fields, would have been disruptive in the short-term and not taken lightly. There is reason to believe that the initiative often rested not with the lords of great estates but with the peasants, or alternatively with minor lords whose income derived from only one or two manors and who were

Figure 1: Forrabury Common (Cornwall). Over 40 strips survive above Boscastle, separated by low stone and earth balks. This is a remnant of open field farming but not of the 'midland system': under the rotation practised here, strips grew crops for two to three years and were then put down to grass to recover.

therefore intimately involved with the fortunes of the settlements to which they were attached. Analysis of field systems in Somerset has suggested that Glastonbury Abbey may have deliberately imposed this arrangement within much of its estate – possibly in the time of the reforming abbot Dunstan in the mid-tenth century – but this was exceptional, since no equivalent consistency can be discerned in the layouts of other settlements and their fields on the estates of the king, the Bishop of Wells or other major landholders in the shire. Elsewhere, and on a broader canvas, the Bishop of Coventry and Lichfield, with an estate which stretched from the 'Central Province' in the Midlands to the 'Northern and Western Province' in Lancashire and Cheshire, can be seen to have drawn his income from settlements and field systems arranged according to local practice, rather than on the basis of any centrally imposed template.[24] By the thirteenth and fourteenth centuries, the authority to order local affairs vested in the 'community of the vill' had become well-established and within this the management of farming bulked large. In 1294, for example, the villeins (unfree peasants) of Brightwalton (Berkshire) collectively reached agreement with their lord the Abbot of Battle over common rights in and around two woods, surrendering their claims to one in exchange for unambiguous entitlement to the other. Similarly in 1410 the lords of Harlestone (Northamptonshire) agreed a revision of land allocations between fields with a committee of village representatives.[25] Although the last case comes from the late-medieval period when the bargaining power of the peasantry was unusually strong – when even 'Warwick the Kingmaker' chose not to reverse a rent reduction achieved on holdings in his manor of Lighthorne close to the heart of his estate[26] – there is no reason to think that their tenth-to-twelfth-century forebears would have been lacking in prowess. By and large, we should look to the local peasant community as the driving force in the organization and reorganization of its own field system.

Exceptions can be found, but they often relate to specific cases where we know that lords had particular incentives to impose a 'fresh start'. The colonizing efforts of incoming Norman landholders in Yorkshire and County Durham in the late eleventh and early twelfth century, which led to the creation of a series of villages on their estates arranged in regular rows, may well have been the context in which new open fields were also laid out in these places, even if the details were left to stewards or the settlers themselves. When Liverpool was founded as a new port by King John, alongside a creek in the Mersey, there was almost certainly a major rearrangement of any open fields already serving the small pre-existing farming and fishing community, if only to cope with the enlarged population; something of the pattern is still discernible to the north and north-east of the planned town, in the spaces between streets such as Vauxhall Road and Scotland Road. A regime of three open fields, with a three-course rotation, was deliberately imposed on

Drakelow (Cheshire), a manor on the Black Prince's estate newly created after 1346 out of two sanctuaries at Rudheath (near Northwich) and Overmarsh (now King's Marsh, near Farndon); these were no longer needed for the recruitment of soldiers to fight the Welsh from among the fugitives who had resorted there.[27] But such circumstances were unusual. If we are seeking reasons why some places continued to farm a mixture of open strips and closes, with various degrees of communal regulation, while others adopted a highly regulated system of working great open fields in common, we should normally focus on the local peasant communities, and on various cultural and psychological influences bearing upon them. Among these may have been a simple wish to keep in step with what seemed to be working well in neighbouring settlements. If only – to quote the great oral historian of the Suffolk countryside, George Ewart Evans – we could 'ask the fellows who cut the hay'.[28]

Whatever the context in which open fields were first laid out, they clearly did not remain static. Typically, not only in the great open fields of the 'Central Province' but also in smaller versions found in other parts of the country, the subdivisions of such fields were very important units within their management. These were often called furlongs (though in places they went under other names, such as flatt, shoot or – confusingly – *feld*) and normally all the strips within a furlong ran parallel to one another, being bounded at either end by a headland which allowed access to them and also served as the turning-area for the plough team. In the northern counties, there is some evidence (for example in names based on words associated with clearings, such as *ridding*) that furlongs originated as the units by which land was reclaimed and brought into cultivation. Conversely, they may have been formed from the subdivision of larger blocks of land, such as the exceptionally long groups of strips found in parts of Northamptonshire, Yorkshire and elsewhere. Some furlongs were given names derived from earlier small settlements – such as those ending in *worth* and *cote* – implying that these had been abandoned as part of the reorganization of the fields, although the relationship between settlement change and the laying out of open fields is a controversial one, to be addressed in the chapter which follows.[29] A key point is that wherever a communally agreed rotation of crops was in operation, this did not require there to be a given number of fields: the furlongs, whether grouped together into great open fields or dispersed in smaller blocks separated by closes of arable or pasture, would be allocated to whatever course of rotation had been determined. At Tarvin and Wybunbury (Cheshire), for example, three-course rotations had been established by the end of the thirteenth century but they covered a multiplicity of small separately named units, 14 in the first case, 12 in the second. Similar arrangements have been found all over the country, including within the 'Central Province' in parts of Oxfordshire, Buckinghamshire, Bedfordshire and Hertfordshire.[30] Even where the classic 'midland system' of two-to-four great open fields is clearly in evidence, these extensive units of land seem to have been formed from the amalgamation for cropping purposes of contiguous furlongs: one field or group of furlongs lying fallow in any one year, while one or more other fields were sown and harvested at communally agreed times. Hardwick (Cambridgeshire) 'which had an impeccable three-field system in 1639, boasted at least seven "fields" in 1251' so presumably there was some significant reordering of the community's arable in the meantime. At Laxton (Nottinghamshire), where a three-course rotation can still be observed in the surviving open fields, it is believed that the strips were organized into furlongs for crop rotation purposes sometime before the fields themselves were designated by grouping the furlongs together; the earliest reference to a field here is to Mill Field not later than 1189, while South Field, first mentioned in 1232, was possibly the last to be created. And notwithstanding the communal rotation scheme, individual furlongs within the great open fields might still grow different crops, typically wheat or rye where winter sowing (before Christmas) had been agreed, barley, oats or legumes – peas, beans and vetch – where there was 'Lenten sowing' in the spring.[31]

Two twelfth-century descriptions of what appear to be the rearrangement of furlongs into fields survive. Both are couched in terms which imply the close involvement of manorial lords, but this does not invalidate what was said earlier about the initiatives likely to have been taken by peasants; these documents may merely be recording the formal confirmatory stage. At Dry Drayton (Cambridgeshire) in the 1150s, the Abbot of Crowland and four other lords agreed on a 'new partition' of the land 'in field and in meadow' because it had been 'dispersed in minute parts and long uncultivated'; it was all rearranged 'by complete fields and by certain boundaries'. In the following decade at Segenhoe (Bedfordshire), where holdings had become highly fragmented and intermixed, 'knights, free men and others' came to one of the two manorial courts in the settlement and 'surrendered their lands under the supervision of the old men and by the measure of the perch, to be divided as if they were newly won land, assigning to each a reasonable share'.[32] Similar references in the following century appear to involve a redistribution of furlongs from two fields to three, probably as part of a switch from a two-course to a three-course rotation which would leave less land lying fallow each year. About 1241, the Abbot of Eynsham was accused of depriving a tenant of his common pasture at South Stoke and Woodcote (Oxfordshire) by dividing into three parts lands which had always formerly been divided into two. At Puddletown (Dorset) in 1292 'a division of the land of the convent [of Christchurch Priory] … was made … in three fields, namely the first near the king's highway 248 acres, another to the east 177 acres, another to the west 205 acres'. Several switches from two fields to three have also been identified in Northamptonshire; for example, Broughton had two fields in 1317 but an extra one, Middle Field, by 1336, while at Kislingbury the East and West Fields of the thirteenth century had been joined by South Field not later than 1340.[33] All this testifies to the dynamism of open field systems during centuries which witnessed climate change and considerable growth and decline in population: it has been well said that 'the boundaries of common fields and the extent of common rights fluctuated like the sea shore'.[34] It also reinforces the impression that the emergence over most of the 'Central Province' of a highly regulated approach to farming would have been a phased process, the product of decisions taken in each community over several generations: an initial sharing of a portion of the available arable and pasture; the introduction of communally agreed practices for farming this shared land, including in time a decision to rotate the crops and the area left fallow; the rearrangement of the arable subject to this rotation into great open fields. Even this model doubtless varied from place to place, just as the pressures which prompted these decisions also differed in points of detail.

By the twelfth and thirteenth centuries, it had become normal for all transfers of freely held land to be recorded in charters, and accordingly references to strips and closes are found as a matter of course. About 1250, for example, William son of Hugh of Thorpe gave the canons of Lincoln Cathedral half a bovate of arable land in Laceby (Lincolnshire), comprising 9 selions (strips) to the south of the village and a further 21 selions to the north of the village, an arrangement which strongly suggests that there were two open fields either side of the settlement. Since a bovate was typically about 15 acres (around 6 hectares), and the total holding here was 30 selions, it is fair to conclude that each strip was probably around a quarter-acre in size. The selions were identified by the furlongs within which they lay, and also by the names of adjoining landholders ('two selions … over Dicfurlanges'; 'two selions over Littelbechill between the land of Hugh son of Ely and the land of Everard'; 'one selion over Doflandes next to the land of Ralf of St Paul'), and there is a good deal to be gleaned from such information. On the one hand, the St Paul family – Ralf or William – occur as neighbours in the references to exactly half the strips in the charter, a circumstance which strongly suggests, when allowance is made for some exchange and transfer down the generations, that there had been a regular sequence to the distribution of the strips when they had originally been laid out. Furthermore, one of the selions ('on the north side of Littelbechill between the land of Henry son of Berengar and the land of Hugh son of Ely') was also identified as 'abutting over the furlong of Ralf of Bradley': a description which implies that one of the furlongs was no longer in the possession of a number of different holders but had come into the hands of one, presumably through the consolidation and exchange of strips.[35] It was initiatives of this sort which could readily lead to the enclosure of the entire furlong, in a reversal of the processes we have already explored.

By the thirteenth and fourteenth centuries we begin to have an understanding of how open fields were actually worked, particularly from local court rolls with their detailed regulations and records of punishments, covering matters such as the dates which governed the annual round of activity and the safeguarding of crops from thieves and straying animals. At Newton Longville (Buckinghamshire) the court met on 1 July 1290 and ordered that 'no-one shall allow his calves to be in the fields in the growing grain ... there shall be no carting at night ... everyone shall see that his stiles and lanes, those nearest his neighbours, are so kept that [no one] incur damage because of lack of such maintenance'. At Chalgrave (Bedfordshire) on 25 July 1303, it was decreed that 'no-one shall carry during the whole of autumn except by day ... no-one shall carry corn except by cart ... all shall close their curtilages and ... no-one may have exit by the curtilage': the last two orders seeking to ensure that the crofts around each house were kept properly hedged or fenced, without allowing direct access to or from the open fields beyond. And on 8 August 1315, the court at Cuxham (Oxfordshire) imposed a penalty of 40 pence (16.7p) if any 'sheep shall come into the field sown with Lenten grain until the Feast of St Michael [29 September]'.[36]

Behind all this lies the story of an English countryside which until the early fourteenth century was under increasing strain as the population continued to grow – though the strain was felt most where there was the greatest dependence on arable farming, without the diversification which abundant pasture or other resources allowed. Analysis of data on the peasantry in the 1279 Hundred Rolls, a governmental survey which in its present form covers much of midland and eastern England, suggests that almost half those with a stake in the fields possessed holdings so small that their families were at or below subsistence level unless income was supplemented from elsewhere.[37] A case in point would be Adam Unwyne on the Bishop of Ely's manor of Willingham (Cambridgeshire). He appears in a survey of the bishop's estate in 1251 owing labour service to his lord each Monday, Friday and occasionally more often – hoeing, mowing, reaping, threshing, sheep-shearing and hurdle-making according to the season of the year – with an obligation to render a hen at Christmas and six eggs at Easter and liability to make additional payments demanded by his lord, all for a cottar's holding of two acres (0.8 hectares) of arable land.[38] New land was of course brought into cultivation: it has been estimated that by the close of the thirteenth century, over 4 million hectares in England were being farmed as arable land, compared to about 2.4 million hectares in 1086 and 3.1 million hectares in 1914.[39] But this must have caused a dangerous imbalance in some parts of the country, given the necessity for plentiful woodland – for fuel, toolmaking and building materials

– and for sufficient meadow and pasture to feed the livestock which pulled the ploughs.

Problems of land shortage for the majority would only be exacerbated if individuals enclosed consolidated blocks for themselves. There is good evidence – as implied by the Lincolnshire charter above but especially outside the 'champion ' regions – that this was already happening by the middle of the thirteenth century.[40] Once the reversal of the population trend in the fourteenth century brought an easing of pressure on resources, many of the brakes on the process were released: marginal land need no longer be ploughed, enterprising peasants could break with community bonds and seek easier terms (if necessary by moving elsewhere), lords tended to lease their lands rather than farm them direct (so loosening their hold on their peasant tenants) and opportunities arose to group strips together into larger holdings. The break-up of open field farming was a natural consequence of all this: having taken some seven centuries to evolve, the open fields were by now embarked upon seven centuries of enclosure. One stage along the way was to leave arable strips, and sometimes whole furlongs, temporarily uncultivated as 'leys', pasture on which beasts could graze – although it was often necessary to keep them tethered so as not to intrude on neighbouring strips. These were frequently the subject of fifteenth- and sixteenth-century village bye-laws, such as those of Dodford (Northamptonshire) in 1463–64 which ordered the restoration to tillage so as 'to increase the amount of corn' of all leys put down to grass in the previous twenty years.[41] From here it was but a short step to withdrawing the strips from the open field regime altogether: a farmer who had acquired several neighbouring strips might well want to hedge them about and work them in a way that did not conform to the communal arrangements. This led to the type of gradual, piece-by-piece enclosure which became widespread in fourteenth- and fifteenth-century England, evidenced by the more frequent references to 'closes' which occur in charters, rentals and court rolls, sometimes in a context which orders the removal of the newly created boundaries. At Great Horwood (Buckinghamshire), for example, there are references to 'uncultivated lands' or 'uncultivated grounds' in court-rolls of 26 April 1374, 15 May 1385 and 31 May 1467, and to peasant farmers' 'closes' by 1 August 1503. In Tilston (Cheshire) on 20 December 1491, Jankyn Williamson of Stretton leased to Jankyn Leche of Carden 'certain parcels of ground … as heretofore been open field' in terms which show that strips (here described as 'butts') had been consolidated together prior to enclosure: 'all the Overtywarts flatt shooting afore the gatehouse of the parsonage of Tilston … one butt cloven in two shooting on the said flatt … and two other butts shooting on the said flatt next to the hedge of a croft of Randall Carden'.[42] Manorial lords themselves faced both challenges and opportunities in these circumstances, as falling population led to a decline in income from rents. While there was limited experimentation with cash-crops, a far less labour-intensive alternative was to convert what they could of the open arable fields to enclosed sheep or cattle pastures, an option also attractive to some of the more substantial freeholders within the local community. Because of its impact on settlements, this process has been left for more detailed discussion in the chapter which follows.

A corrugated pattern on the surface of permanent pasture – broad ridge and furrow, at least 5 metres across from one furrow to the next, with a shallow curve to its course along the length of the ridges – can usually be identified with some confidence as evidence of medieval open arable strips, even though (strictly speaking) what we see in the pastures today are the fossilized remains of these strips from the last time they were ploughed. The sinuous course, normally a gentle reverse-S, represents the line taken by the plough team, which approached the headland terminating each strip at an angle in order to save space when turning around. The ridges themselves were created quite deliberately by ploughing a consistent line back and forth so as to repeatedly turn soil to the right, usually working clockwise out from the centre. This was achieved by the heavy wheeled ploughs with a mouldboard for turning the sod, introduced in mid-Saxon times, which are apparently being described in a riddle preserved in the tenth-century anthology known as the *Exeter Book*: 'I go sniffing along … borne on a wagon … I leave green on one side and black on the other'.[43] All this had the effect over successive seasons of shifting soil towards the centre of each ridge, accentuating the furrows on either side of it, although a point would have been reached where measures would have had to be taken to prevent the ridges becoming too steep. On some lighter soils, such the Breckland and indeed across much of East Anglia, this conscious ridging up of the arable land seems not to have been employed, but on heavier soils it certainly assisted with surface drainage, the ridge and furrow normally being ploughed across rather than along the contours so as to facilitate run-off. Comparison with village plans of open fields, which survive from the sixteenth century onwards, strongly suggests that in origin a single ridge was equivalent to an individually held strip (or 'land'), although this correspondence was liable to be obscured over time by farmers' acquisition of neighbouring ridges to create wider strips. The furrows between the ridges would serve not only as drainage channels but also as dividers between one strip and the next, this being reinforced as the critical time of harvest approached if the corn stood high on the ridges but grew relatively poorly in the wetter furrows: a typical midlands open field, with strips in blocks of furlongs running in different directions, would certainly have displayed a much more 'striped' and 'patchwork quilt' effect in early summer than an extensive modern cornfield today.[44]

There are, however, dangers in leaping to conclusions on all this without supporting documentary evidence. Ridge and furrow which is narrower and straighter than that described in the previous paragraph is likely to have been created after the middle ages, and as already said even that of medieval origin is left to us in the form it took when it was last ploughed. This might be any time up to the early nineteenth century before the open fields were enclosed prior to conversion to pasture. It might be the later nineteenth century if farmers were concerned to maintain the ridges to aid surface drainage of these pastures. It might even be the twentieth century if there was some short-term ploughing insufficient to eradicate the ridges altogether. Cheshire's pastoral farmers in the 1840s are known to have created small extra ridges down the middle of the furrows, so as to improve the run-off of water, or to 'split the ridge' with an extra furrow down the centre, techniques which can still be observed in the surface of the county's pastures today, as in the old Town Field area of Tilston, where arable strips survived till the late eighteenth century.[45] Nevertheless, whatever alterations may subsequently have been made to the ridges and furrows, their underlying medieval pattern remains and serves as important evidence both of the lengths of strips and of the extent and distribution of former open arable farming (Figure 2). Even where ridge and furrow has now disappeared – a victim of deep ploughing or of deliberate flattening to ease the harvesting of a grass crop – traces of headlands sometimes survive; vertical aerial photographs, notably a survey by the RAF in 1947, are also available as excellent evidence of the former extent of ridge and furrow. But – to reinforce the point – caution is needed when interpreting all this. On the one hand, we cannot assume that all the ridge and furrow in a particular locality was in use as ploughed strips at the same time. On the other, without documentary evidence we cannot know how far the strips were worked in common.[46]

We may also be able to detect former arable strips in the landscape from a pattern of reverse-S hedges – planted in between the strips as part of the process of piecemeal enclosure – or from the zigzag course of a lane or boundary, which formerly marked the line of the headlands between the furlongs. There are few sequences of reverse-S hedges as spectacular as that at Brassington (Derbyshire), where the curving ridge and furrow can also be discerned in alignment with them, but field boundaries of this nature are widespread wherever the strips were enclosed by agreement between neighbours rather than through coercion or a commissioners' award. As for zigzag lanes, an excellent illustration is to be found in the former Town Field area of Clotton (Cheshire) – shown as still partly 'open' on an estate map of 1734 – where the minor road known locally as 'corkscrew lane' plots a course between the surviving reverse-S field boundaries (Figure 3). Those who use such tracks today are quite literally following in the footsteps of the peasants who ploughed the fields on either side.[47]

Another feature of the modern rural landscape which may take us right back to the activities of these medieval farmers are lynchets (terraces on

Figure 2: Ridge and Furrow near Wigston Parva (Leicestershire). Melting snow accentuates the broad, reverse-S ridge and furrow characteristic of medieval open fields, near where Watling Street (now the A5) crossed the Fosse Way. In the foreground, a headland serves to terminate the ridges and furrows, which take advantage of natural gradients to facilitate surface drainage.

Figure 3: Field System, Clotton (Cheshire). This RAF photograph of January 1947 shows a small planned settlement along the main road (the A51) with a row of adjacent tofts, a back lane which then zigzags along the headlands of a former open field system, and several reverse-S hedges caused by the piecemeal enclosure of strips. (English Heritage NMR RAF Photography.)

hillsides where arable strips ran along the contours, rather than up and down the slope). These are normally interpreted as extensions to the open fields to feed a growing population, and they survive because they were allowed to revert to pasture in the population downturn of the late middle ages. Examples abound over much of the country, among the more readily accessible being the lynchets in the beechwoods of the Gog Magog hills of Shelford, south of Cambridge, those on the slopes below Housesteads Roman fort (Northumberland) and those associated with the deserted medieval settlement of Hound Tor on Dartmoor, where a sinuous reverse-S course can still be discerned. In a few places open arable strips are still being worked, though without the former communal regime – as at Soham (Cambridgeshire), 8 kilometres south-east of Ely, where the North Field was never enclosed, and the aforementioned Forrabury (Cornwall) (Figure 1).[48] However, the best demonstration of communal arable farming remains that at Laxton, where three great open fields are still worked by tenant farmers who hold intermingled strips, meet annually in early December in a manorial court (the Court Leet) presided over by the lord of the manor's steward, and mostly live as neighbours to one another, in farms which line the main road through the village. Even so, as an echo of the medieval 'midland system', this demands qualification: each Laxton farmer now has the bulk of his land in enclosed fields outside the system of strips, the 'fallow' field grows a grass crop as forage for animals and in place of communal access to meadows the practice since 1730 has been for patches of common grassland (sykes) near watercourses to have their hay crops auctioned off to the highest bidder. Anyone with the slightest interest in medieval farming should visit Laxton, ideally between March and June when the strips are most easily distin-guished: but what the visitor sees is not a fossilized open field system, but one which has evolved over the centuries as all such systems did. Laxton is special because of the remarkable survival of three open arable fields, albeit in truncated form, and of a court to regulate farming within them.[49]

Pasture, meadow, marsh and fen

Medieval pastures took many different forms. Some were extensive areas of rough grazing on lightly settled moorlands and heathlands or were to be found in wetlands unsuitable for cultivation. Others were managed intensively by their local communities, among or beyond the arable fields, and were liable to be ploughed up if demand for arable outstripped supply. Some pastures served as greens around which settlements clustered. Yet others were temporary leys created within open arable fields, intended not only to feed livestock but also to renew the fertility of the soil. Meadows, by contrast, had a more uniform appearance, normally fairly flat, located next to a watercourse and prone to flooding. By the time documentation becomes fairly abundant, it is clear that in all parts of the country some pasture and meadow was liable to be held in closes, managed exclusively for a lord or one of his acquisitive freeholders, and it is a measure of the importance of these resources – pastures for grazing and sometimes the collection of fuel, meadows for hay as winter feed – that such private holdings were often valued more highly than equivalent areas of arable: in the Essex manors of Latton and Bocking, for example, either side of the year 1300, while an acre (0.4 hectare) of arable was valued at sixpence (2.5p) per annum, private pasture was reckoned at a shilling (5p) per acre per annum and private meadow at two or four shillings. As with arable, however, at least a portion of the available pasture and meadow was normally managed in common, and where the 'midland system' prevailed it was fully integrated into the highly regulated regime, with livestock having to be moved on and off by appointed dates. The Bishop of Ely's estate survey of 1251, for example, listed private and common resources separately, including at Little Gransden (Cambridgeshire) where there were 25 acres (10.1 hectares) of private pasture 'called *Gravis*, where the plough-oxen of the parson of Gransden can feed with the bishop's oxen' along with 'a certain pasture called *Langelund*, and it is common to all the village'. Similarly, on his manor of Barking (Suffolk), four areas of private pasture were listed, plus 'a certain common of pasture which is called Berkingetye' of 90 acres (36.4 hectares).[50] Barking Tye survives as a common to this day, governed by District Council bye-laws which forbid the posting of notices on trees, the snaring of birds and – except by 'lawful authority' which essentially was the case in the middle ages as well – the keeping on the common of cattle, sheep or other animals. Today, some 3% of the land surface of England is registered as common land, including precious survivals such as the Commons in south London – Clapham, Wandsworth, Tooting, Streatham – all saved ultimately because of acquisition by the Metropolitan Board of Works in the 1870s and 1880s and reminders of a string of discrete settlements, each of which had its own mention in the Surrey portion of Domesday Book.

Domesday was, however, inconsistent in its handling of pasture. Only one circuit, that covering south-west England, appears to have attempted systematic coverage, although fairly full details are given for some counties elsewhere. Measurements vary from acreages (often in round figures, like the 200 acres – about 81 hectares – of Lyneham, Oxfordshire) to linear estimates (such as 17 furlongs by 17 furlongs – about 3420 metres each way – at Frome, Dorset, or one league in length and breadth at King's Nympton, Devon). Such differences make comparison very difficult, although Oliver Rackham has calculated that perhaps one-third of the landed area of

England was treated as pasture in 1086, if upland moors and heaths are included. Where a rental value is assigned, such as two shillings per annum at Kempston (Bedfordshire) or 40 pigs at Abinger (Surrey), it is possible that the reference is to privately held pasture, but this cannot be the case everywhere since at Oxford the burgesses paid 6s 8d (33.3p) per annum for what is specifically described as common pasture outside the town wall. There are several other explicit references to common pasture – in 12 places in Devon, for example – and its existence may also be inferred from use of the phrase 'pasture for the livestock of the vill', often found in Cambridgeshire, Hertfordshire and Middlesex, or 'pasture for sheep' in East Anglia, especially Essex. Domesday also reveals that intercommoning arrangements between settlements were in place, usually so that those short of pasture could access that available elsewhere. Benton and Haxton (Devon) had common pasture in neighbouring Bratton Fleming; Hardington and Hemington (Somerset) used one another's common pasture; there was pasture in the Suffolk hundred of Colneis common to all men of the hundred. It has also long been recognized that many of the 'pasture for sheep' entries for inland Essex manors were in fact referring to entitlements to graze the coastal marshes of Canvey, Foulness and Wallasea Islands.[51]

The Domesday commissioners dealt more comprehensively with meadow than with pasture but inconsistencies in the way different Circuits handled their material again pose problems: most entries for meadow give their acreage, but others describe them by the number of plough teams they could sustain or use linear measurements. However, a more serious difficulty is the suspect nature of the information which is presented. Occasionally, we are specifically told that a manor had no meadow (as at Orwell Bury, Hertfordshire, or Stockton, Yorkshire), a circumstance which presumably meant resort to the intercommoning already encountered with pasture, but it is more usual to find cases where the resource is simply omitted. Accordingly, on the face of it there was no meadow at all in Shropshire (despite the richness of the Severn floodplain) and a paucity of it in the Welsh marches generally, in Cornwall and in much of East Anglia. It is impossible to believe that the royal manor of Hingham (Norfolk), with 60 villeins and 29 bordars holding 20 ploughs between them, had only 8 acres (3.2 hectares) of meadow, or that in Thetford, straddling the Little Ouse river which forms the boundary between Norfolk and Suffolk, a small portion in ecclesiastical hands had 12 acres (4.9 hectares) of meadow but the remainder, shared by king and earl, had none at all.[52] At Shocklach, a dispersed settlement in Cheshire adjoining the modern Welsh border, there is to this day a 16-hectare meadow still managed communally and until recently with boundary stones demarcating the ends of the surviving 'doles' or shares: this is appreciably more meadow than there apparently was in 1086, when only half an acre (0.2 hectares) was recorded (Figure 4).[53]

Figure 4: Gwern-y-ddavid, Shocklach Oviatt (Cheshire). The meadow (bounded to the west by the Welsh border) still retains unenclosed 'doles' owned by different farmers, despite some consolidation since this photograph was taken in July 1971. As a township of dispersed settlement, Shocklach demonstrates communal farming of shared resources outside the context of a nucleated village. (Copyright 2006 Cheshire West and Chester Council & Cheshire East Council ©. All rights reserved. Flown and captured by Hunting Surveys Ltd., 8 July 1971.)

There is no certain answer to the conundrum, particularly since variation is apparent even within particular Domesday circuits: the Essex folios, for example, demonstrate that there were meadows in excess of 40 hectares for settlements in the north-west of the county watered by rivers such as the Stour and the Colne, but give much smaller amounts further down these rivers towards the east coast.[54] It may be that the management of grassland as meadow was not well-developed in some parts of the country, but it is also possible that what the Domesday commissioners were sometimes attempting to record was not the whole of a community's meadow but a discrete portion of it, such as that held privately by the lord alone or (conversely) that held from him and subject to communal regulation. A focus on meadow shared as one of the assets of the manor might explain the contrast between north-west Essex where there were later to be some affinities to the 'midland system' and the rest of the county where there were not, and also the relative scarcity of recorded meadow in north-west Warwickshire where individual rather than communal holdings would later be much more significant than elsewhere in the midlands.[55] But it would be unwise to press this too hard and wrong to dismiss the Domesday figures altogether. Whatever vagaries there may have been in the collection and presentation of data, a striking contrast in the overall character of landscape and economy is clearly apparent between Cornwall on the one hand, with its scattered references to odd acres of meadow, and the valley of the Thames with its tributaries in Oxfordshire and Berkshire on the other, rich in the extensive meadowland which helped to sustain a thriving medieval cheese-making industry.[56]

Where meadows were held in common, stakeholders were assigned 'doles' or shares from which to take their hay, but had to complete their mowing before the date designated for the animals to be allowed in to graze in common; apart from the Shocklach example cited above, the North Meadow at Cricklade (Wiltshire) is a good surviving illustration of such a meadow divided into doles. From elsewhere in Oxfordshire, at Shifford, comes evidence of the distribution of such doles: about 1360, a meadow called Twelve Acres was divided into 12 shares, the lord having in one year the first, third, fifth, seventh, ninth and eleventh shares while two tenants held the remainder, with the distribution alternating from one year to the next. Communal access to meadow was certainly found even in areas where arable farming was not practised in common; at Rivenhall (Essex), where the norm was for small enclosed fields to be worked independently, there is map evidence from 1716 of meadows along the River Blackwater divided into strips.[57]

With the growth in population in the centuries following the Norman Conquest, more land was needed to feed both people and livestock, and meadow was no exception: it has been calculated that some 4% of the surface of England was managed as meadow by the mid-thirteenth century, compared to about 1.2% according to the figures in Domesday Book.[58] As early as William the Conqueror's reign, his own religious foundation, Battle Abbey, was having to purchase some 12 hectares of meadow 8 kilometres away at Bodiam (Sussex) because, as its chronicle put it, 'the area around the church was wholly dry and well-watered meadows were scarce'.[59] This sort of arrangement, for both meadow and pasture, became ever more frequent. Within the heavily arable county of Northamptonshire, for example, a survey of 1290 informs us that Hemington (west of Peterborough) was having to supplement its limited supply of meadow by accessing that in four other places nearer the River Nene, at Barnwell, Southwick, Warmington and Yarwell. Peterborough Abbey's Borough Fen, to the north of the town, supplied extensive common pasture each summer to the people of the entire hundred and to the abbey's tenants elsewhere; in 1310, for instance, there were 32 cows from Kettering grazing there.[60] An appreciation of the value of pasture and meadow as scarce resources often led to dispute if attempts were made to privatize what was held in common. Henry II's Assize of *Novel Disseisin* of the 1160s, which gave freemen deprived of their holdings redress in the royal courts even against their lords, was interpreted from the outset as protecting rights of access to common pasture, and it was accepted that hedges or banks enclosing old-established commons could lawfully be demolished without resort to the law courts provided that this was done without delay. Thirteenth-century legislation, in the form of the Provisions of Merton (1235) and second Statute of Westminster (1285), removed any absolute prohibition on lords enclosing pastures, but permitted it only if free tenants and neighbours were left with sufficient to meet their common entitlements.[61]

It was the abundance of rough pasture to be found in the moorlands that enabled them to make a significant contribution to the country's agricultural economy, despite their reputation in popular culture as marginal 'wastes' fraught with danger for those who ventured into them.[62] For much of the middle ages moorlands were largely controlled by the crown or other great landholders as reserved hunting areas (the royal 'forests' or private 'chases' to which we shall turn later) but provision was also made for a limited amount of settlement and livestock grazing, especially for the benefit of lower-lying villages or hamlets elsewhere on their estates. For example, the forest administration of Dartmoor, which passed from the crown to the Earls (later Dukes) of Cornwall in the thirteenth century, was less concerned with hunting (there was better sport elsewhere) than with regulating and levying charges for communal grazing; in 1403–4 the Duchy derived an income of £66 from the 6,400 cattle, 95 horses and indeterminate number of sheep, mostly from parishes away from the moor, formally permitted to graze there. In the Vale of Pickering, a distinctive pattern of long narrow parishes stretching up to the pastures in the North York Moors from the villages below strongly suggests activity deliberately planned from the time the settlements were established.[63] Meanwhile in Cumberland, great estates were arranged so as to combine upland portions which the lords kept for themselves ('in demesne') and lowland portions where manors were sub-let to free tenants. Furness Abbey's estate, for example, was divided into lower-lying 'Plain Furness' leased to local manorial lords and the upland 'Furness Fells', managed for the monks largely as a sheep ranch; the abbey had a licence for the export of wool by 1230. Other Cumberland baronies within Copeland, where there was a similar contrast between upland and lowland tenurial arrangements, have yielded evidence of summer pasturages (shielings) in the lords' moorland fells, many established in the thirteenth or early fourteenth centuries. The footings of rectangular stone huts, and place names derived from the Scandinavian word *skali* for such a temporary hut – itself the origin of the word 'shieling' – are legacies of this activity, the two coming together in the present-day landscape at places such as Scale Close, Borrowdale and Scales, Gosforth.[64]

Commercial vaccaries – specialized cattle farms – also appeared on the moors and were widespread by the early fourteenth century. Fountains,

Furness and Calder Abbeys all had them in Cumberland by this time, as did the Countess of Aumale, whose vaccary at Gatesgarth, supporting 40 milk cows and managed for her as a demesne farm from 1267 (at latest) till her death in 1293, is probably associated with the huge enclosure of Gatesgarth Side east of Buttermere, twice the size of the lake below and now marked by a drystone wall. Vaccaries of similar date have been identified – to name but a few examples – in Wyresdale and Blackburnshire forests (Lancashire), around Barnard Castle (County Durham) and in upper Calderdale (Yorkshire).[65] Beyond these, we have the example of Edward the Black Prince, who established a cattle enterprise intended mainly for the commercial production of plough beasts on his demesne manor of Macclesfield (Cheshire) in 1354. Nine years later the herd was at its maximum size (707 head of cattle) before declining to the eventual termination of the project in 1376, the year of the prince's death. The probable locations of his three vaccaries have been identified in the landscape today, at Macclesfield park to the west of the town, at Harrop in Rainow township to its north-east and at Midgley in Wildboarclough on the Cheshire-Staffordshire border. Alongside the surviving series of annual accounts, these stand as evidence that on the edge of the Peak District in what at first sight might appear to be an inhospitable tract of countryside, a profit could be made even in the decades immediately following the Black Death.[66]

In the expansionist era of the thirteenth and early fourteenth centuries, there was certainly a good deal of colonization of moorlands to create new settlements, necessarily with some arable land as well as pasture. On Dartmoor, for example, a new hamlet for five peasants 'in the waste of the king' at Dunnabridge can be dated by its appearance in a manorial account of 1306 when there had been no reference to it two years earlier.[67] More remarkable is the fact that such colonization continued into the late middle ages, deliberately encouraged by lords keen to find an alternative use for the land. Former monastic granges in Yorkshire, bases for substantial sheep and cattle grazing concerns in the twelfth and early thirteenth centuries, were being leased to peasant settlers by the fourteenth, under the combined pressures caused by indiscipline among the lay brothers who staffed them, difficulties in recruiting these lay brothers as population fell, and the insecurity of the northern border. Thus, the abbey history of Fountains records the permission given by the Cistercian Order in 1363 to 'found new vills in place of the ruined granges at Aldburgh, Sleningford, Sutton, Cowton, Cayton, Bramley, Bradley, Kilnsey and Thorpe' so that 'demesne lands previously maintained by the abbey at these places should henceforth be let out to laymen' for annual rents.[68] Lay lords followed suit. In the forest of Sowerbyshire (Wakefield, Yorkshire), the Duke of York abandoned his deer park at Erringden and leased it to eight tenants as farms between 1449 and 1451. In Cumberland, what had at the beginning of the fourteenth century been four demesne vaccaries at Wasdalehead in Copeland forest had become 19 tenant farms by 1547.[69] There were certainly compensations for those prepared to take up these leases, beyond whatever advantageous terms they were offered, since the moors offered distinctive plant material which could be put to good use: peat (as an alternative fuel to woodland which was normally in short supply), bracken (for thatch, bedding for cattle and – if burnt to ash – for the making of soap) and heather (for brooms, thatch, fuel and baskets).

An abundance of pasture, meadow and various other resources was also a feature of marshlands and fenlands – though here with plenty of arable as well. In marshlands, located beside the sea from which they were protected by man-made embankments, peasants engaged in salt-panning, fowling and fishing, but provided that farmland was properly drained they also enjoyed the benefit of rich clay and silt soils. Accordingly, in Lincolnshire in 1332, the tax assessments for the marshland wapentakes (districts) of Holland far exceeded those in other parts of the shire, while the highest rural assessments in Norfolk two years later were in the western marshland portion of Freebridge Hundred, in places such as Terrington, Tilney and Walsoken.[70] It is no coincidence, therefore, that both here around the Wash and also in the Romney marshes of Kent there was intensive settlement and extensive arable cultivation. Around the Wash this was largely in the form of open fields, with long strips of up to 1.5 kilometres extending into reclaimed land, bounded by drainage dykes. In Romney, the reclaimed arable fields took the form of small irregular closes indicative of individual rather than communal enterprise: oats (especially), wheat, barley, peas, beans and vetch are all known to have been grown here by the early fourteenth century. By contrast, areas such as Halvergate (Norfolk) and marshlands along the coasts of Suffolk, Essex and Sussex were characterized by extensive pastures, especially for sheep. Much of this was commercial demesne farming for the profit of lords such as the Earl of Norfolk and the Abbot of St Benet's, Holme, both of whom had flocks of over 1,000 sheep grazing on Halvergate in the thirteenth and early fourteenth centuries, although it sometimes represented common pasture detached from the inland parishes which desperately needed this additional resource. After the Black Death, even those marshlands noted for arable farming became increasingly important as sheep pastures, so taking on the character they continue to have except where arable has returned in recent decades.[71]

Fenlands could also offer a good living to their inhabitants. Fens were and are distinguished from marshes by being inland, waterlogged, low-lying areas of peat soils; in medieval times settlement was confined to drier 'islands' within them. However, since the peat lacked the acidity found in a 'peat-bog', there was again the potential for drainage to yield fertile soil suitable for both arable land and pasture, and there is plenty of evidence of reclamation to create additional holdings: the Bishop of Ely, for example, had 60 'new' tenants on his manor of Littleport, 13 'new' tenants at Downham and a further 111 'new' tenants at Doddington (all in Cambridgeshire) recorded in 1251.[72] Seasonal flooding, so that a distinction was drawn between 'winter ground' which could be farmed all year and 'summer ground' which could not, was accepted by lords and peasants alike in their management of the fens: such flooding, though potentially disastrous for the corn harvest, was of some benefit to pasture and especially to meadow, and this made pastoral farming in fenlands particularly important. Crowland Abbey, for example, had considerable demesne sheep flocks in and around Cottenham (Cambridgeshire) until the early fourteenth century and one of the settlements involved, Landbeach, appears to have been originally developed as a sheep ranch where cultivation could also be undertaken if neighbouring parishes' fields were flooded. Cattle were also abundant in the fens, some being brought in from neighbouring areas to be fattened for the market.[73]

Like their marshland cousins, medieval fenland families could supplement an income from agriculture with fishing and fowling; they also had access to peat as a fuel, to wood, reeds and sedge both as building materials and as fuel, to hemp and flax as fibres, to woad as a dye, and to the opium poppy to relieve the notorious 'fen ague', although it was doubtless put to other use as well. The twelfth-century *Liber Eliensis*, a history of his community by a monk of Ely, records the netting at sluices of eels, water wolves (*lupi aquatici*), pickerels (pike), perch, roach, burbots, lampreys and – as hearsay – sturgeon, along with the taking of geese, coots, dabchicks, watercrows, herons and ducks using nets and snares. Other sources add bustards, swans, cranes and bitterns. There was considerable profit for manorial lords from all this – the Cambridgeshire folios of Domesday Book, for example, record 27,150 eels per annum rendered from the manor of Doddington, 24,000 from Stuntney and 17,000 from Littleport – but it seems clear that the peasantry also enjoyed common rights to these creatures. On Crowland's manor of Cottenham in 1391 seven men, including one from neighbouring Histon, were accused at the manorial court of fishing when they did not have common right to do so: the implication being that others did enjoy these rights.[74] Similarly, trouble in manorial courts over fowling seems to have concerned abuse of the common right, not the right itself, as in a case at Waterbeach in 1522, where an order was made that wild fowl should not be sold outside the manor without first being offered to the lord. It was access to such resources – along with the inherent fertility of the soil – that enabled some peasant populations to survive on very small arable holdings, notwithstanding the systematic expansion of the arable area through reclamation which characterized the eleventh, twelfth and thirteenth centuries: the 1279 Hundred Rolls show 91% of the peasantry in Waterbeach with less than two hectares of arable, well below what would have been regarded as subsistence level in the midlands.[75]

Although the focus here has been on the extensive and relatively well-studied fens north of Cambridge, a similar story could be told about fenlands in other parts of the country, such as Axholme in north Lincolnshire, the Lancashire and Cumberland mosses, the Norfolk Broadland and the Somerset Levels. Reclamation through drainage schemes proceeded apace: for example, Southlake moor in the Somerset levels was reclaimed by Glastonbury Abbey in the thirteenth century, as were parts of Pilling Moss (Lancashire) by Cockersand Abbey. Peat-digging was a major activity in the Broadland – much to the profit of the major landholder St Benet's Abbey, Holme – and this has left us the 'Norfolk broads', with their ragged edges along the sides of the former trenches, as the flooded legacy; almost 20 million cubic metres of peat are estimated to have been dug from the Broads by the early fourteenth century, after which the activity declined.[76] Axholme was another area noted for this, with Thornton Abbey (Lincolnshire) prominent in the enterprise; the droveways which extend into the fen within long narrow parishes such as Ousefleet and Swinefleet were in origin the access-ways to these former peat-diggings. As in the Cambridgeshire fens, so in Axholme, many farmers had very small holdings but with access to other resources, including fish and fowl, they were (according to a later account) 'very happy respecting their mode of existence'.[77]

Marshlands and fenlands did change in the later middle ages. Despite their protecting banks, marshes were affected by rising sea-levels, first apparent from a 'super-surge' in December 1287 which had a catastrophic effect on the Netherlands (where the Zuider Zee developed its present form as a result) but which also hit east Norfolk and Romney in particular. Overall, there was the same trend towards greater emphasis on pastoral farming as in much of the country: the accounts for the marshland manor of Wisbech Barton (Cambridgeshire), for example, show the Bishop of Ely increasingly reliant on income from sheep rather than grain production as the fourteenth and fifteenth centuries wore on.[78] Reduced population also affected the availability of labour to keep banks and ditches in good repair and this, allied to widespread confusion over who was responsible – lords, peasants, neighbouring settlements – contributed to an apparent increase in disputes and complaints on this score. The competing interests of fishers and fowlers who wanted to let water in and farmers who hoped to keep it at bay only made things worse. A remedy was sought through the periodic authorization by the crown of Commissions of Sewers, normally local landowners who were to order the construction, repair and maintenance of drainage works, if necessary by levying a tax, although these seem to have had only a limited impact. The General Sewers Act of 1531 acknowledged that existing provisions were 'none of them … sufficient remedy', and empowered commissioners to enact local legislation 'after the laws and customs of Rumney marsh in the county of Kent or otherwise by any ways and means'.[79]

The basic problem was that long-term drainage improvements required concerted effort and major capital investment. The dissolution of the monasteries in the 1530s did not help matters, since it removed from the scene some major landowners who could offer a co-ordinated approach. However, it would be unfair to suggest that grand enterprises had never been undertaken. The remains of sea banks, for example, can readily be found in the marshland landscapes as indicators of large-scale land reclamation schemes from late-Saxon times onwards: there are good surviving examples of such banks representing medieval intakes from the Wash in Lincolnshire, at Wrangle, Lutton and near Gedney Drove End, and also in Norfolk, where in the villages of West Walton and Walsoken the communal obligation to repair the sea bank, at a rate of several feet per annum for every acre held, is recorded in 1348. Elsewhere, in the Cambridgeshire fens, Morton's Leam, apparently built about 1490 on the initiative of the local divine John Morton, still runs today as an artificial channel alongside the River Nene from a point east of Peterborough to Guyhirn: an early attempt to hasten the flow of river-water to the sea to prevent it flooding surrounding farmland (Figure 5). This

Figure 5: Morton's Leam near Whittlesey (Cambridgeshire). This 20-kilometre channel, diverting water from the River Nene east of Peterborough, was initiated by John Morton, successively Bishop of Ely and Archbishop of Canterbury in the late fifteenth century. The first major project to drain the fens since Roman times, it still contributes to the overall drainage network.

was the principle taken up again in the great drainage schemes of the Dutch engineer Cornelius Vermuyden, in Axholme and in Cambridgeshire, during the seventeenth century. Yet these fenland drainage schemes have deprived us of a bountiful and distinctive landscape which now survives, imperfectly, only in pockets such as Wicken Fen (Cambridgeshire), Redgrave and Lopham Fen (on the Norfolk-Suffolk border), and Thorne Waste (Yorkshire). The loss of the fenland meres, such as Whittlesey Mere near Peterborough, described in Domesday Book as hosting fishing boats belonging to the Abbots of Ramsey, Peterborough and Thorney, and still over 600 hectares in extent in 1786 when it was home to summer regattas and winter skating, is particularly regrettable. This was drained between 1851 and 1853, an enterprise which caused the surrounding peat to dry out and sink, with the result that nearby Holme Post is, at nearly 3 metres below sea level, claimed to be the lowest land point in England: a dubious distinction which hardly compensates for what has disappeared.[80]

Woodland, parks and warrens

As with other resources, discussion of the coverage of woodland in Domesday Book is bedevilled by different measurement systems. However, despite some woodland being described in acres, some by linear measures and some in terms of feeding swine, an authoritative estimate by Oliver Rackham suggests that about 15% of England's surface was wooded in 1086: coverage ranging from less than 4% in Lincolnshire, Cambridgeshire, Leicestershire and Cornwall to over 30% in Staffordshire and Worcestershire and possibly 70% in the Weald. The national figure should be compared with estimates of 33% woodland cover in the late sixth century and perhaps only 10% by the mid-fourteenth.[81] These figures are a reminder of growing pressure on a precious resource. 'Assarting' – bringing land into cultivation, usually through the clearing of woodland or scrub – was the stuff of everyday life for over 700 years prior to the Black Death and an activity the crown was content to profit from, rather than prohibit, when it took place within the confines of a royal forest. But cutting down trees and then failing to proceed to cultivate the land – probably because removing the stumps was far harder than the initial felling – was frowned upon as 'waste'. Henry II's treasurer, Richard fitz Nigel, wrote that:

> if woods are so severely cut that a man, standing on the half-buried stump of an oak or other tree, can see five other trees cut down round about him, that is regarded as 'waste', which is short for 'wasted ... an offence, even

in a man's own woods … considered so serious that he … must all the more suffer a money penalty proportionate to his means.[82]

It is this which seems to lie behind occasional references to 'wasted wood' (*silva vastata*) in the Essex folios of Domesday Book and to the sums levied from those who had caused 'waste forest' – damage to woods within the king's forest – by Henry II's exchequer.[83] All these entries do, however, cover different types of woodland reflecting diverse management practices, and in places these distinctions are still recognizable today.

There was little or no 'natural' woodland (wildwood) left in England by the Norman Conquest: 'natural' in the sense that, having regenerated after the Ice Age (mostly as small-leaved lime, oak, hazel, ash and elm, plus alder in wet low-lying areas) it had not been influenced by human activity. The last such wildwood to survive may have been in the Forest of Dean, and even this did not outlast the thirteenth century.[84] Virtually all the woodland of Domesday Book – and all woodland anywhere in England by 1300 – was there because of a conscious decision to retain and manage it as a resource. On the other hand, somewhere between one-third and two-thirds of the woodland recorded in 1086 is thought to have been 'primary', that is the direct descendant of the post-Ice Age prehistoric woodland, rather than 'secondary', the result of planting or regeneration on ground previously cleared and put to alternative use. Where those who felled such 'primary' woodland to bring land into culti-vation left narrow belts as field-boundaries, they were effectively preserving portions of it and for this reason hedgerows composed of 'primary' woodland survive to this day, especially among the irregularly shaped fields of formerly wooded areas such as the Arden district of Warwickshire and the Kent and Sussex Weald.[85]

'Secondary' woodland may sometimes be recognized by consulting early maps, which allows the first record of its appearance to be dated, or by the presence of ridge and furrow within the wood showing its former cultivation. It may also be necessary to use pollen analysis to establish the matter: it is this technique which has led to the conclusion that there are very few woods in chalk or limestone districts of southern England which were not preceded by a phase when the countryside was largely open. The concept of 'primary' and 'secondary' needs to be distinguished in turn from that of 'ancient' woodland, a term applied to woods in continuous existence since 1600. But whatever its origins, the presence today of a wood which existed in the sixteenth century or earlier is of obvious interest, not least because of the distinctive flora associated with this habitat. Studies under different soil conditions of 'ancient woodland indicator' plants, such as small-leaved lime and wild service among the trees, and dog's mercury, wood anemone, oxlip, herb paris and lily of the valley among other flora, have established that they are not uniformly reliable across the whole of England (not all grow in every region in any case), but a cluster of such plants is at least a starting point for enquiry into the longevity of a wood. At Swithland (Leicestershire) there is a good, well-studied, example of an ancient wood which contains many of these indicators, even though part of it is clearly 'secondary' in origin, as shown by the ridge and furrow in its northern and south-eastern portions.[86]

The Domesday commissioners were not, of course, concerned with the niceties of how woodland came about, but when they recorded it they normally had one of two types in mind. One was coppiced woodland, managed to ensure a constant supply of rapidly regenerating, easily collected wood – termed 'underwood' and used mostly for fuel alongside fencing, toolmaking and the wattle of timber-framed buildings. A tract of woodland was divided into sections, with the trees in each section being cut back to their stumps ('stools') in rotation; from each stool there would be a vigorous regrowth of sprouts ('poles') which would then be harvested after an interval which in medieval times was usually of four to eight years, in places much more. At Bradfield Woods (Suffolk), where coppicing has been recorded since 1252, the poles are now cut every eight to ten years (Figure 6). Coppicing was normally managed, in practice, as coppice-with-standards, whereby certain trees were allowed to grow for many decades towards their full height without being coppiced, eventually being felled for use mostly in buildings, as rafters and timber frames. Another practice was pollarding, the trees being periodically cut some 1.8 metres or more above ground and allowed to sprout in the same way as those which were coppiced; this had the disadvantage that the harvesting of the regrowth was more laborious but the advantage that the sprouts were out of reach of grazing animals. For this reason, pollarded trees were often found in deer parks and on the edges of woods adjacent to an area of pasture. All this can still be seen not only at Bradfield but also at Hayley Wood near Longstowe (Cambridgeshire), where there are interpretative panels to explain the processes involved.[87]

The other woodland type was wood-pasture: woodland which certainly yielded fuel and building materials but also served as pasturage for livestock, in other words 'pasture with trees'. Because animals grazed the young shoots, woodland regeneration was sparser and more intermittent than it was in coppiced woodland, but pollarding was often practised to combat this and could lead to the woodland cover persisting for centuries even if no new trees grew. In many rural communities, wood-pasture was, in essence, a particular form of common pasture, to which the peasant farmers had communal rights of access: Ebernoe Common and The Mens (both in Sussex) and Naphill Common (Buckinghamshire) are three survivors from

Figure 6: Bradfield Woods, Suffolk. These woods, which belonged to Bury St Edmunds Abbey in the medieval period, have been continuously managed as 'coppice-with-standards' since the thirteenth century. The stumps ('stools') in the foreground have been coppiced to produce the 'poles' which either lie on the ground or are propped against remaining standard trees.

their medieval communities' mixed farming regimes, and may be added to the examples of extant common pasture mentioned above.[88] Wood-pasture was also found in parks, forests and chases, whether or not there was any common access to this resource. Essentially, forests were the king's hunting reserves (especially for the hunting of deer) and they extended far beyond his demesne holdings. Settlements practising mixed arable and pastoral farming were certainly located in forests, their inhabitants living with restrictive laws, accompanying payments and the threat of damage from hunting parties passing through. Chases were similar private hunting reserves held by lords other than the king, again with a good deal of farming going on within their bounds, the Bishop of Lichfield's Cannock Chase (Staffordshire), where he received hunting rights within the royal forest in the late thirteenth century, being a case in point. Practice was not, however, fully consistent, for the term 'forest' was and is sometimes used in preference to 'chase' for the hunting reserves of a subject, especially one of the royal family such as a Duke of Cornwall or Lancaster. Examples of surviving wood-pasture in this context include Birklands and Bilhaugh within Sherwood Forest, where there are late-medieval pollarded oaks still to be seen; at its maximum Sherwood covered a fifth of Nottinghamshire and seems to have been the 'shire wood' with pasture available to everyone with common rights in the county. Parks were generally more wooded than forests or chases in proportion to their total area, certainly by the time of maximum population pressure on resources by the close of the thirteenth century, but also had a crucial role to play as pastures for the herds normally kept within them awaiting slaughter for sport and for meat.[89]

The word 'forest' derives ultimately from the Latin *foris*, meaning 'outside'. They were areas set aside outside normal jurisdiction, and in many ways belong in a book on the law rather than the landscape. As Rackham has put it, many of the 142 forests and chases he has identified (82 of them royal forests) extending at their maximum under Henry II to a third of the landed area of England, covered 'ordinary farmland' and 'ordinary countryside'; despite the importance of some forests as wood-pasture, others had very few trees, being primarily moorland (like Dartmoor, Exmoor and those in the Peak District and Lake District), heathland (like Wolmer, Hampshire) or fenland (like Kesteven, Lincolnshire).[90] The traditional belief that William the Conqueror introduced forests in this legal sense to England is now under challenge; hunting itself, for wild boar and hares as well as for deer, seems to have been popular in pre-Conquest England and there were certainly areas where entitlement to do so was restricted to the privileged few. But if the Normans were building on late-Saxon precedents they certainly took them to a new level in terms of rigour and extent: as the *Anglo-Saxon Chronicle* explained in the Conqueror's obituary, 'he loved the stags as dearly as though he had been their father' and 'set up a vast deer preserve and imposed laws concerning it'.[91] Domesday Book duly mentions forests in over a dozen shires, though often in passing because they did not fit easily into the schedule of the inquiry. Subsequent kings extended the designated area (by the process of 'afforestation') without changing the landscape other than indirectly through the introduction of deer, but such was the inconvenience which resulted, to the detriment of lords' incomes as well as peasants' livelihoods, that they bred seething resentment. Henry II's Assize of the Forest of 1184, for example, placed restrictions on the clearance of woodland and the pasturing of cattle within the king's forests, even where these were not part of the royal demesne, and made provision for officers to patrol and protect his forest rights in a way which must have been seen as highly intrusive by those who lived there.[92] In practice, even Henry II was prepared to see some of his forests cleared of woodland for an appropriate payment – his annual exchequer accounts, the pipe rolls, are full of payments for 'assarts' to create clearances for cultivation within the royal forests – and his successors went further, regarding the sale of charters of 'disafforestation' as a means to bring in much-needed income. Thus, Richard I received 200 marks (£133.33) for the partial disafforestation of Surrey and £100 for the total disafforestation of Ainsty wapentake, Yorkshire, thereby lifting the legal restrictions imposed on these forests and facilitating the subsequent removal of trees. King John extended the process to Lancashire, Yorkshire, Devon, Cornwall, Essex, Shropshire, Staffordshire and Lincolnshire. But popular antagonism towards the forests and their officials remained so strong that concessions had to be made both in *Magna Carta* in 1215 and in separate Charters of the Forest of 1217 and 1225 (promising for example to curb oppressive conduct), a clear signal that the tide had turned. The extent of royal forest early in Edward III's reign was only about two-thirds of what it had been in Henry III's and in the late middle ages the application of 'forest law' withered away [93] – only to be partially revived in the sixteenth and seventeenth centuries because of the potential for raising revenue. Indeed, tracts of designated forest survived well into the nineteenth century, when a drive to extinguish common rights and allocate portions to the crown as timber plantations led on the one hand to a series of enclosure measures and on the other to campaigns to save them, largely for recreational purposes. The New Forest and Epping Forest Acts of 1877–78 were early examples of conservationist legislation.[94]

While medieval forests and chases were basically shared land – farmed by lords and peasants like the rest of the country but under the obligation of respecting the privileged hunting rights which pertained within them – parks were normally areas over which a lord had exclusive control, though even here some common entitlements might persist and grazing rights could be leased for an appropriate payment. The royal park at Woodstock, for example, supplied not only building timbers for the king and those he patronized (like the nuns of Godstow, who were given 15 oaks in 1275) but also fuel for the tenants of neighbouring manors who were allowed to collect it.[95] Domesday Book recorded 37 parks, all in the hands of the king or great ecclesiastical and lay barons, a figure which was certainly too low, partly because there are occasional examples of known parks which were left out, partly because the northern Circuit VI chose to omit reference to them altogether, and partly because most of the features termed 'hays' – numbering well over a hundred – were evidently deer enclosures and thus, in effect, parks by another name.[96] Thereafter, parks proliferated, to an estimated total of over 3,000 by the end of the thirteenth century, descending the social scale to embrace some of the more modest religious houses and lords best regarded as 'country gentry' although remaining disproportionately in the hands of the élite.[97] Although various fish, fowl and other animals were kept within them, deer, especially fallow deer, were prized above all. In one sense, parks offered 'subsistence farming' at an élite level, for venison hardly ever found itself onto the open market, unless it was placed there by poachers. Lords valued the deer from their parks as meat for their own table, as means (dead or alive) to impress their guests and as a vehicle for patronage through gifts of stock to others.

But they did not always pay their way in strictly economic terms: it was the hunting they offered, as sport and as spectacle, which was their principal *raison d'être*.[98]

Many of these parks have left their mark in the landscape today, not least some huge royal parks, such as Henry I's Woodstock, which later grew to over 11 kilometres in circumference, and Windsor Great Park, which under Henry III occupied just under 150 hectares, with a circumference of about 8 kilometres, but then doubled in size during the fourteenth century. A more typical size for a medieval park, especially one in private hands, was between 40 and 120 hectares, although the Bishop of Ely's Hatfield Great Park (Hertfordshire) first appears in 1251 as at least 400 hectares in extent. Other survivals widely used today include Sutton Park, immediately to the west of Sutton Coldfield (Birmingham), first recorded in 1315 as belonging to the Earl of Warwick 'enclosed and fenced, with a fishpond and outwoods' but a corporation park since the sixteenth century; the formerly monastic Kirkstall Abbey Park in Leeds; and Ashbourne Memorial Gardens and Park (Derbyshire), within which the medieval manor house stood at the eastern end of the town.[99] Park boundaries often continue, since with deer capable of leaping up to six metres in length and three metres in height, some massive banks with internal or double ditches were constructed. Examples range from the spectacular, like the 3.7 metre-high southern boundary bank at King's Somborne (Hampshire), a park which at one time belonged to John of Gaunt, to the more subtle, such as part of the eastern boundary of the park associated with the Bigod family's Framlingham Castle (Suffolk), where the bank now stands under one metre high[100] – although it would originally have supported an additional pale, a structure for which oak was the favoured timber. Where stone was readily available, walls would typically be built on top of the banks, as may still be seen in the Yorkshire examples of the Home Park of Fountains Abbey (the 'Monk Wall') and Capplebank Park, West Witton, where the boundary bank and wall are sited along the top of a steep slope within the southern confines of the park, so denying the animals a run-up to leap out. Even if little else survives, park boundaries such as these may still be discernible in the landscape from large enclosures surrounding a group of fields or from the diversion of routeways – like the loop in the old road from Whitchurch to Telford as it passes through the village of Hodnet (Shropshire) and so skirts Hodnet Hall Gardens, successor to the park around which the diversion was made in 1256.[101]

The question still remains, however, of what exactly went on in a medieval park. Sixteenth- and seventeenth-century park plans by the cartographer John Norden and others indicate the importance of wood-pasture but also show gardens nearest the principal residence, pools (attracting birds and fish), areas of open ground (the launds or lawns), coppiced woodland, and sometimes arable or common land.[102] There might also be some industrial activity. Iron mining and smelting were notable features of Yorkshire parks in the fourteenth century, such as Rothwell Park and the Old and New Parks at Wakefield, with lords being prepared to lease rights to tenants to undertake the work, although it is fair to add that this did have its drawbacks: at Rothwell in 1322 the parker reported that herons no longer nested there because of the forges, while in 1331 four tenants in New Wakefield Park were fined for failing to backfill 19 iron-mining shafts. Parks could also serve as quarries for stone, a well-preserved example being that from which Bolton Castle was built between 1378 and about 1396.[103]

Above all, however, parks should be seen as places for leisure and pleasure, especially that to be derived from hunting deer. Forests and chases, where the terrain might be unfamiliar, the quarry was wild and there was a sporting chance for the beasts to escape, probably offered a greater thrill, but declining numbers, at least of red and roe deer, made a successful outcome increasingly uncertain by the end of the thirteenth century. Despite some limitations on space, hunting in parks offered acceptable sport for the lord's family and his guests, with an almost guaranteed end-product. 'Coursing', with small numbers of deer or hares – sometimes single beasts – being chased by hounds along a prepared course, was ideal as spectator sport: Samson, Abbot of Bury St Edmunds from 1182, liked to 'watch the hounds run' when entertaining guests in his parks and a sinuous route marked by earthworks and field-boundaries in a former park at Ravensdale (Derbyshire) has been identified as just such a course. Alternatively, deer could be driven towards stationary archers waiting to take aim, or hunting could be undertaken on foot. It has been suggested that, along with falconry, park hunting was regarded as suitable sport for women, whether or not accompanied by male suitors;[104] parks must also have been the places where a lord's children learned to ride and shoot.

Beyond this, some lords undoubtedly looked on their parks as a private retreat. This was doubtless part of Henry I's motivation at Woodstock, for which expenditure on the 'king's buildings' is recorded in the 1130 pipe roll. This was 'a remarkable place which he had made a dwelling-place for men and beasts', including his own menagerie of porcupines, camels, lions, and lynxes, forerunner of the collection of exotic species subsequently moved by King John to the Tower of London; from here, it eventually settled at Regent's Park to become London Zoo in 1831.[105] For most – from kings with rare animals downwards – parks also provided opportunities to display wealth, status and taste, and analysis of the approach from nearby Salisbury to the royal residence at Clarendon Park, as redesigned under Henry III, suggests a deliberate attempt to show off the elevated royal palace to best effect. The views from the residence might also be important. Examination of what could be seen of the adjoining deer parks from the highest rooms within the castles at both Castle Rising (Norfolk) and Okehampton (Devon) show that the boundaries were invisible, so giving the impression that the parks extended much further. The balcony constructed in 1354 at Woodstock specifically to allow Isabella, daughter of Edward III, a better view of the park, and a fifteenth-century stone viewing platform at Harringworth (Northamptonshire) overlooking the centre of the park and an extensive lake,[106] also testify to the significance of having a prospect of the park, whether to admire the landscape or to watch the hunting.

The centrality of hunting as the principal purpose of most parks is reinforced by the fact that many of them were located in or very close to forests or chases, so that they could be managed together. As Henry II's treasurer put it, 'it is in the forests that the king's chambers are, and their chief delights. For they come there, laying aside their cares now and then, to hunt, as a rest and recreation'. His king had work done on his residences in the parks of both Woodstock and Clarendon almost as soon as he came to the throne.[107] The royal park at Havering was located within the forest of Essex, the Earl (later Duke) of Lancaster's park at Quernmore was within the forest of Quernmore (Lancashire), the Courtenay family's Okehampton Park lay within the chase of Okehampton, and so on. In August 1357, because the Black Prince's park at Peckforton (Cheshire) was 'so stocked with game that the pasture thereof is insufficient for their sustenance', orders were given to release some animals through the boundary 'for the replenishment of the prince's forest there'. 400 deer are known to have been driven in the other direction – from the New Forest into the New Park – prior to a hunt by Richard III in the 1480s.[108] Since gates were liable to be left open either by accident or design, access into the park for the deer was commonly achieved by the construction in the surrounding barrier of a deer-leap over which they could jump. Analysis of deer-leaps at Quernmore, in what appears to be a surviving remnant of the medieval park wall, shows them to have been 14 yards (12.8 metres or two customary rods) long and suggests that deer were driven from the forest into the park using temporary fencing to funnel them towards the leaps, which were located on a downslope making it easier for the deer to jump over. The design of the leaps, and the fact that – as we have already seen at Capplebank Park, West Witton – the slope from within was uphill, meant that it was impossible for the deer to jump out again (Figure 7).[109]

A significant feature of many parks – though not confined to them, since they were also constructed on common pasture or on demesne land close to a lord's hall – were rabbit warrens. When first reintroduced to England following the Norman Conquest, and from thereon until the early fourteenth century, rabbits (or 'coneys' as they were properly called, 'rabbit' being the term used for the young) were regarded as luxury items, to be kept – like

Figure 7: Deer Leap, Quernmore Park (Lancashire). Although somewhat dilapidated, the 'Low Stile' deer leap, at a zigzag in the park's drystone wall boundary, gives an impression of the required height: intended to allow deer to leap into the park if driven downhill from outside, but sufficient to prevent escape if approached uphill from within. (Photograph by kind permission of Mike Derbyshire.)

deer – primarily for the lord's table by special permission of the king. Though reared in all parts of England, these early rabbits were ill-suited to the climate and in need of nurture and protection, their custodians, the warreners, being relatively well-paid specialist officials. Enclosed within the boundaries or compartments of a park, or by banks, streams and ditches elsewhere, they raised few concerns about risks to the surrounding countryside, being seen as fragile creatures, unlikely to stray.[110]

However, all this changed during the course of the fourteenth century. In the Breckland, where dry sandy soils were better suited to rabbit-keeping than to other forms of farming, Ely Cathedral Priory's warren at Lakenheath (Suffolk) traditionally produced no more than 50 rabbits per annum, exclusively for the monks; by the last two decades of the century, it had an annual average output of over 3,000, with 80% being sold for profit. At nearby Brandon, where the warren belonged not to the prior but to the Bishop of Ely, the decade immediately before the Black Death generated an annual average of 158 rabbits, of which 89% went to the lord; by contrast, the 1380s and 1390s yielded well over 2,000 rabbits per annum with some 85% produced for the market. Although the evidence suggests that production and profits generally fell back in the fifteenth century, the Duchy of Lancaster's warren at Methwold (Norfolk) appears to have been a wholly commercial enterprise from the 1390s right through to the 1460s. These East Anglian businesses were particularly favoured by proximity to the London market, meeting a buoyant demand for both meat and fur, but there is no reason to suppose that the rising living standards of the mass of the population, in town and countryside, did not encourage a similar response to rabbit-production on tracts of less fertile soils elsewhere. Alongside all this there are clear signs that increasing rabbit populations, as the animal became acclimatized, led to greater incidence of crop damage from escapees and a welcome, if occasional, supplement to some peasant and labouring families' diet through poaching; by 1521, the Scots writer John Major could describe Britain as an island where 'rabbits swarm' as nowhere else.[111]

The most obvious legacies of medieval rabbit farming in the landscape are the fifteenth-century warreners' lodges at Thetford (Norfolk) and Mildenhall (Suffolk), both remnants of defensible tower-houses which could be used as look-outs, storehouses and accommodation, both for the warrener's household and, on occasion, for a hunting party. Associated earthworks are more subtle. Although natural features, or those inherited from the past (such as the early-Saxon linear earthwork known as the Fossditch, which forms the western boundary of Methwold warren) were frequently used to confine the rabbits, man-made enclosure banks can sometimes be detected, as at High Lodge Warren near Thetford. Better-known are the so-called 'pillow mounds' – low, flat-topped mounds, usually rectangular with a surrounding ditch to aid drainage and hardly ever more than ten metres across. Over 2,000 have been identified in England and Wales, in more than 500 groups, although the majority are post-medieval in origin: examples on Dartmoor at Merrivale in Walkhampton and Yalland in South Brent (Devon), the Cotswold sites of Crickley Hill (Gloucestershire) and Castle Combe (Wiltshire) and two apparently linked to religious houses at Isleham (Cambridgeshire) and Sawtry (Huntingdonshire) are among those which through documentary references or association with other features are likely to be of medieval date. Their regional distribution is uneven, surviving examples tending to be in the moorlands of the south west, the Cotswolds and the chalk downlands, as well as in Wales: far more in the west of the country than in the east, a circumstance attributable in part to subsequent ploughing-out in arable areas but also to the fact that they were built to help the rabbits to find burrows in areas of damper soil, an effort less necessary in the drier east of England. They are very scarce in the Breckland, for instance, despite the known popularity of rabbit farming here. It remains the case, however, that the principal means of catching farmed rabbits in the medieval period, by sending in ferrets and netting them as they fled from their burrows, was easier if the burrows were constructed beneath a pillow mound to a predetermined pattern rather than if left to the rabbits to develop themselves, and this was almost certainly another factor in their construction.[112]

Milling

Before we leave the subject of farming, we should discuss the activity essential to processing the grain from the fields. Mills are commonly associated with peasants' obligations to their lords,[113] but many of them were at least in part commercial enterprises which relied on paying customers: apart from industrial mills – to which we shall return in the next chapter – some corn mills were held not by a lord but by tenants, while others operated in boroughs away from any manorial regime. That said, Domesday Book, which records just over 6,000 mills, does treat them as profitable assets for their lords, and they continued to be so for much of the middle ages; at least 5% of manorial lords' income is reckoned to have been derived from their mills by the end of the thirteenth century. The erection of three mills in Cambridge by the sheriff Picot, yielding £9 per annum, led to complaints recorded in Domesday Book over encroachment on common pasture, destruction of houses and the loss of mills belonging to the Abbot of Ely and Count Alan of Richmond. To judge by the provision made for legal redress for nuisance caused by watermills, entered in the late-twelfth century lawbook 'Glanvill', this was a far from isolated case.[114] The millers themselves, who normally paid fixed sums to the lord which they recouped by charging a 'multure' on each customer – typically one-sixteenth – were notorious for dishonesty with their weights and measures: Chaucer was repeating a commonplace when he wrote that his burly, boorish miller, 'well versed in stealing corn and trebling dues … had a golden thumb'.[115]

Horse mills can rarely be discerned in the landscape but such documentary references as there are suggest that they were often utilised when for some reason other forms of power were inappropriate. A horse mill was installed at Carlisle Castle in 1194 in case the garrison was cut off from the mills on the river below, and in the mid-thirteenth century one was built for St Albans Abbey because the stream feeding the watermill had found another course. It has also been suggested that several new horse mills were introduced towards the end of the middle ages, in places where population had declined to the point where manorial water- or windmills were no longer economic to run. There is some evidence that they were favoured for the grinding of malt for brewing, as was the case with the horse mill belonging to Margery Kempe, who was a leading brewer in King's Lynn (Norfolk) in the 1390s before devoting her life to pilgrimage and mysticism; the surviving early-sixteenth-century brewhouse at Middleham Castle (Yorkshire) preserves a circular horse track for just such a mill.[116]

Most watermills depended for their power on fresh flowing water, but along the coast tide mills were sometimes built, reliant on the ebb and flow of the sea to turn the wheel which drove the machinery. Tide mills are elusive in the archaeological record, but 37 examples (none of which survive) have been identified from documentary references before 1300, among them one at Fareham (Hampshire) which was unambiguously described as a 'sea-mill' in 1210–11. One of the main drawbacks of these mills was their vulnerability to storms and excessively high tides; towards the close of the thirteenth century, at both Walton (Suffolk) and Milton Hall (Essex), new windmills had to be built to replace tide mills wrecked by the sea.[117]

Inland watermills, by contrast, tended to be long-lasting and even if no structures survive they can often be recognized by the diversion and damming of streams, to create 'leats' and millponds so that a head of water could be released to drive the wheel: although it is fair to add that there is a risk of confusion with the creation of water features for aesthetic purposes, as may be the case at the site of the deserted medieval village of Ingarsby (Leicestershire).[118] The *Luttrell Psalter* of about 1340 shows a small timber-framed building with thatched roof and overshot wheel (plus eel traps in the millpond) and if this modest structure is representative of most medieval watermills it is no surprise that their survival is so rare. There are standing remains at Fountains Abbey, where some twelfth-century masonry survives and the original plan of the mill, straddling the watercourse with symmetrical chambers on either side, is still to be seen, but this was unusually substantial. More typical is the late-medieval stone and cob building beside a leat, little more than 6 metres by 3.5 metres in size, which was later incorporated into the industrial site at Sticklepath (Devon).[119]

Watermills were fairly evenly distributed across England, reaching an estimated total of at least 9,000 by the end of the thirteenth century. By contrast, the 4,000 or so windmills built from the late twelfth century onwards tended to feature in the eastern half of the country, where supplies of running water were less readily available.[120] One of the earliest references to them, in the 1190s, relates to a dispute between Abbot Samson of Bury St Edmunds and a dean, Herbert, who 'set up a windmill at Haberdun [within the abbey's area of jurisdiction] and when the abbot heard this, he grew so hot with anger that he would scarcely eat or speak a single word'. This was precisely the type of dispute over competing mills sparked by Picot the sheriff in Domesday Cambridge, and despite Herbert's protestations that 'free benefit of the wind ought not to be denied to any man' – presumably a novel argument at the time – and that 'he wished to grind [only] his own corn there and not the corn of others, lest perchance he might be thought to do this to the detriment of neighbouring mills' he was obliged to have it pulled down. It is a sign of the proliferation of a novel form of milling just at this time that Pope Celestine III (1191–98) was obliged to weigh in with a decretal stating that windmills were liable to the payment of tithe.[121]

Although no medieval windmill now survives – except possibly the ruined bases of some tower mills, noted below – their appearance is known from illustrations and later surviving examples. The earliest type was the post mill, the whole body of which was rotated so as to catch the prevailing wind. These are known from illustrations both in the 'Windmill Psalter' of about 1270 (so named in the 1890s by its then owner William Morris) and in the *Luttrell Psalter* some 70 years later, from various depictions in stained glass, brasses, bosses, wall-paintings and carvings, and from post-medieval examples such as those at Bourn (Cambridgeshire), recorded in 1636 and possibly the oldest surviving in England.[122] The base of the post was supported by cross-pieces set into a flat-topped mound, and these low 'windmill mounds' – which served to elevate as well as to stabilize the mill – are occasionally identifiable today. A good example can be seen at Cold Newton (Leicestershire), inconveniently sited amid ridge and furrow but in the best place for the wind (Figure 8).[123] Tower mills, in which the body of the mill is fixed but the cap at the top, to

Figure 8: Windmill Mound, Cold Newton (Leicestershire). As a base for a post mill, the mound is characteristically flat-topped and positioned at an exposed high point. Medieval ridge and furrow runs either side of the mound but also stops short of it, suggesting that strips continued to be ploughed after the windmill had been established.

which the sails are fixed, can be rotated according to the wind, are known to have been built from the late thirteenth century: accounts survive for the construction of a stone mill at Dover Castle (Kent) in 1294–95, which must have been of tower design, and there are illustrations of them in late-medieval wall paintings and stained glass, as in a window of Stoke-by-Clare Church (Suffolk). Truncated stone towers at Tidenham (Gloucestershire) and Burton Dassett (Warwickshire) may be the remains of former medieval tower mills.[124] Yet while it is tempting to regard windmills as an advance on watermills, because they were introduced later, they were never as popular: watermills were of greater potential size and (except in the specific case of tide mills) generally more reliable, since if they were well-positioned the source of power could usually be controlled. Accordingly, when let out for rent, water-mills normally commanded higher sums than windmills.[125] In this as in every other agricultural activity, there was good sense behind the decisions taken by our medieval ancestors, however surprising they sometimes seem to us today.

3

The landscape of rural settlement

If Leonardo da Vinci's ornithopter, which he drew about 1485, had actually been built and – more to the point – had ever got off the ground, a flight over the late-medieval English countryside would have revealed a rich variety of settlement patterns: from places where, to quote William Harrison in 1577, 'the houses … lie uniformly builded … together, with streets and lanes' to those in which 'they stand scattered abroad, each one dwelling in the midst of his own occupying'.[1] Scholars have coined the terms 'nucleated' and 'dispersed' to describe these different forms of settlement, though in reality there were, and still are, various gradations between the two extremes and in some contexts a lack of clarity over whether a given group of dwellings constitutes one settlement or many. Ultimately, a settlement was defined by its own sense of identity, carrying a place name intended to distinguish it from others, even if it was part of a greater unit (such as a parish or township) to which its inhabitants formally 'belonged' for administrative purposes. Even today, isolated farmsteads – settlements in their own right according to most definitions used by scholars today – are known not by numbers but by names. There is also no consensus on how to distinguish 'hamlet' from its perceived superior, 'village', some preferring size (such as a dozen households as the dividing line between the two), others function, a village being the 'local centre of secular and ecclesiastical authority … the primary place of a particular manor or parish' upon which hamlets were dependent.[2]

The *Atlas of Rural Settlement*, discussed in the previous chapter, relies largely on nineteenth-century one-inch Ordnance Survey maps to divide the country into regions of different settlement types. This is based on the premise that the pattern of settlements can be classified according to the extent to which they were either nucleated or dispersed, the former embracing those in which dwellings were clustered together in relatively large units (typically villages or large hamlets) with tracts of scarcely inhabited countryside in between, the latter covering scattered farmsteads and small hamlets: in areas of dispersion, the density of settlements might be greater, but the settlements themselves were very small. This raises a host of issues, because as the authors fully recognize there are realities on the ground which defy neat classification. But the *Atlas's* broad division of England into three zones – a 'Central Province' largely comprising nucleated villages, a 'South-Eastern Province' of both 'scattered nucleations' and high density-dispersion, and a 'Northern and Western Province' in which dispersed settlement clearly predominates – carries conviction, however much debate there might be over the 'sub-provinces' and 'local regions' into which these zones are further broken down. Also very helpful are the estimates for England as a whole of between 10,000 and 12,000 villages and large hamlets, and between 3,000 and 4,000 communities (vills) consisting solely of dispersed settlements, at the zenith of medieval population early in the fourteenth century. All this provides a basis for further analysis, while leaving a lot of questions to be answered by ongoing research.[3]

Dispersion and nucleation

Most discussion of rural settlements treats them together with their associated field systems, the general argument being that nucleated villages were found in medieval England alongside the great open fields of 'champion' country, dispersed hamlets and farmsteads with the mixture of small open fields and closes encountered elsewhere. This fits with much of the evidence of medieval farming and settlement seen in the landscape today: travelling through the midlands, for example, one often passes through discrete villages each surrounded by extensive ridge and furrow or by straight hedges resulting from the parliamentary enclosure which did away with the open fields. It also fits with our understanding of what would have been most convenient to those working the land. If each householder's strips were intermixed with those held by others, and distributed across the open fields, it made sense for everyone to live as neighbours in a centrally placed nucleated settlement, with the fields arranged around it. Conversely, if holdings were at least partly consolidated, into compact groups of closes with perhaps a few unenclosed strips, farmers would want to be near to where their land was concentrated; this would lead to a more dispersed settlement pattern. In broad terms, the link between settlements and field patterns is well-established and accordingly – as we saw in the previous chapter – the three great 'Provinces' of the

Atlas of Rural Settlement provide a useful framework for the study not only of the distribution of villages and hamlets but also of the layout of their accompanying fields. But it was certainly possible to manage shared resources collectively from dispersed hamlets or farmsteads, and equally possible to farm individually held closes while living in a nucleated settlement. In any case, the coincidence of a particular settlement pattern with a specific type of field system does not prove that they arose together.[4] While we need to be alert to the fact that settlements and their associated fields were intimately connected, as different aspects of local land use, the origins of each deserve consideration in their own right.

There is now general agreement among scholars that in the first few centuries following the arrival of Anglo-Saxon settlers, rural England was essentially a land of dispersed hamlets and farmsteads. Given a free choice, the favoured mode of settlement in the countryside was to live in isolated dwellings or – at most – small hamlets, with handfuls of buildings clustered together in any one place at any one time. This isolation is familiar to most farmers in England today, as it is to those wealthy enough to buy or build palatial homes with scant regard to cost. Indeed, as far as rural areas are concerned, nucleated settlement has been described as a 'short and aberrant episode in the long history of dispersed settlement which characterized all of this country'.[5] Many early Anglo-Saxon settlements also appear to have been relatively short-lived, lasting perhaps 250 years at most before their sites were abandoned in favour of others in the vicinity.[6] The story of how, when and why this changed to a settlement pattern which was more static and, over much of England, significantly more nucleated than hitherto is a complex one. As with the field systems discussed in the previous chapter, it involved a staged process in which different factors predominated at different times in different places. It seems clear that population increase was one important factor, leading to the growth of villages, generation by generation, out of one or more previous farmsteads and hamlets. Sometimes these small outlying settlements were abandoned in favour of one which expanded into a large 'central place', their names perhaps living on in the furlongs of open fields which spread over them. Sometimes they survived, grew and coalesced into 'polyfocal villages' with several nuclei connected by streets and lanes, a phenomenon first identified at Great Shelford (Cambridgeshire) through Christopher Taylor's work with a WEA/Cambridge University Extra-Mural Board class there in the late 1960s.[7] However, this did not happen everywhere: outside the 'Central Province' of the *Atlas of Rural Settlement* (especially to its east where growth was highest), population increase led not to widespread nucleation but chiefly to an intensification of a dispersed settlement pattern, with new hamlets and farmsteads proliferating. So other factors were certainly involved.

The contrast between the midlands, with its village nucleations, and more-densely populated East Anglia, with its many small settlements, has been explored by Tom Williamson. He sees the technological advance represented by the introduction of a heavy wheeled plough with mouldboard – essential to the cultivation of the clay soils increasingly exploited from the eighth century onwards – as a significant development, because a large team of oxen was needed to pull such a plough; since most peasant farmers did not have enough animals of their own, they were obliged to pool their resources. In the midlands, he argues, there were advantages in settlement nucleation with peasants living as neighbours because a rapid, co-operative, response was needed to the limited opportunities available within a relatively short ploughing season and because there was abundant meadow to support fairly high concentrations of livestock. Conversely, where meadow was scattered and in short supply, as in much of the *Atlas*'s 'South-Eastern Province', there was a tendency for hamlets and farmsteads to hug the edges of 'greens', pockets of damp ground which offered a precious – but dispersed – resource from which some of them took their names. These common greens served both as pasture and as an alternative to meadow and were generally associated with smaller settlements and field systems, although there was considerable density to their dispersion across much of East Anglia and the south east.[8] Williamson was not primarily concerned with the 'Northern and Western Province' but his comments could also apply to some areas of dispersed settlement in this region as well, such as parts of the west midlands and Welsh marches where, again, several place-names ending in 'Green' are to be found. These ingenious theories have been challenged because they do not fit everywhere: within the midlands, the siting of settlements in the Whittlewood area on the Northamptonshire-Buckinghamshire border show no consistent correlation with the distribution of meadow, while in East Anglia there is an imperfect match between the greater density of nucleation, and greater development of open fields, in Norfolk and the greater abundance of meadow further south.[9] But if such considerations were irrelevant in some parts of the country, they may have been highly influential in others: they do not provide an all-embracing rationale for the diverse development of nucleated and dispersed settlements but neither does any other explanation. In tackling this subject, it is best to reject a monocausal approach.

Attention has been drawn to administrative changes from the late-ninth and tenth centuries onwards, as much of midland and northern England initially fell under Scandinavian occupation, only for Anglo-Saxon royal government embracing the whole of the country eventually to emerge stronger in response. This was a period when great estates broke up into smaller units, when the lords of those units sought to exploit them more efficiently (as the 'manors' of Domesday Book) partly because of the revenue demands of the crown, and when the Church began to develop a parochial system based on local communities. These developments, all tending towards a reorganization of the way local resources were managed, have sometimes been seen as encouraging settlement nucleation.[10] There can be no doubt that the construction of manor houses and parish churches – the latter increasingly 'built to last' (in stone) after 1000 – introduced new focal points within a settlement around which housing might congregate.[11] But while there was stabilization of settlement in response to these circumstances – with sites coming to be occupied long-term rather than being abandoned after a couple of centuries – nucleation was far from being the inevitable consequence. In Cornwall, for example, 'much of the emerging medieval landscape of settlement and agriculture appears to have been organised around ... newly established churches' but these ecclesiastical centres became 'focal points in landscapes of highly dispersed settlement' rather than village nucleations.[12] Herefordshire appears in Domesday Book with many of the ingredients which might be expected to lead to the development of nucleated villages with great open fields: a density of population similar to that in much of the midlands, relatively high amounts of arable land pressing on resources, and scarcely any 'freemen' among the peasantry who might have been inclined to resist the imposition of manorial control. It also has the highest incidence in the country of castle earthworks in close proximity to churches, which implies – if the present features can be taken as successors to pre-Conquest equivalents – that there had been some deliberation over how the settlements were laid out. Yet this is a county essentially of dispersed, not nucleated, settlement, much of it indeed 'high and very high density dispersion'.[13] So as with the field systems considered in the previous chapter, we should abandon any attempt at determinism and envisage various cultural and perhaps psychological factors coming into play, as decisions on the arrangement of the community's housing were taken in the light of the diverse demographic, environmental and administrative pressures outlined above. And just as with the fields, while we may envisage these decisions being taken sometimes by lords or their representatives, sometimes by peasant communities, sometimes by both together, they would have been based on the experience of neighbouring settlements and a perception of what would work best.[14]

So what was the chronology of any rearrangement of rural settlements, and how did this relate to changes in the layout of fields? In particular instances there is always the possibility that villages and their fields were planned together, but this does not appear to be typical. On the one hand, where nucleation occurred it often seems to have been a phased process: the initial development of a village lacked any obvious plan, but in due course there was replanning according to a more regular form. On the other, while it is tempting to see the fields as having been rearranged at the same time as their parent settlements, only occasionally is there good evidence of this having happened. If we take the analogy of the well-documented process of parliamentary enclosure in the eighteenth and early nineteenth centuries – in many respects the reverse of what we are discussing here, but comparable in its overall impact as a 'landscape revolution' – the great replanning of a community's fields on geometrical lines was normally preceded by small-scale piecemeal enclosures of irregular form which served to illustrate what could be achieved. And the rebuilding of farmsteads away from the old village centres in among their new consolidated holdings, while clearly linked to the enclosure process, was often not a coincident development but – as Hoskins pointed out in *The Making of the English Landscape* – one which followed a generation or two later.[15] In a medieval context, there is much to be said for a model which sees settlement forms, like field systems, undergoing a series of changes which influenced one another but were only contemporaneous in the most general terms.

One influential excavation of a deserted settlement site was that of Goltho (Lincolnshire) in the late 1960s and early 1970s. Here, a planned medieval village – with streets at right angles to one another and regularly laid out enclosures for peasant housing – was interpreted as having originated in the tenth or eleventh century, but to have been preceded by a short-lived ninth-century settlement whose arrangement bore no resemblance to it and over which successive manor houses were later built; the fact that the dating of these developments has subsequently been challenged (as too early) does not undermine their essential sequence. Detailed investigations in central Northamptonshire, at places such as Braunston, Daventry and Higham Ferrers, have also led to the conclusion that the original nucleations probably date to before 850 and subsequent replanning to the tenth century. At Cottenham (Cambridgeshire), an apparently eighth-century nucleation (still the site of the church) was subsequently abandoned in favour of a new ninth- or tenth-century centre to the south, laid out according to a radial plan; further planned extensions followed in the twelfth century. Wharram Percy (Yorkshire), Brandon (Suffolk), Chalton Down and Bishops' Waltham (both Hampshire) are other early nucleated settlements which appear to have undergone 'second-phase' replanning, though in the latter case not until the eleventh century.[16] These later reorganizations may well have occurred in the context of intensified manorial control – a drive to apportion house-plots systematically in relation to government tax assessments and the demands of the local lord – but there must have been other reasons for the initial clustering of houses together, albeit in an irregular, unplanned pattern. It is tempting to suggest that peasants were motivated by a heightened sense of interdependence, whether for mutual protection, the sharing of equipment or ready access to specialist skills and services, including in some places those provided by a newly built church.

As for any connection between these processes and the rearrangement of the fields, clear evidence of a link between the two is remarkably elusive. At Shapwick (Somerset), the existence of a planned settlement whose arrangement changed little from the eleventh century to the eighteenth, set conveniently between two great open fields, lends itself to the suggestion that these were all laid out at the same time, but the investigators acknowledge the possibility of alternative explanations, one of which is that the village and its fields both developed in stages.[17] Where we have documentary evidence of a replanning of the fields, there is no sign that this extended to the accompanying settlement: for example, the twelfth-century accounts of the deliberate rearrangement of the open fields at Dry Drayton and Segenhoe – encountered in the previous chapter – make no reference to the layout of the housing. Conversely, we read in the *Battle Abbey Chronicle* a detailed description of a post-Conquest planning initiative which created a new town but did not change the fields outside. Many of these fields were already being worked as part of neighbouring manors before being granted to the abbey and – as was usual in the Weald – they were arranged in closes held by individuals rather than in common. Successive abbots were certainly prepared to promote further woodland clearance and to rearrange tenancies to their own advantage, but no attempt was made to reorder these closes into open, communally worked, fields; instead, we are told in the *Chronicle* that 'in Petley there is one wist ... which a man called Oter formerly held; it is forty-eight acres in size', and that 'next to Strellewelle are four acres which Gilbert the stranger held and his heirs after him'. We have here a nucleated settlement laid out without significant alteration to the pattern of its accompanying fields: and since the prevailing custom of the area was to farm in closes, that pattern remained.[18]

Of course, circumstances might sometimes arise where it made sense to arrange a settlement and its fields at the same time, such as the colonizing schemes in northern England noted in the last chapter. It is possible that in some other cases of late nucleation, where concentrated settlement cannot be demonstrated before the twelfth century – Faxton and Lyveden (Northamptonshire), Wawne (Yorkshire), Gomeldon (Wiltshire) – the open fields were planned together with the village, along lines by then well-established in their respective areas. Much the same has been suggested for the settlements around Whittlewood on the Northamptonshire-Buckinghamshire border, where evidence for nucleation is lacking before the late-ninth and tenth centuries; here, the investigators suggested that these communities may – in effect – have skipped the earliest phase of inchoate nucleation and partial establishment of open arable strips and arranged their settlements and field systems together within a coherent plan. As at Shapwick, these are attractive theories, but they cannot be proved. The reality is that no model of how settlement nucleation linked to field patterns applies everywhere: 'a connection between the two is likely … but we still do not know what that relationship was'.[19]

Another reality is that, however convenient it is to distinguish nucleated and dispersed settlements one from the other, much of England displayed characteristics of both. Even the *Atlas of Rural Settlement*, which relies on that distinction for its methodology, accepts that, of 'the eight varied ways in which a single township may be settled', four of them embraced 'mixed settlement patterns' between the two extremes.[20] Within the 'Whittlewood' area, though part of the 'Central Province' with its emphasis on nucleation, the parish of Leckhamstead (Buckinghamshire) had six small but identifiable settlements prior to the mid-ninth century, most of them sufficiently distant from each other to categorize this as an example of dispersion. The changes of the late ninth and tenth centuries led to fewer and larger foci than before, one apparently with a planned row of tofts, but Leckhamstead is regarded by its investigators as a 'dispersed village', described in Domesday Book as three separate manors, each with its own ploughlands, meadow and woodland.[21] In Norfolk – within the 'South-Eastern Province' – a tendency has been observed for villages apparently created as nucleated settlements in or around the eighth century subsequently to become more dispersed, as farmsteads, attracted by the availability of a scarce resource, migrated to the edges of commons and greens. Longham (near East Dereham) and Stanfield (near Wymondham) are examples of places where such migration meant that the earlier nuclei had already been abandoned by the eleventh century, leaving their churches standing in isolation. Alternatively, as at Weasenham St Peter (near Fakenham), the settlement around the church remained but subsidiary foci developed around the common. The medieval field systems associated with these settlements were largely open arable farmed in common – though lacking some of the rigorous consistency associated with the 'midland system' – but they were not attached to single nucleations: 'for much of northern East Anglia, the era of villages was short-lived'.[22] Meanwhile in Cheshire, part of the 'Northern and Western Province', we have the example of Tilston, where the evidence in the landscape is of a row of house-plots (tofts) adjacent to the medieval parish church, a second small nucleation around Tilston Green the best part of a kilometre to the north, and dispersed settlement in the form of farmsteads and other dwellings at various intersections of routeways elsewhere within the township. This pattern of small nucleations surrounded by scattered hamlets and farmsteads was widespread in medieval Cheshire, as demonstrated by archaeological work at the deserted settlement of Tatton, a 'straggling … interrupted row … with scattered halls and hamlets elsewhere in the township'.[23]

So any survey of rural settlement across medieval England between the years 1000 and 1540 will embrace a variety of patterns of nucleation and dispersion: a complexity sufficient to challenge even the hardiest exponent of categorization. However, as has already been alluded to, one recurrent characteristic of medieval settlements is the impact of at least a degree of deliberate planning in their layout. This is most obvious where the present-day settlements retain a recognizable pattern of straight streets and geometrically shaped village greens, lined by tofts of consistent dimensions with continuous 'back lanes' forming predetermined rear boundaries. Such a pattern is often encountered in north Yorkshire and the north east, where it has been attributed to deliberate resettlement following William the Conqueror's 'Harrying of the North' in 1069–70, and also in Cumberland, where the context may be William Rufus's annexation of the area from the Scots in 1092, after which he sent 'very many peasants thither with their wives and livestock to settle there and till the soil'; no one who visits Milburn, just off the A66 some 14 kilometres east of Penrith, can fail to be impressed by the regularity of a layout in which housing still surrounds on all sides a large rectangular green, a place of safety for the animals once penned within it.[24] But similar evidence of planning can be found embedded in many villages all over England which have since expanded far beyond their original form. In the Fylde area of Lancashire, for example, what are today quite diversely arranged settlements such as Clifton, Elswick and Longton were originally laid out in rows, each with territorial boundaries embracing a share of open field arable, marshland and mossland, possibly as part of another post-Conquest colonization initiative following violent incursion by the Scots in 1061. At the opposite end of the country, Chobham, Egham and Great Bookham are all in the Surrey commuter belt today, but all contain within them in the vicinity of their parish churches 'excellent illustrations of regular two-row plans', with peasant tofts aligned either side of a main street and back lanes behind. The fact that they were all within Chertsey Abbey's estate suggests that here at least it was the lord rather than his tenants taking the lead in imposing a plan.[25]

Yet there was much more to planning than setting out geometrical patterns of streets and house-plots. Rashleigh (Devon), duly entered as a manor in Domesday Book with a recorded population of 15, consisted in the mid-eighteenth century of a small hamlet and several farmsteads mostly grouped around and within an identifiable oval enclosure, roughly 700 metres by 450 metres, by then held in separate portions. This may well be a settlement in which the oval enclosure – possibly representing the original intake for cultivation – previously housed the communally farmed open arable, with the peasant houses being systematically grouped around it so as to allow easy access to other resources beyond. Stanfield (Norfolk) is another settlement where the open arable fields seem to have been deliberately developed within a large oval, in this case just to the north west of the church and manor house, with peasant settlement being located 200 metres and more west of the church at the periphery of the oval, at its interface with the common pasture beyond.[26] These are not obviously 'planned' but there was certainly some forethought, and communal decision-making, behind the placing of the peasants' houses. As Christopher Taylor has written, we need to be alive to the possibility that 'many thousands of villages whose layouts do not show any elements of planning could nevertheless be the result of deliberate development'. At first sight, Raunds (Northamptonshire), which had several nuclei in the medieval period, does not look to have been planned systematically. Yet detailed analysis of former tofts in different parts of this settlement has shown them to have been very carefully laid out according to a 16 ½ feet (5.03 metres) rod, both in length and in breadth, seemingly as part of a deliberate reorganization in the tenth century.[27] We also find evidence of planning in settlements so small that they would normally be described as examples of dispersion: Halton Shields near Corbridge (Northumberland), a former shieling settlement for upland summer grazing, was reorganized – probably in the early sixteenth century – as a row of seven uniform tofts along the line of Hadrian's Wall,[28] while in Cheshire the neighbouring settlements of Clotton and Burton near Tarvin, each with only a few adjacent house-plots, still exhibit all the characteristics of a deliberate arrangement (Figures 2, 9). And planning certainly played a large part in the extension of settlements to cope with increased population, as at Cottenham (Cambridgeshire), where the boundaries of additional tofts are derived from the sinuous course of the former strips, at Burwell (also Cambridgeshire) where North Street (first recorded in 1351 as a northwards extension of the village) appears to follow the line of a headland between furlongs of the open field, and at Cestersover (Warwickshire) and Walgrave (Northamptonshire) – the former a deserted settlement – where house-plots alongside streets leading away from the core of the village incorporated traces of the ridge and furrow of the former open fields.[29] Given their impact on communal farming arrangements, it is hard to believe that these extensions could have gone ahead without 'planning consent' granted by the 'community of the vill', whether or not the lord or his representative was also involved.

Turning to dispersed settlement as a whole, we encounter a story of infinite variety, every bit as important for the study of rural settlement as that of the nucleated villages which have traditionally received more attention. Although growing population and more organized manorial administration were certainly factors which led to settlement nucleation, most places responded to these issues not by replacing their dispersed settlement pattern but by intensifying, adapting and refining it. Thus, at the isolated farmstead of Berry Court in north-east Cornwall, occupation has been traced back to the ninth century; in Essex, at hamlets such as Asheldham, pottery dating to

Figure 9: Burton near Tarvin (Cheshire). This hamlet has changed little since the RAF took the photograph in January 1947. It retains much of its medieval character as a planned settlement, with a row of tofts between the main street and a back lane to the north, and farmers living as neighbours to one another. (English Heritage NMR RAF Photography.)

before the tenth century has been found at or very close to the subsequent settlement sites; in Staffordshire, scattered settlement around Shenstone, as at Hilton and Upper and Lower Stonnall, has been postulated to have been in existence by the eleventh century, even though the first documentary references to some of these places are much later.[30] All this suggests that, as part of a reorganization of the landscape paralleling that which was taking place in the 'nucleated' regions, dispersed farmsteads and hamlets, with their accompanying fields, were 'settling down' in fixed locations. The date when this happened varied, but that was the case with village nucleation as well. The process is nowhere better demonstrated than in Rivenhall (Essex), where the existing pattern of dispersed farmsteads and hamlets has been shown to have been largely in existence by the eleventh or twelfth centuries, preceded by a series of earlier Romano-British and early Saxon farms in different positions.[31] The fact that, in medieval Cornwall, dispersed settlement was associated with a landscape of open strips – possibly covering as much of 60% of the land surface at their maximum extent – while in Essex the countryside was dominated by hamlets, farmsteads and enclosed fields, with limited evidence of open arable over most of the county,[32] reinforces the dangers of attempting to link types of settlement and field system together.

Beyond the hamlets and farmsteads of the eleventh century onwards which can be shown to have had Saxon or earlier predecessors – in the immediate vicinity if not on exactly the same site – there were a host of dispersed settlements in medieval England which were the result of systematic clearance and colonization to feed a growing population. Much of this activity (like the settlement of Hound Tor on the lower slopes of Dartmoor) dates to the eighth-to-eleventh centuries, before it was captured in documentation. But once we have charters, surveys and other estate records there is no difficulty in illustrating this all over the country, as hitherto unrecorded settlements appear for the first time – sometimes incorporating the element 'new', sometimes words associated with woodland, enclosure, farmstead or shelter; the fact that they already bore names by the time they were first recorded suggests that they were almost invariably older than the dates to which they can be assigned.[33] It was this phenomenon which saw population in parts of the wooded Arden region of north-west Warwickshire, for example, increase fourfold between 1086 and 1279; detailed study of one parish within Arden, Tanworth, has shown a sustained attack on the woodland in this period, resulting in a landscape composed largely of single farmsteads each with their own separately held closes. Although each farmer held on average only about two hectares, this was supplemented by the resources of the surviving woodland and at least partially redeemed by the free status granted to those who cleared the land. In the similarly wooded environment of Hanbury, Worcestershire, where population doubled between about 1170 and 1299, several new place names had appeared by the middle of the thirteenth century in areas of woodland clearance, such as Blickley, Broughton and Becknor, all being treated as separate units of estate administration and evidently distinct hamlets; over 60% of the peasant tenants in Hanbury were freeholders by the close of the thirteenth century.[34]

A similar process took place in the wetlands of eastern England, where there were some astronomical population increases over the same period, occasioned by the construction of banks to prevent flooding both from the sea and from inland watercourses, and by the drainage of what could thereby be reclaimed. An extra 250 square kilometres is believed to have been brought into cultivation within the Lincolnshire parts of Holland between 1170 and 1240, and in one parish here, Moulton, the parent village spawned two hamlets during the course of the thirteenth century (Moulton Chapel and the aptly named Moulton Seas End) as well as several farmsteads, all protected by banks. Similarly in the Cambridgeshire fens, 13 new free tenants were recorded in 1251 at *Apesholt*, a hamlet on a gravel ridge which had been set up in the outlying parts of the Bishop of Ely's manor of Downham.[35]

Colonization was sometimes undertaken as a project led by lords of the manor – who saw the potential for profit by allowing peasants and others to win new land for cultivation in return for the grant of free status and future payment of rents – sometimes as a matter of individual or collective enterprise. Charters give the impression that lords were in control, but there must be a suspicion that in many cases they were merely regularizing a situation which had arisen already and ensuring that they received some rent in return. Sometime between 1200 and 1213, Amaury Earl of Gloucester gave to Richard de Crespi 'ten acres of land of my assart at Nurstead (Kent) next to the house of William Huryng'; at around the same time in Devon, a peasant freeholder, Benedict son of Edric Siward, was granted by Guy de *Brittevilla* lord of Cornwood 'all my land of Cholleswyht' by closely defined boundaries, evidently the origins of the now-deserted hamlet of Cholwich over 200 metres above sea level on Dartmoor; on 25 May 1219, the Bishop of Lincoln granted to a more substantial figure, Walter fitz Robert (later described as a knight) and his heirs 'all the assart made or to be made of our wood of Harthey' (Huntingdonshire) with provision for the men and houses there to be treated as part of the bishop's manor of Buckden, and later allowed Walter to build a chapel there.[36] In every case, an annual rent was specified, and in every case we have a glimpse of a new settlement, with its own name, coming into being, but there is at least a hint that the grants were retrospective. Even where lords clearly played a more active role in promoting colonization, a point would be reached where some responsibility was handed over to the incoming settlers. Thus, the ridgeway villages of Mayfield, Wadhurst and Ticehurst on the Sussex Weald all seem to have originated from thirteenth-century market grants obtained by their lords, who laid out the market areas in unoccupied parts of their estates but then left settlers to congregate around these nuclei without any further planning on their part: these have been described as 'permissive settlements', whose residents were encouraged to take advantage of the trading opportunities provided but without any lordly direction over their layouts.[37] When it came to taking decisions over how to occupy new land, organize settlement and arrange field systems, we must expect the peasantry, doubtless with some of the better-off freeholders playing a prominent role, to be fully capable of exercising initiative – with many of their lords happy to let them get on with it, content to benefit from the extra rent which would accrue.

Industrial settlements

Industrial activity in medieval England – if we exclude agriculture from the definition – was largely a rural affair, since it needed ready access to raw materials and to waterborne power supplies and these tended to be found in the countryside. Accordingly, any discussion of rural settlement must take this into account. Obviously, there were many urban-based craftsmen and (especially before the thirteenth century) several towns active in the manufacture of cloth but – as we shall see in the next chapter – it was primarily as centres of commerce and administration that most towns flourished. The rural focus of industry meant that those engaged in mining or manufacture usually did so part-time, alongside their farming duties. Well over 1,000 coastal *salinae* (saltworks) are recorded in Domesday Book, mostly along the east and south coasts between the Humber and Plymouth Sound where there were a host of settlements engaged in the organized evaporation of seawater, but except in Devon and Dorset no specific *salinarii* (saltworkers) are mentioned: the implication must be that the rural peasantry – villeins, bordars or however they are recorded – were doing this work while also tilling the land. Crockerton (Wiltshire) bore a place name derived from its reputation as a pottery-making centre, but the population in 1234 was still listed according to its landholdings, which at less than two hectares for each peasant household would have made a second income imperative. Excavation of the deserted village of Lyveden (Northamptonshire) has revealed evidence of tile kilns and furnaces for the smelting of iron ore, but the structure and layout of the housing was typical of a peasant farming settlement – which, to a large extent, it remained. Blast furnaces, introduced at the end of the middle ages as a technological advance in the smelting of iron ore, had to await the completion of harvest before being 'blown in' after their annual summer service. Mining was also predominantly a seasonal occupation: fourteenth- and fifteenth-century lead miners have been reckoned to extract at most two tons of ore per annum, mainly in the period between mid-April and July when spring ploughing and lambing were over and haymaking and harvest had not yet begun. Stone quarries were worked not speculatively but in response to specific demands, so the labour was intermittent and ideally suited to men who had alternative work on the land. And, from the thirteenth century onwards, one of the major attractions of the countryside to the entrepreneurs who controlled the cloth industry was that some of the key processes, notably spinning and weaving, could be undertaken in the home as part-time family activities, free of the restrictive practices of urban gilds.[38]

The consequence of all this is that industrial activity, though it sometimes left a considerable legacy in the landscape, is usually thought to have had limited impact on the pattern of rural settlement. It relied mainly on a workforce which was also engaged in farming and was already established in existing villages, hamlets and farmsteads. There are, for example, extensive tracts of 'saltern mounds' along the Lincolnshire coast, created by the distinctive method of saltmaking – found here and in the Solway Firth – of washing out the salt from saturated mud and sand, leaving dumps of waste matter behind: but the associated settlement pattern, of hamlets and farmsteads colonized from parent villages inland, is essentially derived not from this ancillary activity but from the opportunities to exploit farmland newly reclaimed from the sea.[39] For their part, stone quarries have typically left a pockmarked landscape, nowhere better illustrated than by the 'hills and holes' of the great Jurassic limestone workings at Barnack (Cambridgeshire), (Figure 10), Taynton (Oxfordshire) and Ham Hill (Somerset), but given the sheer weight to be transported there was every incentive to locate them as close as possible to established routeways and population centres. Corfe (Dorset), a planned settlement where two streets fan out from the castle established here after the Norman Conquest, still has various trackways which led from these streets to the local Purbeck marble quarries, while Barnack, which lies immediately adjacent to its former quarries, has the regularly laid-out peasant house-plots typical of countless farming villages of the midlands.[40]

As for mining, the landscapes of Cornwall, Devon, the Peak District, the north Pennines and elsewhere are enriched through the pits, trenches and spoil heaps generated by extraction, and through the slag heaps produced by subsequent smelting.[41] However – notwithstanding the 3,000 men employed in the Penwith-Kerrier area of west Cornwall for much of the fifteenth century – the mining industry mostly involved low numbers at any one location, and

Figure 10: Barnack Quarries (Cambridgeshire). Now a nature reserve, the 'hills and holes' are the product of the Jurassic limestone quarries adjacent to the village, worked from Roman times until the early sixteenth century. The durable stone was prized for high-status buildings, including Barnack's own parish church with its late-Saxon tower.

once the raw material could no longer readily be extracted from the surface it made sense to try somewhere else in the vicinity. This meant that miners did not put down permanent roots next to anything as ephemeral as a mine: they generally walked between their home settlements and their movable places of work, a daily commute by foot of perhaps a few kilometres each way. The earliest record of a coalminer ('carbonarius') in England, in the *Boldon Book* (a survey of the Bishop of Durham's estates) of 1183, places him at Escomb (County Durham), which to judge by its fine Saxon church had been a settlement since the seventh century; he had his own house-plot with four acres (1.6 hectares) of land and was expected to find coal as fuel for ironworking. As this form of mining spread, first through the north east during the thirteenth century and over most of England's known coalfields thereafter, the raw material proved to be so readily accessible that there was no need to abandon familiar dwellings and fields. There might, however, be temporary shelters at the mines. 'At dinner tyme ... they syt downe together beside theire tynwork in a little lodge made up with turves covered with straw' wrote Thomas Beare, a commentator on the south-west tin industry, in 1586; 'many little howses ... shrowd them in neere the worckes' recorded the topographer and surveyor for the Duchy of Cornwall, John Norden, in 1610. Traces of these shelters, roughly 5 metres by 3 metres with drystone or turf walls and often some evidence of a fireplace, have been found in the south west on Dartmoor and Foweymore and while not necessarily medieval can be taken as representative of a longstanding tradition.[42] A variation on this theme – temporary dwellings though in this case providing sleeping accommodation – were the *shiels*, or summer lodgings, of lead miners on Alston moor, which suggest that mining was being combined with the tending of livestock in their summer pastures. Small complexes of buildings also accompanied forges and furnaces for the working of iron, where constant supervision was required. Thus, in 1240 William of Lancaster gave to the Augustinian priory of Conishead 'one acre of land next to the stream ... for a forge with a yard and for building other houses there, necessary to it'; in 1377 William son of Elias of Bramley was granted rights to take loppings from trees in the wood at Calverley (Yorkshire) 'for baking and brewing for his servants at the forge and for his supervisors there'. Out of all this, very little seems to have emerged as new permanent settlement, although the present-day hamlet of Pounsley near Framfield (in the Sussex Weald), where there was a 'bloomery' furnace for the smelting of iron ore by the 1540s, may have originated in this way.[43]

These references to temporary settlements, and even to one which may have developed from temporary to permanent, are ample demonstration that medieval England was not lacking in 'industrial settlements'. The cloth industry certainly had them. What at the beginning of our period was largely a female domestic craft developed into a complex series of processes, from the initial grading, washing and beating of wool, through carding or combing, spinning into yarn and weaving, and then on to the fulling of cloth (to scour and thicken it), tentering (drying and stretching), teasing (raising the nap), shearing (to remove raised fibres) and finally – if required – dyeing. Much of this became specialist skilled work, carried out by full-time urban or part-time rural wage-earners under the co-ordination of entrepreneurs, who employed the workers, supplied them both with raw material and with equipment and invested in new technology; those responsible for the later stages, such as fullers and dyers, tended to emerge in this role.[44] For spinning, hand-driven spinning wheels, because they produced an inferior yarn and demanded full-time attention, only slowly replaced the traditional distaff and spindle – the *Luttrell Psalter* of the 1340s illustrates both methods – but for weaving there was a clear advance with the introduction of the horizontal treadle loom by the thirteenth century, producing a tighter weave in one-third of the time taken by the previous upright loom.[44] Mechanization was introduced to fulling in the twelfth century and to teasing in the fifteenth, with waterwheels providing the power in both cases. While the significance of these developments in stimulating rural industrial activity has been exaggerated, it remains true that they were especially to be found in the countryside, with several towns continuing to favour conventional 'walking' (treading the cloth by foot) as a method of fulling: Norwich did not acquire its first mill for the purpose until 1429.[45] A dedicated fulling mill in use in the fifteenth century has been identified from excavation at Beaulieu Abbey (Hampshire), with arched drains serving deep stone-built processing tanks, but these technological advances have usually left little obvious trace today, not least because fulling mills and gig mills (for teasing) cannot readily be distinguished from corn mills on the basis of surviving remains and many performed different functions in different periods.[46] It is the settlements which hosted the cloth industry which are its principal legacy in the landscape.

For much of the medieval period, Flanders – though heavily reliant on the import of wool from England – led the way in European cloth production, despite the efforts of English manufacturers during the thirteenth century to cut costs by turning increasingly to a rural workforce so as to bypass the collective power of urban gilds. However, after 1300 the Flanders cloth industry went into decline, hit by war, civil unrest and high export duties imposed on English wool. Cloth manufacture within England prospered in response, stimulated in part by the improved living standards following the Black Death which – in the eyes of scandalized contemporary observers – saw peasants dressing far better and more fashionably than was right and proper.[47] Economic fortunes fluctuated thereafter, but by the 1430s the value of cloth exports had outstripped that of wool and England had become indisputably the major European cloth producer. Both urban and rural communities benefited from this revival, though with greater geographical concentration than hitherto: in the countryside it was regions such as the West Riding of Yorkshire, Suffolk, Kent and the Cotswolds, favoured either by abundant local wool supplies or by easy access to the London market, which became especially important. And it is in some of the villages associated with cloth-making in this late-medieval period that we find the industry's lasting impact. Analysis of relative wealth in different parts of the country on the basis of tax assessments has shown cloth-producing shires such as Suffolk, Somerset and Wiltshire, middle-ranking at the beginning of the fourteenth century as the last two were in the late twelfth century as well, to have been in the 'top ten' by the early Tudor period.[48] Economic growth on this scale did not necessarily lead to a significant increase in population in these places, but it was certainly reflected in the quality of building.

Minchinhampton (Gloucestershire), for example, was already by 1200 developing as a cloth-making centre based in new dispersed settlement along the Stroud valley, below and apart from the original village nucleus where the church and manor house remained. There were at that time four fulling mills beside the river and during the following century several manorial tenants are recorded as engaged in fulling and in digging fuller's earth; in addition, any weaver living by his craft and in need of a home was allowed to enclose part of the common. By the late fifteenth century the many fulling mills and dye works located down in the valley were responsible for the finishing of internationally renowned 'Stroudwater' cloths, the growth of their associated hamlets fully compensating for the desertion of some 50 houses in the old village centre above. Similarly, Castle Combe (Wiltshire) had 31 messuages (houses for those with a stake in the open fields) and 20 cottages (for wage-earners, especially those engaged in cloth-making), along with three corn mills and a fulling mill, according to a manorial survey of 1340: the craftsmen's cottages were in 'Nether Combe' close to the stream which drove these mills, while the peasant farmers' messuages were in 'Over Combe' adjacent to the open fields on a nearby hill, a clear sign that the cloth industry was having a significant impact on the shape of the settlement. By 1447, despite the dramatic fall in population on a national scale over the preceding hundred years, there were still 28 messuages, 19 cottages, one gig mill and three fulling mills; by 1507, 50 houses and two fulling mills; by 1547, 51 with four mills. In the 1450s we learn that the lord Sir John Fastolf had made substantial purchases of cloth annually from the village craftsmen, mainly as livery for his retinue of soldiers in France, and so had facilitated 'the common wealth of the said town and of the new buildings raised in it', among them a new church tower and '50 houses newly rebuilt', forerunners of the Cotswold stone houses which still dominate the village today. Far from suffering decline and depopulation, this was a village which was attracting incomers and sufficiently thriving for the lord to engage in major improvement to its housing stock. A comparable story could be told of Kersey (Suffolk), a village laid out on opposite sides of a valley between the parish church at the southern end and the Augustinian priory at the northern, with a stream crossing the street which links them. Here the cloth industry does not seem to have made any obvious impression on the overall layout, although it certainly enhanced the importance of the watercourse, which can be seen to this day as clear and shallow, ideal for the cleansing of the wool and cloth at various stages of production. The making of a distinctive light and narrow cloth which took its name from the village undoubtedly sustained Kersey in the late middle ages, helping to preserve the plan and contributing to the wealth reflected in the rebuilding of many of the half-timbered houses which survive (Figure 11).[49]

These three places all had a farming element within their local economy, but they all depended for their late-medieval prosperity not on agriculture but on cloth manufacture. They remind us that, even if they did not owe their original existence to industry, they ought really to be regarded by the late middle ages as 'industrial villages'. It was cloth for which they were known far afield and cloth which seems to have provided employment, including what we must presume to have been plenty of full-time employment, to a

Figure 11: Kersey (Suffolk). Essentially a single-street settlement laid out across a valley, with a church at one end and a stream as a focus for industrial activity, Kersey had a market from 1252 and by the fifteenth century was prospering from the production of the distinctive hard-wearing cloths which bore its name.

substantial portion of the population. At Minchinhampton with its hamlets away from the parent village, and at Castle Combe with its separate cloth-making quarter, the industry gave a new shape to the pattern of settlement and at all three there was a superior quality to much of the late-medieval house building. If we turn to other industries, we can see a number of communities which seem to have had a similar specialist focus. In Furness, a place called Orgrave (ore-diggings) appears in Domesday Book as an outlier of Earl Tostig's estate based on 'Hougun' (probably to be identified as Haume near Dalton-in-Furness); this subsequently passed to the monks of Furness Abbey, whose Coucher Book refers to the surface working of iron by ditch and trench. On a larger scale, the villages of Danby (Yorkshire), Horsham (Sussex) and St Briavels (Gloucestershire), while not owing their origins to the iron industry, appear on both documentary and archaeological evidence to have been major centres of production in the thirteenth and fourteenth centuries, to the point where their viability, and the livelihood of their inhabitants, depended far more on industry than on agriculture. At Danby, medieval slag heaps (dated by pottery sherds) survive as indicators of the extensive ironworking enterprises in upper Eskdale undertaken both by the canons of Guisborough and by lay lords such as the de Brus and Latimer families. Both Horsham and St Briavels were major suppliers of arrows to the king's armies and in each case the centre of activity has been identified: at Horsham a dedicated area just to the east of the settlement, at St Briavels just over a kilometre south-south-west of the castle on a sloping site with a source of running water.[50]

Inland salt production, based on the boiling in lead salt-pans of brine taken from the local rivers, was another industry which focused on a limited number of locations. Domesday Book leaves us in no doubt that *Wich* (later Droitwich) in Worcestershire and the three *Wiches* in Cheshire (Northwich, Nantwich and Middlewich) were very special places: Droitwich was covered in a series of separate entries which demonstrate that a host of different landholders, mostly in Worcestershire but some in neighbouring shires, had a stake in its salt-making activities, while those in Cheshire were dealt with separately from the general run of estates and were described in highly distinctive terms. Although there must have been some inhabitants who farmed the surrounding land, Domesday Book does not tell us about them, nor does it see fit to record any assets for these places other than those connected with salt; they were recognized, in 1086 and throughout the middle ages, as places of national importance for the production of a commodity invaluable as an ingredient of foodstuffs and essential to their preservation. The network of trackways leading from the various *Wiches* – identifiable by names such as Saltway (Oxfordshire) and Saltersford (Cheshire) – are testimony to their far-reaching significance. Even along the coast, where as we have seen most salt-making seems to have been a part-time activity, there may have been some specialist places, such as the Dorset settlements of Lyme Regis (where 27 *salinarii* or salt workers were recorded) and Ower (where the 13 *salinarii* were the only inhabitants mentioned).[51]

Two industrial activities have been left for separate treatment because there are particular stories to tell about their impact on rural settlement. Among the extractive industries, the mining of silver had certain peculiarities. It was found in small quantities within several lead fields at various times during the middle ages, being dug from the surface under the control of local landholders and those individuals to whom they had granted mining rights. However, the crown had a particular interest in silver – essential to the minting of coins, normally a royal prerogative – and was prepared to invest heavily in deeper mining using a full-time workforce. The output of ore of a fourteenth- and fifteenth-century silver miner in west Cornwall has been calculated to be well in excess of that of others – 24 times more than that of a tin miner, for example, six times that of a lead miner, and much more consistent throughout the year, figures which imply work undertaken full-time, or largely so.[52] The major source of silver in twelfth-century England was the Alston moors below Nenthead (Westmorland), which expanded rapidly owing to new discoveries in the early 1130s to become – temporarily, during the second half of the twelfth century – the most important area of silver production in the world; activity also spread into Northumberland and County Durham. Collectively known as the 'Carlisle minery', since the border town was the headquarters from which the operation was overseen and annual payments were made to the crown, the enterprise greatly impressed contemporaries; the mid-twelfth century writer Robert de Torigni, though based in Normandy, was aware of 'veins of silver ore discovered at Carlisle' and of 'miners who dug for it in the bowels of the earth'. It clearly changed the face of the rural landscape in the vicinity of the mines, with perhaps 1,000 miners in total at work by the 1160s. Yet it seems to have had no lasting impact on the settlement pattern, since within 30 years the industry was in severe decline, as the mines became ever more challenging and costs exceeded the profits to be made: by the 1220s mining here was almost entirely confined to lead, not silver, and had been reduced to the part-time and seasonal activity which was characteristic of the rest of the country.[53]

Another illustration of the precariousness of this industry, albeit on a much smaller scale, can be seen at Carreghofa, near Llanymynech on the Wales-England frontier. Here, just east of Offa's Dyke – on land now used as a golf course – the discovery by lead miners of a vein of silver-lead ore led in 1193 to the justiciar Hubert Walter, who was running the country for the absent King Richard I, declaring this a royal mine and ordering the refortification of the border castle, which was garrisoned so as to offer protection. By summer 1194 three miners were at work here, at the relatively good wage of four pence (1.67p) a day, and the mint at Shrewsbury had reopened to coin pennies from the silver they produced. But, again, the activity proved to be ephemeral. There was not sufficient ore to sustain silver production long-term and the venture petered out during the reign of King John, though lead-mining continued as a part-time occupation for local peasant farmers. The prospect of a major enterprise on the Welsh frontier died almost as soon as it arose.[54]

There is, however, one area where we can speak with greater conviction about the long-term legacy of silver mining, partly because the enterprise lasted a considerable time (from the end of the thirteenth century to the early sixteenth, though with a break after the Black Death) and partly because it has been thoroughly researched. This is the Birland peninsula between the Tamar and Tavy estuaries in south Devon, not part of the royal estates but a place where in 1292 the crown exercised its prerogative to take control of mineral extraction, recruiting miners from Derbyshire, north-east Wales and elsewhere and also tinners from the south west who were skilled in drainage work; within six years there were over 300 miners and about 100 tinners employed. The mineworkings themselves have been identified, mostly shallow shafts and open trenches of which good examples survive at Cleave Wood just north of the Tamar estuary; evidence of the adits (almost horizontal tunnels) used to drain off water from the deeper workings, and even of an air-shaft leading off one of these, have been found at Furzehill (south west of Bere Alston). Of particular significance is the 16-kilometre Lumburn Leat, constructed in the late fifteenth century to carry water from a point west of Tavistock in order to power suction-lift pumps installed in the more northerly of the Birland mines, by then using shafts which could not be drained by adits and were too deep for water to be lifted out manually. The fact that these pumps were the latest technology – invented in Italy earlier in the century – and that the leat was on a scale which makes it unique in medieval England is testimony to the importance attached to the continued operation of these silver mines, even when supplies were becoming more difficult to extract.

Yet despite all this, evidence of purpose-built settlement remains very limited. There are documentary references in the very early years of the enterprise to housing and administrative buildings first at Maristow then at Calstock, apparently for the use of managers and refiners, and in 1360 the sheriff of Devon was instructed to ensure that there was no hindrance to the provision of housing for mineworkers, but no archaeological trace of settlement in the immediate vicinity of the mines has been found. All the signs are that we are looking again at temporary dwellings which left no lasting impression on the landscape, or the absorption into the existing dispersed pattern of some additional accommodation for miners. A fifteenth-century list of named places within the parish which covered the Birland peninsula, compiled for the purpose of organizing a rota for hearing confessions, gives no indication that there were at that time 'extra' hamlets close to the mines, now unknown because they disappeared once mining ceased; it does suggest, however, that the established settlement pattern had been influenced to the extent that hamlets relatively near the mines had tended to become larger than the rest. One exception stands out – though better regarded as a town than a village – in the shape of the Bere Alston, close to the northern end of the mines, founded about 1305 by Reginald de Ferrers, lord of the manor whose silver resources were now being exploited by the king. This already existed as a small settlement with open fields, but, following the grant of a weekly market and annual fair in 1295, burgage-plots were laid out over some of the strips to its east and south, evidently in an attempt to salvage some profit for the lord from all the crown-sponsored activity on his estate. The fifteenth-century confessions rota shows this to be the largest settlement in the parish and the unusually small size of the burgage plots (37–49 metres long by about 10 metres wide) reinforces the impression that many of them would have been leased to working miners. This was certainly a place which, largely if not entirely, owed its existence to the mining industry, and it is rightly acclaimed as 'probably … the first specialist mining town in Britain'.[55]

The final group of 'industrial villages' which ought to be considered, also along the coast, are those based on fishing. Longshore fishing in distant waters was certainly known in medieval England, but for most of the period seems to have been a full-time occupation for men living in those towns which served as coastal ports. East and West Looe (Cornwall), for example, were deliberately founded as new settlements, carved out of the manors of Pendrym and Portlooe in Talland respectively, on opposite sides of the Looe estuary; both were in existence by 1201 and despite temporary decline in the later fifteenth century they thrived for much of the period both as ports for trade with France, Spain and Ireland – drawing on a hinterland which included the tin-producing area of Bodmin Moor – and as bases for Atlantic and inshore fishing. It was reported in 1555 of West Looe, generally regarded as the lesser of the two, that 'most part of all the … country between Exeter and Bridgwater are served with fish from the haven'.[56] Outside the ports, sea fishing is generally regarded for most of the middle ages as having been a part-time activity, though one seen as sufficiently important for inland manors to retain detached portions of shoreline in a way familiar from the arrangements made for access to extra woodland, pasture or meadow. A detailed study of the south Devon coast, for example, has shown how at Stokenham (inland from Slapton Sands) both fishing and also 'fish-watching' – to report the movement of a potential catch – seem to have been imposed as manorial obligations, though elsewhere it was a small-scale activity for middle-ranking freeholders acting independently. Key to their success were the storage arrangements on the shore for boats, nets and other fishing gear, in huts known as cellars, as a reminder of which Coombe Cellars on the Teign estuary survives as a place name. But these were at best temporary dwellings for those who lived inland.[57]

The picture changed towards the end of the middle ages with the foundation of some dedicated 'fishing villages'. Mevagissey and Gorran Haven (Cornwall) were both in existence by the early fifteenth century, established as secondary coastal settlements attached to manors based inland. Dittisham, Hallsands, Westwood, Middlewood and Cockwood (Devon) have all been identified as former cellar settlements transformed into permanent villages towards the end of that century. But the reasons for the development of these permanent sites differed from one county to the other. Mevagissey and Gorran Haven appear to have been speculative ventures by manorial lords seeking an alternative income in the post-Black Death era: Mevagissey, despite its twisting streets, seems to have been planned around a market-place and had a pier and quay provided by the lords of the manor of Treleaven, while Gorran Haven was supplied with a new church. The Devon examples, on the other hand, have been interpreted as a response to a local upsurge in population from about 1480 which (it is argued) led those who could not be accommodated on the land to seek an alternative livelihood, meeting what would have been a parallel increase in demand for food. These were definitely 'unplanned' settlements, as houses were built by incomers close together (without gardens or crofts) wherever there was space between the beach and the fields behind, and to this day there are narrow winding lanes, successors to the gaps left between one dwelling and the next: they have been described as 'a close-knit disarrangement of buildings'. Elsewhere along the English coastline, a similar tendency for temporary settlements to become permanent can occasionally be glimpsed from the place name element *scela* (Old English) or *skali* (Scandinavian) meaning a 'temporary hut', which though normally referring to seasonal pastures may indicate the fishing origins of coastal settlements in Cumberland such as Sandscale and North Scale, both near Barrow-in-Furness, and Seascale just south of Sellafield. The process can be demonstrated very well in the case of North Shields (Northumberland), which according to a case heard by parliament in 1290 had begun as 'three huts (*sciales*) only' made on the bank of the River Tyne by fishermen; here, the prior of Tynemouth as lord had clearly taken an interest since he proceeded to erect further buildings, so that it had developed into a port which the burgesses of Newcastle-upon-Tyne now saw as a threat.[58] In fishing, at least, we can point with some conviction to the sort of temporary settlements which housed workers in a variety of enterprises taking on a permanence which gave a legitimate claim to the title 'industrial village'.

Houses and their plots

Whatever the overall arrangement of housing within a rural settlement, dwellings were usually – though not invariably – located inside an enclosed plot. Among lesser folk, the enclosed area was generally known as the toft; a separate area, the croft, was often – but again not always – attached to the toft. At an élite level, that of a lord of a manor or a substantial freeholder, the plot on which the house stood might be recognizable today as a platform enclosed by a moat. On a national scale, the distribution of moated sites can tell us a great deal about the incidence of dispersed settlement, since this was the context in which most were created. About one-fifth of the 5,000-plus moats identified in England are in Suffolk and Essex, shires characterized by their multiplicity of dispersed hamlets; in Dennington (Suffolk) immediately north of Framlingham, for example, there are no less than eight moated sites, and in the next parish to the north, Laxton, a further five, all apparently associated with a fragmented pattern of both lordship and settlement within the territories concerned. Elsewhere, such as the Welsh borders and the west midlands (notably the Arden area of Warwickshire) a relatively high density of moated sites appears to have been the consequence of sustained woodland clearance, again resulting in a proliferation of small settlements each marked by the presence of one dwelling set apart from the rest by its moat. Conversely, in areas of nucleated settlement, generally with more concentrated lordship, moats are less abundant, and where they occur there is commonly only one per parish.[59]

The broad chronology of moat construction suggests that, after a slow start around the middle of the twelfth century, the 'peak period' ran from 1200 to 1325, when manorial incomes were at their most buoyant and many new settlements were being established. Despite their proliferation in areas of dispersed settlement, environmental factors should not be omitted from any analysis of their distribution: whatever the national picture, at a local level they are scarcely found wherever the subsoil is freely draining, or where there are outcrops of chalk, limestone, sand or gravel. Rather, they are associated with sites, especially on clay land, where the water table could readily be reached by digging and the soil would compact into a firm broad and deep ditch; while not every moat was 'wet', within a given locality the wetter spots seem deliberately to have been sought out. Moats facilitated drainage of the house platform within, offered some protection against casual violence and theft, and were a source of water both for keeping fish and for extinguishing fires. Their ultimate purpose, however, was almost certainly that of status symbol: an expression at the level of manorial lord or substantial freeholder of the same desire to impress which motivated the designers of castles (Figure 12).[60]

Figure 12: Weeting Church and Manor House (Norfolk). The moat in the foreground was added in the mid-thirteenth century to a fortified manor house of about 1180. The round west tower of the adjacent parish church is characteristic of early Norfolk churches, although this example was rebuilt in the 1860s.

As for the configuration of the tofts and crofts associated with the mass of the rural population, we can take as our starting-point a regional analysis first published in 1988, on the basis of excavations conducted up to that time. This provides a framework which is still useful, even though it bears little resemblance to the zones of dispersion and nucleation represented by the Provinces of the *Atlas of Rural Settlement*. 'Region 1', embracing the south-west peninsula, is wholly within the 'Northern and Western Province' of mainly dispersed settlement and its eastern boundary exactly follows that with the 'Central Province' as shown in the *Atlas,* but the other three regions cut across the Provincial boundaries. The clear evidence of regional charac-teristics makes it likely that ideas on the arrangement of these plots spread by emulation, by copying from other examples in the neighbourhood, much as seems to have happened with the overall layouts of settlements and field systems: but if so, a different sequence was followed, except possibly in the distinctive context of the south west.

Accordingly, we find in 'Region 1' that the norm was for the settlement area as a whole to be walled off, partly to prevent uncontrolled access by animals, and that within this enclosure there was no obvious plan to the positioning of individual houses. Sometimes they lacked any property boundaries of their own (as at Okehampton, Devon), sometimes they had their own irregularly shaped walled plots (as at Hound Tor), though without the dual arrangement of both toft and croft. 'Region 2', however, straddling the 'Central' and 'South Eastern' Provinces of southern England and the south midlands, was characterized by generally well-defined rectilinear tofts and crofts associated with each house, though with occasional exceptions such as Bullock Down, a short-lived hamlet on the Sussex Downs where (as in parts of the south west) there was no separation of the two. In the north and north west of England, 'Region 3', distinct rectilinear tofts and crofts for each house were again encountered (though merged as one at a Northumberland site, West Hartburn), while in 'Region 4', the east midlands and northern part of East Anglia grouped around the Wash, it was usual for houses to occupy 'squarish' plots which seem to have been regarded as toft and croft combined. When this model was first suggested, the four 'Regions' did not cover the whole of England, but there have been refinements since: recent work on dispersed farmsteads on Denge Marsh (part of Romney Marshes), for example, has shown them to lie within small tofts without accompanying crofts, a conclusion which suggests that this should be regarded as a southern extension of 'Region 4'.[61]

Where there were crofts as well as tofts, they seem to have served either as paddocks, gardens or (occasionally) as additional ploughed areas, as was apparently the case at Holworth (Devon), where there was a ramp in one corner of each croft seemingly giving access to the open fields. Whatever their precise role, they gave the peasant householder some independence from the communal farming regime, to grow what he chose or to enclose livestock which, for whatever reason, were best kept away from the common pastures. Where there were no boundaries delineating a separate croft, there might still be some cultivation or the grazing of penned or tethered livestock within the undivided enclosure, but the toft's principal function was always as a base for the house and ancillary buildings of an individual family. There is good archaeological evidence that tofts were associated with fierce independence and a desire for privacy: an antidote to the communal farming arrangements which, especially in 'champion' country, affected so much of peasant life. Repeatedly, the boundaries between tofts, and those which separated them from their street, were prominent statements: deep ditches (at Grenstein, Norfolk, and Riplingham, Yorkshire), banks topped by hedges (Grenstein again), stone walls (at Thrislington, County Durham), timber palisades (at Hangleton, Sussex). Within them, evidence has been found of cobbled pavements which served as hard standing work surfaces (as at Anstey, Leicestershire), of outdoor ovens or kilns for drying crops or malting barley (as at Hound Tor on Dartmoor, West Hartburn in County Durham, Gomeldon in Wiltshire and Faxton in Northamptonshire), of digging for building materials (as at Wharram Percy in Yorkshire, Caldecote in Hertfordshire, and the aforementioned Grenstein and Bullock Down), of private water supplies from pits (for example at Goltho and Riseholme in Lincolnshire, Barton Blount in Derbyshire and Wroughton Copse in Wiltshire) and of the burial of infants (as at Thrislington, Gomeldon and Upton, Gloucestershire).[62] The widespread occurrence of these features, across all regions and within hamlets as well as villages, is striking.

There is also a broad consistency across the country, or at least some common themes, in the design of the housing which occupied these plots. For some three centuries beginning about 1200, a plan based on four elements was remarkably widespread among families all over England, from the ranks of the middling peasantry to those of gentry lords of the manor. This plan was based upon a house being wholly or partly one-storey and one room deep. It embraced, first, a central space open to the roof with hearth in the middle; second, a separate private area at one end of the building; third, a cross passage accessed from at least one but usually two opposing doorways located at the far end of the central space from the private area; and, fourth, another separate area (often with a 'service' function such as food prepa-ration or storage) at the end of the building beyond this cross passage. Such matters as the size of the structure (including elaboration at one or both ends, to accommodate extra rooms vertically or horizontally), the quality of materials and construction, and the nature of any decoration, served to differ-entiate the status of those who dwelt in such houses, and as we have seen manorial lords and those who aspired to copy them had a liking for putting moats around their houses by the thirteenth and early fourteenth centuries. But the basic plan itself can be found time and again, to the point where it is sometimes difficult to assign a status to excavated examples. Thus, at Wintringham (Huntingdonshire), a small house dated to around 1200, aligned north-south, had a central space with hearth in the middle, opposed doorways creating a passage between them, and a screened-off area beyond this passage at the southern end. By the mid-thirteenth century the central space (again with hearth in the middle) had been realigned west-east, this time with what can clearly be interpreted as separate service rooms to the west but with the passage between two doorways at the other end of the building. By about 1300 another, larger, house had been built, this time north-south, with the service rooms to the north, cross passage between two doorways adjacent to them, a screened-off central space with hearth in the middle, and then a separate private area at the southern end. This last version had a moat around it and was probably a manor house, but it would be unsafe to assume that the earlier structures had been. While, for convenience, it is helpful to discuss manor houses separately from the dwellings of the masses in the paragraphs which follow, this essential conformity of plan – not ubiquitous among peasant houses but frequently encountered – should always be borne in mind.[63]

For over 800 years until the close of the middle ages, a lord (or his steward or other representative) exercised authority and social control by using the central space within his house – the *aula* or hall – as a public area for eating, entertaining, doing business and sitting in judgement. For the Venerable Bede in the early eighth century, the hall was where the lord would sit at dinner with his counsellors, while a 'comforting fire' blazed in the midst. In the thirteenth century, Robert Grosseteste, Bishop of Lincoln, advised in his *Rules for Household and Estate Management* that the lord (or in this case the lady) should 'make your own household to sit in the hall as much as you may … and sit you ever in the middle of the high board that your visage and cheer be showed to all men … eat you in the hall afore your many, for that shall be to your profit and worship'. By the second half of the fourteenth century, William Langland was deploring a tendency for some lords to 'abandon the main hall which was made for men to eat their meals in', but his comment was balanced by another which suggested that communal eating with large households remained popular.[64] Even where the lord was an absentee, there was an obligation on his tenants or retainers to guard the hall – as recorded on the estates of Gloucester Abbey and St Paul's Cathedral either side of the year 1200 – since it still served as an administrative centre.[65]

It is therefore quite wrong to envisage medieval manor houses as isolated features divorced from their surroundings, even if this is sometimes how they appear today: whether as a permanent residence or as the base for the lord's local administration, they were intimately associated with the neighbouring settlement from which the lord drew an income. At Wharram Percy, for example, a stone manor house dated on both documentary and archaeological grounds to the 1180s was built at the north end of the row of peasant house-plots laid out at that time on a plateau above the parish church, in a planned extension to the village west of its earlier focus around the church, stream and mill. But in the thirteenth century there was further expansion of the village northwards, over a furlong taken out of the open fields, and a new, larger manor house was erected, again at the northern end of this new row of peasant dwellings; the previous manor house was replaced by a succession of peasant houses.[66] The 'Whittlewood project' located the sites of several medieval manor houses in the vicinity of churches, for example at Wick Dive at the northern end of the settlement and at neighbouring Wick Damon at the southern end, while also suggesting that in some cases earlier peasant houses had been demolished to make way for them.[67]

There is evidence both from excavation and from standing remains that eleventh- and twelfth-century manor houses were not arranged according to the standard plan outlined above, the hall being treated instead as a discrete, freestanding building within a complex of domestic and service structures: the manor house was a series of rooms, but they were not under the same roof. At Goltho (Lincolnshire), successive tenth- and eleventh-century halls within the manorial complex were detached from other buildings such as the bower, kitchen and sheds. Surviving stone halls of late-eleventh or twelfth-century date, like Westminster Hall and Minster Court (Kent) – although hardly typical as royal building and monastic grange respectively – support the conclusion that these early halls were usually separated from other domestic structures, and examples of such freestanding structures can be found as late as the beginning of the fourteenth century, the manor house at Wasperton (Warwickshire) being a case in point.[68] By then, however, the standardized plan for manorial halls and their ancillary rooms had emerged. The central hall was open to the roof with hearth in the middle, between separately defined 'solar' and 'service' ends. The solar end was positioned behind the lord's high table and served as private chambers for his family and privileged guests. The service end typically comprised separate rooms for buttery and pantry, supplied from a kitchen beyond; this was often detached because of the risk of fire. Between the service end and the hall was a cross passage (also known as a screens passage) running between two opposing doorways which gave access to the hall; this passage was separated from the hall by a partition, which might be a permanent structure but could be no more than a movable screen.

The evolution of this plan can be traced through the twelfth to early fourteenth centuries from several manor house excavations.[69] Among examples still standing, however, it is usual to find greater elaboration, with a central hall open to the roof flanked by two-storey wings at one or both ends to form an L-, T-, H- or half-H shaped plan, the last being where the wings project forwards but not back from the hall; in all these, the concept of service and solar areas was retained but the accommodation therein was greatly enhanced. The so-called 'hall-and-cross-wings' H- or half-H shaped plan was especially popular, well-established over much of the country by the fourteenth century, sometimes built anew in that form, sometimes developing in stages from a T or L: in Yorkshire, for example, Rawthorpe Old Hall, Dalton, of the early sixteenth century, has been identified as an example of a single-build, Sharlston Hall near Wakefield as a case where the original hall of about 1425 had one wing added around 1450 and the other about 1500. And by the end of the middle ages, there was a growing tendency to elaborate further by adding appendages to the cross-wings, and in a few cases to extend these wings and add a fourth side to create a full courtyard. Penhallam, Jacobstow (Cornwall), part of the complex at the aforementioned Berry Court, is a very early example of this phenomenon: excavation has shown the evolution of a hall-and-cross-wings plan, in place by the middle of the thirteenth century, to a full courtyard with gatehouse commanding a drawbridge over the moat, by (at the latest) the early fourteenth. More typical timing was that at the manor house at West Bromwich (Warwickshire), which is known to have developed from an original T-plan in the thirteenth century to an H-plan by around 1425; by 1500 further annexes, including a chapel, had appeared on both wings and early in the seventeenth century the addition of a gatehouse completed the courtyard.[70]

Turning from here to the homes of the majority, we need to say first that some of the conclusions reached in the 1960s – admittedly with an expectation that they would be overturned by further work – have not stood the test of time. One of these is the classification of different types of peasant dwelling. Excavations up to that time suggested that there were recurring patterns in peasant house types, ranging from the humblest dwellings (labelled 'cots' and presumed to be for the poorest peasants or 'cottars') which might be one-roomed at about 5 metres by 3.5 metres or two-roomed about 10 metres by 4.5 metres, to 'longhouses' (for the most populous group, the 'villeins') anything up to 30 metres in length and distinguished by having space for animals at one end, on to 'farms' where living standards were sufficiently high for humans and animals to occupy separate buildings within the same toft: though whatever their length these buildings were at most 6 metres wide because of the constraints of available timber to span their roofs. Work since then has challenged the assumption that different house-types and house-sizes can automatically be assigned to particular categories of peasant, has pointed out that ancillary buildings – indicative of 'farms' – can be found in tofts and crofts associated with various sizes of dwelling (not necessarily the largest) and has demonstrated that not all long narrow houses were necessarily 'longhouses' in the sense of being intended to shelter livestock at one end: to be identified as longhouses under this tight definition, there needs to be evidence that animals were actually kept within them, such as substantial open drains, tethering rings or post-holes for stalls.

The other major change in our perception of peasant housing is a rejection of the idea that much of it was not built to last. In the pioneering days of medieval settlement excavation, archaeologists were impressed by recurring evidence of repeated rebuildings, seemingly every few decades, as at Wharram Percy where in 'toft 6' the original twelfth-century timber house gave way in the late thirteenth century to a small stone dwelling and thereafter to what was interpreted as one longhouse after another, also in stone; similarly, in 'toft 10', on the site of the late-twelfth-century manor house, a sequence of peasant dwellings was subsequently erected – first of timber, then of stone, then of timber-on-stone – with some rebuildings being on a completely different alignment. Likewise at Hangleton 'building 9' apparently moved from an alignment sideways to the street and a position at the back of the toft in the thirteenth century to appear gable-end to the street and at the front of the toft by the fifteenth.[71] But further documentary and archaeological work has questioned much of this. The small 'cots' which allegedly preceded longhouses in tofts 6 and 10 at Wharram Percy have been reinterpreted as portions of once longer dwellings and – given difficulties with dating and identification of function – there has been a challenge to the idea that the presence of several differently aligned buildings within a toft necessarily indicates sequential development: might we not be seeing contemporary structures, that is one or more houses (perhaps a second one for a retired couple) and an ancillary farm building or two? Excavation has certainly revealed medieval peasant houses which passed down several generations, as at Great Linford (Buckinghamshire); the pattern here was for modification but not wholesale rebuilding, with the result that houses whose basic structure was of timber frames on low stone walls lasted from the thirteenth or fourteenth centuries to the seventeenth.[72]

In terms of construction technique, the thirteenth century is now seen as a time when the practice of placing timber uprights in 'earthfast founda-tions' – that is directly into the ground, so creating the postholes which can sometimes be identified by archaeologists – was replaced by setting them on stone walls or, if stone was scarce, on individual padstones. This did not happen everywhere – in Cheshire and Lincolnshire earthfast techniques seem to have persisted while in parts of the midlands they were succeeded by a phase of resting timbers on the ground surface without any intervening stone.[73] But the phenomenon was widespread, despite the different types of stone available in different regions and resort in some places, such as Norfolk, to the building of 'clay lump' walls to support the timbers instead. This development implies a new expectation that houses would last longer than their predecessors, whose timber uprights had rotted in the ground. The impression that peasants were prepared to invest heavily in houses built for the long term is also apparent from the popularity over much of England of cruck construction, based upon the walls and roofs being dependent upon massive curved timbers set in bays at intervals through a house, for which there is both documentary and archaeological evidence from the thirteenth century onwards. The essential point about cruck construction is that the walls were built as screens without load-bearing responsibilities: they might frequently be rebuilt but this did not mean that the dwelling as a whole was being rebuilt, if the basic structure dependent on the cruck frames remained intact. This is possibly what happened in 'toft 6' at Wharram Percy, where the excavation of successive longhouses has been reinterpreted as revealing padstones to support a series of crucks: the apparent rebuildings of this longhouse actually involved the replacement of its walls but not of the essential cruck structure.[74] Crucks in themselves were major investments, based on the trunks of standard trees which might well have been over 100 years old; it is unlikely that they would have been replaced in a shorter period than the timbers themselves took to grow.

The picture which emerges from all this is one in which, at least from the thirteenth century, a high proportion of peasant houses were substantially built, many incorporating large timber crucks and, at ground level, some local stone if available. It would be wrong to forget the small one-roomed 'cot' altogether: for landless wage-earning labourers, whether working on farms or engaged in an industrial activity, this might be all that could be afforded and – with the addition of one or two outbuildings within the toft – all that was needed. Excavation of the deserted village of Tatton (Cheshire) suggests that modest dwellings often of one room only, built of local timber, straw and earth 'obtained without money changing hands and erected without specialist assistance' sufficed for most of the population, with any livestock being housed separately; comparisons have been drawn between this peasant accommodation and that on the Solway Plain in north-west Cumberland.[75] But more substantial houses, of which the 'longhouse' with animals at one end was one version, were widespread elsewhere, even among those whose holdings in land were small. Late fourteenth- and fifteenth-century building agreements in the west midlands, where lords required incoming peasant tenants to repair or rebuild houses if there had been dilapidation, show the dimensions of some 80% of those listed to have been at least 4.6 metres by 9.2 metres (15 x 30 feet) but more usually 4.6 metres by 13.8 metres (15 x 45 feet); some of the longer houses went to the holders of 12 hectares or more but others to tenants of only a quarter of this. A key point is that, at least from the thirteenth century, peasants seem to have been prepared to engage in the market to buy building materials (especially the major timbers) and employ skilled workers (among whom professional carpenters were most prominent). It has been reckoned that by the early fifteenth century one of the typical longer houses in the west midlands would have cost between £3 and £4 to build – almost a year's annual income for a carpenter, half as much again for a building labourer.[76]

Against this background, we can return to the standard plan of central space, cross-passage between opposing entrances, and private and service ends, this time in the context of the houses of freeholders and of peasants in general. Excavated examples of houses which show the classic four components, but appear to have had no association with a manorial lord, have been identified at Monkton (Kent) in the late twelfth century, and at Hangleton (Sussex), Tattenhoe (Buckinghamshire) and Meldon near Okehampton (Devon) during the thirteenth. From the fourteenth century onwards, houses are still standing, much altered since medieval times but with the essentials of this arrangement apparent. At Woolstaston near Church Stretton (Shropshire), for example, an L-shaped house with open hall and solar wing at one end, known on documentary evidence to have been occupied by freeholders, has had the construction of its timber framework (including crucks) dated to the 1390s. All the basic components of service end, cross-passage, open hall and private end (the latter two-storeyed) can be identified in a surviving fifteenth-century house known as Forsters in Bridewell Lane, Shapwick, considered to 'have been suitable for a prosperous yeoman farmer, a tenant of [Glastonbury] abbey'. And many of the surviving 'Wealden' houses of Kent and Sussex had their origin in late-medieval freeholders' dwellings, built in the local style whereby the two ends projected on jetties at first-floor level, with a central hall open to the roof between them.[77]

Before leaving this subject, a final word should be said on longhouses. Among the examples of non-manorial houses mentioned in the previous paragraph, only that at Meldon in Devon can confidently be described as a longhouse in the strict sense of having accommodated animals at the end beyond the cross passage. In the others, this end was used for other purposes, perhaps for storage or as a workshop. Longhouses narrowly defined take us back to the regionalism we encountered in connection with the layout of tofts and crofts: Regions 1 (the south west) and 3 (the north and north west) were areas where they were common, Regions 2 and 4 (the south, south east and midlands) were areas where animals tended to be either left outside or housed in a separate building. One possible explanation for this contrast is that the drier and milder climate of the south and east allowed cattle to be overwintered without the need to bring them inside the house, a suggestion which accords with what may have been late-medieval enclosed 'crew-yards' for the keeping of cattle through the winter, found within tofts at the 'Region 4' sites of Barton Blount and Goltho.[78] Even in 'longhouse' regions, however, there appears to have been a tendency by the later medieval period for those who could afford to house their livestock in a separate building within the toft to do so, not necessarily because of any objection to having animals under the same roof but to increase their domestic space. There is no suggestion, for instance, that the wealthy freeholders who occupied the late medieval L-shaped house at Woolstaston chose to share their accommodation with animals, even though they were in an area with a 'longhouse tradition'.

It is worth adding that a move away from living under the same roof as livestock would not be the only example of dynamism in the approach taken to rural housing. A significant late-medieval change in the positioning of hearths has been detected, the central open hearth being replaced by one set against the partition which separated the hall from the cross passage: a switch apparent in Goltho and Barton Blount by the fourteenth century, in the Halifax-Huddersfield area of Yorkshire in the fifteenth century, and further north in West Whelpington (Northumberland) by the end of that century. In this respect, freeholders and peasants can be regarded as 'ahead' of many lords of the manor, who retained an open hall with central hearth throughout the middle ages. The construction of a hearth against the cross passage was to continue to be a feature wherever longhouses continued to be built, as they did in some quantity in the south west into the seventeenth and the north until the eighteenth centuries. By then, however, there had been a fundamental change in house-type elsewhere, in the direction of dwellings which were not only intended solely for human habitation but were almost entirely two-storey: a sixteenth- and seventeenth-century 'Great Rebuilding', involving the roofing of the hall and the insertion of fireplaces, which made the medieval plan redundant and evidence of its former existence correspondingly hard to find.[79]

Late medieval adjustment

The story of rural settlements from the early fourteenth century onwards is often told as a series of local reflections of national population decline: most contracting, some becoming deserted altogether, as disease and out-migration took their toll. Archaeological work at West Whelpington, for example, has shown the division of an area adjacent to the green into several new tofts in the expansionist thirteenth century, but the abandonment of the west end of the village and construction of a new boundary bank to delineate the reduced settlement thereafter. Yet in any specific case, the story is never as simple as it might seem. One reason for contraction at this site was almost certainly the impact of fourteenth-century Scottish raiding parties, as implied by the discovery of a cache of five silver coins apparently hidden in a drystone wall. And despite sometimes being labelled a 'deserted medieval village', West Whelpington did in fact survive the middle ages, only finally being abandoned about 1720. It was in good company in doing so, for several other now-abandoned medieval settlements – around 15 in Northamptonshire, for instance, perhaps six in Norfolk – continued beyond the sixteenth century, only later to fall victim to the landscaping of parks or other 'improving' initiatives.[80] Nuneham Courtenay (formerly Newnham, Oxfordshire), which some have argued is represented by 'sweet Auburn' in Oliver Goldsmith's 1770 poem *The Deserted Village* after the residents had been removed nine years earlier, is one well-known example, although here again reality is complex: strictly speaking this was not a deserted settlement but a shifted one, since a replacement was built about 2.5 kilometres away along the Oxford to Henley turnpike road.[81] But whatever the circumstances in which settlements failed, their sites offer opportunities for study which still-occupied ones cannot. Their earthworks can be recognized from the patterns of roughly rectangular tofts (surviving sometimes as house platforms, raised above their surroundings, sometimes as enclosing banks and ditches) with hollow ways (worn-down trackways) between them; very occasionally they bear evocative names such as Cold Newton (Leicestershire) – although this survives in much-shrunken form as a hamlet – and Hungry Bentley (Derbyshire) now represented only by Bentley Fields Farm (Figure 13). Also in Leicestershire, Whatborough, on a summit 230 metres above sea-level, has the distinction of being the subject of the earliest known plan of a deserted settlement, drawn up for All Souls College, Oxford in 1586 when its title to the large enclosure which had super-seded the village and its fields faced a legal challenge; many of the features shown on the plan can still be recognized in the landscape today (Figure 14).[82]

The phrase 'deserted village' is now used with caution, since it is acknowl-edged that depopulation was widespread in areas of dispersion as well as nucleation and that the majority of abandoned medieval settlements were in reality small hamlets and farmsteads. Cheshire and Essex, for example, are virtual blanks on the 1968 map of 'Deserted Medieval Villages' helpfully repro-duced in the *Atlas of Rural Settlement*, yet the current Historic Environment Records show 93 'deserted settlements' in the former county, 101 in the latter. Even within the 'Central Province', analysis of place names in the east

Figure 13: Hungry Bentley (Derbyshire). Earthworks characteristic of a deserted medieval settlement are clearly visible in a field of permanent pasture, including a pronounced hollow way – presumably the 'main street' – the roughly rectangular banks and ditches of former tofts (house-plots) alongside it and the ridge and furrow of medieval and later ploughing beyond. (©webbaviation.co.uk)

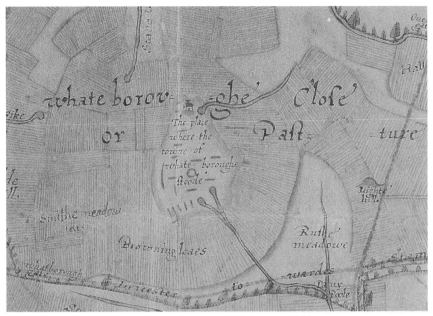

Figure 14: Plan of Whatborough (Leicestershire), 1586. This plan, produced for an Elizabethan lawsuit, depicts the landscape of a deserted settlement ('the place where the towne of whatebroughe stoode') with enclosed pastures where there had previously been open arable fields. The ridges and furrows of former strips are indicated either by hatchings or by annotations. (Photograph from Hovenden Map I:19 by permission of The Warden and Fellows of All Souls College, Oxford.)

midlands has shown that those with the element *thorp* or *throp* (generally indicative of an origin as a small, secondary settlement) were far more likely to be deserted than those featuring *ingaham* or *tun*, which tended to develop into parochial centres and to survive; further west in Warwickshire, it is known that 73% of places which ultimately became deserted were not the principal settlements within their parishes.[83]

Among reasons for settlement desertion, the Black Death seems only occasionally to have been directly to blame. At Earnshill (Somerset) in 1352, the curate asked the bishop effectively to combine his duties with those at the neighbouring church of Curry Rivel because there was no one left on account of the recent pestilence. Similarly, at Tusmore (Oxfordshire), the lord was given permission in 1357 to 'enclose his hamlet ... and the highway ... passing through it, the hamlet having been inhabited entirely by [his] bondmen but now void of inhabitants since their death in the pestilence': but here numbers were already falling in the first half of the century, since it had arable land lying uncultivated in 1341, before the Black Death literally dealt a killer blow.[84] Other catastrophes – natural or man-made – were sometimes responsible, among them William the Conqueror's creation of the New

Forest (an unusual example of afforestation having a direct, negative, impact on rural settlement), late-thirteenth-century inundations from the North Sea into Norfolk and Cambridgeshire, and fifteenth-century French raiding on the Sussex coast.[85] It is also clear that some places were deserted because of the deliberate actions of their lords. Osmerley (Worcestershire) and Budley (Somerset) fell victim to park creation in the early thirteenth century,[86] while in the 1180s Henry II's courtier Walter Map castigated the Cistercian monks for clearing settlements either to create solitude for their abbeys or to replace them with granges worked by lay-brothers. Map had a personal grievance against this order and some of his language was certainly 'over the top', especially on the wider social consequences; in fairness it should be added, first that the Cistercians often made alternative arrangements for the displaced peasants and second that they were not the only religious order to act in this way. But his words would have rung true with some of those who read or heard them.

> How gratefully do they enter upon lands that are given them … they proceed to raze villages, they overthrow churches, and turn out parishioners … Those upon whom comes an invasion of Cistercians may be sure that they are doomed to a lasting exile … they are left destitute … some are hooked into robbery or theft [and into] poverty which … defiles towns with thieves, arms forests with robbers, changes lambs to she-wolves, drives women from the marriage-bed to the brothel.

In reality, experiences differed from one place to another. At Accrington (Lancashire) in the 1190s, the monks of Kirkstall evicted the inhabitants to create a grange, the dispossessed promptly destroyed it and the monks then rebuilt it over again. Conversely, although the foundation of Rufford Abbey (Nottinghamshire) in 1147 led to the destruction of Rufford itself and also of neighbouring Cratley, all eight men of Rufford were given money in exchange for their lands and a new settlement, Wellow, grew up as a replacement.[87]

It was similar action by lords in the late middle ages which caused particular outrage. Around 1490, the Warwickshire antiquary John Rous wrote in his *History of the Kings of England* that he had been petitioning successive parliaments since 1459 on the subject of 'spoliators' who 'have ignominiously and violently driven out the inhabitants' from villages and hamlets in his neighbourhood, listing 62 within a radius of 20 kilometres of Warwick which were 'either destroyed or shrunken, which is to be deplored'. This behaviour was responsible for shortages and consequent high prices of grain, deaths from starvation, and (with echoes of Map) an increase in idleness, begging, and prostitution: even the security of the realm was under threat from a lack of available manpower.[88] About the same time, parliament legislated on the subject, passing the 'Act against the pulling down of towns' in 1489, which railed against the 'desolation and pulling down and wilful waste of houses and towns ... and laying to pasture lands which customarily have been used in tilth' and prohibited the demolition of any house to which 20 or more acres (at least 8.1 hectares) of arable had been attached within the past three years. Further legislation followed at intervals over the next half-century, with the *Domesday of Inclosures* of 1517–18 being the product of a government enquiry into offences committed. This tells us, for example, that in March 1489 (contrary to the Act of that year) the Prior of Bicester destroyed the five houses remaining at Wretchwick (Oxfordshire)

> and lands formerly used for arable he turned over to pasture for animals, so that 18 people who used to work on that land and earn their living there and who dwelled in the houses have gone away to take to the roads in their misery and to seek their bread elsewhere and so are led into idleness.

Similarly at Wormleighton (Warwickshire) on 6 October 1498, the royal courtier and lord of the manor William Coope enclosed 12 tenements

> with hedges and ditches on all sides, and those tenements still remain enclosed, and he willingly allowed those messuages and cottages aforesaid to be wasted fall into decay and ruin, and still they remain so. And he converted the aforesaid arable land ... into pasture ... whereby twelve ploughs which were fully engaged in cultivation of these lands are completely idle and sixty persons who lived in the aforesaid houses ... were compelled tearfully to depart, to wander and be brought to idleness.[89]

Thomas More's satirical remarks in *Utopia*, eventually translated into English in 1556, illustrate the widespread understanding of the problem at the time, while also implying that more substantial settlements were liable to attract most attention, especially if they left churches as isolated features in the landscape (Figure 15).

> Sheep that were wont to be so meek and tame and so small eaters ... be become so great devourers ... that they eat up and swallow down the very men themselves ... devour whole fields, houses and cities, tempting nobles and gentlemen and even abbots to throw down houses ... and leave nothing standing, but only the church to be made into a sheephouse.[90]

Contemporary commentators deserve credit for raising the subject but they were attacking the symptoms not the cause. The population downturn had profound effects upon labour supply and the demand for land and goods

Figure 15: Heath Chapel and Deserted Settlement (Shropshire). The two-cell Norman church, which retains its early tiny windows and round-headed doorway, stands isolated apart from earthworks which include house platforms and hollow ways. Seven families were taxed here in 1327 and there was still some occupation in the late eighteenth century.

– all impacting upon the course of wages, rents, prices and the remnants of unfree status – and it inevitably affected settlements as well, with a tendency for peasants to leave less-favoured locations in search of easier terms and conditions elsewhere. This seems to be the principal reason why smaller settlements were most vulnerable to late-medieval desertion: they had less of a cushion against loss of population to begin with. It would not take much death and departure to wipe out a hamlet of (say) four families in total and even larger communities could soon reach a point where there was no longer a 'critical mass' to sustain farming and other collective activities. In response, some peasant families moved elsewhere, others stayed on and turned to alternative, more individualistic, less labour-intensive types of farming, such as sheep and cattle grazing: an option which might also be available to their lords. It was the latter who were vilified by the commentators, but enterprising freeholders and peasants were also keen to accumulate land, enclose it and convert it to pasture. For example, Compton Verney, listed by Rous among the formerly populous villages from which the inhabitants had been driven out, is known in 1407 to have had several smallholdings of pasture of varying sizes, in the hands of about 20 households, at least some of which was probably composed of abandoned open field strips.[91]

In some places, lords did their best to keep the settlements on their estates alive: it was peasant behaviour which killed them off. A good case in point was Chapel Ascote (Warwickshire), where the ladies of the manor, the nuns of Nuneaton Priory, far from seeking to destroy the settlement, kept ordering their tenants to keep their buildings in good repair and fining them if they did not; but despite this effort, evidenced in manorial court rolls for much of the fifteenth century, they were fighting a losing battle. The disappearance (for whatever reason) of the last ale-selling brewer in 1451 may have been both a factor in, and a consequence of, the terminal decline of the Chapel Ascote community, and it illustrates the critical breakdown in services which might lead to the demise of a settlement. No smith, no wheelwright, no miller: why stay when there was a larger settlement with vacant holdings a few kilometres away, which had access to them all? In similar vein, attention has recently been drawn to the effects of low morale and anti-social behaviour among peasant communities when settlements were in decay and there were not enough people left to sustain normal life: at Barcheston (Warwickshire), for example, another place to lose its last brewer in the middle of the fifteenth century, the handful of peasant households still in residence through the 1470s and 1480s were suffering encroachment onto their pastures from the neighbouring town of Shipston-on-Stour, seem to have themselves ignored customary regulations on grazing, and were having to endure the presence among them of one violently aggressive family who quarrelled not only with their neighbours but also allegedly assaulted the sons and daughter of the lord. For all Thomas More's lamentations, this was the old order overturned before the settlement was deserted, not as a result of it, and it is small wonder that the lords of Barcheston decided to lease the manor to a grazier in the 1490s and sell it outright in the 1500s. The result was that the new owner, a wool merchant, had the five remaining houses removed and all remaining arable land converted to pasture.[92]

It is clear that, while virtually every settlement suffered some decline in population during the fourteenth century, the long-term effects were more serious for some than for others. Those with some inherent vulnerability – unfavourable location, small size, limited access to communal services – tended to witness slow out-migration of the remaining population, though the removal of the last few inhabitants might be the result of lordly decision and involve some coercion, in the interests of making the place more viable from an economic point of view. Wretchwick, where we have seen that the Prior of Bicester was officially blamed for the desertion, had already shrunk from 12 households in the 1430s to the five cited as being evicted in 1489 and similar steady decline is apparent in many other deserted settlements: at Woolashill (Worcestershire) where 20 households in the thirteenth century had fallen to 13 by 1426, nine by 1442 and two by the middle of the sixteenth century; at Upton (Gloucestershire), over 200 metres above sea level, where the bishopric of Worcester recorded 11 households in 1170, 16 in 1299, eight in 1327, four in 1334 and none at all in 1383; and at Barton Blount (Derbyshire) where the distribution of pottery shows the last occupation of houses to have spanned the late fourteenth to the late fifteenth century.[93] Analysis of admissions from the residents of surrounding villages and hamlets to the Holy Cross Guild of Stratford-upon-Avon, through the fifteenth and early sixteenth centuries, allows the process of desertion to be tracked by the decline of certain settlement names: the broad picture is one of gradual decay for much of the fifteenth century, especially before 1450, as entrants became ever less frequent, but sudden disappearance in three or four cases around 1500, when admissions from these places cease abruptly and it is likely that an enclosing lord had indeed taken the decision to evict the remaining inhabitants and switch to commercial pastoral farming.[94] There were certainly some financial incentives for a lord to get rid of the last few peasant families. Ingarsby was valued at £50 per annum as a working community on the eve of enclosure by Leicester Abbey in 1469 but at £81 as depopulated sheep pastures in the *Valor Ecclesiasticus*, the government's survey of church property, in 1535. According to the *Domesday of Inclosures*, Wormleighton's value to William Coope as lord increased from £40 to £60 per annum as a result of the depopulation he carried out in 1498.[95]

Recent distribution maps of deserted settlements suggest that nowhere was immune from the impact of shrinkage of population and local decision-making and that villages and hamlets could disappear on all sorts of soils and terrain. Within the confines of one small county, Rutland, settlement desertion has been shown to be fairly evenly spread across soils favouring arable, pasture and a mixture of the two.[96] It is however a truism in business that when times are hard product diversification is the best recipe for success, and there is good reason to think that those places which enjoyed a mixed economy suffered less overall. The late-medieval increases in population in Cotswold cloth-making and Devon fishing communities have already been noted. Elsewhere, the wooded Arden district of north-west Warwickshire, an area characterized by dispersed settlement and reliance on cattle grazing, coalmining, metalworking and charcoal burning as well as on arable cultivation, fared much better than the Feldon district to the south east, an area of 'champion country' and nucleated villages heavily dependent on cereal growing: with the result that by 1524–25 the Arden district had increased its percentage contribution to the county's taxation compared to 200 years previously, while the Feldon had declined.[97]

To return to Wormleighton, there is, in fact, a twist in the tale, since in 1507 following its enclosure and depopulation William Coope sold the lordship to the cattle-grazier John Spencer (ancestor of Diana, Princess of

Wales) who petitioned the crown against any punishment which might be imposed as a result of the *Domesday of Inclosures* enquiry. This was not an isolated example of the Spencers acting in this way: it was clearly policy to acquire already-deserted or at least partly depopulated sites for use as cattle pastures, but they were not necessarily responsible for causing or hastening the depopulation. The outcome of Spencer's petition is unknown, but he claimed energetically to be restoring the settlement, rebuilding the church, replanting woodland and erecting five new houses, one of which was for himself. As a result, 20 people now lived there. This is a warning against over-simplification of the 'deserted settlement' story but it does not undermine it. Wormleighton did suffer depopulation as a mixed-economy settlement at the end of the fifteenth century, Spencer bought it for cattle grazing and the landscape which resulted was that of a country house with park plus some cottages for retainers. What is to be found there today is the modified Spencer house and a nineteenth-century 'estate village' (successor to the cottages he built) on a hill less than a kilometre from the settlement Coope had destroyed.[98] But in its own way Wormleighton has survived: like every medieval rural settlement still on the map as an inhabited place today, it has had to adapt to do so.

4

The landscape of towns and trade

In the two and a half centuries which followed the compilation of Domesday Book, the proportion of England's population living in towns rose from 10% to between 15 and 20%. Despite the decline in absolute numbers and improvements in rural living standards thereafter, somewhere between one in five and one in seven were still dwelling in towns under Henry VIII.[1] This is a clear sign of the continuing attraction of urban living. Toponymic surnames recorded in some east midlands towns in the thirteenth and early fourteenth centuries show them acting as magnets for settlers from within a radius of some 25–30 kilometres, with larger centres such as Nottingham and Lincoln drawing them from over 100 kilometres away; there was also significant immigration from Wales to towns in the western half of England by the fifteenth century.[2] But all these figures are dependent on an answer to the question: 'what was a town?' Most historians today are sceptical of definitions based on the legal-constitutional privileges of a 'borough', essentially because some very small places enjoyed this status during the middle ages when other, more economically vibrant, centres did not.[3] And in seeking alternative means of distinguishing urban from rural settlements, scholars have to accept that just as every village had some people who made a living from craftsmanship – even if only part-time – so every town had people who worked the land, whether gardens and orchards within their plots or the fields outside. The small Staffordshire town of Rugeley in 1380–81 had a total of 81 taxpayers, 16% of whom were cultivators with the remaining 84% engaged in some manufacturing activity or working as labourers and servants. At the close of the middle ages, 35% of those who left wills in the Kentish towns of Ashford, Hythe, Milton and Sittingbourne included some agricultural land among their bequests.[4]

However, the balance between farming and other activities was different in a town from a village and medieval society did recognize a distinction between the two. For Susan Reynolds in the 1970s, a medieval town was 'a permanent settlement' in which 'a significant proportion' of the population lived off 'trade, industry, administration and other non-agricultural occupations' and where there was a 'social distinctiveness' based on 'common interests' which set the inhabitants apart from the countryside, in their own perception and that of their rural neighbours. That distinctiveness was expressed through associations of traders and craftsmen, and through various forms of self-determination, ostensibly for the benefit of the members of the urban community. At the turn of the millennium, the *Cambridge Urban History* adopted a broadly similar definition of a town as 'a permanent and concentrated settlement [which] normally lives, at least in part, off food produced by people who live outside it', while acknowledging that to some extent recognition as a town was a matter of perception: 'the inhabitants ... regard themselves, and are regarded by the inhabitants of predominantly rural settlements, as a different sort of people'. More recently, in grappling with the phenomenon of the 'small town', Christopher Dyer has looked not only to 'occupational diversity' but also to 'high densities of buildings, rows of houses closely packed along street frontages ... peculiar street patterns including the accommodation of market places' and the frequency of two-storey buildings as features which, collectively, mark them out from villages.[5] Notwithstanding the inevitable borderline cases, and the fact that some settlements effectively changed their status in one direction or the other over the course of time, these working definitions provide a basis for the exploration which follows.

Domesday Book and beyond

Domesday Book has been reckoned to provide evidence of 112 boroughs in 1086, but the figure should be treated with scepticism. It is derived not only from places specified as a *civitas* or *burgus*, but also those for which there are passing references to burgesses or which have a claim to be regarded as boroughs for other reasons. Bury St Edmunds, for example, is counted among the 'boroughs' because of Domesday's reference to 'bakers, ale-brewers, tailors, washerwomen, shoemakers, robe-makers, cooks, porters, agents', all indicative of a thriving commercial centre, even though the words 'borough' or 'burgess' are absent. It would in any case be pointless to speculate on what precisely constituted a 'borough' at this time. More profitably, we should note that some 60 places appear from Domesday Book to have had markets and a good proportion of these – places such as Abingdon (Berkshire, now Oxfordshire), Faversham (Kent), Bampton (Oxfordshire) and Ilminster (Somerset), none of which are reckoned among the 112 'boroughs' – almost certainly functioned economically as towns, albeit on a smaller scale than Bury St Edmunds. When one realizes that the list of markets must be woefully incomplete – Domesday mentions no markets at all for some counties, such as Cambridgeshire, Huntingdonshire, Surrey and Essex – this only increases the sense of inadequate recording of towns. To inadequacy may be added inconsistency, for in contrast to their handling of rural estates the Domesday commissioners obviously had no template of standard questions to guide them when it came to surveying the towns. We learn about governing *judices* or lawmen at Chester, York and Cambridge, about local laws and customs at Chester, Hereford, Lincoln and Oxford and occasionally about trading activity, such as the import of marten pelts to Chester and the 42 men associated with the market in Tutbury (Staffordshire). However, all this is done in such a way that comparisons can scarcely be made between one town and another. London, Coventry (Warwickshire) and Peterborough (Cambridgeshire) seem to have been omitted from the Survey, and Winchester appears only in passing.[6]

Of course, we should be grateful to Domesday Book for such information as we can glean. Its listings of houses provide some basis for an estimate of population, suggesting that – after London as the largest urban centre – York, Lincoln, Norwich, Thetford (Norfolk) and Oxford were all sizeable places, although in every case numbers seem to have fallen in the two decades since 1066, apparently through a combination of economic dislocation, castle-building and fires. The population of York is estimated to have dropped from some 8,000 on the eve of the Conquest to 5,000 by 1086, that of Lincoln from 6,000 to 4–5,000, Norwich from 6–7,000 to 5,000, Thetford from 5,000 to 4,000 and Oxford from 5,000 to 2–3,000. Oxford may have been no bigger in 1086 than some other middle-ranking towns, such as Exeter, Gloucester, Leicester, Nottingham, Stamford (Lincolnshire) and Wallingford (Berkshire); others, including Cambridge, Chester, Huntingdon and Ipswich were perhaps a little smaller but still above 1,500. There were a number of lesser Domesday boroughs which presumably had a local commercial role but seem to have housed under 1,000 people – places like Berkhamsted (Hertfordshire), Ilchester (Somerset), Lydford (Devon), Malmesbury (Wiltshire), Romney (Kent) and Tamworth (Staffordshire) – and these may fairly be embraced within any reasonable definition of a town. However some others, with populations of burgesses in single figures – among them Stanstead Abbots (Hertfordshire) and Penwortham (Lancashire) – would have been smaller than many rural settlements and hard to distinguish from them in function or appearance.

Urban defences are discussed further in Chapter 6 but it is worth noting here that Domesday Book is also useful for passing references to the repair of town walls at Chester and Oxford and (more significantly for those with an interest in urban topography in general) to the presence of houses 'outside the walls', a phenomenon noted at Colchester, Hereford, Leicester and Oxford. There were houses 'outside the city' at Canterbury and Lincoln and people named as *suburbani* at Winchester.[7] This is not necessarily evidence that the room available within the walls had been filled: late-eleventh-century intramural Winchester had more open space than built-up area except in the very centre.[8] But these references suggest that towns were already growing outwards and there is no doubt that the overall story down to the early fourteenth century is the usual one of expansion – growth of the existing urban settlements and the foundation of new ones – though with an added dimension in the efforts made by several of these communities to secure and enhance the privileges of self-government.

As we have seen, most towns relied on their adjoining fields for at least part of their sustenance: Domesday Book duly reports that the burgesses of Cambridge lent their ploughs to the sheriff and that their counterparts at Huntingdon, Oxford, Shrewsbury, Steyning (Sussex), Tamworth, Totnes (Devon) and York all worked their land in one way or another. However, it was their non-farming activities which set towns apart from the surrounding countryside, and made for a population normally larger, more diverse in composition and more densely packed than in a rural settlement, with a sense of corporate identity which encouraged the development of separate administrative and judicial arrangements. Town walls, ditches or other boundary markers often had as one of their main functions the delineation of the area within which tolls were liable to be paid and the urban administration held sway. And as centres of population at the focal point of trade routes, towns were also liable to be chosen as the places where kings and lords built their castles for regional governmental purposes, and where the larger churches came to be founded, so adding to the diversity of urban function, though sometimes at a cost to those whose houses were in the way. Domesday Book mentions the removal of houses to make room for new castles in no fewer than 11 boroughs – such as the 166 'destroyed on account of the castle' at Lincoln – and the physical legacy of this can often be seen in the town's layout today.[9] Cambridge's castle, still the site of county administration in an elevated position to the north of the river, obliterated the streets of the earliest urban settlement here. That at Winchester was built into a corner of the town walls, removing lengths of street running alongside those walls. And the Norman policy of relocating cathedrals to the most important towns in their dioceses meant that in Norwich, for example, most of the pre-Conquest settlement to the south of the river was taken over for the construction of a new cathedral priory and its associated buildings, at the expense of at least two pre-existing churches and several streets.[10]

The network of towns in existence in England at the beginning of the second millennium, and that recorded in Domesday Book, owed a great deal to a series of authoritative decisions over the previous 400 years or more. Places which had been chosen by the seventh century as centres of royal and ecclesiastical administration, such as Winchester for the kingdom of Wessex and Canterbury for the kingdom of Kent – both utilizing former Roman sites – would certainly have hosted substantial non-agricultural activity from the outset, as did the coastal or inland ports which were apparently deliberately fostered by kings at this time: towns such as Ipswich (serving a royal centre at Rendlesham), Sandwich (serving Canterbury) and Southampton (originally named *Hamwic*, serving Winchester). All these included the element *wic* in early spellings of the name, and so did London (*Lundenwic*) and York (*Eoforwiceastor*), in both of which the functions of trading port and royal-ecclesiastical centre were combined, based in different parts of the town.[11] By the end of the eighth century, there had been further encouragement to urban development through the establishment of a network of fortified *burhs* as protected market towns and communal defences against the threat of Viking raiding along estuaries and rivers. For their part, the Vikings themselves, as they occupied much of northern and eastern England during the course of the ninth century, proved to be considerable stimulants to urban growth: it has been argued that they were responsible for developing linear trading extensions to earlier *burhs*, as happened, for instance, at York (where the 'Jorvik' excavations have revealed the growth of a major trading settlement south east of the earlier centre), at Lincoln (where Wigford arose as a trading area across the river to the south of the fortified area), at Cambridge (where settlement was also extended south from an earlier *burh* across the river), and at Huntingdon, which seems to have been developed as the river-port for its already-established neighbour, Godmanchester. In their turn, the kings of Wessex (Alfred the Great in the late ninth century, his son and successor Edward the Elder in the early tenth century) and the rulers of that part of Mercia not under Scandinavian occupation embarked upon fresh schemes of *burh* creation, initiatives which embraced both new sites (such as Wallingford) and existing ones (like Worcester, where the local bishop had already fostered a trading settlement). Thereafter, as Viking-held territory fell to the English, there was a rebuilding and enlargement of some of the *burhs* they had held, among them Bedford and Cambridge, where the defences were extended further south, and Thetford, where they now reached further north. It was also in the tenth century that some of the great religious houses, among them the nunnery at Romsey (Hampshire) and the monasteries at Hartlepool (County Durham), Whitby (Yorkshire), Durham and Peterborough, founded towns around market places deliberately established at their gates, seeking to benefit from the commodities traded therein and to profit from the rents and tolls which could be charged.[12]

The expansionist era

From this pre-Conquest background, which created the heterogeneous picture of urban activity Domesday Book struggled to express, towns continued to grow in size and number – though with fortunes which varied from one to another. Twelfth-century assessments to *auxilia* (or 'aids'), levied by the exchequers of Henry I and Henry II, show a familiar hierarchy of London, Lincoln, York and Norwich as the leading urban centres, to which Bristol can be added on the basis of similar levies in the thirteenth century. By the time of the Lay Subsidy of 1334, Newcastle-upon-Tyne and Boston (Lincolnshire) had joined the leading group, with Coventry also prominent. When the Subsidy was assessed again in 1524–25, London, Norwich, Bristol, Newcastle-upon-Tyne and Coventry still led the way, but York, Lincoln and Boston were well down the list of contributors.[13] There are problems with the interpretation of these figures, which as tax assessments are not necessarily the fairest reflections of towns' respective economic fortunes; their significance for an understanding of late-medieval developments is discussed towards the end of this chapter. Here, we should note the importance of an involvement with international trade: Bristol, Newcastle-upon-Tyne and Boston were major coastal ports, along with others prominent in the earlier assessments like King's Lynn, Yarmouth (both in Norfolk) and Southampton, while York, Lincoln and Norwich were leading inland river ports. Other towns were famed for their international fairs, their specialized manufacturing or their importance as administrative centres, the greater among them hosting the courts for the shires to which they gave their names, or fulfilling a governmental role on the national stage: not only London and Westminster, but also places like Winchester, Worcester, Oxford and Northampton, all of which played host to sessions of the king's exchequer during the twelfth century and subsequently to meetings of parliament.[14]

Towns built on their commercial and administrative functions to establish distinctive identities. In the twelfth century, Henry of Huntingdon was impressed with the reputation of Winchester for wine, Worcester for fruit, Exeter for metals and Bath (as a spa) for 'pools'. His near-contemporary, the anonymous author of the *Gesta Stephani* (Deeds of Stephen), praised Bath for its 'little springs … creating in the middle of the town baths of agreeable warmth' where 'the sick are wont to gather … from all England to wash away their infirmities in the health-giving waters'. Even relatively small towns could attract the attention of a thirteenth-century merchant whose travels around the country left an impression of each one: 'blanket of Blyth … ruffs of Bedford … quilts of Clare … mead of Hitchin … tiles of Reading' and so on, though the reliability of all this is tempered by the fact that he ended his list by declaring that 'there's … too much to drink and … my wits are away'.[15] Even so, he was right to acknowledge the importance of these lesser towns, since it has been reckoned that by the end of the thirteenth century about as many people in total lived in England's roughly 600 'small towns' (defined as having populations of between 300 and 2,000) as in the 50 or so 'large towns' which exceeded them in size. In the less populous parts of the country, they were the only urban presence; medieval Cumberland, Westmorland and Lancashire, for example, are thought to have had about 40 'small towns' in total by that time, among them Manchester and Liverpool alongside such as Cockermouth and Penrith.[16]

Crucial to the viability of a town was its market. Since markets were a source of income to whoever was entitled to charge stall-rents and tolls, the right to hold one was supposed to be a privilege specially conferred – by the twelfth century normally only by the crown. Even in the troubled reign of King Stephen, we find a series of royal market grants, such as in Eynsham (Oxfordshire), Ledbury (Herefordshire) and Lichfield (Staffordshire) all on a Sunday, in Cobham (Surrey) on a Tuesday and Ross-on-Wye (Herefordshire) on a Thursday.[17] In all, some 2,800 markets are estimated to have been formally granted by the crown to settlements in England and Wales between 1200 and 1500, the majority before 1275, with the peak period coming in the middle decades of the thirteenth century: of 28 places in medieval Derbyshire to be accorded market rights, for example, no less than nine received their grants during the 1250s. Most of the places concerned never had the social and economic diversity characteristic of a town – and after 1300 far more of these 'village markets' were closing down than were being set up – but every town certainly had a market. While the international ports and fairs were, in reality, markets writ large, the majority of towns served a local or regional hinterland. Yet this usually weekly gathering was not only vital (literally) to the country dwellers who needed to turn surplus produce into cash or commodities but also provided the context in which non-agricultural activities could flourish, enabling those who lived by trade, craft, manufacture or administration to obtain at least some of their food without having to produce it themselves.[18]

Despite the impression of there being overall control from above, some market grants were clearly attempts to regularize informal gatherings of traders already taking place, commonly on the Sabbath because of the opportunity to combine trade with worship: a customary Sunday market held in the churchyard of Reepham (Norfolk), for instance, is known only from Henry III's order in 1240 that it be removed. According to the thirteenth-century lawyer Henry Bracton, who was concerned to offer guidelines in order to limit their proliferation, a new market would be a nuisance if set up within six and two-thirds miles (10.7 kilometres) of an existing one, because 'a reasonable day's journey consists of twenty miles' and, if this is divided into three parts, 'the first part, that of the morning, is to be given to those who are going to the market, the second is to be given to buying and selling … and the third part is left for those returning from the market to their own homes' before nightfall.[19] In practice, this limitation seems to have been neither observed nor enforced – innumerable markets were closer to one another than this, and some commodities were traded further afield – but it enshrines the notion that, while producers often welcomed a choice of outlets, close proximity could lead to rivalry and resentment. By the middle of the thirteenth century, Welsh cattle drovers were taking their beasts to Ross-on-Wye's Thursday market, then going on to Gloucester and Newnham markets on the following Saturday and Sunday, before trying to sell any which remained at Gloucester's Wednesday market on their way home. In the half-century prior to 1346, grain from the Wiltshire manors of Longbridge Deverill and Monkton Deverill was finding its way not to one local market but several, at Frome, Shaftesbury and Hindon, within a radius of up to 17 kilometres. But early in Henry II's reign, objections by the men of Wallingford and Oxford to a market at nearby Abingdon led to a violent confrontation in the town and eventually a judicial hearing before the king, settled in Abingdon's favour on the basis of reliable memory of a market here in Henry I's time.[20]

Initially, the Church seems to have had no problem with 'Sunday shopping': all Stephen's grants of Sunday markets noted above were for the benefit of a local cathedral or abbey. From the early thirteenth century, however, it led a drive against the practice and also against the holding of markets in church-yards, despite their evident popularity. The Statute of Winchester of 1285, for example, laid down that 'from henceforth neither fairs nor markets be kept in churchyards, for the honour of Holy Church'. This concern sometimes led to new market places having to be created, as had already happened in Northampton in 1235, when Henry III had ordered that the market in All Saints' churchyard be moved to 'an empty and waste place' to its north; today, the (rebuilt) church duly occupies a site just to the south of the town's Market Square, where open-air trading continues to thrive. But it was not easy to curb the enthusiasm for buying and selling on the Sabbath. When in 1353 Edward the Black Prince ordered a Sunday market at Malpas (Cheshire) to be switched to a Tuesday – or any weekday other than Monday so as not to compete with neighbouring Whitchurch – he conceded that 'all men may buy and sell bread, ale, fish and small victuals every Sunday, as they used to do'. In 1368, the Archbishop of Canterbury had to order the closure of a Sunday market held near the church at Sheppey (Kent), the 'tumult' from which was disrupting the mass. Similarly, it was alleged in 1416 that a market held on Sundays and feast days in the churchyard of St Michael le Belfry, York – close to the Minster – was causing a nuisance from horse manure and the clamour of 'those that stand about'.[21]

As with markets, the grant of the right to hold a fair was normally reserved to the crown. Fairs were annual events, usually held during the summer and typically lasting two or three days, although this should be qualified by saying that some towns held more than one 'annual fair' (commemorating different saints) and that some fairs could run for a fortnight or more: in 1136, Winchester's St Giles fair, for example, was extended to a total of 14 days in all. Among King Stephen's charters was one for Walden Priory (Essex) which specified that their fair, in this case of two days in late July, was to be held 'at the church'[22] but the same concerns over disturbance as we have already encountered meant that it was more usual to find them in designated market places. This was the case, for example, at Lincoln, where St Botolph's fair, internationally renowned in the thirteenth and fourteenth centuries, became established on Newport Green, a cigar-shaped market place in a suburb to the north of the town. It also applied in the case of St Werburgh's fair at Chester, though here the abbey gatehouse opened onto the market area. It may have been this proximity which led to precision about the opening and closing times and about arrangements for the monks to put up stalls and lease them to traders, all set out in charters of the first half of the twelfth century; these confined activity to the period 'from nones on the vigil of St Werburgh until vespers on the day following the festival', that is, mid-afternoon on 20 June to early evening on 22 June.[23] Fairs sometimes spilled over into neighbouring streets (as did St Ives fair, Huntingdonshire), or were held on common land on the outskirts of town (like the Midsummer fair at Cambridge which led to the area on which it was held, Greencroft, changing its name to Midsummer Common). But unlike markets which often had their own spaces deliberately created, it is hard to claim that fairs have left a direct imprint on the landscape today. Given that rival claims to a levy on all the wine consumed at Boston fair was worth taking to the king's court in 1189,[24] their immediate impact while they were in full swing would have been a different story.

Routeways

Trade was of course dependent upon a transport infrastructure. Coastal ports were heavily involved with internal as well as overseas commerce, especially Newcastle-upon-Tyne, King's Lynn and Southampton which all had thriving seaborne links with London; fairly accurate measurements of the distances between ports all the way from Yorkshire to Cornwall (such as eight miles from Sandwich to Dover, seven miles from Winchelsea to Hastings, equivalent to 12.9 and 11.3 kilometres respectively) were recorded by the end of the twelfth century.[25] The economist Adam Smith's calculation in the

1770s that a ship would take about six weeks to carry 200 tons of goods from London to Edinburgh, while a heavy wagon would carry only four tons by road in roughly the same time, is probably a fair guide to medieval performance as well, and emphasizes the value of coastal shipping. It has also been calculated that bulk transport of grain in the fourteenth century would normally have cost only two pence (under 1p) per ton per mile by sea, against seven pence (3p) by river and at least one shilling (5p) by road – a reminder that the network of navigable rivers was also very important. Most parts of England were within 25 kilometres of a navigable waterway, and there were particularly good connections feeding the Humber, the Trent and the Wash; the Trent itself was navigable inland as far as Burton and was linked via the Foss Dyke to Lincoln and on via the Witham to Boston.[26] Considerable efforts were made in places to maintain or improve navigability: there was a canalization scheme at Beverley (Yorkshire) between 1115 and 1130, and the River Nene was kept navigable as far inland as Northampton during the thirteenth century, though this was not the case later on. Urban fortunes were certainly at stake in all this. Shrewsbury prospered from being on the navigable Severn while Ludlow, on the unnavigable Teme, did not. Henley-on-Thames also did well during the thirteenth century as a place where grain from the surrounding countryside was gathered in for shipping downriver to feed London. Isleham, on the fen edge in Cambridgeshire, was another successful inland port, and here there is evidence of an artificial channel having been dug to link the River Lark with a complex of wharves to the north of the town.[27]

Yet for all this, most movement was by road. The four great highways which in Anglo-Saxon times had come to be known as Ermine Street, Watling Street, the Fosse Way and Icknield Way received special mention from Henry of Huntingdon in his early twelfth century *Historia* and they also appeared schematically in a mid-thirteenth-century map drawn by Matthew Paris, monk of St Albans Abbey; however, neither discussed the road network further.[28] The Gough Map, a depiction of England, Scotland and Wales of about 1360, is much fuller, showing some 4,700 kilometres of road in total. These included links from London to Exeter and St Ives (Cornwall); to Reading on to Bristol; to Oxford on to Gloucester and thence to St Davids; to Coventry, Warrington, Lancaster and ultimately Carlisle; to Huntingdon, Stamford, and on to Pontefract and Penrith; and to Cambridge, Bury St Edmunds, Thetford and Norwich. A route is also shown serving the Welsh marches from Worcester to Liverpool, another from Bristol through the midlands to Grantham, another along the south coast from Southampton to Canterbury. Considerable detail is given on local roads around York and Lincoln. But the Gough Map is variable in its coverage, weak on thinly populated areas of the Weald, Hampshire Downs and Chilterns and hazy on the Scottish and Welsh coastlines. The important London to Dover road is missing, and so is the York to Newcastle section of the road to Scotland, besides the networks which certainly served major ports like King's Lynn and Lincoln.[29] Even the Fosse Way and Icknield Way are absent, although – as cross-country routes – this might reflect a decline in their significance with the growing importance of London as a hub.

It should not be assumed, either, that the presence of a route between two major towns – whether or not indicated by a red line on the Gough Map – means that there was only one road along it: parallel versions might develop. The Great North Road through what is now Cambridgeshire, where it skirts the western edge of the fens, has been shown to have had three roughly parallel branches, one running through Ogerston (duly mentioned on the Gough Map), another forming the main street of a string of villages such as Sawtry and Glatton, a third through Stilton on the line of Ermine Street. It was the latter which was turnpiked and which (bypassing Stilton) eventually became the dual-carriageway A1. This in turn has now been superseded by the A1(M) and B1043, running alongside each other for some 13 kilometres between Alconbury and Norman Cross: an interesting survival to the present day of the concept of parallel routes, since the minor road can still serve as a diversion if the major one is blocked. Similar stories can be told of the London to Norwich route through the Breckland, where there were three different crossing-points of the River Lark in Suffolk (the present A11 crossing at Barton Mills and two more to the south east), and of the route south of Chester towards Malpas, where a meandering trackway now surviving as a long-distance green lane, a former Roman road and the route eventually turnpiked which has become the A41 were all available.[30]

Some 16,000 kilometres of road are estimated to have been in use in Britain in Roman times; this network survived imperfectly, with much falling into disuse, and the medieval pattern differed considerably from it. Even former Roman towns came to be linked by roads which diverged from the Roman course. A medieval journey to London from Exeter or Gloucester, for example, would follow the old Roman road for a few kilometres east out of town but then take a different route, which in Gloucester's case was akin to the modern A40. Travellers from Chester to London in Roman times headed south to Whitchurch and Wroxeter before picking up stretches of what is now the A5 in the direction of St Albans; their medieval successors also used the equivalent of the A5 into St Albans but reached it by a more easterly route through Newcastle-under-Lyme and Lichfield.[31] Some of this divergence arose from the decay of Roman roads, but most from the fact that the growth of new urban and rural settlements – especially towns such as Oxford and Coventry which were not on Roman routes – necessitated the development of new roads to provide the links between them. And far from avoiding towns, in the manner both of modern motorways and trunk roads and of some long-distance Roman roads like the original Fosse Way, medieval routeways served the needs of travellers in search of markets and places to stay overnight, by leading them into every town centre along their way.

As for the condition of these roads, it is easy to point to shortcomings since – outside the towns – their maintenance was largely reliant on the fulfilment of manorial obligations. Medieval roads were rarely 'made' in the sense of being laid with stone or gravel, although there were rudimentary efforts to fill in the ruts: one method of repair seems to have been to lay planks or branches across wet areas and to fill the potholes with sand. Essentially these roads were earthen tracks, which from heavy use (especially from livestock being driven to market or between manors) could easily become 'hollow ways'. As we have seen, in some circumstances such as wet or open countryside, these roads might branch out into several alternatives running roughly parallel to each other. Around 1520, a Lollard critic of the late-medieval practice of pilgrimage – itself responsible for plenty of traffic, especially to and from famous shrines such as those at Walsingham and Canterbury – said that journeys were undertaken 'more for the green way than for any devotion', an interesting comment on the appearance of the roads.[32] Inevitably there were complaints, such as those which prompted Edward I in 1285 to order the Prior of Dunstable to repair the high roads through his vill which are 'so broken up and deep by the frequent passage of carts that dangerous injuries continuously threaten'; in 1339 parliament had to be suspended because members found a spell of bad weather had made roads impassable.

This does, however, give a misleading impression of a road network which, however imperfectly, stood up reasonably well to the demands placed upon it. There was occasional government interest, such as a decree of Henry I that major highways should be wide enough to allow two wagons to pass each other and for 16 knights to ride side by side; the Statute of Winchester of 1285 required any hedges and ditches (where 'a man may lurk to do hurt') to be set back 200 feet (61 metres) from major roads – so allowing for detours around ruts – and specifically authorized travellers to divert over neighbouring land if the beaten track was impassable. By the late fourteenth century, royal grants of pavage were allowing tolls to be levied for limited terms of years to be spent on the upkeep of some major roads, mostly those running north and west of London: an anticipation of the turnpike trusts of the early modern period, even to the extent that the same roads were involved, such as the 11 kilometres of Watling Street (the A5) between Fenny Stratford and Stony Stratford (Buckinghamshire), which featured both in pavage authorized by Edward III and in one of the earliest turnpike acts of 1706. Charitable giving also played an important role, like Sir Gerard Braybrooke's bequest in 1427, leaving £100 'to foule ways in Bedfordshyr and Buckinghamshir and also in Essex'. Haphazard though all this might appear, in general terms it seems fair to say that medieval roads were just about sufficient to cope with the volume of traffic; most of the evidence points to travellers of all sorts, from tradesmen to the royal household, moving about with some frequency without major impediment, at all times of year. By the mid-fifteenth century professional hauliers with horse-drawn carts were routinely plying their trade between London, the midlands, Oxford, Bristol, Salisbury and Southampton; indeed, over 1,600 carts per annum were passing through Southampton's gates by this time, all year round, with the peak activity in February and March.[33]

The success of the roads rested, of course, on there being effective means of traversing rivers and streams, and at the very end of our period the traveller John Leland recognized as much by repeatedly celebrating the crossings he encountered. In the course of what he calculated as a two-mile (3.2 kilometre) journey from Kettering to Geddington (Northamptonshire), for example, 'I rode over another bridge of tymbre wher rennith a broke' then 'passid over a broke that cummith from Ardingworth' (presumably by a ford), then on arriving at Geddington 'I passid agayne in the middle of the toun over Ardingworth water, that there rennith under a stone bridge'. This bridge, built in the middle of the thirteenth century, is still in place, though ironically with a ford beside it still used by vehicles too wide for the bridge. Then as now, bridges had the capacity to inspire awe as feats of design as well as of engineering, and Leland was prone to break off his accounts of progress by road to enumerate the various examples along major rivers. Some of his observations are of real significance, such as his comments on a three-arched bridge over the River Ure at Bridge Hewick near Ripon (Yorkshire), which is the only record of its existence, and his mention of another three-arched bridge crossing the Tees at Piercebridge near Darlington (County Durham), the earliest datable reference to a magnificent structure which survives to this day.[34]

Bridge-building proliferated in England from the ninth century onwards, mostly in response to quickening trade and the growing demand from horse-drawn carts for safe and dry river crossings. Bridges at London, Rochester (Kent), Chester, Huntingdon, Cambridge and Nottingham, most with Roman forerunners and all in existence at important river crossings by the early tenth century (notwithstanding many subsequent replacements), appear to have been the result of royal initiatives and in every case an obligation was placed upon their associated shires to contribute to their upkeep: in Chester, for example, Domesday Book specifically mentions that 'for the repair of the city wall and the bridge, the reeve used to call out one man to come from each hide in the county' on penalty of a prohibitive £2 fine to be imposed on the lord of any man who did not come.[35] However, most medieval bridge construction, and their upkeep thereafter, relied on individual generosity, spurred by a mixture of self-interest and altruism often laced with a sense of pious duty:

over 100 bridges in medieval England had chapels built on and adjacent to them, mostly as chantries so that prayers could be said for benefactors. Similar considerations applied to causeways, usually over flood-plains leading to bridges, for which the same Old English word *brycg* was sometimes employed. About 1130, Alexander Bishop of Lincoln was given permission by Henry I to build a new bridge at Newark-on-Trent (Nottinghamshire), clearly as part of a concerted effort to develop an urban centre here, since he also built a castle and obtained a royal grant of a five-day fair; his initiative led to a permanent diversion of the Great North Road away from Ermine Street so as to cross the Trent at Newark, as the A1 still does today. It was also in Henry I's reign that Ramsey Abbey is thought to have built a new bridge over the River Ouse in Huntingdonshire in order to encourage access to their market and fair at St Ives; its fifteenth-century successor, complete with chapel, still stands (Figure 16).[36] Beyond this, the provision of bridges frequently relied on bequests in wills and special fund-raising efforts from the sale of indulgences, which remitted the penance due following confession of sins: in 1479, for example, the Archbishop of York granted 40 days' indulgence to anyone who contributed to a new bridge – the equivalent of the modern M6 Thelwall viaduct – over the 'very great and swift river' Mersey near Warrington, which was having to be built afresh.[37]

Figure 16: St Ives Bridge (Huntingdonshire). A River Ouse crossing was established here when a new market-town was developed in the twelfth century, though the present bridge, with its chapel, is early fifteenth century (and the rounded arch dates to 1716). The previous settlement, Slepe, is marked by the church some 500 metres north-west of the bridge.

A common problem was that bridges, once built, were left without adequate arrangements for their ongoing maintenance. An enquiry in 1350 into responsibility for the upkeep of Egham causeway in Surrey, which led from the town of Egham to the bridge of Staines and was also a flood defence, found that it had originally been built and kept in repair during Henry III's reign by Thomas of Oxford, at his own expense, but that there had been no provision for its upkeep thereafter. By 1385 the causeway was found to be 'so destroyed and broken that the loss of all the adjacent country is to be feared,' so the sheriff of Surrey issued a public proclamation 'that all persons, ecclesiastical as well as secular, shall each, according to the extent of his holding, cause the same to be repaired with all haste.' Thereafter, the crown made various grants of 'pontage' to named individuals, empowering them to levy tolls, and the causeway survives to this day (Figure 17).[38] Elsewhere, we find that from the early eleventh to the late fourteenth century – when responsibility passed instead to a charitable trust – the upkeep of the bridge over the River Medway at Rochester on the London to Dover road was vested in a series of landholders within the lathe of Aylesford, an administrative subdivision of Kent, who each had a stake in particular arches: the Bishop of Rochester was responsible for the first arch and its piers, the king for the fourth, the Archbishop of Canterbury for the fifth and ninth, and various

Figure 17: Egham Causeway (Surrey). Originally built through an individual's generosity in the mid-thirteenth century, the causeway was intended to carry east-west traffic crossing the River Thames at Staines and also to protect Egham if Runnymede (to the right) was flooded. The Egham bypass was opened along this extension to the causeway in 1935.

manors in and around Gillingham for the remainder. This had the obvious disadvantage that the bridge would be of variable quality, but at least responsibility for this important crossing did not rest on one source alone.

Another form of maintenance was through alms given to a hermit living on or near the bridge who was expected to keep it in repair, such as John 'Leper' who was authorized by the town of Oxford in 1377 to maintain the Grandpont over the River Thames. William Langland's late-fourteenth century poem *Piers Plowman* criticized those who 'paraded as hermits for the sake of an easy life' but at least some of these men could alternatively be described as 'professional bridge-wardens'. Many claimed to live by the thirteenth-century papally approved *Rule of St Paul,* which enjoined them 'to avoyde idleness … and to repair ways and brigges to youre power' and were subject to formal appointment processes: in 1423 the mayor of Maidenhead presided over an installation ceremony at which the new hermit, Richard Ludlow, swore to keep away from taverns and spend all he received as gifts, beyond basic sustenance, on the repair of the town's bridge and roads. As a variant of all this, in 1457–58 a circular went out from the mayor and governing body of Nottingham soliciting alms for repair of the town's bridge, with a promise that the priest at the chapel on the bridge would celebrate divine service daily for the benefit of all who contributed.[39] So when the Statute of Bridges of 1531

Figure 18: Packhorse Bridge, near Barrow-in-Furness (Cumberland). This late fifteenth-century 'Bow Bridge' over the Abbey Beck, 3.2 metres wide, is a rare survival of the type of modest crossing widespread in medieval times. It gave the monks of nearby Furness Abbey access to a mill but also served an important packhorse route to the coast.

lamented the fact that 'decayed bridges' were liable to 'lie long without any amendment to the great annoyance of the King's subjects' and enacted that, unless an alternative obligation could be demonstrated, maintenance must always be the responsibility of the corporate town or shire within which the bridge stood,[40] it was arguably giving a misleading impression of the efforts made over the previous centuries to keep bridges in repair. Medieval engineers and those who engaged them have left us perhaps 200 bridges still functioning in England today and – like roads – they were maintained in a state sufficient to allow them to serve their society reasonably well.

In considering the structure of medieval bridges, we must of course acknowledge that many minor crossings serving packhorse routes would have been by ford or by the use of modest structures which rarely survive: tiny narrow arched bridges such as Bow Bridge near Furness Abbey (Cumberland) (Figure 18) or simple stone slabs, to create a clam bridge (with one span) or a clapper bridge (with two or more), like Postbridge clapper over the East Dart River on Dartmoor. Among more elaborate structures, timber was favoured for both bridges and causeways in the pre-Conquest period and although less durable than stone it offered a cheaper building material; accordingly, wooden bridges continued to be erected throughout the medieval period. Stratford-upon-Avon had a timber bridge until the end of the fifteenth century and in 1540 the majority of bridges over the Thames were still built of wood. However, stone was already in use by the end of the eleventh century, sometimes in conjunction with timber superstructures carrying the roadway but increasingly as the exclusive building material. There are a few examples of medieval bridges built in brick (as at Mayton Bridge, Norfolk over the River Bure) or of brick mixed with flint and stone (as at Moulton Bridge, Suffolk, over the Kennett), but these are exceptional: small, late and almost entirely confined to East Anglia.[41]

From the many surviving examples of medieval stone bridges, it is possible to see some technological development over the centuries. Similar techniques were used for the construction of arches as were employed in ecclesiastical buildings, and the same masons may sometimes have worked on both – as at Durham where Bishop Ranulf Flambard's new stone bridge over the Wear in the early twelfth century was built at the same time as the cathedral nave, or at Chelmsford in 1372, where the rebuilding of Moulsham Bridge over the River Can was entrusted by the Abbot of Westminster to Henry Yevele, also responsible for remodelling the naves of Canterbury Cathedral and Westminster Abbey. It is no surprise, therefore, that bridge design mirrored that found in churches, with the semi-circular arches of the twelfth century – such as those within the Exe Bridge in Exeter, England's earliest surviving stone bridge (albeit disused and incomplete) – giving way to pointed ones thereafter. Pointed arches allowed spans to be varied in width so that piers could rest wherever the firmest foundations within the river were found, while allowing a level road surface to be maintained above. A further advance came in the form of segmental arches – rounded but less than a full semi-circle – which were introduced in the fourteenth century. These presented a flatter profile and allowed broader spans which caused less interference to river traffic. Good examples of pointed-arched bridges are those at Bakewell (Derbyshire) of about 1300 and at Huntingdon, rebuilt at various dates during the fourteenth century. Farndon (Cheshire), dating to 1339, and the fifteenth-century bridges at Ludford (in Ludlow, Shropshire) and also at Wadebridge across the Camel demonstrate segmental arches. All include projecting triangular-shaped piers which served to deflect flowing water away from the uprights and allowed refuges for pedestrians part way across.

A further dimension to all this was the greater boldness of engineers in the north of England when it came to the height and spans of the arches. The late-fifteenth-century stone bridge at Bideford (Devon) uses no less than 24 arches to cross the River Torridge, and there are similar examples of the use of multiple arches at roughly contemporary structures at Barnstaple (also in Devon) and Stratford-upon-Avon. But in the northern uplands long low bridges like these would have been vulnerable to flash floods and river surges, so fewer piers and greater arches were favoured: as at the late-fourteenth-century Devil's Bridge at Kirkby Lonsdale (Westmorland), with two of its three arches having spans in excess of 16 metres; the Twizel Bridge over the River Till in Northumberland, built about 1500 as a single arch with a span of around 30 metres; and the Piercebridge over the Tees first noted by Leland, composed of three arches, the central one with a span of some 22 metres. With its precisely cut masonry and skilful use of several arch rings (counter arches) to support the superstructure, this last example has been described as 'the climax of medieval bridge design'.[42] In company with some of the other bridges listed here, it deserves to be ranked alongside great castles and churches among the best illustrations of medieval structural engineering.

Urban self-government

When the Statute of Bridges in 1531 obliged what it described as a 'town corporate' to maintain any which stood on its land, it was recognizing the collective powers which many urban communities had acquired by that time. A book on the landscape is not the place to explore these powers in any detail, but the story may briefly be told. Essentially, the market activity of a town necessitated a special court if only for the resolution of trading disputes, a corporate identity developed among traders in common pursuit of commercial advantage, and it was unrealistic for lords to enforce within towns the labour services and other obligations associated with servile tenure, so properties came to be held 'freely' for money rents with little restriction on their transfer. Much of this can be glimpsed in Domesday Book – albeit with the benefit of hindsight – but it was from the twelfth century that these corporate privileges were refined, defined and enshrined within charters which, collectively, can be regarded as conferring 'borough status'. A very early example is a charter of Henry I for the men of Beverley, datable 1124–33, confirming 'free burgage according to the free laws and customs of the burgesses of York, and also their gild-merchant with its pleas and toll, and with all its free customs and liberties in all things as Thurstan the archbishop gave to them'. Nearly 50 royal charters to English towns survive from the reign of his grandson, Henry II, with the right to a gild-merchant, freedom from toll, burgage tenure and various borough customs (usually modelled on those elsewhere) as the standard fare. Oxford, for example, not later than 1162, was specifically confirmed in its entitlement to a gild-merchant, freedom from tolls all over England and Normandy and other 'customs, liberties and laws which they have in common with my citizens of London' including provision for court cases to be settled according to London law: a clear message to the king's sheriff of Oxfordshire, based at the castle in the south-west quarter of the town, not to interfere.[43] What all this meant, in practice, was that the leading tradesmen were free to form an association for their mutual benefit – the gild-merchant – burgage properties within the town were to be held for money rents without any vestige of 'unfree tenure', there was an opportunity to trade free of toll wherever specified, and a series of local laws and customs would apply within the borough under the jurisdiction of its own officers.

Another concession, which featured less regularly and was liable to be revoked and then restored according to political necessity, was the right of a borough to answer for its own farm to the royal exchequer. What this meant was that the farm – a lump sum rendered annually to the king, covering rents and various customary dues – would be accounted for not by the sheriff (who was also responsible for the 'shire farm' and who stood to profit from any excess collected) but by officers of the borough: any surplus raised, over and above the farm required, could then be used for the borough's own purposes. Gloucester is known to have enjoyed this right by the 1170s and by the close of Edward I's reign in 1307 no less than 50 boroughs did so, as part of a proliferation of concessions during the course of the thirteenth century which, in addition to those itemized above, might include the right to elect a mayor and entitlement to levy murage, pavage or pontage for the upkeep of walls, streets or bridges respectively. All this added to the sense of corporate identity and activity; Lincoln, for example, was able to pave 'the high road through the … town' in 1286. By the fourteenth century, some boroughs were regularly sending representatives to parliament, while by the fifteenth it was normal for charters to include a right for the borough collectively to hold land, possess a common seal and issue its own bye-laws.[44]

Reality was of course more complicated that this brief account might suggest, since boroughs differed on many points of detail. Gilds-merchant varied in the extent of their exclusivity and in their precise relationship to the governing authority of the town: effectively the same body at Winchester and Worcester, for example, but kept distinct at Exeter. Most boroughs, especially those which acquired their key privileges after the twelfth century, never formally had a gild-merchant, but the leading merchants still formed themselves into a governing assembly to discharge the corporate respon- sibilities which had been conferred. Even the status of 'burgess', with a right to trade freely within the borough, differed from town to town: open to any man born there at Colchester, but more usually by the thirteenth century a privilege acquired by inheritance, apprenticeship or purchase. The prevalence of sub-letting increasingly distanced this status from possession of a 'burgage plot' within the town, a topic to which we return below. It is also the case that, while the greater towns acquired more independence to become by the fourteenth century substantial self-governing communities, smaller market towns lagged behind. Even some economically flourishing places found it difficult to secure the grant of significant liberties, especially if they were located on the demesne of a lord other than the king. The abbeys of Abingdon, Bury St Edmunds and St Albans were most reluctant to grant any substantial self-governance to the towns at their gates; the consequent resentment led to violence in all three places during the Great Revolt of 1381. Leicester, though a substantial midlands town which profited from the wool trade, failed to gain the autonomy of comparable places until its lordship had passed to the crown with the accession of Henry IV in 1399. That said, some smaller towns did manage a measure of corporate activity, one example being Towcester (Northamptonshire) which, although governed by successive lords of the manor outside the royal demesne, obtained the king's permission in the mid-fifteenth century to pave its main street with limestone.[45]

Town planning

This discussion of urban privileges is a necessary prelude to any treatment of the phenomenon of the 'medieval new town'. Maurice Beresford's pioneering book on the subject, first published in 1967, defined them as the result of 'decisions ... to plant towns where no settlement existed' and identified no less than 171 examples in England, with a further 200-plus in Wales and

Gascony. The distinction drawn was between new urban settlements on previously unsettled land, where plots were laid out and prospective settlers offered attractive terms on which to build their houses, and the larger number of organic 'villages-turned-town' which lay outside the scope of the book. Among the 'new towns' of England, the foundations of some 44 were dated to the period 1066–1140 (the Norman Conquest to the onset of the civil war of Stephen's reign), a further 96 from the end of that war in 1153 to the accession of Edward I in 1272, another 16 during Edward's reign to 1307, but only six during the rest of the medieval period, with none after 1368.[46] This ground-breaking study has predictably attracted criticism from those it has stimulated to engage in further research on the subject. Apart from its serious neglect of pre-Conquest initiatives, the book makes a distinction between 'new' and 'organic' towns which in reality was rarely clear-cut. At Higham Ferrers in 1250–51, for example, there was already an established village community before the Earl of Derby took a series of preconceived steps to free the villeins and start an annual fair, effectively converting it into an urban centre: there was no 'plantation' here, but there was certainly a deliberate decision to found a 'new town'.[47] Indeed, the concept of an 'organic' town is itself open to challenge, if by this is meant an urban settlement which grew of its own accord without any direction by the king or other lord: a village could certainly prosper from its agricultural activity and outstrip its neighbours in size of population, but a market was an essential prerequisite to support the crafts and trades which characterized a town and as we have seen this was a privilege the grant of which was supposed to be controlled from above, whether in the defended *burhs* and at the monastic gatehouses of the pre-Conquest period or during the centuries which followed. So there is a sense in which every medieval town was a deliberate creation on the part of the king or other lord on whose estates the settlement lay; as an added incentive to utilize the market, the privileges of borough status outlined above might also be conferred as part of a package, designed to attract settlers and maximize the lord's profits from rents and trade.

It ought to be said at the outset that despite the proliferation of urban initiatives, especially in the twelfth and thirteenth centuries, not every feudal lord chose to exploit his estates in this way. A study of borough foundation across the northernmost shires of England has shown that, while the Bishop of Durham was very keen on such ventures, there were several northern baronies – like those based on Embleton and Wark in Northumberland – which declined to develop them, whether from inertia or from careful calculation of likely returns on investment.[48] Nor were all foundations bound to succeed, even at times of burgeoning growth in population. Oversley (Warwickshire) was established by the Boteler family in the middle of the twelfth century, when they built two roads to link their castle to the major midlands routeway known as Ryknild Street and provided a chapel and burgage plots alongside these roads. However, the settlement was not located at a crossing of the nearby River Arrow and proved less attractive to settlers than Alcester, 1.5 kilometres to the north, which was. In the event, several plots were not built upon and the settlement was abandoned by the early thirteenth century.[49] As for whether the layout of a town's street pattern was deliberately planned, we now know that the relationship between this and the foundation of new urban settlements is by no means straightforward. Some new creations of the pre-Conquest period, such as Thetford and Sandwich, lacked any rigidity of plan[49] and even where a deliberate layout seems obvious it often resulted from a staged process over several generations. Close analysis of the grid plan at Ludlow, for example, has shown there to have been at least four different phases to the laying out of the town, from the twelfth century onwards, while at Burton-on-Trent the local abbey originally created a single-street town only then to add four further sections, the last of which, in the late thirteenth century, failed for lack of settlers. Likewise Durham, though dominated by its cathedral and castle in a loop of the River Wear, has been described as 'a series of village scale units … a series of separate borough entities'.[50] The vast majority of cases of medieval urban planning actually represent either enlargements of, or replacements for, towns or villages which existed already, their claim to be 'new' often being compromised by the fact that the same fields were being farmed as hitherto: Beresford himself drew attention to this in the cases of New Sleaford (Lincolnshire) and New Malton (Yorkshire).[51] Genuine examples of 'new towns' in the sense of urban settlements consciously founded and laid out as separate entities on uninhabited land are by no means widespread.

Prime examples of what may fairly be called 'burghal extensions' – planned appendages to established settlements – are the significantly named Eynsham Newland and Sherborne Newland (Oxfordshire and Dorset respectively), both ventures of the thirteenth century, both adjacent to but outside the confines of a pre-existing town, and both represented by 'Newland' street names today. Elsewhere, at Appleby-in-Westmorland, a new town was laid out early in the twelfth century on the west bank of the River Eden, with a castle at the southern end some 30 metres above the river, a new parish church of St Lawrence near the bridge at the northern end, and a broad market street ('Boroughgate') running downhill between the two; but an earlier, pre-Conquest settlement survived east of the river, was referred to in a thirteenth-century lawsuit as 'Old Appleby where the villeins dwell' and still preserves the name Bongate (bondmen's street). Another example is Downton (Wiltshire), where in 1086 there was a substantial village with a recorded population of 131 on the east bank of the River Avon and where the Bishop of Salisbury proceeded to develop a 'new market' and 'new borough' on the west bank in the early thirteenth century: there were 40 burgage plots here by 1211-12 and 89 by 1218-19, occupying the long straight street leading from the bridge, still known locally as 'The Borough'.[52] At Ashbourne (Derbyshire), the Domesday settlement north of the Henmore Brook is marked by the presence of the parish church, but during the thirteenth century the Ferrers family developed a long street running east, roughly parallel to the brook, incorporating a triangular market place and culminating in a manor house and park at the opposite end of the town: this initiative took advantage of traffic passing between the midlands and the north west (including that attracted by lead and silver mining in the area), leaving the original settlement as no more than the church-end of Ashbourne, without an identity of its own. At about the same time in Shropshire, the Abbot of Shrewsbury developed 'Newtown' as a planned appendage to Baschurch; with its straight streets and carefully delineated parallel house-plots, it still presents a marked contrast to the parent settlement. And as late as 1447, the construction of a new bridge over the River Severn prompted the development of Bewdley (Worcestershire) as a planned replacement for Wyre Hill, less than a kilometre to the west; almost a century later, Leland described Bewdley as 'a very new towne, and that of old tyme there was but some pore hamelet' which he implied had disappeared – although here at least Wyre Hill persists as a street name within Bewdley today. New developments like these have recently been described as 'medieval enterprise zones' which remained attached to their parent manor, and drew much of their population from within that manor; as far as the founding lord was concerned, the old and new settlements were both important sources of income, offering alternative revenue-streams.[53]

If we are seeking genuine 'new towns', as opposed to extensions of, or replacements for, existing settlements, we need to look for speculative ventures at some distance from other communities, often located at the boundary between different jurisdictions and sometimes bearing a name which has the hallmarks of having been deliberately imposed. These can still be seen as 'enterprise zones', with incentives being offered to those prepared to move in and build on the plots made available, but at least the new settlement had an identity which clearly set it apart. In this group we can certainly include Battle (Sussex), which would not exist had William the Conqueror not founded an abbey on the site of his victory over Harold Godwinson in 1066, and the monks not proceeded to develop a town outside their main gate following the grant by the king of a Sunday market in 1070–71. A similarly speculative venture was Devizes (Wiltshire), founded by the Bishop of Salisbury probably in the 1130s to attract trade in the vicinity of his castle, named the *burgus de divisis* because it straddled two episcopal manors. So was Baldock (Hertfordshire), established by the Knights Templar (who named it after Baghdad) in the mid-twelfth century at an important crossing on the Great North Road on the edge of two parishes. Mountsorrel (Leicestershire), a castle town probably of the mid-twelfth century located where two parishes met, and Brigg (Lincolnshire), named from a bridge which by 1235 had been built across the River Ancholme at the junction of four parishes, appear to be other examples of this type. The crown was not, of course, to be left out of the picture. About 1119 Henry I issued a charter encouraging settlement at the intersection in Bedfordshire of Watling Street and the Icknield Way, where he had a lodge called Kingsbury, promising burgage tenure and the liberties and privileges of the city of London; a weekly market and annual fair are mentioned here by the end of the reign. The place probably took its name, Dunstable, from a *stapol* or post which stood at the crossroads to point out the four ways.[54]

Royal initiatives of this sort were especially important along the coast, although here again some foundations were really replacements for earlier towns no longer viable because of the vagaries of the sea: such as New Romney (Kent) already in existence by the end of the tenth century, and the Sussex towns of New Shoreham (founded by Philip de Braose about 1100) and New Winchelsea (founded by King Edward I in the 1280s), all of which replaced 'Old' versions with the same name which could no longer function effectively. More convincing as 'new' were sea-ports given the names of local features, like Portsmouth at the entrance to the Wallington estuary where there was already a harbour at Portchester further upstream, and Liverpool at a tidal creek in the Mersey known as *le pool*; Richard I's foundation charter for Portsmouth in 1194 granted burgage tenure with the privileges of Winchester and Oxford, adding a market and fair, while Liverpool received a foundation charter from John in 1207 which promised privileges to those who took up burgage plots 'as any free borough on the sea coast of England then enjoyed'. Edward III took an alternative approach by honouring his wife when founding Queenborough on the Isle of Sheppey (Kent) in 1368; conversely, his grandfather Edward I, developing a port at the point where the River Hull entered the Humber, had called it Kingston. At this point, however, a cautionary word should be entered, since Kingston upon Hull was not really new, but an extension of an already successful port called Wyke upon Hull, which the king had bought from the Cistercian abbey of Meaux in 1293. In this instance, it was the monastic foundation, rather than its royal successor, which was truly the 'new town'. Liverpool is also thought to have been preceded by a small fishing and farming settlement, whose open fields it took over and extended.[55]

How was all this expressed in the landscape? As we have seen, a key feature of any medieval town, whatever its origins, was a place to hold a market: sufficiently large to accommodate stallholders but with access-points narrow enough to control entry and exit, so that stall-rents and tolls could be collected. Many market grants to existing settlements must have assumed that the residents and traders would find a suitable location for themselves, hence the initial appeal of churchyards, but – as we have seen – by the thirteenth century ecclesiastical pressure was requiring other solutions. An obvious location was at the intersections of routeways, and the triangular market places at Bampton (Oxfordshire), Taunton (Somerset) and Ashbourne may have arisen in this way, not necessarily through deliberate planning. Where the main thoroughfare broadens into an elongated cigar shape, as at Henley-in-Arden and at Chard (Somerset), this may also have been a gradual, unplanned, development, the outcome of steady pressure by stallholders to encroach on either side of the street. However, market places with a more obvious rectilinear shape have the appearance of being consciously planned, all the more so if – as at St Ives (Huntingdonshire), Chipping Sodbury (Gloucestershire) and New Thame (Oxfordshire) – the main thoroughfare has clearly been diverted to ensure that travellers passed that way. Drivers using the main A44 between Evesham and Oxford are still forced to snake through the broad medieval market places of Moreton in Marsh (Gloucestershire) and Chipping Norton (Oxfordshire), both deliberately laid out with burgage plots on either side some distance from the original settlement nuclei marked by parish churches, and in Moreton's case by the significant name 'Old Town' (Figure 19). We can also be confident that the market place was part of an overall plan where it was located just outside the precincts of a castle or abbey – like those at Battle, Devizes, Ely and St Albans – or occupied one block, or *insula*, within a grid system of streets, as at Castleton (Derbyshire) and Salisbury (Wiltshire).[56] That said, the original shape of a market place could quickly be transformed by structures built within it: the Abbot of Bury St Edmunds, for example, was in dispute with his townsfolk in the 1190s over the erection of what appear to have been permanent shops and booths, causing 'so many and great encroachments in the market place'.[57]

This does not mean that all urban trade was restricted to the market place, since those who lived and worked within a town – as opposed to those who came in from outside – would frequent certain streets and quarters and carry out their businesses from there. William fitz Stephen's description of London, dating to Henry II's reign, explained that 'those that ply their several trades, the vendors of each several thing, the hirers out of their several sorts of labour are found every morning each in their separate quarters and each engaged upon his own peculiar task'. This phenomenon, which has given many English towns their distinctive trade-related street names, persisted throughout the middle ages, whether because of some local amenity (like the riverside locations favoured by the dyers of Salisbury and Winchester) or because they were compulsorily excluded from the

Figure 19: Moreton in Marsh, (Gloucestershire). Traffic on the A44 (bottom left) and A429 (bottom right) still passes through the wide market place laid out astride the Fosse Way, with burgage plots either side, in the early thirteenth century. The 'Old Town' with church is away to the right, secluded from this deliberately planned 'burghal extension'.

town centre on the grounds of hygiene or fire risk.[58] The capacity to trade in these locations outside the principal market was facilitated by the fact that medieval streets were often fairly broad. When Stratford-upon-Avon was laid out at the end of the twelfth century it was to have streets at least 50 feet (15.2 metres) wide, while in 1480 William of Worcester on a visit to Bristol paced out several streets of 20 steps (about 10.7 metres) or more in width: one only 5 steps (about 2.7 metres) across was specifically named 'Narrow St Thomas's Street'. The impression sometimes given that medieval towns were a crowded network of narrow streets is false, being more characteristic of the sixteenth and seventeenth centuries, by which time street frontages had often crept forward. At Winchester, where the main thoroughfare was protected against encroachment but the side streets were not, the present-day High Street retains its eleventh-century breadth but streets leading off it funnel out: narrower towards the High Street where there was most advance from buildings either side, broader further away.[59]

The layout of the streets within a medieval town was determined by factors such as local topography and the pattern of converging roads, but there was usually an element of deliberate planning at some stage. The most obvious signs of this are to be found in those 'new towns' established on supposedly virgin sites which displayed a rigorous grid pattern of streets.

New Winchelsea is often cited as a prime example (though even here there was a previous small settlement called Iham), partly because no less than 39 chequers can be identified from the original grid plan, and partly because surviving documentation allows us to tell the story of how Edward I, convinced that continued expenditure on the existing port of Winchelsea was a waste of money, acquired some 60 hectares on Iham hill and in 1281 commissioned a surveyor to 'plan and give directions for streets and lanes, and assign places suitable for a market and for two churches'. On 25 July 1288 he duly transferred some 795 new house plots, arranged by streets and quarters, to the burgesses of the old town, though the initial promise that no rent would be collected for the first seven years seems not to have been honoured.[60] Similar stories doubtless lie behind other towns with grid plans, even if many of the details of their foundation are unknown.

There is a convention that in order to be classified as having a 'grid plan', a town must have at least three streets of equal importance running in each direction, and at least nine chequers or *insulae*. By these criteria, just over 20 medieval 'new towns' in England (including three in the Isle of Wight) exhibited the form, ranging in date from New Romney (Kent) by 960 to New Winchelsea as the last of the type. But failure to achieve nine chequers does not in itself mean an absence of planning. Plenty of urban foundations display some evidence of a grid and although these are not on the scale of three streets by three a deliberate overall plan seems more plausible than an assumption that the pattern arose as a result of piecemeal expansion. Both Bishop's Castle (Shropshire), where the Bishop of Hereford founded the town in 1127 (Figure 20) and Hartlepool, where a pre-Conquest town was re-founded by the Brus family about 1180 as a port for the nearby settlement of Hart, had simple grids based on a principal street, one or two back lanes and several cross streets.[61] Elsewhere, such minor grids with few chequers might form only part of what is known to have been the medieval town, suggesting an element of planning but not necessarily the foundation anew of the town as a whole. A limited criss-cross pattern of this type can be discerned outside the west gates of the abbeys of Bury St Edmunds and Peterborough, the former attributed to the years prior to the Domesday Survey, the latter to Stephen's reign when the abbot is reported (in one translation) 'to have changed the site of the town to a better position'.[62]

A tiny number of newly planted towns can be said to have had a 'radial plan', with streets fanning out from a dominant castle towards the surrounding defences: Richmond (Yorkshire), Pleshey (Essex) and Devizes, all dating to the twelfth century, conform to this pattern, although the precise arrangements differ.[63] By far the commonest plan, however, was that based on a single main street, usually accompanied by a market place either at one end or part way along it. This plan was also frequently encountered among nucleated villages,

Figure 20: Bishop's Castle (Shropshire). This twelfth-century planned town was laid out between the Bishop of Hereford's castle to the north and a church (off-picture) to the south. Three roughly parallel streets run downhill from the castle – the central one broadening out to accommodate a market – with cross streets providing links between them. (© The GeoInformation Group.)

so we find it where an existing settlement, like Higham Ferrers, was effectively granted urban status by its lord. It was also common where towns had been established along major routeways to take advantage of passing trade: witness the twelfth-century foundations of Uxbridge (Middlesex) where the London to Oxford road crossed the river Colne, described in Leland's *Itinerary* as 'but one longe streate', and also Boroughbridge (Yorkshire) and Baldock, both on main roads from London to the north. Thirteenth-century examples include the Bishop of London's Chelmsford (Essex), where the London to Colchester road crossed the River Chelmer, and Newmarket (founded by the Argentein family on the Suffolk-Cambridgeshire border). Several castle towns were also based around a single main street. Among these is Arundel (Sussex), apparently established between the Norman Conquest and the compilation of

Domesday Book; here, a main street runs down from the castle on the east to a river crossing and quay on the west, with a market place created where the street splays out near the bridge. Newcastle-upon-Tyne (a royal foundation sometime after 1080) and Pontefract (Yorkshire), a baronial new town which appears in Domesday Book, are other early castle-based towns, both with broad market streets running away from the castle gates. The late foundation of Queenborough in 1368 on 'a broad and deep arm of the sea convenient for ships to put in at' was constricted by its estuarine site to a simple main street between the castle and the sea.[64]

Even where the street pattern within a medieval town implies minimal overall planning, a sure sign that there has been some authoritative direction is the presence of 'burgage plots', the series of long narrow enclosures for housing, arranged next to each other along the principal streets. In theory, these plots were held by the burgesses, the freeholders who (if there was a measure of self-government) contributed through their rents to the town's corporate funds and might also participate in collective decision-making – though in practice, subletting made for greater diversity. Analysis of the size of burgage plots has shown that they were normally laid out by standard measures, partly to facilitate equitable calculation of rents. Each community would have had its own measuring 'rod, pole or perch' and although in the countryside this varied in length (in Pembrokeshire, 10 feet or about 3 metres, in Cheshire 24 feet, some 7.3 metres), in towns the 'statute perch' of 16 ½ feet (5.03 metres) seems to have been widespread; indeed, by the close of the thirteenth century, a statute acre (4840 square yards) was also being recognized, on the basis of 4 statute perches by 40. Accordingly, the Bishop of Worcester's foundation charter for the new town of Stratford-upon-Avon in 1196 stated that each of the plots should cost one shilling (5p) annual rent and measure 3 ½ perches by 12 perches (equating to 18 by 60 metres, or just over a quarter-acre in size); although several plots had been subdivided lengthways into halves or thirds within 50 years of the grant of this charter (creating frontages to the streets of 6 or 9 metres), these basic dimensions still govern property boundaries in the centre of the town today. Similarly, the foundation of Burton-on-Trent (Staffordshire), about the same time as Stratford, was accompanied by a stipulation that the burgage plots should measure 4 perches by 24 (about 20 metres by 121 metres). Where no such specifications exist but plots can be measured on the ground today, similar dimensions have been found in towns as far apart as Evesham (Worcestershire) and Totnes (Devon).[65] Not all burgage plots respected the 16 ½ feet perch: different lengths have been noted in Alnwick (Northumberland), in York and in Oxford, where there was a contrast between a short perch inside the walls and a longer one in extra-mural Broad Street.[66] But whether the statute measure or a local alternative was used, the key point is that we are in the presence here of substantial urban planning.

Studies of the configuration and dimensions of burgage plots are helpful for the reconstruction of the stages by which a medieval town developed, as in the Bail, the 'Upper City' of Lincoln on the site of the former Roman fortress, where the southern part of Bailgate immediately to the east of the castle was probably laid out in the middle of the twelfth century and the northern part towards the Newport Arch – where the plots are wider – some years later. Bailgate was under the jurisdiction of the castle constable on behalf of the crown, but – notwithstanding the well-recorded example of New Winchelsea – we should beware of assuming that the 'authority' which took the initiative in urban planning was always an extraneous lord. The 'Lower City' of Lincoln, occupying the slope between the Bail and the River Witham to the south, was reconfigured in the first half of the eleventh century, with streets such as the Strait and Steep Hill coming into existence, presumably under the direction of the 12 'lawmen' referred to in Domesday Book who governed this part of the town. In twelfth- and thirteenth-century Sandwich, the town's council seems to have been heavily involved in the realignment of streets to accommodate a westward extension of St Peter's Church and the repositioning of the fish market: a custumal of 1301 mentions the council's powers to move a market if its place 'be too much crowded or too narrow … as was the case with the fishmongers in the new street'.[67] This was collective responsibility in action.

Whatever their origins, all towns reflected the growth of population down to the early fourteenth century by extending the built-up area. Along rivers, this sometimes took the form of reclamation of the waterfront, above all in London where over 1.5 kilometres west of the Tower around Queenhithe were the subject of successive schemes from Roman times onwards; indeed, medieval London is estimated to have increased its surface area by 15% through extending into the river, creating space for new dwellings, wharves and warehouses, mostly before 1350. Similar efforts have been identified at King's Lynn, Hull, Newcastle-upon-Tyne and Norwich.[68] More widespread was the growth of suburbs beyond the boundaries which delineated the urban nucleus. Suburbs clustered around the main roads as they approached a town, with a pronounced 'goose-foot' funnelling effect to these roads if the town walls restricted access to a limited number of gates. As early as the 950s, the area known as Wigford was stretching for almost a kilometre along the main road running southwards from Lincoln and it was further extended thereafter; by the later twelfth century main roads leading out of Canterbury and Winchester passed through suburbs of similar extent. As has already been noted, several towns were recorded as having suburbs in Domesday Book, although whether this settlement beyond defined limits implied some freedom from urban jurisdiction is unclear. On the north side of Lincoln, the suburb of Newport was developed soon after the Norman

Conquest, based on a street running out from the walled area of the town which broadened into a market place and later hosted the great St Botolph's fair, but this remained under the authority of the governing council. Escape from urban control is more obvious at Shrewsbury, where the abbey was granted at its foundation in the 1080s 'the whole suburb outside the east gate'. Although there is little evidence of deliberate suburban planning on the part of the monks, they hosted a rival fair to that of the town across the bridge for much of the medieval period and inevitably attracted to the vicinity some of the economic activity which would otherwise have flourished over there.[69]

In general, whether or not they were subject to an alternative authority, suburbs tended to be more spacious in their layout of streets and properties than town centres; they often acquired boundaries of their own, in the form of banks, ditches and bars across roads, but they were often perceived to lie outside the town gates, with trading allowed free of urban tolls. They might house a considerable proportion of a town's population – a quarter of Exeter's total in the 1520s and over a third of Winchester's in both the 1140s and the 1340s – with many of their residents engaged in industrial activities: an archaeological site at Alms Lane, Norwich, for example, has revealed suburban growth in the thirteenth century over rubbish dumps and quarry pits north of the town, and evidence thereafter of brewing, skinning, pottery-making and working in iron, leather and bone, before the area was abandoned after the Black Death and then developed for housing instead.[70]

As urban authorities increased their powers during the course of the middle ages, they certainly took an interest in what were, in effect, local planning measures intended to help people live harmoniously in close proximity to one another. The earliest known urban building regulation comes from ninth-century Canterbury, where a space of two feet (0.6 metres) between each house was required, but they are best known from London, where an Assize of Buildings was issued about 1189. As detailed regulations evolved from this, they came to insist that party walls between stone houses should be at least 3 feet (0.9 metres) thick and 16 feet (4.9 metres) high, roofs be tiled or at least not have flammable reeds and straw exposed, and the mouths of cesspits be at least two and a half feet (0.75 metres) away from the property boundary. Good evidence for the enforcement of all this survives both from the excavation of London dwellings obviously built to conform, and also in the record of offences, nearly a quarter of which in the fourteenth and early fifteenth centuries concerned drainage and water disposal. There is, for example, a fascinating glimpse of sanitary arrangements at London's Queenhithe in August 1314, where rainwater and other waste from houses and the street were channelled into a gutter designed to cleanse a public convenience 'on the Hithe'; Alice Wade, who had fitted a pipe from her own domestic privy so that this would discharge into the gutter, was ordered to remove it, since the gutter 'is frequently stopped up by the filth therefrom, and the neighbours under whose houses the gutter runs are greatly inconvenienced by the stench'.[71] Apart from foul water, what concerned regulators most was the risk of fire: it is some tribute to their success in this regard that whereas there had been five 'great fires of London' in the eleventh and twelfth centuries, there were none at any time between 1212 and 1666, nor any similar catastrophic conflagrations in the major towns of York, Bristol and Norwich through the thirteenth and fourteenth centuries. An ordinance of 1467 in Worcester forbade thatched roofs and timber chimneys within the town walls, while the Building Assize for Newcastle-upon-Tyne, apparently late-medieval in date, orders that the ground and first floor of buildings must be of stone at least three feet thick; again, archaeological investigation of structures of this date suggest that the rules were being observed.[72] This corporate concern for general welfare mirrors the readiness to act in concert for mutual benefit which we have already encountered in rural settlements, and to which we shall return.

Urban buildings

It is easy to have a false impression of the appearance of medieval towns since the survival rate of buildings from the period is in inverse proportion to their frequency at the time: rare, highly untypical houses persist (including some castles, to which we shall turn in Chapter 6), the mass of humble dwellings have all but disappeared. There remain, for example, some exceptional urban dwellings for the élite, such as St Mary's Guildhall, Lincoln, built as a royal residence not later than 1157; the thirteenth-century stone palace of the Bishops of Wells; Lambeth Palace, the London residence of the Archbishops of Canterbury, of the thirteenth and fifteenth centuries; and Gainsborough Old Hall, built in the 1470s and 1480s by a nobleman who served both Richard III and Henry VII. All these were highly unusual in an urban context because of the lack of any serious constraint on space: the grounds of Gainsborough Old Hall occupied a full quarter of the town, the episcopal palaces were within ecclesiastical enclaves, and the royal house at Lincoln was built in the developing suburb of Wigford, away from the more densely occupied town centre.[73] Yet in one sense these élite buildings were in the mainstream of urban house design, for they were all laid out in one way or another around a hall: the motifs of the countryside applied in the town as well, at all levels above the humblest in society.

For merchants, the hall was a place for such business as did not need to be kept confidential, and it must also have conveyed an impression of status equivalent to that of the lord of a rural manor. Twelfth-century merchants' houses survive in stone, for example, as Wensum Lodge, Norwich, where the original two-storey range had a single-storey aisled hall added along the street front, and as the Norman House and Jew's House, Lincoln, which both had halls on the upper floor.[74] Nos. 3–4 West Street, New Romney is an early fourteenth century example, reproducing in stone the standard manorial plan of single-storey central hall, cross passage and service end, with the other end of two storeys, comprising undercroft with chamber above. Among new buildings of the fifteenth century, when timber had come to be regarded as a more fashionable, flexible and economical material than stone, Little Hall, Lavenham, Great Porch House, Devizes, and the Merchant's House, Bromsgrove – each one of which can be linked to prominent local mercantile families – all boast an open hall and a two-storey wing for services below and one or more chambers above. In all these cases, the building plots were sufficiently wide to allow the halls to be set parallel to the street, and, where space and funds allowed, buildings of this type might be enhanced by the development of courtyards behind. Thus, the fifteenth-century Salisbury merchant's house now known as Church House in Crane Street had a particularly wide passage between hall and service end, to allow horses and carts to gain access from the street to the courtyard beyond. What might be called communal town residences – inns, colleges, hospitals – particularly favoured the courtyard plan to maximize accommodation, while always retaining a hall as an essential element within the overall layout.[75] The fourteenth-century New Inn, Gloucester and fifteenth-century Pilgrim's Inn (otherwise The George) Glastonbury are good surviving illustrations of this arrangement, as are the hospital of Holy Cross, Winchester (founded in the 1130s) and several Oxbridge colleges, where the fourteenth-century Mob Quad at Merton (Oxford) and Old Court at Corpus Christi (Cambridge) both have grounds for claiming to be the earliest survivors in a university context.[76]

Lower down the social scale, the hall was also a key feature of urban buildings which combined the functions of residence and shop (or workshop). Tackley's Inn, (106–7 High Street) Oxford, apparently intended partly as student accommodation from the time it was built around 1320, had a hall with screens passage and chamber running parallel to the street, all of which was fronted by five shops with a vaulted undercroft below; a passage between two of the shops gave access from the street to the hall but there appears to have been no direct interior link between hall and shops, suggesting an intention to rent them out as separate units. Similarly, at nos. 38–42 Watergate Street, Chester, also of the 1320s, a run of shops had a hall, with screens passage and service end, occupying the full width behind them; the shops had chambers above and undercrofts below but in all but one case there was no internal link to the hall, again implying a renting-out arrangement

(Figure 23). Conversely, at nos. 48–52 Bridge Street, Chester, where again there is a hall running parallel to the street fronted by shops over undercrofts, a series of internal doorways to the hall, apparently giving access to each of the shops, imply that they were all under the owner's direct control. An alternative layout, well-suited to narrow burgage plots created by subdivisions and for a situation where house and shop were held by the same person, was for the hall to be set at right-angles to the street, with a single shop at the front and private rooms extending behind. A late thirteenth-century example is the so-called 'eastern house' of Booth Mansion (nos. 28–34 Watergate Street), Chester, which had a shop facing the street, with undercroft below and chamber above, then hall with services at the back. The merchant's house at No. 58 French Street, Southampton, of the late thirteenth and fourteenth centuries, had an undercroft largely below street level, and above that a shop accessed from the street with hall and two-storey chambers behind (Figure 21). Some aspects of this arrangement were replicated, albeit on a smaller scale, in a terrace of at least 23 houses built about 1450 in Tewkesbury as a speculative development by the nearby abbey; many of the units still survive as nos. 34–50 Church Street, with shop at the front facing the street, chamber above the shop and open hall at the back, though in this case undercrofts were missing (Figure 22). A similar terrace development, though with some differences in the internal layout, survives as The Abbot's House, Butcher Row, Shrewsbury, also of the 1450s and again with the local abbey in the role of building speculator.[77]

Two widespread features of these timber-framed commercial buildings are worthy of note. One is the repeated use of the jetty, an extension of the beams supporting the upper storey so that it projected beyond the ground floor frontage; in multi-storey buildings this could be repeated from one storey to the next. Jetties were an ingenious way of winning extra accommodation space without encroaching on the street below. They are first recorded in London not later than 1246, and were widely adopted in other towns from about 1300: an innovation in design where towns were clearly ahead of the countryside.[78] The other is the frequent, though not invariable, provision of a stone undercroft, absent altogether from some towns with surviving medieval houses such as Salisbury and York but found in Oxford, Southampton, Stamford and elsewhere; a variation at Norwich is that the undercrofts were built of brick. Where they existed, they seem to have served as fireproof storage areas, which might also be used as additional retail outlets, workshops or taverns. They also helped to give a stable and level platform for the superstructure of the house, commonly being found on sloping ground, beneath that part of the house towards the bottom of the slope. This is the case, for example, at Pride Hill, Shrewsbury, where a series of thirteenth- and fourteenth-century halls with accompanying shops have

Figure 21: No. 58 French Street, Southampton. Built in the 1290s, and now restored to its mid-fourteenth century appearance, this merchant's house is arranged gable-end to the street, with a jettied chamber projecting over a ground floor shop, below which is an undercroft. Behind the shop is an open hall, with chambers beyond for further accommodation. (English Heritage Photo Library.)

Figure 22: Fifteenth-century terrace in Church Street, Tewkesbury (Gloucestershire). This is an early surviving example of uniform building development, as shown by the consistent line of the jetty. The terrace was erected as a commercial venture for leasing to tenants by the Benedictine abbey of Tewkesbury, whose magnificent mid-twelfth century central tower appears in the background.

undercrofts not under the shops but at the rear of the plots, where the land falls away to the River Severn.

All this helps to give a context for the peculiar arrangements at Chester, where not only are there as many as 180 surviving stone undercrofts but access to the shops above them is from continuous galleries, the so-called 'Rows', which in the fourteenth century ran along both sides of the four main streets and even today, though reduced in extent and much-altered, remain prominent features of the town. The result was, and remains, a sequence of shops at two levels, one series occupying the undercrofts partly below ground and accessed from the street, the other series above them accessed from the galleries, which cut through the structural front portion of each building and – as has been observed by commentators ever since John Leland and William Smith in the sixteenth century – allow shoppers to stay dry whatever the weather (Figure 23). Similar arrangements have been found in single buildings or short stretches, both in England and on the continent, and it is possible that Kendal (Westmorland) might have offered a close parallel had it preserved its 'galleries hanging over the street' described by the early eighteenth-century antiquarian William Stukeley. However, the coherence of the system at Chester, embracing all its main streets, makes the town unique.

Chester's Rows appear to have developed in stages through the second half of the thirteenth and first half of the fourteenth centuries, in a context in which – partly because of the natural terrain but mainly through the accumulation of debris left from the Roman occupation – the streets were effectively broad hollow ways; this allowed an undercroft to be inserted along the street front while the Rows themselves were at the same level as the ground at the rear. Acute shortage of space within the town's walled area, exacerbated by Chester's role as a base for the Edwardian conquest of North Wales, seems to have made a two-tier arrangement of shops an attractive proposition, but it is still remarkable that a series of individual owners would co-operate in allowing continuous galleries to be built, especially since these became public thoroughfares enclosed within the structure of private buildings. In this connection, it is surely significant that, on the one hand, the town's powers of self-government steadily increased during the thirteenth century – with rights to take over vacant house-plots being vested in the governing assembly by a royal charter of 1300 – and on the other that, before and after this date, a small group of merchant families came both to dominate the assembly and to

Figure 23: Watergate Street Row (nos. 38–42 Watergate Street), Chester. The shops with walkways ('the rows') above occupy the undercrofts of three separate units, behind which was a single hall running parallel to the street. The cross-passage beyond the Art Shop slopes upwards to a level at the rear which matches that of the 'rows' at the front.

buy up properties for redevelopment along the main streets. It was probably on the initiative of this locally powerful group, acting together for private gain and public good, that the distinctive Rows system came about.[79]

Away from grand schemes such as this, the dwellings of the remainder of medieval urban society – the families of poorer craftsmen and labourers – are only rarely to be seen in towns today. These tended to be built away from the areas set out as burgage plots, or to occupy small subdivisions within them. Lady Row, Goodramgate, York, was built in 1316 within the churchyard of Holy Trinity Church in order to provide funds to support a chantry, and survives today as a two-storey series of single rooms (probably shops) below and domestic accommodation above, the latter projecting on jetties into the street. Although the structures do not survive, a similar design of ground-floor room with first-floor jetty is implied by a lease dated 1370, whereby the Prior of Lewes contracted with a carpenter to build two rows of shops within the grounds of an inn in Tooley Street, Southwark, each shop to be 12 feet (3.7 metres) deep. Surviving fifteenth-century terraces include 157–162 Spon Street, Coventry, on an important approach road to the town, which is a range of six small dwellings each with a frontage of no more than 5 metres, embracing a hall open to the roof in one half of the house and a two-storey compartment – perhaps shop and upper chamber – in the other half, and 13–23 Upper Lake, Battle, built over a former quarry to a broadly similar plan though with a frontage of 8.5 metres.[80] These were not, however, the humblest of urban dwellings, none of which survive above ground. One excavated example is a terrace of four thirteenth- or early fourteenth-century cottages in Lower Brook Street, Winchester, the stone footings of which show them to have been little more than 5 metres square, with partitions to demarcate living and sleeping areas. Excavated buildings of about the same date in Powick Lane off Deansway, Worcester, apparently timber-framed on dwarf stone walls, some with evidence of workshops behind them, have been interpreted as the dwellings of artisans or unskilled labourers; these had one- or two-room floor plans and were of similar dimensions to those in Winchester. Tiny fifteenth-century stone dwellings excavated at St Peter's Street, Northampton, have also been interpreted as the homes of the urban poor. Beyond this, from surveys of parts of London by the cartographer and surveyor Ralph Treswell between 1607 and 1614, we know of the existence of many dwellings of only one room in plan, arranged like those of the Victorian urban poor around courts and sometimes running to several storeys in height. However, this was probably unusual, since as has been pointed out in a recent survey of Sandwich, one of the distinguishing features of many of the poorest houses, especially those away from town centres, would have been their construction of one storey only. In a context in which towns stood out from the surrounding countryside partly because of the proliferation of two- or multi-storey buildings – exceptional in a rural context outside the southern counties, even at the end of the middle ages – possession of an urban one-storey dwelling was a tangible reminder of one's lowly status in society.[81]

Turning from domestic to public buildings, we need deal here only briefly with parish churches, since they figure prominently in the chapter which follows. Many towns already flourishing before the Norman Conquest have an embarrassing surplus of churches to deal with today and even in the middle ages provision must have seemed excessive. In due course, medieval Norwich and Winchester both acquired 56 parish churches, York 39, Cambridge 16, Oxford 13, the origins of most of them dating to before the Gregorian reform movement of the late eleventh and early twelfth centuries. Prior to this, each lord who held property within the town was liable to build a church attached to his estate: multiple lordships led to multiple churches, which were treated as assets by the founders and their descendants. But the revived papacy of the 1070s onwards was committed to the exclusion of secular lords from interference in ecclesiastical affairs, so that parish churches came increasingly to be seen as independent of those on whose estates they lay – unless these were religious houses – the clergy now being answerable in most respects to the pope's local representatives in the diocesan admin- istration. While these measures were not entirely successful – many lay patrons retain an interest in the appointment of parish priests to this day – they removed some of the incentives to further church foundation, except where there were new settlements to be served. And since post-Conquest town plantations normally resulted from the initiative of a single lord, they customarily began either with a chapel dependent on the church of the parish within which they were created, or at most with only one parish church. Boston (Lincolnshire), founded by Alan, Earl of Richmond on the east bank of the River Witham around 1100 appears to have had its own parish church, St Botolph's, from the outset: indeed the church gave its name to the town and (after late-medieval rebuilding) its tower ('the Stump') still dominates the place today. Conversely, Bewdley, with a position overlooking the Severn which made a great impression on John Leland – 'at the rysynge of the sunne from the este the hole towne gliterithe, being all of new buyldinge, as it wer of gold' – had 'but a chappell of ease … of tymber in the harte of the towne' while the parish church remained at Ripley some 1.5 kilometres away.[82]

Parish churches were often the only 'public building' a community could claim to have, frequently being used (like their churchyards) for trade or other secular activities. An alternative did however exist in the form of a guildhall, wherever a religious or mercantile gild was sufficiently prosperous to build one. There is a fine example at Thaxted (Essex), a timber-framed structure built by the Cutlers in 1390 with an open space below for use as a covered market. Another late-medieval survivor is that at King's Lynn, where a fire in 1421 destroyed the previous hall of the Holy Trinity Gild, which had been established in the Saturday market place in the original heart of the town. Over the following 16 years the present guildhall was built to replace it, as a hall with undercroft below, the lower storey of stone, the upper of brick but faced on the south gable overlooking the street with a chequer-board pattern of light and dark squares of flint. Four late-medieval guildhalls also survive in York, all clearly retaining their early features despite a measure of restoration.[83] In practice, the prominence of some mercantile interests in urban government often meant that guildhalls came to be used for meetings of the town assembly, as happened for example with the hall in Lavenham market place, built by the local Gild of Corpus Christi following its foundation in 1529. The magnificent stone guildhalls of London (begun in 1411) and Norwich (built from 1407) were however intended from the outset as meeting-places for the urban assemblies, not for any individual gilds, and stand as testimony to the self-confidence of these local authorities.

Late medieval adjustments

The story of England's towns in the two centuries following the Black Death is a complicated one, since the country's economic fortunes fluctuated in that period and the experience of individual places differed. Certainly there was a significant drop in the number of functioning markets, with less than 40% of those recorded before the pestilence still operating in the early sixteenth century. Most of the contraction would have been among the 'village markets' but Leland duly recorded several losses in towns, such as at Bideford (Devon) where there was now 'no weekly market at a sette day' and at Chorley (Lancashire), home to a 'wonderful poore or rather no market'.[84] Nearly all towns suffered significant loss of population between the early fourteenth and early sixteenth centuries, and this inevitably affected their physical appearance. Even taking as a baseline the post-Black Death figures obtainable from the 1377 poll tax assessment – themselves reflecting a sharp decline over the previous fifty years – there were some notable falls by the time of the Lay Subsidy of 1524–25: a reduction from about 5,000 to under 2,000 at both Boston and Beverley, some 6,500 down to 4,000 at Lincoln, over 13,000 down to little more than 6,000 at York, and over 4,000 to under 3,000 at Leicester.[85] Besides the national downturn, there were local reasons behind these figures: Leland duly noted, for example, that 'good cloth making at Beverle … is nowe much decayid' and that Boston 'hath … beene manyfold richer then it is now', its 'steelyard' quayside area being largely unoccupied.[86]

Lincoln's suburbs and back streets were by the early sixteenth century largely abandoned; the number of active parish churches fell from 46 in the early fourteenth century to nine by 1549. York, which was petitioning the crown for relief in the late fifteenth century on the grounds that 'ther is not half the nombre of good men within your said citie as ther hath been in tymes past', had witnessed a virtual halt to new house-building in preceding decades.[87]

Even towns which fared better than those listed above faced severe problems. Coventry prospered as a cloth-making centre in the late fourteenth and early fifteenth centuries but went into prolonged decline thereafter, with two particularly serious depressions from the 1440s to the 1470s and (after brief revival) during the 1510s and 1520s. Though it remained one of the towns most heavily taxed by the 1524–25 Lay Subsidy, it was claimed locally that assessments on this scale were unrealistic. As early as 1442 the governing authority was imposing fines on landlords who failed to rebuild houses they had demolished, only to reverse the policy in 1473 by encouraging them to be pulled down if 'in doute to fall'; by 1523 no less than 565 vacant houses were identified. Leland summed up its position neatly when he reported that 'the towne rose by makynge of clothe and capps, that now decayenge the glory of the city decayeth'. Norwich, despite a catastrophic fall in population during and immediately after the Black Death, recovered in the role of regional adminis-trative and commercial capital and (after London which was not a contributor) featured as England's largest town in the 1524–25 Lay Subsidy in terms both of total assessment and the number of recorded taxpapers: yet early in the sixteenth century there were complaints that 'many houses, habitacions and dwellynges … grue to ruyn'.[88] Canterbury, servicing the headquarters of the country's southern ecclesiastical province, and Newcastle-upon-Tyne, with an important coastal trade link to London, were better placed than most to ride out economic depression and having been leading tax contributors before the Black Death broadly maintained their rankings in the 1524–25 Subsidy; Canterbury's population may well have increased between 1377 and the early sixteenth century. Both, however, had large numbers of vacant properties within them, along with unpaid rent arrears, as the fifteenth century drew to a close. Colchester, another cloth-making town, was generally faring well until the middle of the fifteenth century only to suffer contraction thereafter; it has been estimated that 'of the 190 years between 1334 and 1524 it is improbable that more than a quarter were years of growth to higher levels of output' and that its overall population fell possibly by as much as one-third between the early fifteenth and early sixteenth centuries.[89] Salisbury, also a cloth-making centre which generally maintained its prosperity through the late medieval period – evidently England's seventh most populous town in 1334 and eighth in 1524, with a good deal of domestic and ecclesiastical rebuilding, much of which survives – suffered a slump in production around the middle of the fifteenth century. Smaller towns also experienced recession, with vacant burgage plots being reported in the late fourteenth and fifteenth centuries at places as diverse as Brackley (Northamptonshire), Shrewsbury and Hartlepool.[90]

Some of the most dramatic urban failures were to be found among those deliberately developed during the expansionist thirteenth century, such as Warenmouth (Northumberland), intended as a port for Bamburgh when founded by Henry III in 1247; this was the centre of some activity into the fourteenth century, but had disappeared by 1575 when an exchequer commission could find no trace of an alleged 'sea town' of Bamburgh. Another case is that of Ravenserodd (Yorkshire), founded by the Earl of Aumale on a recently created sandbank on the Humber in the 1240s, briefly a serious rival as a fishing and trading port to Grimsby only 8 kilometres away, but swallowed up by further shifts in the course of the river little over a century later: 'this was an exceedingly famous borough … adorned with more ships and burgesses than any of this coast', according to the *Meaux Abbey Chronicle* of the 1390s, but now it had been 'reduced to nothing by the merciless floods and tempests'.[91]

Yet for all this pessimism, we need to remember the point made at the beginning of this chapter that, taken as a whole, towns broadly maintained the 15–20% share of the total population which they had attained by the early fourteenth century. Some towns managed to avoid significant population decline and even in those places where economic indicators point to depression, this was not always reflected in the urban landscape. By the early sixteenth century, Halifax, Wakefield, Leeds and Bradford in west Yorkshire, Hadleigh and Lavenham in Suffolk, Crediton, Totnes and Tiverton in Devon were among the rising centres of cloth production which certainly functioned as towns in social and economic terms, benefiting both from a weak gild tradition – so making them attractive to capital investors – and from a boom in cloth exports to the continent in the early Tudor decades. As contributors to the 1524–25 Lay Subsidy, Lavenham ranked fifteenth, Totnes eighteenth and Hadleigh twenty-seventh; none had featured as towns in the pre-Black Death Subsidy of 1334 but – admittedly not without protest at the burden in the case of Lavenham – they now outstripped places like Oxford, Shrewsbury and Southampton. Long-established ports and market-towns such as Exeter and Ipswich also benefited from the proximity of these cloth-manufacturing centres: both were far more significant contributors to the 1524–25 Subsidy than they had been in 1334, and while this does not mean that they had necessarily experienced net growth between those two dates it does suggest that they were faring better than most.[92] Various forms of metalworking – pinmaking at Sherburn-in-Elmet (Yorkshire), cutlery at Thaxted (Essex) and diverse forms of ironmongery at Birmingham – appear to have found a ready market which helped to sustain their respective towns through the late medieval period. To set against Leland's account of decayed markets were some he reported upon in very favourable terms: Worksop (Nottinghamshire) had been 'made a market town more than 30 yeres ago', Cirencester (Gloucestershire) had the 'most celebrate market in al that quarters' and Warrington (Lancashire) enjoyed a 'better market than Manchestre'; these must all have profited from local opportunism and enterprise which set them apart from less-fortunate neighbours.[93] An excellent example of this has been demonstrated at Buntingford (Hertfordshire), a hamlet in the thirteenth century but a small town of at least 350 people by the early sixteenth, to which date the oldest timber-framed buildings in the modern settlement have been assigned. The fact that Buntingford stood on land partitioned between several manors, so that there was no dominant lord, meant that its affairs were directed by what has been described as 'an informal … co-operative' of craftsmen and traders, 'an independent community of the vill', which benefited from a well-placed market on Ermine Street while nearby Chipping and Standon declined.[94]

Beyond this, there are many examples of building schemes which proceeded apace during the fifteenth century, leaving us not only with the bridges and gildhalls mentioned already and the rebuildings and enlargements of parish churches to be discussed in the next chapter, but also with what we can fairly call 'public utilities'. Common latrines covering a mill-leat on Exe island were provided by the town authorities of Exeter not later than 1467, while conduits supplying townspeople with fresh water – initiatives previously associated with cathedrals or monasteries (as at Lichfield from the twelfth century, Bristol from the thirteenth and Exeter from the fourteenth) – became increasingly common, the outcome either of the generosity of rich benefactors or the enterprise of the urban government. These are known to have been in place in Bristol by 1400, Coventry by 1483, Exeter by 1441 and Ipswich by 1451; the incorporation of Lichfield by royal charter in 1548 had been preceded three years earlier by the establishment of a Conduit Lands Trust, designed to guarantee a regular water supply to the town independent of that supplied by the cathedral. This corporate spirit is also seen at Coventry in 1524 when, concerned at the slump in the local cloth industry, four rich citizens contributed £125 between them 'to goo to a Comen Welthe for makyng of Clothe', which implies some sort of collective employment scheme. As evidence of civic pride and concern for the welfare of the urban community as a whole, these initiatives add an extra dimension to our understanding of England's late-medieval towns, to set alongside the data on generally declining prosperity and population.[95] Demographic and economic forces had a profound impact on the medieval urban landscape, but so did the collective decisions of those in power.

5

The landscape of religion

Since nearly everyone in medieval England had a belief in the teachings of Christianity – even if their observance was often crude, careless or inextricably bound up with folklore[1] – and since the Church had a pervasive influence in society, as political and spiritual adviser, landholder, builder, patron, and creator of written records, it is somewhat artificial to devote a separate chapter to the 'landscape of religion'. After all, the Church, with its estates and buildings, appears throughout this book. Nevertheless, it is convenient to treat the features specifically associated with worship in a chapter of their own and accordingly the focus here is on religious houses, cathedrals and local churches: their buildings and their context. Between 1000 and 1540, religious edifices towered over most other elements in the landscape, just as the Church and its teachings dominated people's lives. And of all the legacies in the landscape bequeathed to us by medieval England, places of worship remain among the most important in terms of frequency of use today.

For convenience, the student of the medieval Church usually draws a distinction between its 'regular' and 'secular' expressions: 'regular' (from the Latin *regula*, a rule) to denote the monks, nuns, canons and friars bound by the rules of their religious orders, and 'secular' to cover the bishops, priests, deacons and those in minor orders who were supposed to serve the laity through the diocesan and parochial systems. The difference between them is by no means clear-cut. The regional 'minster churches', key to the Church's pastoral care and mission from the seventh century to the eleventh, before the widespread development of parishes, were staffed by clergy many of whom adhered to a monastic rule, and this tradition lived on among those 'regular canons' and friars whose express purpose was to offer a direct, practical ministry to the laity; moreover, throughout the medieval period, even the most reclusive 'regulars' would have claimed to serve the world at large through their regimes of prayer. For their part, the 'seculars' embraced many within their ranks who could not obtain a benefice – a post within the Church carrying a guaranteed income – so had to scratch a living outside the formal ecclesiastical structure. By the thirteenth century, there were also groups of lay mystics, such as the Beguines, a movement of religious women which had arisen in the Low Countries but were found in parts of East Anglia, whose life was one of piety and devotion akin to that of nuns, but without a formal rule and without enclosure from the world.[2] The eremitical tradition of early Christian monasticism also persisted in medieval England, in the form of the hermits who looked after isolated chapels, patrolled woods and maintained roads and bridges, and in the various anchorites, both male and female, who were to be found dwelling in cells attached to particular churches, increasingly located in towns rather than the countryside as the middle ages wore on.[3] All this adds colour to the overall picture, but the basic division between 'regulars' and 'seculars' remains helpful as a basis for discussion.

Religious houses

Monasticism – accepting this as a general term covering the lifestyles of those men and women bound by the rules of a religious order – was intended to appeal to people who sought a life of perfection in this world as preparation for the next, without the distractions of secular life. It had been part of Christian observance since the end of the third century, characterized by extreme asceticism, but about 530 Benedict of Nursia drew up a rule for a monastic house he had founded at Monte Cassino in central Italy which was not only rational, clear and comprehensive but also moderate in its demands. It envisaged a monastery as a self-governing, self-sufficient, community in which the brethren elected their own abbot and consumed the produce of their own fields, and so was equipped to survive in a variety of contexts, whatever the condition of the world outside. The essential humanitarianism of the *Rule of St Benedict* shines through any number of its chapters, and only a few extracts can be quoted here.

> When they get up for the Work of God, they may quietly encourage one another since the sleepy are given to making excuses.

> We read that wine is not at all a drink for monks, yet, since in our days it is impossible to persuade monks of this, let us agree ... that we should not drink our fill, but more sparingly.

Clothing should be given to the brethren according to the nature of the district where they live and the climate, because in cold places more is needed and in warm ones less.[4]

A rule couched in these terms had obvious appeal: it did not make excessive demands upon its adherents and it could be adapted to meet local conditions. Accordingly, Benedictine monasticism spread rapidly through western Europe from the sixth century onwards, superseding previous rules, often with government encouragement in the interests of promoting stability and conformity. So when Edgar (king of the whole of England from 959 to 975) and his senior ecclesiastics deliberately revived monasticism in England following its total collapse during the conflicts with the Vikings, it was determined that every new house was to follow Benedict's *Rule*. By the end of the tenth century, there were about 30 houses of monks and eight houses of nuns in the kingdom, all Benedictine.[5]

By then, some of the simplicity of the original *Rule* had been lost, with monks spending more time in worship and far less time on agricultural work than initially envisaged. As they spread through Europe in the ninth and tenth centuries, Benedictine houses were well-endowed with land, inevitably bringing them into daily contact with their local society and economy. Far from being self-sufficient communities which could survive whatever storms were raging beyond the monastic gatehouse, they became landlords of peasants, employers of servants and regional centres of learning, offering prayers for their benefactors and hospitality to travellers but necessarily bound up with the political and economic vicissitudes which affected everyday life. And in the absence – till 1215 – of anything resembling a constitution to bind the members of the order together, 'families' developed: houses which shared a common interpretation of the *Rule*, following a particular model. By the Norman Conquest there were some 40 abbeys of Benedictine monks in England, which between them held about one-sixth of the landed wealth of the country: places like Westminster, Ely, Peterborough, Crowland (Figure 24) and St Augustine's Canterbury were major corporate institutions, others such as Christ Church Canterbury and Worcester also served as cathedrals. The 13 Benedictine nunneries at this time were less well-endowed.[6]

One significant contribution made by these pre-Conquest Benedictine houses was to popularize a 'standard monastic plan', whereby church and ancillary buildings were arranged around secluded cloisters. The key features of this plan are found in a ninth-century manuscript kept at St Gall, Switzerland, and nearly all religious orders went on to adopt it, unless their particular circumstances dictated otherwise. The cloisters – a courtyard with a surrounding covered walkway – were usually located on the sunnier, southern side of the church, with a chapter-house (for meetings) and communal

Figure 24: Crowland Abbey (Lincolnshire). The abbey and village occupied an island above the surrounding fenland, which in its undrained condition grew no corn within 8 kilometres but was rich in fish, fowl and pastures. The monks had several territorial disputes with neighbouring houses of the same Benedictine Order over this valuable 'unimproved' land.

dorter or dormitory on the eastern side, communal frater or refectory on the side opposite the church, and storerooms and various types of alternative accommodation to the west. Additional rooms typically included a calefactory (warming-room) and parlour (where talking was allowed) usually along the eastern range, a kitchen positioned near the refectory, a rere-dorter (latrines) as an extension to the dorter, and an infirmary located separately away from the cloisters; a covered passage through the eastern side, the slype, gave access to buildings and cemetery beyond. Anyone visiting a medieval monastic site today will encounter this plan time and again, to the point where signage is hardly necessary, but also worth looking out for are the elaborate water management systems which underpinned it, such as the conduits and channels which provided drinking water and serviced the *lavatorium* (the trough for washing hands before entering the frater), kitchens, baths and rere-dorter.[7]

From 1066, England was linked to a duchy which had itself witnessed a monastic revival since the turn of the millennium. This led to a certain 'Normanization' of English religious houses, in matters such as the personnel appointed as abbots, modifications to the liturgy and the imposition of military quotas on several larger foundations, obliging them to distribute portions of their estates to knights who would fulfil this commitment. But the newly enriched conquerors – profiting from the acquisition of a kingdom four times the size of Normandy – proved to be enthusiastic benefactors, and by 1100 there were about 150 Benedictine houses in England, all but 17 of them for monks. Many of these were subordinate priories or cells administering estates given to Norman mother houses, such as Clare (Suffolk) and Frampton (Dorset), dependencies of Bec and of St Stephen's Caen respectively. But some were major independent abbeys, among them Battle, founded by the Conqueror himself in 1067 on the site of his victory the previous year – colonized by monks from Marmoutier – and Shrewsbury, established by the local earl Roger de Montgomery about 1087 and colonized from Séez. Again, the nunneries they founded were fewer in number and smaller in scale, but Elstow (Bedfordshire), established by the Conqueror's niece Countess Judith about 1078, was to grow into a house of some size, with 19 nuns in residence as late as 1442. Of particular significance were the new foundations which – for the first time – carried Benedictine monasticism north of the Humber, such as Selby about 1070, Whitby about 1080, Tynemouth about 1083, and St Mary's York about 1086; Benedictine monks were also introduced to the cathedral at Durham in 1083.[8] The Benedictines continued to prosper after 1100, to the extent that by the population climax of the early fourteenth century they had some 225 houses of monks and 80 houses of nuns in England and Wales as a whole. However, from the early twelfth century onwards they were competing for benefactors and recruits with alternative orders and most of the subsequent new foundations were small-scale, often dependent priories intended to manage distant landholdings. The abbeys of Reading (founded in 1121) and Faversham (1148), established by Kings Henry I and Stephen respectively, were well-endowed exceptions.[9]

All this had a major impact in the form of intense building activity. It has been well said that 'the sheer volume of construction in the first generation after the Conquest must have turned the country into a vast building site' and it certainly made an impression upon contemporaries. The early twelfth-century Benedictine monk William of Malmesbury, for example, described the monasteries 'ancient in religion but modern in their buildings' which now peppered the landscape, while acknowledging 'the mutterings of those who say it would have been better if the old had been preserved in their original state than new ones raised from their demolition and plunder'. Thus, a new church was begun in 1070 at the monastic cathedral of Christ Church, Canterbury by the incoming Norman archbishop Lanfranc, to a design based on that of the abbey at Caen from which he had been recruited. Similarly, at St Albans in 1077, the arrival as abbot of Lanfranc's nephew Paul, a monk of Caen, immediately signalled the commencement of a new church. These examples could be multiplied time and again, but it would be wrong to associate the reconstruction effort solely with newcomers from Normandy: from 1084, the monastic cathedral at Worcester had its pre-Conquest church replaced by Bishop Wulfstan, one of the few English prelates to retain his position.[10] Whatever the sentiment, the result of all this activity was that architecture characteristic of Norman Romanesque proliferated across the country, still recognizable most obviously in round-headed doorways and arcading, often with minimalist, geometrical, decoration, by apsidal east ends sometimes accompanied by radiating chapels, and (in the rare cases where these have survived later alteration) by tiny, very narrow, vertical window openings. The style continued to dominate ecclesiastical architecture in England until the last quarter of the twelfth century, and among the finest examples still to be seen of its deployment in a monastic context are the nave of Peterborough, the transepts at Ely and the nave, tower and west front of Tewkesbury (Figure 22).[11]

After the Conquest as before, Benedictine houses formed themselves into 'families', following particular elaborations of the original *Rule*. Detailed *Constitutions* drawn up by Lanfranc for the monks of Christ Church Priory, Canterbury,[12] for example, were adopted by several other abbeys, among them Battle, Crowland, Durham and St Albans. The story of monasticism from hereon is largely one of groups of monasteries which chose to take the Rule in a particular direction, sometimes to the extent that they were eventually recognized by the papacy as a separate order. This happened, for example, with the houses which modelled themselves on the Benedictine abbey of Cluny in Burgundy, founded in 910, which established a reputation for its zealous observance of lengthy and magnificent ritual and grew rich from the endowments of those eager to benefit from the prayers of the monks. By the end of the tenth century, these Cluniac houses had become a distinct, papally authorized order, with a constitution which signalled their subordination to Cluny: hence the designation of most of them as priories rather than autonomous abbeys. There were nine houses of monks in England by 1100, 35 by the early fourteenth century. Among the earliest were the priories of Lewes (Sussex), Castle Acre (Norfolk) and Much Wenlock (Shropshire), all founded between 1077 and 1089. Their architecture tells us much about the Cluniac approach, which assumed that a monk worked hard for most of his waking hours at communal worship, offering prayers on behalf of the living and the dead, so was entitled to eat well and to dwell in large, well-appointed, buildings. Accordingly, we find the completion of the church at Castle Acre in the 1160s heralded by an elaborately decorated west front, dominated by blind arcading. Similarly at Much Wenlock, although the ostentation of the church itself can only be glimpsed in fragments, there is some fine blind arcading of about 1140 in an interior wall of the chapter house, where the rounded arches interlock to create a precocious pointed-arch effect.[13]

Such ostentation was anathema to another order which traced its origins to a Benedictine house in Burgundy, the Cistercians. The story here is of a group of monks breaking away from their community at Molesme in 1098 and settling in the woods at a place they called Citeaux from the 'boggy ground' they found there. Under their first abbot, Alberic, the monks sought to revive a literal interpretation of the *Rule of St Benedict*, stripped of all the elaborations which had accumulated over the centuries. They wore a grey-white habit of undyed wool, unlike the black habits of the Cluniacs and their fellow-Benedictines, so came to be known as the 'White Monks'. They simplified the church services and restored manual work so that the monks had a day divided into three roughly equal parts (worship, manual work and private study), as originally envisaged by Benedict. They also tried to avoid anything not specified in the Rule. All this made for a life of simplicity and austerity, which other houses in the area duly took as their model to follow. But what turned the Cistercian fraternity into a distinct order, and a highly successful one at that, was, first, the provision of a constitution which facilitated expansion while retaining control from the centre, and, second, a brilliant propaganda campaign. The constitution, the *Carta Caritatis* (Charter of Love) devised about 1117 by the second abbot of Citeaux, the Englishman Stephen Harding, decreed that all should follow the *Rule of St Benedict* as interpreted at Citeaux and provided for lasting affiliation between a mother house and the communities which it had originally colonized.[14] The propaganda was led by Bernard, who from 1115 until his death in 1153 was abbot of one of Citeaux's earliest daughter-houses, Clairvaux, but who spent much of his time travelling across Europe as an adviser to popes and princes, popularizing the order and attracting huge numbers of benefactors and recruits. By 1152 – when the general chapter forbade any more new foundations without permission from the centre – there were over 300 houses in Europe, including almost 50 for monks and a further eight for nuns in England. The first English house, at Waverley (Surrey), was colonized in 1128 by monks from L'Aumône, a Cistercian abbey near Chartres, but more influential was to be the next foundation in 1132 at Rievaulx (Yorkshire), a daughter of Bernard's own abbey of Clairvaux. Rievaulx would produce five daughters of its own, in Scotland and northern England, and through these a total of 11 'granddaughters', with further 'great-granddaughters' to follow. The equally famous abbey at Fountains, some 30 kilometres or so south-west of Rievaulx, was established at about the same time.

Aelred, abbot of Rievaulx from 1147 to 1167, encapsulated the appeal of the Cistercian lifestyle in his *Speculum Caritatis* (Mirror of Love):

our food is scanty, our garments rough; our drink is from the stream and our sleep often upon our book. Under our tired limbs there is but a hard mat; when sleep is sweetest we must rise at a bell's bidding … [but] everywhere peace, everywhere serenity, and a marvellous freedom from the tumult of the world.[15]

Cistercian houses were characterized by their remote sites, by churches which were small and lacking in ostentation, and by domestic buildings arranged around the cloisters in distinctive fashion; the frater was typically placed at right angles to the cloister walk on the opposite side to the church, with kitchen and calefactory inserted either side of it, and the western side of the cloisters was given over to accommodation for the lay brothers who were admitted (mostly from local peasantry) to a vocation of manual work, particularly in the fields. This at least was the intention, and a glimpse of this idealism is still to be seen, for example, in the ruins of Buildwas Abbey (Shropshire), founded in 1135 within the Savignac Order (which merged with the Cistercians 12 years later) and structurally one of the least altered religious houses in the country. At this site, the buildings on the opposite side of the cloisters from the church have disappeared above ground, but a good deal of the remainder can still be seen. The church has a low, squat, central tower, in keeping with the express prohibition by the Cistercian general chapter in 1157 of steeples and belfries, and is only about 60 metres long, with short transepts flanking the crossing; the chancel at the east end is only one bay in length. There is also evidence of a screen separating the lay brothers in the nave from the fully professed monks in the choir.[16] Elsewhere, at the abbeys of Furness (Cumberland) and Coggeshall (Essex) we can still find another distinctive Cistercian feature, the gate chapel – located at the gatehouse, deliberately isolated from the main monastic buildings, because the Cistercians discouraged pilgrims and other visitors from worshipping in their monastic church.

But this early idealism was not to last. Orderic Vitalis, writing in Normandy about 1135, was already worried about the Cistercians' reputation, seeing them as victims of their own success: 'many seek to be numbered with the true servants of God by their outward observance, not their virtue; their numbers disgust those who see them and make true monks seem less worthy in the faulty judgement of men.'[17] Those who visit Cistercian remains today often have some difficulty in recognizing the spirit of asceticism, for several houses within this order grew rich from the estates eagerly bestowed upon them by benefactors, especially during the height of their popularity in the twelfth century. At Rievaulx, for example, the ruined church we now find on the site is some 113 metres long and the three-storey, seven-bay chancel to the east of the crossing occupies over one third of the length of the church: this was built in the early thirteenth century, a clear indication that initial restraint and austerity had already been cast off. Meanwhile, the west range of the cloisters shows evidence of private rooms on the ground floor and a granary above. At Fountains, the landscape is dominated by a magnificent 52-metres-high tower at the northern end of the north transept of the church, a striking refutation of the decree of 1157 and of the thinking encountered at Buildwas. The story, of course, is one of development over time. The original church at Rievaulx, revealed by excavation, had a modest chancel, only two bays long, while the west range of the cloisters here is the result of redesign in the fifteenth century, after lay brothers had ceased to be recruited (Figure 25). At Fountains, the church tower was built very late in the monastery's history, around 1500 when the abbot, Marmaduke Huby, was energetically recruiting more monks, repairing and rebuilding the abbey's property, and leaving his mark as a reforming visitor on the order in England as a whole. 'Huby's Tower' gives us an insight into the mixed motives of the builder, carrying both his own initials and emblems and an inscription to the glory of God.[18]

It took a highly selective approach to admissions and to the acquisition of estates if an order's early inspiration was to be sustained, but among the more successful in this respect were the Carthusians, modelled on a house at Grande Chartreuse in south-east France which had been founded in 1084. This order combined personal isolation and collective organization:

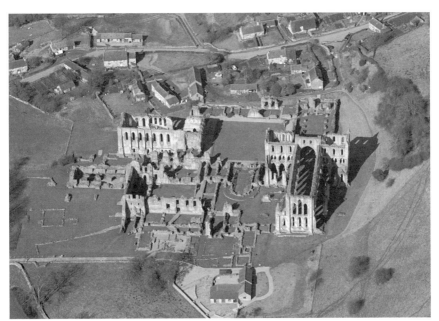

Figure 25: Rievaulx Abbey (Yorkshire). Set in a wooded valley, the abbey developed an extensive farming enterprise, leading in turn to the aggrandizement of its buildings. Accordingly, the church (right) grew into a three-tier structure, with an elongated chancel (in foreground); the frater (to left of the square cloisters) was also substantially remodelled. (English Heritage Photo Library.)

the monks lived as a community but had individual cells where they spent most of their time. Recognized by the pope as a new religious order in 1133, the Carthusians deliberately kept recruitment and expansion under strict control, with individual houses typically restricted to a prior and 12 brethren – echoing Christ and his apostles – plus 16 lay brothers, a few elderly monks and a handful of domestic and farm servants. This restrained self-sufficiency was also characteristic of the early Cistercians, but the difference with the Carthusians is that they succeeded in keeping to their rules. Accordingly, the order grew very slowly but mostly remained above criticism. Only nine houses were established in England in total, the earliest at Witham (Somerset) in 1179, but seven of them between 1343 and 1414 when monasticism as a whole was declining in numbers, income and morale. Among these was the best surviving example, Mount Grace (Yorkshire), where we can still see the distinctive Carthusian plan of a cloister surrounded by individual cells, each with its own garden, and the remains of a church, chapter house and frater which were all modest in scale (Figure 26). It is no coincidence that, of all the orders of monks, it was the Carthusians which gave Henry VIII most trouble during the 1530s; 18 of their number were executed or starved to death in prison for refusing to take the oath acknowledging Henry's royal supremacy over the Church in England, and their houses had to be forcibly suppressed.[19]

Figure 26: Mount Grace Priory (Yorkshire). Carthusian monks spent most of their time in solitude within their own cells. This view of the north cloisters at Mount Grace shows the cell foundations, set within individual garden enclosures, and in the distance the monastic church, beyond which were the south cloisters composed largely of service buildings.

A different form of religious life was espoused by communities of regular canons. In origin, these were groups of priests dwelling together in order to serve a church, or sometimes a school or hospital. There was an attempt early in the eleventh century to impose greater discipline on these communities, with Wulfstan Archbishop of York drafting legislation that canons should live chastely and eat and sleep in communal rooms,[20] but it was only after 1074, when Pope Gregory VII issued a code based on the writings of the fifth-century North African bishop Augustine of Hippo, that such aspirations come to fruition. Houses of 'Augustinian' canons – houses which regarded themselves as following St Augustine's *Rule* in however modernised a form – spread thereafter through France and Italy, either as new foundations or as a result of existing communities accepting the imposition of the rule. The movement reached England about 1100, although there is uncertainty over which was the first house established here: St Botolph's, Colchester, St Mary's Huntingdon and St Gregory's Canterbury, the first two represented by serving churches today, all have a claim. The order became very fashionable during Henry I's reign (1100–35) when a further 40 houses were founded, three-quarters of them by members of the royal court.[21] Prominent among these was Carlisle, established by the king in 1122 and made a cathedral for a new border diocese 11 years later, although the church today is much shorter than it was before a visit by the Scots in the 1640s.[22] Another was Runcorn, founded by William fitz Nigel constable to the Earl of Chester in 1115 to serve his castle chapel and minister to pilgrims and other travellers crossing the River Mersey. After 19 years, this community moved to a more secluded site four kilometres away at Norton; although the original duties remained, it is hard not to see the move as illustrating a tendency within the order generally to withdraw to the more isolated lifestyle normally associated with monks. Norton went on to become one of the larger Augustinian houses in England, with over 20 canons in residence by the thirteenth century, and in 1391 was granted the status of abbey by the pope. Archaeological excavation has revealed a church with domestic buildings arranged around a cloister in customary fashion, the original structures of the mid- to late-twelfth century being partly replaced by, partly incorporated within, larger-scale buildings erected during the course of the thirteenth century, all of which can be visited at the site today.[23]

These survivals of Augustinian buildings are comparatively rare, since although numerically the canons were almost as popular as the Benedictines – about 200 houses and 2,600 professed canons in England and Wales by 1300, compared to some 225 houses for 3,300 Benedictine monks – they made less impact upon the landscape. Augustinian houses were on average only one-third as well-endowed as those of the Benedictines, since after the initial patronage by the royal court the order descended the social scale, becoming the favourite of merchants and gentry who could not afford lavish foundations.[24] This was inevitably reflected in the more modest scale and elaboration of their buildings, which – given that many were in populated areas – have also tended to fall victim to demolition for re-use of the stone; exceptions such as Haughmond and Lilleshall, about 30 kilometres apart in Shropshire, owe their continued existence – albeit in ruins – largely to their location away from major settlements. However, the canons' churches have often outlived them. A case in point is Bridlington (Yorkshire), where the canons' nave continues to serve St Mary's parish; the crossing, east end and most other monastic buildings were pulled down following the dissolution. Another notable example is St Frideswide's Priory, Oxford, closed in 1524 so that it could be incorporated into the college Cardinal Wolsey founded on the same site, with the church later being made a cathedral for Henry VIII's new diocese of Oxford. The Augustinian priory churches at Bristol and Southwark have also survived, from the crossing eastwards, and at Bristol the canons' chapter-house is also extant; both churches have become cathedrals, Bristol under Henry VIII, Southwark in 1905, although both now have Victorian naves.[25]

Like the Benedictines, the Augustinians lacked a formal constitution; an Augustinian house was one acknowledged to be following the *Rule of St Augustine*. At the Fourth Lateran Council in 1215, Pope Innocent III provided for triennial meetings of heads of houses in those orders where such assemblies did not already take place, with the Cistercians initially to advise on how they should be run: a measure which ensured that there was at least a framework to bind communities together.[26] But – as with the Benedictines – Augustinian houses tended to develop families, modelled on particularly influential foundations. The Premonstratensians, for example, began in this way. Named after a house at Prémontré in north-east France founded in 1120, they were heavily influenced by the Cistercians: the canons opted for austerity, wore undyed habits and developed a constitution similar to that of the *Carta Caritatis*, which enabled the various affiliated houses to function as a separate order. Like the Cistercians, they favoured underpopulated areas, which meant that, as canons, they were often to be found ministering on the margins of settlement. Some of their best work in Europe was in carrying Christianity to the Slavonic peoples of the east, but they were under-represented in England, where less than 40 houses were established in all. The first of these was at Newsham (Lincolnshire), dating to 1143, though the slightly later Welbeck (Nottinghamshire) was eventually recognized by pope and king as the principal house of the order in England. The Premonstratensians do not feature prominently in the landscape today, but a fifteenth-century battlemented gatehouse is to be found in a typical frontier location at Alnwick (Northumberland), while at a secluded coastal site at Cockersand (Lancashire), an octagonal thirteenth-century chapter house survives; excavations here in the 1920s revealed a simple, aisleless church, with buildings arranged around the cloisters much as in a Cistercian house (see Figure 27).[27]

All religious communities professed to be engaged in a fight against the Devil – normally through prayer – but a distinctive expression of this was provided by the military orders. The best-known, the Templars and the Hospitallers, both arose in the aftermath of the First Crusade of the 1090s. While their bases in Syria and Palestine were fortified for military action – providing a religious vocation for knights more suited to fighting than to prayer – their houses across Europe were used primarily for the administration of estates, for hospitality to pilgrims going to or from the Holy Land, as recruitment and training centres, and as retirement homes for aged members of the orders. The first Templar foundation in England was in London in 1128, the first for the Hospitallers at Clerkenwell (Middlesex) about 1144. The Templars were eventually suppressed by the papacy in 1312, following accusations of heresy and scandalous behaviour, much of their property

Figure 27: Cockersand Abbey (Lancashire). This bleak windswept site, originally used for a hermitage, gives an impression of the secluded environment favoured by the Premonstratensians: the abbey stood on a sandstone outcrop beside the Lune estuary, with poorly drained mosses on the landward side. The cloisters lay between the surviving chapter house and the shoreline.

passing to the Hospitallers, who had 55 houses in England at their peak on the eve of the Black Death. Archaeological investigation of sites associated with the military orders show that, while their houses had churches and a variety of domestic and agricultural buildings, they did not normally follow the standard monastic plan. At Denny (Cambridgeshire), for example, where the Templars took over a small Benedictine priory about 1170, the refectory and dormitory were not arranged around cloisters in conventional fashion, although such cloisters were eventually built after the house had become a Franciscan nunnery in the early fourteenth century.[28]

Nunneries have tended to receive less attention in studies of medieval monasticism as a whole, largely because their communities were fewer in number, generally smaller in size, and lacking most of the variety which characterized the male religious life. By the middle of the twelfth century the 13 houses of 1066 had risen to about 70, mostly Benedictine, Cistercian or Augustinian in their affiliation.[29] However, the allegiance scarcely matters, since the lifestyle varied little and none were admitted to a share in the government of the order: Cistercian abbesses, for example, did not attend the annual general chapter. In the medieval period, all nuns were supposed to lead an enclosed life, 'withdrawn from the world' to spend their time in prayer: the nun as nurse or teacher is largely a product of the sixteenth-century 'Counter-Reformation'. Although in Scotland and Wales there were a number of royal and aristocratic foundations of nunneries during the course of the twelfth century, in England the founders were normally drawn from the ranks of the gentry, with endowments correspondingly modest. This in turn means that the surviving buildings of medieval nunneries tend to be small-scale and fragmentary. Particularly regrettable is the lack of any evidence above ground of buildings associated with the Orders of Fontevrault and Sempringham – the latter also known as the Gilbertines and an order confined to England, indeed the only one to originate here. Both developed during the twelfth century, their distinctive feature being the provision of separate church and cloister complexes for the nuns on the one hand and the canons who led their worship on the other; in other orders, nunneries usually employed chaplains among their male servants. This double-cloister arrangement can still be seen at Fontevrault itself, where Henry II and his family lie buried, but in England it is known only from archaeological investigation: excavations at the Gilbertine sites at Sempringham itself (in Lincolnshire) and Watton (Yorkshire) have shown the nuns' church to be divided lengthways down the middle, so nuns and canons could access it from their separate cloisters without seeing each other, while aerial photography suggests a similar arrangement at another priory of this order, Shouldham (Norfolk).[30] Nor is there any obvious trace of the nunnery founded in 1415 by Henry V at Syon (in Isleworth on the north bank of the River Thames), the only house in England of the strict contemplative Bridgettine Order. This was replaced by the Elizabethan and Georgian mansion on the site still known as Syon House, although the community stayed together in exile after the dissolution and – from its current base at South Brent (Devon) – can claim a continuous history ever since.

Nevertheless, a few medieval nunneries have left good surviving remains. The church of the Benedictine house at Romsey (Hampshire), a pre-Conquest foundation, continues because in 1545 it was purchased by the town as its parish church; the nave, transepts and east end here are fine examples of Norman Romanesque work, the product of major rebuilding from the 1120s onwards.[31] The Benedictine nunnery in Cambridge, originally founded early in Stephen's reign but subsequently endowed about 1160 by Malcolm IV King of Scotland and Earl of Huntingdon, who was responsible for the dedication to the Poitevin saint, Radegund, also survives in part because several of its buildings, including the cloisters, church and refectory, were incorporated in modified form within Jesus College, Cambridge, founded at its dissolution in 1496 by the Bishop of Ely. The church here, though only partially remaining as the College chapel, is more modestly proportioned, with a squat central tower and short narrow chancel. Brewood White Ladies Priory (Shropshire), an Augustinian nunnery founded probably in the late twelfth century, is also represented today by the remains of its church, but this was mean in size and never had a central tower built over the crossing.

Whatever the affiliation, every house of monks, canons or nuns in medieval England held estates which sustained it, and no study of monasticism should neglect the impact on the landscape beyond the precinct walls. The Cistercians have attracted a good deal of attention in this respect because they established granges to house lay brothers working the estates away from the vicinity of the house itself. Many of these granges controlled extensive tracts of scarcely populated land, allowing the Cistercians by the last quarter of the twelfth century to become famed for their vast sheep flocks which supplied the wool export trade to Italy and the Low Countries; in 1193, the English houses collectively contributed one year's wool crop to King Richard I's ransom. Typically, a grange comprised a chapel, dormitory, barns and dovecote – the latter a reminder (along with monastic fishponds) of the prohibition in the *Rule of St Benedict* on eating four-footed creatures, and hence the importance within the monastic diet of those with two feet or none. First mentioned in England in 1145, a total of 75 such granges are known to have been established in Yorkshire alone by 1200, no less than 24 of which were associated with Fountains; among surviving remains of these Fountains granges are a gatehouse at Kilnsey on the River Wharfe, a chapel at Bouthwaite on the River Nidd, and a barn at Sutton above the River Ouse.[32] But the Cistercians were not of course alone in exercising direct control of extensive tracts of land. The Benedictine nuns of Minchinhampton

(Gloucestershire) had a flock of 2,000 sheep before the first 'White Monks' set foot in England and while this was dwarfed by the 15,000 sheep being kept by Fountains in 1286, Benedictine Peterborough and Crowland had even greater numbers (at least 16,000 each) around 1320. Nor was reliance on granges peculiar to the Cistercians, for wherever a community kept land for its own farming purposes – as opposed to leasing it to tenants – this was a sensible arrangement as a base where hired labourers could live and work. For example, a Benedictine grange at Cumnor (Oxfordshire), part of Abingdon Abbey's estate, has been subject to archaeological investigation and the reeve's house, the farmworkers' cottages, barns, a cowshed, dovecote and fishponds have all been identified. Nor should we envisage every grange as exclusively agricultural in purpose: the Fountains grange at Bradley near the confluence of the Rivers Calder and Colne, for example, oversaw a metalworking site at Smytheclough, functioning by 1194, where a dam, watercourses and slagheaps have all been identified. Whatever the enterprise – farming, quarrying, mining, metalworking – religious foundations brought long-term stability to estate management. Unlike lay families' estates, they did not break up as a result of royal displeasure or the failure of heirs. So planning could be long-term and investment could be made with confidence for what seemed an infinite future.[33]

The fruits of all this can still be seen in the profusion of monastic buildings which date to the expansionist era of the thirteenth and early fourteenth centuries: the era when recruitment was buoyant, new land was being won for cultivation, and an increasing population fuelled rising incomes whether through the sale of agricultural produce or the granting of leases to lengthening queues of aspiring tenants. The correlation between trends in the rise and fall of population and the initiation of cathedral and abbey building works during the course of the middle ages is striking.[34] These buildings – often additions to or replacements for Norman Romanesque structures of the previous century – were in the styles conventionally known as Early English and Decorated, characterized by pointed arches and arcading, fluted columns and (in contrast to the Romanesque apse) straight-sided east ends to their churches; but where the Early English style is recognized by its tall narrow lancet windows, the Decorated boasts much broader windows, with elaborate tracery, and intricate sculptural detail. Among present-day cathedrals which served as medieval monasteries, the east end at Southwark, rebuilt following a fire in the church in 1207, the west front of the church at Peterborough, completed by 1238 as a façade to the Romanesque nave behind, the chapter house at Chester, finished by 1250, and the east end at Ely, which replaced a much smaller Romanesque apse and was ready by 1252, are among the finest examples of the Early English style. The octagonal central tower at Ely, successor to the Norman tower which collapsed in 1322, and the Lady Chapel here, completed in the 1370s and almost detached in a corner of the north transept, can scarcely be surpassed as an illustration of the Decorated. Elsewhere, the church of Westminster Abbey harmonizes aspects of both the Early English and the Decorated styles, and does so with remarkable uniformity for most of its length despite a 100-year break in construction after the death of King Henry III in 1272. This is because the western parts of the nave, built in the late fourteenth and fifteenth centuries, deliberately – but unusually – followed what by then was the 'outdated' style already established in the rest of the building.[35] Nor was grandiose building confined to the monastic church: the magnificent octagonal chapter house at Westminster Abbey, for example, built in the 1250s, bore an inscription comparing it to a rose among flowers and was described by the community's historian Matthew Paris as 'incomparable', though admittedly this was paid for by Henry III as a setting fit for a king to address his subjects.[36]

Capitalist enterprise and elaborate building schemes inevitably provoked further reaction, and it came in the first half of the thirteenth century, when the papacy began to recognize new orders of friars. There was a fine line to be drawn between various radical groups which arose in western Europe about this time, all claiming to imitate the lives of Christ and his disciples as itinerant preachers who begged for their sustenance, and both the Humiliati of Provence and Lombardy and the Waldensians (or Poor Men of Lyons) of southern France were initially condemned as heretics in 1184. It was to the credit of Pope Innocent III that in 1210 he was prepared to approve a simple rule drawn up for another such group, the Poor Men of Assisi, because he appreciated their effectiveness in combating heresy: in effect, they could reach the parts the Church usually did not reach, by going onto the streets and into private houses. This was the origins of the Franciscan Order of Friars, named from their founder Francis of Assisi, a drop-out from his father's prosperous cloth business. In their turn, the Franciscans inspired other friars' orders, most notably the Dominican, Carmelite and Augustinian ('Austin') Friars, for whom rules were approved by the pope in 1216 and during the 1230s and 1250s respectively. The Dominicans arose from a team of canons preaching against the Cathar heresy in southern France and the order continued to stress the importance of preaching, and of academic study to underpin it, thereafter. The others represented attempts by the papacy to impose some discipline upon disparate individuals and small congregations who were living outside any formal ecclesiastical control. But whatever their origins, and any subtleties of emphasis which divided them, all were distin-guished from other male religious orders by their less constrained lifestyles and their stress upon corporate as well as personal poverty: they were supposed not to depend upon the estates accumulated by their houses but to rely instead on alms given in return for their ministry to the laity, as preachers in streets and confessors in homes. In practice, this meant that there was considerable freedom for the individual friar in how and where he spent his time, liberated from much of the daily routine of worship which characterized traditional communities: a liberation which led in turn to permission for many to become students and teachers at Europe's universities, among them Paris, Oxford, Cambridge and Bologna, during the first half of the thirteenth century. By contrast, the small number of nuns who affiliated to these orders – by the dissolution there were only one Dominican and three Franciscan nunneries in the country – led enclosed lives similar to those of their sisters in the traditional orders.

But how is all this reflected in the English landscape? There were Dominican ('Black') friars in England by 1221, Franciscans ('Grey Friars') by 1224, Carmelites ('White Friars') by 1242, Austin friars by 1249. Given their reliance upon alms to support their life as mendicant (begging) preachers, one might expect to find them predominantly in centres of population, and numbers of friars' houses established is indeed a rough and ready guide to the relative size of medieval towns. All four orders mentioned above – the only four orders officially recognized by the papacy after 1274 – were to be found in London, in the two major centres of learning, Oxford and Cambridge, and in several of the top-ranking towns in the 1377 poll tax returns, including York, Bristol, Norwich, Lincoln, Boston, King's Lynn and Newcastle-upon-Tyne. Towns with three orders of friars (among them Gloucester, Leicester, Shrewsbury, Yarmouth, Ipswich) were drawn from the middle ranks of the 1377 returns, while smaller towns such as Lichfield, Ludlow, Derby and Southampton supported only one or two orders each.[37] As for the friars' legacy in these places today, there have inevitably been considerable losses. Despite the initial concern to renounce corporate possessions, the friars did in fact amass sufficient property and income – held for them where necessary by third parties – to allow them to build some substantial churches and accompanying domestic buildings, similar in plan to those of the traditional orders. But their location predominantly in towns means that most of their buildings have disappeared, or at best can be detected only within subsequent structures. Thus the site occupied by the Dominicans of Cambridge was used in 1584 to found Emmanuel College as a 'spearhead of puritanism'. The founder, Sir Walter Mildmay, wanted as little as possible of the friary to survive and ensured that the new College chapel would not be on the site of the friars' church; there are traces of it instead within the College buttery.[38] Elsewhere, however, their churches do sometimes survive and street names are often a clue to their former presence: the early fourteenth-century Greyfriars Church on Friar Street, Reading (Berkshire) is a prime example of both.

As with other religious orders, it is not difficult to find contemporary criticism whenever standards slipped. The friars were particularly vulnerable to gossip because they used their wits to solicit alms and win invitations into private houses, were disliked by parish clergy as 'rival attractions' liable to divert burial fees to their own churches, and were despised by conventional monks and canons: witness the depiction of the friar as a fox in the misericords of the Benedictine Abbey church of Chester (now Chester Cathedral), which date to about 1380. They also squabbled among themselves, notably over the boundaries of their respective begging districts in towns – the 'limits' which led to Chaucer's depiction of a friar as a 'limiter', who would 'go around the houses, poke and pry', dispensing 'flummery and hokum'.[39] But all this negativity must of course be unfair to many individuals, none more so than the members of the Franciscan Observants, a new order founded as a breakaway from the Franciscans in 1415 in an attempt to recapture the original idealism. Six houses existed in England by the early sixteenth century, all forcibly suppressed in 1534 after their members had refused to accept the royal supremacy and, in some cases, had preached against the king's marriage to Anne Boleyn. Most of the friars were imprisoned, either in gaols or in other Franciscan houses, and at least 32 were put to death.[40] All this is worth remembering as we consider the evidence for a decline in monastic observance towards the close of the middle ages.

From the thirteenth century onwards, it was required of bishops that they conduct visitations of religious houses in their dioceses: every few years the members of each community would be summoned individually before their bishop to answer his questions about what was amiss and the bishop would then issue injunctions (instructions) to address what he perceived to be faults. These records were never intended for publication and are liable to give a negative impression because their deliberate purpose was not to praise the good but to correct the bad. But when due allowance is made, the overall impression is that by the late middle ages, while outright scandal was rare, complacency, apathy and demoralization were widespread. Time and again, we are told that religious houses were struggling to run their estates efficiently and to maintain their fabric adequately. Bardney Abbey (Lincolnshire) was visited sometime in 1437–38, when the bishop was told that 'the dorter, frater, cloister and the other buildings of the monastery are much dilapidated, in so much that the rain comes in' and visited again in 1440, when there were complaints about the failure to enclose woodland copses after felling so 'the stumps, when they sprout again, are destroyed'. At Huntingdon Priory in 1439, tensions between the prior and his deputy were all too apparent, as the sub-prior complained that 'the church, cloister, chapter-house, frater, dorter and all the houses, offices, glass and all the buildings of the granges, manors and appropriated churches belonging to the priory are utterly in ruin in the prior's default', an allegation with which several of his colleagues concurred.[41]

Yet the evidence of fifteenth- and early sixteenth-century monastic account rolls suggests that, while estates were now run largely through leasing land rather than by farming direct, most religious houses were able to balance income and expenditure satisfactorily, with sufficient to meet repairs and other contingencies and to keep debts to manageable proportions. Nor is it difficult to cite examples of substantial building work in the late medieval period. Much of Gloucester Abbey, including the cloister walk where fan vaulting was introduced, was rebuilt in the century and a half from the 1330s onwards (Figure 28).

The church of Bath Abbey is the product of an entire rebuilding, begun in 1499 after its much larger predecessor had fallen into decay. A new west front and nave were built at Winchester between 1350 and 1410, after subsidence had afflicted the previous Norman building; the chapter house at St Augustine's Canterbury was rebuilt following an earthquake in 1382; a massive central tower was erected at Durham from the mid-1460s after its predecessor had been struck by lightning; a crypt was inserted into the west end of Glastonbury Abbey church about 1500; a new nave, cloister, west transepts and central tower were constructed at Christ Church, Canterbury between 1377 and 1497; Chester's cloister walks were rebuilt in the 1520s.

Figure 28: Gloucester Abbey Cloisters. This Benedictine abbey, now a cathedral, was remodelled in Perpendicular style from the 1330s onwards. The work embraced new cloister walks with innovative fan-vaulting and major alterations to the church, including a new central tower. Monastic buildings such as (from left) the chapter house and slype, were less affected.

All serve today as illustrations of the so-called Perpendicular style of the late middle ages, instantly recognizable by the large broad window openings with horizontal transoms and the withdrawal from elaborate, naturalistic sculptural decoration. Yet while all this work suggests that several monastic communities retained their self-confidence – a counter to the impression of demoralization noted above – it is worth stressing that much of it arose either out of necessity, or in special funding circumstances: Gloucester Abbey, for example, profited immensely from pilgrimages to their shrine of the murdered King Edward II, as Christ Church, Canterbury continued to do from housing the shrine of Thomas Becket. It is also fair to say that these examples come from the richest communities: the smaller, less well-endowed houses, including most nunneries, saw far less building activity.[42]

In general terms, with due regard to these outstanding exceptions, the great age of monastic construction had passed by the middle years of the fourteenth century. Visit any monastic site in England where the foundation predates 1300 and the story is likely to have several common themes. An initial building phase will have embraced the church and the range around the cloisters. The thirteenth century, when numbers were growing and estates were generating a good income, will have seen considerable activity, often involving the replacement of previous buildings: the east end of the church was commonly rebuilt on a grander scale, and domestic accommodation was often enlarged. This phase might continue into the early fourteenth century, but after the Black Death, with reduced numbers and diminished estate income, the picture was generally one of consolidation: repairs where necessary, the adaptation of certain buildings often in the direction of more private accommodation, but few great building schemes.

There are clear signs in all this of the ways in which religious houses changed their appearance to reflect changing roles and – to some extent – the changing lifestyles of their members. As the Cistercians encountered growing difficulty in recruiting lay brothers – especially once population fell in the fourteenth century – so their western ranges were converted to storerooms and private accommodation. And, increasingly, rooms had to be found by the late middle ages for 'paying guests' to help make ends meet: 'corrodians' who paid a lump sum for admission and were then maintained by the house for the rest of their days. Obviously, the short-term solution could beget a long-term problem, especially since these people could turn out to be a considerable distraction. The bishop's visitation of the Benedictine nunnery of Langley (Leicestershire) in 1440 records several complaints about the disruption to worship caused by Lady Audeley bringing her dogs to church, while an inventory drawn up at the dissolution of Lilleshall Abbey (Shropshire) in 1538 shows this Augustinian house to have been accommodating, besides the canons and their servants, a schoolmaster, three gentlemen and four gentlemen's sons. Lilleshall also had nine private chambers listed and seems to have become, in effect, a small boarding school and retirement home.[43] Circumstances such as these would be well-known in the neighbourhood. They would not necessarily generate hostility: it could be argued that the religious houses were 'moving with the times' in offering a useful service to their local communities, at least to those who could afford it. It is clear, also, that several religious communities continued to be highly valued as sources of relief to the poor. But by the early sixteenth century most members of religious orders did not pretend to be living a life of austerity; this at least was what Benedictine monks told Cardinal Wolsey, the only exceptions in their eyes being the Carthusians, Franciscan Observants and Bridgettines. All this would foster a climate of scepticism about their *raison d'être* and provide the context in which dissolution could be contemplated.[44]

Cathedrals

Arrangements such as those described in the previous paragraph reinforce the point made at the beginning of the chapter that the supposed distinction within the Church between 'regulars' living apart from 'the world' and 'seculars' living as part of it, was easily blurred. This was nowhere more evident than in the phenomenon of the 'monastic cathedral', whereby the principal church of a bishop's diocese also served, and was served by, a monastic community. Such an arrangement was peculiar to England and meant that, of the 17 cathedrals in existence for most of the middle ages, those at Bath, Canterbury (Christ Church), Durham, Ely, Norwich, Rochester, Winchester and Worcester were also the churches of Benedictine monasteries, while that of Carlisle belonged to a house of Augustinian canons. In some cases, these provisions pre-date the Conquest – as at Canterbury, Winchester and Worcester – in others they reflect arrangements made by the incoming Normans: Ely, for example, was raised to cathedral status in 1109, Carlisle in 1133. The bishop was titular abbot, but the administration of the house was effectively in the hands of the prior, hence the designation of these foundations as 'cathedral priories'. They offered a contrast to the remaining cathedrals, staffed by secular canons in a manner familiar to this day: Chichester, Exeter, Hereford, Lichfield, Lincoln, London, Salisbury and York, to which may be added Wells, a cathedral till 1090 and restored to that status – to accompany Bath in the same diocese – in 1244.

It is questionable whether a lay person, visiting a cathedral as a pilgrim to a shrine, or as a worshipper in the nave hearing services chanted beyond the *pulpitum* (screen), would have noticed much difference between the two.

The 'secular' cathedrals were well-endowed with estates and built on a grand scale, like their monastic counterparts, and even the domestic buildings bore certain similarities. Cloisters, for example, were added – for processional and ornamental reasons – to the cathedrals of Salisbury in the 1270s and Lincoln in the 1290s, though some, such as Lichfield and York, never built them. A chapter house was also a necessity, so that the secular canons, led by a dean and his key officers, the precentor, chancellor and treasurer, could meet to conduct business; examples can be seen at Lincoln, Salisbury and York, all dating to the thirteenth century and all of polygonal design. But the life of a secular canon lacked – by definition – the full commonality of his 'regular' counterpart, so a communal refectory and communal dormitory were inappropriate: the canons lived instead in separate houses nearby.[45]

As for the cathedral churches themselves, many have already been mentioned in their monastic context. For the 'secular' cathedrals, the story is broadly the same, with vigorous building campaigns in the century following the Norman Conquest creating structures which were subsequently modified as fashion and funding permitted. York Minster, for example, was rebuilt on a new site between 1080 and 1100, but its progress to become the largest medieval church building in the country is attributable to a series of projects of the first half of the thirteenth century, the first half of the fourteenth century, and the late fourteenth and early fifteenth centuries, which collectively obliterated all trace above ground of the earlier Norman work. As buildings, what especially set both secular and monastic cathedrals apart from all but the greatest abbey and parish churches was, on the one hand, their sheer size and, on the other, their significance as places where new construction techniques and new architectural styles could be introduced or developed as models to be copied elsewhere. Every medieval church was intended to be an earthly representation of the heavenly Jerusalem, destination of those souls which would be saved after the Last Judgement as described in the Revelation of St John, but the grandeur of cathedrals, and especially their great height, equipped them particularly well for this role: 'beholde, the tabernacle off God is with men, and he wyll dwell with them', as Tyndale's illegal translation of 1526 put it.[46] The pointed rib vault – a device which allowed extra height to the roof while containing the lateral thrust – possibly originated at Cluny Abbey but the earliest surviving example anywhere in Europe is that over the nave at Durham Cathedral, built between 1120 and 1133; this was the precursor of the pointed arches, as well as pointed roof vaults, which came to dominate the various styles of 'Gothic' ecclesiastical architecture throughout the middle ages. The late-twelfth and early thirteenth-century rebuilding of much of Lincoln cathedral, badly damaged in a collapse of 1185, was in a distinctively English (as opposed to French) Gothic style, conventionally known as 'Early English'; with its emphasis on verticality (notably in sequences of lancet windows) this would also be the style adopted at Salisbury, where a completely new cathedral was erected between 1220 and 1284 following papal permission to abandon its Norman predecessor at Old Sarum.[47] When Exeter Cathedral was almost entirely rebuilt in the century after 1275 – retaining only its Romanesque transept towers but respecting the original Norman dimensions of nave and crossing – it became the country's supreme example of the Decorated style, characterized by the use of the ogee arch and by elaborate decorative carving especially in canopies over portals and in the flowing tracery of windows. The octagon designs used in the first half of the fourteenth century for both the lantern over the central tower of Ely Cathedral and for the Lady Chapel at the east end of Wells Cathedral, although not adopted elsewhere in English churches, are also testimony to a readiness to experiment and to innovate on an elaborate scale. Much the same could be said of the distinctive 'scissor-arches' inside Wells, a brilliant solution to the problem of supporting an overweight central tower, built in the decade before the Black Death. There is an exception to the story of cathedrals as innovators in the case of the Perpendicular style which prevailed from the late fourteenth to the early sixteenth century: a style which may owe its longevity partly to the fact that the skilled craftsmen needed for the best Decorated work were by now in short supply. This was introduced in the 1330s not at a cathedral but at an abbey – as it then was – for the remodelling of the south transept at Gloucester in the 1330s. However, the naves of Canterbury and Winchester Cathedrals, rebuilt either side of the year 1400, were to be among the finest examples of this style in the country.[48]

There were, of course, mixed motives behind these developments. Several rebuilding schemes were prompted by urgent necessity, such as the collapse of Lincoln's Romanesque central tower in the 1230s, but by the close of the thirteenth century England hosted 12 of the 40 richest dioceses in Europe – partly because of their unusually large size – and there was undoubtedly a strong element of competition, as well as imitation, in projects undertaken ostensibly to the glory of God. And possession of the relics of a saint offered the prospect of a lucrative income from pilgrims, while also providing both an opportunity and an obligation to house them appropriately. Thus, the lavish reconstruction of the east end of Canterbury Cathedral followed both the canonization of Becket in 1173 and a major fire in 1174. Lincoln Cathedral's reconstruction after 1185 was supposed partly to honour its first Norman bishop Remigius and thereafter, with greater conviction, the late-twelfth-century Bishop Hugh, canonized in 1220. As for the master masons, the architects of the buildings, they had to solve structural problems while delivering an aesthetically pleasing result; there is good evidence both that they were left a fairly free hand to interpret their patrons' briefs and that they borrowed freely from comparable buildings they had seen, and in some cases had worked upon. The late-twelfth-century historian Gervase of Canterbury has left us an account of the rebuilding of the choir area of Canterbury Cathedral after 1174 which shows that the master mason William of Sens knew only too well how to secure a building contract and then get his own way. The story could have been spun very differently by a less sympathetic narrator, but the outcome was the first 'Early English' structure in the country.

> French and English articifers were … summoned, but … differed in opinion … Some undertook to repair the [fire-damaged] columns without mischief to the walls above. On the other hand, there were some who asserted that the whole church must be pulled down if the monks wished to live in safety … However, amongst the other workmen there had come a certain William of Sens [whom] they retained, on account of his lively genius and good reputation … He … carefully surveying the burnt walls … did yet for some time conceal what he found necessary to be done … and when he found that the monks began to be somewhat comforted, he ventured to confess that the pillars rent with fire and all that they supported must be destroyed if the monks wished to have a safe and excellent building. At length they agreed, being convinced by reason and wishing to have the work as good as he promised.[49]

William of Sens is believed to have worked previously on the abbey church of St Denis, near Paris, as well as the new cathedral at Sens in Burgundy, and his achievements at Canterbury were to influence, in turn, the master mason responsible for the rebuilding at Lincoln from the 1180s onwards. Similarly, in the early thirteenth century, Salisbury Cathedral drew heavily on the contemporary reconstructions of both Lincoln and Wells, almost certainly through the use of shared personnel. By the later middle ages, several master masons are known by name, among them William Ramsey (died 1349) who worked on St Stephen's chapel in Westminster Palace and the cathedrals at Lichfield and London (St Paul's), and Henry Yevele (died 1400), whose work embraced (besides some bridges, as we saw in the previous chapter) Westminster Abbey, Canterbury Cathedral and St Paul's. By such means were architectural ideas spread across the country: even the beating-up by local rivals of William Colchester, a southern master mason previously at Westminster Abbey who was appointed to York in 1405, did not prevent his remaining in charge until 1419, overseeing new buttresses to the tower and (internally) new stone screens, all in Perpendicular style.[50]

Much of the best work left by these men can only be seen inside the buildings and so is outside the scope of a study of the landscape as a whole. However, towers and (less frequently) spires allowed cathedrals and other great churches to advertise their presence far and wide, while also posing some of the greatest problems to medieval masons and their patrons. Chichester's south-west tower, adorning its west front, fell down in 1210; Lincoln's central tower, completed about 1200, had partially collapsed within four decades; Ely's Norman central tower did so in 1322; Durham's central tower had to be rebuilt after destruction by fire following a lightning strike on Easter Day, 1459; Salisbury's slender spire of the early fourteenth century would have long since gone but for ingenious reinforcement by Sir Christopher Wren and others. But such was their symbolic importance in pointing the way to heaven and emphasizing the Church's authority over those on earth below that enthusiasm for towers and spires was unabated: and since they were not strictly necessary to the performance of the liturgy, they could be added as separate projects whenever funds permitted. So the three towers of Lincoln Cathedral, visible over much of the county, are later additions to a largely twelfth- and thirteenth-century structure: the present central tower was completed between 1306 and 1311, the two western towers followed about 1400. Salisbury's tower and spire were not finished until two generations or so after the rest of the building. Durham's present central tower belongs to the 1460s to 1480s, much later than most of the church. Similarly, the three spires at Lichfield, erected over central and twin western towers in the first two decades of the fourteenth century, were late additions to a church predominantly in an earlier style.[51]

Scarcely less impressive were the façades added to the west ends of cathedrals and other great churches, often adorned with statues of Christ and the saints and invariably intended to overawe approaching pilgrims and worshippers as they headed for the entrance to the nave. Their impact was sometimes enhanced not only vertically through the addition of western towers but also horizontally by extending them well beyond the width of the nave and aisles concealed behind. The west front of Wells Cathedral, built in the 1230s, is packed with statues in niches, and flanked by twin towers – themselves late additions – which stand outside the lines of the outer walls of the church itself. The enlargement of the west front at Lincoln Cathedral, in the following decade, with room for a chapel and courtroom in the spaces behind the screen which outflanked the main structure, created a comparable effect.[52] There was ostentation in all this, but even today these buildings have the power to inspire reverence and awe. Buildings of such magnificence, breadth and height, soaring towards the heavens, must have seemed miraculous in their style, in their scale and in the messages they conveyed about the relationship of God to Man and the Church's role as intermediary between the two.

Local churches

Cathedrals had to be managed as landed corporations and – like the religious houses discussed in the earlier part of this chapter – as the profitability of their estates declined in the later middle ages, so did the scale of their building ambitions. With the exception of Bath, every medieval cathedral in England retains a fair proportion of work from before the fourteenth century: it was far too costly to be replaced. The point is worth stressing, because this could not be said of local churches, any number of which survive with little trace of their pre-1300 structures surviving. The contrast takes us to the heart of the difference between cathedrals on the one hand, with their regional (diocesan) role, and local churches on the other. Some of these had the status of 'parish churches', with obligations to their surrounding localities – their designated parishes – and entitlements to draw income from them. Others were administratively dependent upon parish churches and so are conventionally called 'chapels'. But all were the servants, and the products, of their local communities and wherever a local community had the will and the means to rebuild – at any stage in the middle ages – its church or chapel would reflect that commitment.

Although the conversion of Anglo-Saxon England to Christianity during and after the seventh century was accomplished from regional 'minster churches', staffed by teams of clergy who went out to engage in missionary activity, the parish system was developing by the tenth century as a means of organising and sustaining local church provision. The story of how an ecclesiastical network which in 900 had been dominated by minsters came by 1100 to be largely replaced by one of local churches is a complex one which has been expertly told elsewhere.[53] Suffice it to say here that there was an interplay of factors such as lords' wishes to exercise greater control over assets on their manors, a growing wish to identify with local church buildings as communities began to settle at fixed locations, and – after the Norman Conquest – enhanced efforts by bishops to exercise control over their clergy through a closely defined administrative system. All this worked in favour of the subdivision of large 'mother-parishes' – focused on churches which could seem distant, run by priests not readily called to account – into several small ones each with an identifiable 'parish priest' serving his own local flock. This process did not happen everywhere – the huge parishes which survived until the Industrial Revolution in much of north-west England show the tenacity of the older system – but where it took place it involved, at one level, the diversion of revenues from the central minster to the parish church, and, at another, the increasing devolution to the localities of rights to baptize and bury the laity. Of most relevance to this book is the major impact of all this on ecclesiastical building, since while old minster churches continued in being, usually serving parishes much reduced in extent, many new places of worship were required.

By the late eleventh century, it seems clear that most villages, and all towns, had at least one church. Domesday Book is inconsistent in its coverage and omitted many places of worship known from other sources, but still mentions more than 2,000 'churches', 'priests' or 'priests with churches'. It has been estimated that over half of all parish churches in England on the eve of the Industrial Revolution were already in existence (albeit as earlier structures) by 1080. There was clearly a concern that ecclesiastical provision should keep pace with demand: in Worcestershire, where the phenomenon has been studied, a correlation has been found between the recorded populations in Domesday Book and the size of the naves of local churches at that time. According to the chronicler William of Malmesbury, the incoming French lords were largely responsible for this building endeavour: 'the standard of religion everywhere in England has been raised by their arrival: you may see everywhere churches … rising on a new style of architecture; and with new devotion our country flourishes.' William's contemporary, Orderic Vitalis, wrote in similar vein. But while the Norman Conquest undoubtedly gave impetus both to the endowment of monasteries and to the building or rebuilding of parish churches in towns and countryside alike, these comments unfairly neglect the efforts made in the two generations prior to the Conquest.[54]

Several minster churches certainly benefited from the patronage afforded by early eleventh-century kings, nobles and lesser lords. Those at Dover (St Mary's, Kent) and Great Paxton (Huntingdonshire) incorporate late-Saxon features apparently endowed by Kings Aethelred II and Edward the Confessor. Others at Coventry and Stow St Mary (Lincolnshire) were reportedly rebuilt by Leofric Earl of Mercia (died 1057) and his wife Godiva. And at Kirkdale (Yorkshire) an inscription of about 1060 survives on a sundial to record that Orm Gamalsson had a 'completely broken and fallen' church 'newly built from the ground'.[55] Among lesser churches, a 'Great Rebuilding' has been identified from about 1040, mainly but not entirely in eastern England, so that structures began to be built to last, using stone in place of timber, according to a standardized 'two-cell' plan of nave and chancel, sometimes with west tower. This layout is apparent for example at Kirk Hammerton and Wharram Percy (Yorkshire), Burnham (Lincolnshire), Wittering (Northamptonshire) and Deerhurst ('Odda's Chapel', Gloucestershire); the last is known from an inscription to have been dedicated in April 1056, the others probably straddle the Norman Conquest in a way which makes conventional categorization into 'late Saxon' and 'early Norman' irrelevant. Much of this was paid for by local lords, but there is evidence – from wills, for example – to suggest that many freeholders were also keen to participate in the endowment of local churches. Enthusiasm for founding churches flourished in a context where they were seen as 'proprietorial' assets from which the owner was entitled to a rent: to the extent that in some rural communities more than one church came into being and in an urban context, as we have seen, they were liable to proliferate even if serving only tiny congregations (Figure 29).[56]

Despite the papacy's attack on lay proprietorship of churches during the late eleventh and twelfth centuries – an attack taken up by diocesan bishops – ecclesiastical building and rebuilding continued, as new parishes were designated to keep pace with rising population and the creation of new settlements: possibly 1,500 of England's 8,000 medieval parish churches were newly built during the course of the twelfth century, mostly in the earlier decades. The result was that, by the end of that century, arrangements whereby a local 'parish church', authorized by canon (church) law to perform the sacraments essential to the neighbouring population (including baptism, marriage and burial), drawing a corresponding income from the tithes and offerings of the parishioners, and with 'glebe' land set aside for the upkeep of the priest, had become well-established. Yet this is too simple a picture since by 1200 about a quarter of all parish churches in England, and by 1300

Figure 29: Two Churches in one Churchyard, Swaffham Prior (Cambridgeshire). This unusual survival is associated with townships, especially in East Anglia, where more than one manorial lord or substantial freeholder wished to endow his own church. St Mary the Virgin with its Norman tower (right) continues in use but SS Cyriac and Julitta (left) is redundant.

over half, had been 'appropriated' by religious houses – normally where the church lay on an estate which had been granted to a monastery; rather than leave the parish priest in receipt of the tithe and other funds, the monastery took on the role, in effect, of an absentee rector, collecting the revenues for itself and engaging a 'vicar' (substitute) to serve as priest. Although bishops initially encouraged this practice, seeing closer monastic control as a means to exclude lay interference and raise standards among the clergy, by the late middle ages they came to deplore it, with monasteries being accused of treating their churches as a mere source of income: a further source of hostility in the decades prior to dissolution.

Several approaches can be adopted to the study of churches as features in the English landscape. One is to examine the factors behind their siting, and their physical relationship to the settlements they served. The medieval Church was adept at utilising features associated with alternative belief systems – the proliferation of crosses along routeways, for example, was at least partly attributable to a drive to replace sacred trees and other folkloric waymarkers – so it is no surprise that sites of past ritual significance were sometimes chosen for the building of churches. Dedications to St Michael (the Archangel who overcame Satan) are worth investigating in this context, especially if they occupy hill-top sites such as at Wadenhoe (Northamptonshire); in St Albans, the church of this name occupies the site within Roman Verulamium where the martyr was believed to have been condemned to death. Elsewhere, the church at Rudston (Yorkshire) was built next to a prehistoric monolith almost 8 metres tall, that at Knowlton (Dorset) within a neolithic henge. 'Holy wells' – springs believed to have had curative or other miraculous powers – also seem to have influenced the siting of several churches of pre-Conquest origin, such as St Margaret's, Binsey (Oxfordshire), St Mary's Stevington (Bedfordshire) and the church at Holywell (Huntingdonshire), whose dedication to St John the Baptist suggests that the water here may have been used for Christian baptisms before the church was built. All this does, however, need to be kept in perspective. Striking though these examples are, instances of churches built over known pre-Christian sacred sites are not in fact widespread, and ecclesiastical authorities were as likely to condemn continuing popular devotion to springs and trees as to attempt their incorporation into formal worship. In particular, the supposed significance of 'ancient yews' in churchyards has been much exaggerated, partly because they can rarely be dated with conviction to a period earlier than the churches alongside which they grow, and partly because the species cannot be proved to have had any association with pre-Christian ritual in any case (Figure 30). In this, as with much else in the historic landscape, it is right to be cautious in drawing conclusions.[57]

Where there are grounds for saying that a church occupies a ritually important position – simultaneously a continuation and an obliteration of what

Figure 30: Rotherfield Churchyard (Sussex). The church's north-eastern chapel (to right) was probably built in the eleventh century, with other parts added later. The massive yew tree on the extreme left, with split and hollow trunk, implies greater longevity for the site as a place of worship but does not demonstrate a pre-Christian origin.

had gone before – it is generally safe to assume that some ecclesiastical authority, such as a minster or bishop, had played a key role in the decision to build on that spot, whoever the formal founder of the church might be. Even here, however, there are exceptions, such as the field outside York where Archbishop Scrope was executed as a traitor against Henry IV in 1405; having become a focus of popular veneration laced with hostility to the Lancastrian dynasty – against the Church's wishes – it had a chapel built on the site once the Yorkist king Edward IV came to the throne. Late-medieval enthusiasm for erecting chapels at or near wells or springs, as at Ingestre (Staffordshire) and St Cleer (Cornwall) around 1500, seems to have derived from the wish of the founders to profit from the pilgrimage trade.[58] But where there were no such considerations, local lords, and those peasant communities left to arrange their own settlements, placed the church where it suited their own day-to-day convenience. The close involvement of a manorial lord in the establishment of a church, before or after the Norman Conquest, is often to be recognized today by its proximity to a former castle or manor house. Nearly 50 instances of churches standing within 200 metres of a motte (the surviving mound of an earthwork castle) have been identified in Herefordshire – Lingen near the border with Shropshire is a good example – and cases can be found, with less frequency, all over the country (Figure 12). Of course, neither the present-day church building nor the surviving domestic remains may date back to the origins of this arrangement and – here again – care needs to be taken over the interpretation. It is tempting to assume that a place of worship initially provided by the lord for his family and retainers, in the plot of land which embraced his own residence, was later converted into the focus of parochial worship and revenue. However, excavations of such complexes at Goltho and Raunds, both dating to the tenth century, clearly show the church with its graveyard to have been built adjacent to, but outside, the manorial enclosure: while they were very conveniently placed for the lord, they were intended from the outset for wider community use.[59]

In many planned 'row villages', the church and manor house are frequently found together at one end: the lord chose to live where there was plenty of available space, semi-detached (as it were) from his peasant tenants, the church he built was positioned alongside, and the villagers looked in the same direction for both secular and spiritual authority. Where this is not the case – where a parish church is integrated within a planned settlement, rather than at one end of it – we may have an explanation in absentee lordship, with the peasant community being left to locate the church to suit itself: Chobham and Great Bookham (Surrey), which we encountered in Chapter 3 on the estates of Chertsey Abbey, are possible cases in point.[60] Elsewhere, in the context of dispersed settlement, the site may have had some symbolic significance or may simply have been chosen as the least inconvenient option. Thus, the small church at Shocklach (Cheshire), dedicated to an Anglo-Saxon saint (Edith), with eleventh- or early twelfth-century nave and fourteenth-century chancel, stands in isolation; the farmsteads and hamlets which still house the parishioners lie up to three kilometres away. This position led to the inclusion of Shocklach in the list of deserted villages in the pioneering book on this subject published in 1971.[61] But no trace of a settlement adjacent to St Edith's has ever been found, and it seems more reasonable to conclude that the church, which stands at the confluence of a network of public footpaths linking the dispersed settlements of the parish, has from the outset occupied an isolated site. Even so, the place name, which is recorded in Domesday Book and means 'the goblin stream (or bog)', implies that there may well have been a folkloric reason behind the selection of this precise location.

Most studies of churches focus on the development of their plans, which can tell us a great deal about fluctuations in the population to be served and the wealth and commitment of those responsible for the fabric. Archaeological excavation of redundant churches consistently shows their evolution to be more complex than is apparent from the standing structures alone: at Asheldham (Essex), 11 phases were identified from a simple two-cell timber church of the pre-Conquest period through to a stone church with chancel, nave, tower and rebuilt porch of the nineteenth century, while at Wharram Percy (Yorkshire) there were 12 phases over a similar timespan. Much can be read from extant buildings, however, even if few retain their original plans. The commonest arrangement before the twelfth century was the single- or two-cell plan: that is, one space without architectural differentiation for both priest and laity, or a building divided into a chancel at the east end for the priest and a nave for the congregation. Surviving examples of the former are to be found at Harlowbury and St Helen's Colchester (Essex), which are rectangular (Figure 31), and at Maplescombe (Kent) and Nately Scures (Hampshire), D-shaped with the east end in the form of an apse. Two-cell churches are more commonly found. This is often because a chancel was added much later to a Saxon or Norman single-cell church – as at Shocklach (Cheshire) mentioned above – but those in which both sections apparently date to the twelfth century at latest include Bengeo (Hertfordshire), Hadleigh (Essex) and Heath (Shropshire), the latter with a rectangular east end, the others terminating in an apse (Figure 15).[62]

Figure 31: St Helen's Church, Colchester (Essex). Incorporating re-used Roman brick, set within Colchester's Roman walls and with a dedication to the Emperor Constantine's mother, the church almost certainly has a pre-Conquest origin, although the present building – an example of a small rectangular one-cell church, never enlarged – is of the twelfth and thirteenth centuries.

A tendency from hereon to enlarge and elaborate may seem entirely predictable but it possibly represents a change of approach from that of earlier centuries, when one response to expanding demand – often for mausolea – had been to build separate structures within the ecclesiastical precincts: the association of the late eighth- or ninth-century St Peter's Church, Heysham (Lancashire) with the broadly contemporary St Patrick's Chapel 50 metres to its west is a surviving example of a phenomenon encountered over much of France and the British Isles at least into the eleventh century.[63] It was the decision to bring all activities under the same roof – to build what became in effect a 'multi-purpose' local church – which led to ever-greater complexity in ecclesiastical planning. At the most basic level was the three-cell plan, with an extra – often square – cell between chancel and nave. The church at Kilpeck (Herefordshire), which dates to the second quarter of the twelfth century, has an apsidal east end, a square bay and a nave, while St Mary's, Iffley (Oxfordshire), apparently of about 1180, has the same three compo-nents, though here a tower rises from the central cell and the chancel is not the original structure. Both these churches appear to have been built to the three-cell plan from the outset, but where a west tower accompanies a two-cell church – already a widespread feature by 1200 – it is not always easy to tell whether it was an original component. Hales (Norfolk) has a fine twelfth-century church consisting of apsidal east end, nave and west tower; the latter – the type of round tower popular within this county – was probably added but may be part of the initial building. St Andrew's, Weaverthorpe (Yorkshire) has rectangular chancel, nave and west tower, which may all have been built together as part of a project known to have been financed by the lord of the manor, Herbert of Winchester, chamberlain to Henry I, between about 1110 and 1130. On the other hand, excavation at Wharram Percy has identified the west tower as a Norman addition to a pre-Conquest two-cell church.[64]

More elaborate churches of the twelfth century, with transepts forming a cruciform plan, are likely to have originated as minsters: a point which can be demonstrated beyond doubt, for example, at Hadstock (Essex), Bishop's Cleeve (Gloucestershire), Wimborne Minster (Dorset) and Hemel Hempstead (Hertfordshire). The last two also had aisles along both sides of the nave, and the provision of these lateral features became widespread from the twelfth century onwards, both in newly built churches such as Ickleton (Cambridgeshire) by 1100, Bakewell (Derbyshire) and New Shoreham (Sussex) by 1150, and through additions to existing structures. Where the provision of aisles can be dated to before 1200, their insertion on the north side of the nave – as at Bibury (Gloucestershire) and Hemingford Grey (Huntingdonshire) – is far more common than on the south side; of 13 churches in Worcestershire which had a single aisle added before 1200, nine were on the north side, while in Hampshire the proportion was four out of six. No single explanation can be offered for this imbalance, although a reluctance to disturb the south door to the nave – commonly used for agreeing marriage and other contracts – or to encroach upon burials close to this door, alongside liturgical associations of the north side with Christ's death and resurrection, may have been relevant factors. Equally, the 'copycat' effect of custom and practice elsewhere may have come into play.

There is some scepticism among scholars over attributing the addition of aisles to the demands of a growing population, since the practice continued well beyond the Black Death. Aisles may have been built partly to accommodate extra altars needed so that prayers could be said for the souls of benefactors; a wish to improve circulation around the nave, possibly for processional purposes, and the basic urge to enhance the appearance and prestige of the local church, are alternative explanations. But rising population had to be accommodated somehow and – besides the building of new parish churches as mentioned above – initiatives such as the provision of outlying chapels without parochial status and the addition of extra bays in order to lengthen naves were certainly attributable to this factor.[65] Whatever the reasons, local churches went on being enlarged and enhanced through the thirteenth and early fourteenth centuries all over England and the contrasting styles which have resulted – ranging from the Norman Romanesque of surviving early features to the Early English and Decorated of later alterations – can be read as evidence of what must have seemed at the time to be a perpetual cycle of building. Most people who survived into their sixties between 1100 and 1340 (admittedly a small minority) would have experienced a building campaign at their local church at some stage in their lives.

Significantly, though rebuilding might take place at either end of a church, the position of the chancel arch nearly always remained constant. During the thirteenth century – earlier in places – it became established that the lay parishioners were responsible for the maintenance, and if necessary the rebuilding, of the main body of the church, while the recipient of tithe (the rector) was responsible for the east end or chancel, from where the mass was conducted. Indeed, the use of some naves outside service times as a combination of village hall, barn and byre (though less common practice once pews began to appear in the thirteenth century) made it particularly appropriate that this part of the church should be a community responsibility: sometime around the year 1000, the homilist Aelfric had been bemoaning the fact that people 'behave foolishly … drink madly … and play disgracefully' within their local church, comments which suggest that they were already being seen as public buildings partly for secular use.[66] Accordingly, this division of responsibility for different parts of the church meant that the demarcation line between the two was normally respected in any rebuilding scheme – as can be clearly seen, for example, through the many phases identified by excavation at Asheldham, Wharram Percy and St Pancras, Winchester.[67]

From the middle of the fourteenth century, churches developed in different ways. In some cases, contraction of population led to contraction in the size of the church, as parts which became ruinous were dismantled and not rebuilt. This process is apparent, for example, at Wharram Percy, where the aisles did not survive the sixteenth century; at Ovingdean (Sussex), where blocked arcades show that a south aisle and a chapel on the south side of the chancel have been removed; and at Hadstock (Essex), where the nave was shortened at the west end. In more extreme cases, of course, churches were abandoned as the settlements they served were depopulated, or – in an urban context – there was a downturn in the fortunes of their towns. Norfolk is thought to have lost nine parish churches during the course of the fourteenth century, a further 20 in the fifteenth century and – partly as 'delayed reaction' to the late-medieval depopulation – nearly 90 during the sixteenth century. Wallingford (Berkshire) had 11 churches before 1300 but only four by 1439. For John Leland as he travelled through the country in Henry VIII's reign, the ruined church became a familiar sight, telling evidence of urban decline.[68]

More relevant to a church's survival than size of population were financial resources, although the two were obviously linked and a petition to the bishop of Lincoln in 1437 for the closure of the church of Dunsthorpe (Lincolnshire) neatly embraced them both. The church was said to be

> so decreased on account of the lack of parishioners ... that it is hardly sufficient for the eighth part of the salary of a stipendiary chaplain, much less of a rector who has to bear the necessary charges; and ... there is no likelihood of its sufficing in the future since the world is going from bad to worse.[69]

But the converse was that, if funds were forthcoming, local churches could counter the demographic trend. Many examples can in fact be found of churches which continued to be enlarged, had components enhanced or replaced, or – to revert to the point with which this section of the chapter began – were entirely rebuilt in the Perpendicular style of the later medieval period: so much so that between a third and a half of all parish churches in England conventionally regarded as of architectural or historical importance are largely or wholly Perpendicular in style.[70]

A clue to the thinking behind much of this building activity is to be found in the Lady Chapel at Long Melford (Suffolk), where an inscription of 1496 records that the cloth merchant John Clopton, who had financed this addition to his parish church, had 'not exhibited these things in order that I may win praise, but in order that the Spirit may be remembered'.[71] In the context of a well-understood doctrine of purgatory, the place of suffering after death to prepare for entry to heaven, there was a widespread desire to ensure that masses were celebrated for one's own soul, and those of one's family, in order to shorten the time to be spent there. Some could afford, as individuals, to finance chantry chapels, where the family would be buried and priests would pray specifically for their souls, and these often involved structural additions to the church rather than the setting aside of an existing space within it. Those of lesser means could join in a collective effort, either as members of a gild or through voluntary contributions to particular projects. The spire at Bridgwater (Somerset) was paid for by parish collections and a series of individual benefactions and small gifts in 1366–67, when the Black Death was both a recent memory and a recurrent threat. Similarly, the building of several chapels flanking the naves and chancels of the churches of Our Lady and All Saints, Chesterfield ('the church with the crooked spire' in Derbyshire) and Holy Trinity and St Michael, Coventry, during the fourteenth and fifteenth centuries, was mostly financed by the various gilds of the towns. Where details survive of the express purposes of the foundation of a gild, church fabric and fittings are often mentioned, as at Pampisford (Cambridgeshire) where the Assumption Gild was committed to raising funds 'for the use and repair of the church which is in poor condition'. Concern to ensure prayers for one's soul was of course nothing new – the doctrine of purgatory had been refined in the twelfth century – but whereas the donations which sprang from all this had traditionally gone to religious houses, with their monks, nuns and canons supposedly praying for their benefactors, the focus had shifted by 1400 towards the local church, where the endowment of chantry masses, and of facilities to hear them, might also be of spiritual benefit to any parishioners who attended. And given the significant rise in the living standards of peasants, labourers and craft workers, and the healthy profits to be made in some regions especially from the cloth industry, it is no surprise that late-medieval ecclesiastical building prospered wherever these funding sources could be tapped.

It was this mixture of motives – insurance for one's own soul but also a community-minded concern for the parish as a whole – which led many benefactors to go beyond the endowment of a new chapel alone. At Cullompton (Devon), a full aisle was added to the church at the expense of local worsted clothier John Lane (died 1528), who had the structure adorned with ships, shears and other emblems of his business and put an inscription along the outer wall calling on God's mercy for the souls of his family. Sir John Leigh, who died in 1523, provided both a new chancel and a chantry chapel for Godshill parish church on the Isle of Wight and had himself buried in the chancel. Such was the opulence of some of the new chapel structures that they outshone the rest of the church. This was certainly the case with the mid-fourteenth-century south aisle chapel built onto Gaddesby Parish Church (Leicestershire) and with the Beauchamp chapels added to the churches at Bromham and Devizes (Wiltshire) during the 1480s, all highly decorated and of considerable size. In an extreme case, in the early 1520s at Layer Marney (Essex), the Marney family's concern to secure a setting for their chantry chapel appropriate to their wealth and status (newly enhanced through service at the royal court) led to the reconstruction in brick of the entire church, complete with fireplace to warm the bedesmen who were to attend the masses: one of the last complete church rebuildings in England before the Reformation drastically curtailed such activity. All this effort redounded to the credit of the founders but also greatly enhanced the appearance of these churches and in some cases substantially increased the space available for worship.[72]

But while there was clearly still money to spare for ecclesiastical endowments in the late middle ages, those primarily reliant on income from landed estates were liable to suffer, as wages rose and rents and prices fell. This often had an adverse effect upon the chancel of a late-medieval parish church: if the rector was an individual, his income from tithe and other offerings fell with the drop in population within the parish, if the rector was a religious house the problem was compounded by reduced income from the landed endowment as a whole. Methwold (Norfolk) and Yatton (Somerset) are examples of churches largely rebuilt on a grand scale at the expense of the parishioners during the course of the fifteenth century, leaving an earlier chancel which now appears mean and diminutive: Yatton, for instance, where reconstruction of the nave was mostly funded by the local Newton family, has a chancel which is small and dark inside compared to the lightness and airiness of the rest of the church. Analysis of bishops' visitations of parishes in Kent in 1511–12 shows that 32% of churches allegedly had problems with the condition of their chancels, compared to only 7% where there were complaints about the nave and 4% where the tower was faulty. In a similar visitation dating to 1518 of Garthorpe (Leicestershire), where the church had been appropriated to the Augustinian priory of Kirkby Bellars in the same county, the chancel was described simply as 'not built'.[73] But this is not, of course, the whole story. At Swaffham (Norfolk), a wealthy rector, John Botright, who was also a royal chaplain, financed the rebuilding of the chancel – apparently complete by 1454 – on a scale and in a style which matched the parishioners' efforts in the rest of the church. And at Cirencester (Gloucestershire), what has been described as 'the greatest of the Cotswold "wool" churches' was very largely rebuilt between 1400 and 1530 as a combined effort between the merchants and others of the town, on the one hand, and the local Augustinian abbey on the other: this ensured that while magnificent structures such as the west tower and nave were provided at the expense of the laity, the chancel was also enhanced by the addition of a clerestory and some remodelling of its arches.[74]

Any observant traveller today should also be able to see that in different regions of the country there are characteristic styles of ecclesiastical building. To some extent, this is a matter of locally available building materials – some more responsive to delicate carving than others – which give us the granite churches in Cornwall, Jurassic limestone churches in the south and east midlands, sandstone over much of the Welsh borders, millstone grit in Yorkshire and the chequer patterns of flint and chalk in East Anglia. Beyond this, it is clear that fashions took hold in particular areas, and features perceived as outstanding examples of their type became models to be copied in the neighbourhood: as in Norfolk with the round towers to which attention has already been drawn, and in Lincolnshire, where distinctive designs of spire cluster in neighbouring villages to the south and west of the county. In the fifteenth century, the urge to emulate one's neighbour can often be demonstrated from building contracts. On the Suffolk coast at Walberswick, for example, the masons in 1425 were to build a new church tower with the walling modelled on the tower at Tunstall (some 24 kilometres to the south west) and west door as good as that at Halesworth (11 kilometres to the west). Within the same county in 1487, the new tower at Helmingham was to have as many storeys as the steeple at Framsden, the next village to the north. Yet another factor was the fluctuating wealth of a region or place. The relative decline of fifteenth-century York, at a time when Norwich maintained much of its former prosperity, can be traced through the number of chantries founded to commemorate the dead – falling in the former, remaining buoyant at the latter – with the result that there is little fifteenth-century church building to be seen in York to this day, but examples in virtually every church in Norwich. The proliferation of the Perpendicular style in the Cotswolds and much of East Anglia is rightly seen as evidence of prosperity emanating from the success of the cloth trade, while at a humbler level, an outburst of building activity in central Cheshire in the 1520s to 1540s – new towers at Little Budworth, Mobberley and Rostherne, substantial remodelling and enlargement at St Chads, Winsford – have been taken as indicative of a localized rise in prosperity in the early Tudor period. By contrast, some parts of the country remained poor and underpopulated throughout the middle ages, leaving churches which retain much of their original appearance: as at SS Protus and Hyacinth, Blisland (Cornwall), where nave, chancel, north transept and the lower stages of the tower are all identifiably Norman, or St Cuthbert, Cliburn (Westmorland), where Victorian windows cannot disguise the Norman nave and chancel.[75]

It is something of a cliché to say that a parish church is 'a reflection of its local community', but this is almost invariably the case – not only in the plaques, monuments and funerary hatchments which commemorate prominent families, but also in the structure itself, the product of centuries of growth and decline in the numbers, resources and commitment of the people it served. Only where there has been a patron of outstanding wealth has a church broken free, so to speak, from its geographical context, to display building materials or architectural styles which cannot be said to be characteristic of its region. Local – and especially parish – churches are, therefore, one of the most tangible means of reaching back to the lives, and the landscape, of our medieval forebears: focal points in their lives, expressions of their sense of community, mirrors to their fluctuating fortunes, and readily accessible for us to experience today. The message they seem to convey is that, in the fifteenth and early sixteenth centuries, popular religion was lively, with plenty of commitment being shown, at all levels of society, to the support of the local church.[76] This contrasted with the apathy and indulgence which – despite many honourable exceptions – was characteristic of much late-medieval monasticism. It is one of the ironies of history that criticism of Catholic observance, in England as on the continent, flourished in a context of popular enthusiasm for it: with profound implications not only for the political and religious development of the country, but also for the appearance of the urban and rural landscape.

6

The landscape of fortification

Asked to draw a quintessential medieval building, most people would probably sketch the outlines of a castle, complete with one or more towers and battlements. Anyone familiar with English Heritage will have encountered its logo, representing the ground plan of a square fortified building. But for all this familiarity – and while for most of the twentieth century a chapter on fortifications in this period would have aroused little controversy – such has been the revolution in castle studies since the 1980s that this is now one of the more challenging aspects of the medieval landscape to discuss. It has been claimed that 'castles are at once the best known and least understood of medieval buildings',[1] so their study is all the more fascinating. Castles were not, of course, the only form of fortification in medieval England – manor houses, town walls, even churches figure in the pages which follow – but an initial focus upon them will provide a context for the discussion of other structures.

A. L. Poole's *Medieval England*, published in 1958, offers a typical summary of how castles have traditionally been viewed. In a chapter entitled 'Military Architecture', A. J. Taylor, then Assistant Chief Inspector of Ancient Monuments, ran through a sequence beginning with earth-and-timber castles (mostly motte-and-baileys) through rectangular then circular stone keeps to the elaborately defended gatehouses and curtain towers of the late thirteenth century, when castles were at their mightiest as defences against armed assault. This was followed by a 'decline from earlier standards of strength and security' through the fourteenth and fifteenth centuries, with increasing emphasis upon domesticity and display.[2] The juxtaposition with a chapter called 'The Art of War', which dealt among other things with various forms of siege artillery, reinforced the message that developments in castle design were largely a response to improvements in the techniques of military offence. While the details have been expertly refined, this basic structure has recurred time and again in subsequent authoritative treatments of the subject.[3]

While focusing on military considerations, these analyses fully recognized a requirement for castles to offer some residential comfort, while also acknowledging the relevance to design of social and financial issues such as the relationship between lords and retainers (reflected in the disposition of buildings) and the affordability of different types of structure in the light of prevailing economic conditions. However, recent work on castles has usually had a very different focus. Attention has been given, for example, to the role of women in the domestic affairs of a castle and their impact upon the arrangement of private chambers, castle gardens and other forms of 'gendered space'.[4] Above all, there has been growing recognition of the role of castles as symbolic displays of royal and lordly power – 'intended to enhance the dignity of aristocracy'[5] – which have come to be seen as more important than their strictly military function: a view reinforced by a series of studies which have demonstrated the significant limitations, in terms of capacity to resist armed assault, of one major castle after another. Very few were built on 'impregnable' hilltops, and even those that were, such as the baronial castles of Peak (Castleton, Derbyshire) by 1086 and Beeston (Cheshire) in the 1220s, may owe their choice of site as much to symbolism as to defensibility. Most were sited in less-naturally defended positions, from which routeways could be controlled, estates administered or towns and counties governed.[6] There continues to be a difference of view between those who believe that 'while castles of all dates had many other functions including self-promotion, it was defence that remained the first consideration of almost every castle-builder throughout the Middle Ages', and those who hold that 'fortresses possessed a total role in medieval England, to which the strictly military contribution was relatively slight': 'the military was but one dimension ... to the motives of castle-building society'.[7] Neither party in this debate rules out a wider role for castles than the one they see as paramount, but they certainly see a difference of emphasis. All this needs to be borne in mind as we approach our own analysis of castle development here.

One of the difficulties in any treatment of castles is to arrive at an acceptable definition of the term. We have encountered similar problems time and again in this book, but here they are exacerbated by the fact that eleventh- and twelfth-century usage of the Latin *castellum* (or *castrum*) and the English *castel* could embrace a broad range of fortified structures, far beyond the stone buildings commonly associated with kings and great lords to which visitors pay for access today.[8] Contemporaries were more concerned with the realities of fortification than with what they were called. On the one hand, the defining line for the Dukes of Normandy in the second half of the eleventh century was the nature of the enclosing barrier and its accompanying ditch, though it remains a presumption that this legislation, which implied a blanket prohibition which could be lifted through specific permission, also applied to their kingdom of England: 'no-one in Normandy shall be allowed to make a fosse in the open country of more than one shovel's throw in depth, nor set there more than one line of palisading, and that without battlements or allures [wall-walks]'.[9] On the other, it is clear that even churches could serve as fortifications in some circumstances. King Stephen had Lincoln Cathedral turned into a castle' ('incastellaverat') in 1140–41 and there remain traces of machicolation on the west front; Geoffrey de Mandeville Earl of Essex is also reported to have fortified Ely Cathedral in some way so that it could be used as a base for his rebellion against the king a year or so later. Beyond this, fourteenth-century church towers, clearly fortified primarily against the Scots, survive at Burgh-by-Sands, Great Salkeld and Newton Arlosh (Cumberland), all with battlements, at Edlingham (Northumberland) which has a series of narrow arrow-loops, and at Bedale (Yorkshire) where there is a portcullis groove at the bottom of the staircase and battlements which extend from the tower to the roof of the nave.[10]

However, if only for the convenience of historians and archaeologists today, we need to know what we are talking about when we refer to 'the medieval castle'. Modern definitions generally assume that a castle was the residence of a lord and his household, while accepting that the greatest lords – kings, bishops, barons – divided their time between several. Castles were also fortified, even though the extent and purpose of the fortification varied. In large part, they were also administrative centres from which the lord exerted authority over the neighbourhood. Additionally – according to circumstance – they might serve as prison, hunting-lodge, mustering point for soldiers and, if the lord or his representative permitted it, a refuge for the local populace. 'Licences to crenellate', issued on behalf of the king as permission to fortify a building through the provision of battlements, might seem to offer an easy means towards delineation and classification, but few such licences are known from before 1200 and among the 500-plus which can be identified thereafter – peaking in the fourteenth century but persisting into the sixteenth – there is poor correlation with the known distribution of fortified residences which by most definitions would be labelled as 'castles'.[11] Yet we cannot proceed without a definition, so let us settle on 'a royal or lordly residence, fortified against the weapons of the day, normally serving as an administrative centre from which the surrounding area was governed'. No definition is perfect, but this will serve as a basis from which to begin the discussion.

The regional distribution of castles is instructive. It is no surprise that Northumberland, Herefordshire, Shropshire and Cumberland are the English shires with the highest densities of recorded castles: their positions near the Scots and Welsh borders provide an obvious explanation, although this had more to do with the prevailing insecurity of a frontier zone where raiding and banditry were (at times) endemic than with any grand scheme for defence against invasion. The fact that the border county of Cheshire had a much lower density – similar to that of Hampshire and Essex – may reflect deliberate policy on the part of the Earls of Chester to restrict castle-building among their own barons, although there is a group of earthwork sites near the western frontier, such as those at Aldford, Pulford, Castletown near Shocklach and Dodleston, which may be interpreted as part of an early scheme to protect the shire, and Chester itself, against incursions from the west. Cambridgeshire has one of the lowest densities in the country, readily explained by the fact that much of it was composed of fenland which was both unsuitable for castle-building and largely in the hands of major religious houses who had no wish to see fortifications proliferate among their tenants; here again, however, there was a local initiative near the southern fen edge at Caxton, Swavesey, Rampton and Burwell, where a chain of earthwork castles appear to owe their origin to King Stephen's efforts against the rebellious Geoffrey de Mandeville, who was eventually killed trying to take Burwell in 1144. The shires with the lowest castle-densities of all probably owe this largely to the restrictions imposed by the prevalence of royal forests (Nottinghamshire and Staffordshire) and to a social structure with a large number of freeholders and relatively few substantial lords with the resources to invest (Lincolnshire and Norfolk).[12]

Attempts have been made to depict the overall distribution of castles in England as part of a co-ordinated system of national defence and it might be expected that royal castles, at least, would be built according to a master-plan. There was clearly a policy on the part of William the Conqueror to establish castles in each major town which was the focus of shire government – urgently so in the areas which rebelled against him early in his reign.[13] Beyond this, however, the idea does not stand up to scrutiny except in highly specific contexts such as those identified in Cheshire and Cambridgeshire in the previous paragraph. For example, the string of castles near the border with Scotland, from Carlisle in the west to Newcastle in the east, were built by different people at different times – Norham by Ranulf Flambard Bishop of Durham from 1121, for example, Wark-on-Tweed by the prominent early twelfth-century northern baron Walter Espec, both a generation later than the royal castles at either end of the chain – and failed to prevent repeated Scottish incursions south of what was in any case a movable frontier. They were designed for local, rather than regionally co-ordinated, administration and defence and – significantly – when both Norham and Wark were success- fully assaulted by the Scots in 1138, other garrisons did not come to their aid.[14] Similarly, castles built at south coast ports, such as those at Dover

(Kent), Portchester (Hampshire) and Southampton, all royal initiatives, were intended to protect key access and departure points for traffic mostly with Normandy, but not as a chain of fortresses which would support one another in the event of invasion. Such a chain was eventually built at the very end of our period, between 1539 and 1543, with the construction of 18 artillery forts along the south coast from Pendennis (Cornwall) to Sandown (Kent) along with supporting minor works in the Thames estuary and elsewhere, the intention being to combat a perceived threat of papally inspired invasion from France and the Spanish Netherlands. However, although several of these forts, such as St Mawes (Cornwall) and Walmer (Kent), are popularly known as 'castles', they were neither individuals' private residences nor administrative centres and are best regarded as garrison bases: key components in England's first co-ordinated scheme for the defence of the realm, but not really castles. It is interesting that the design of these forts – all 'burly, rounded, hollow, roofed bastions' surrounding a 'tall cylindrical keep' – are open to criticism as militarily backward compared to angle-bastioned fortifications, already developed in Italy, from which the entire field beneath the walls could be commanded. It is possible that this conservatism was the result of personal involvement in the specifications by Henry VIII himself: that it was his preference for some of the traditional features of castles, such as battlements and portcullises – of marginal relevance in this context – which led to their incorporation into the structures.[15] If so, it is a striking demonstration of the way in which, even in fortifications which were of the highest military importance, other considerations could enter into their design.

Early castles

Most historians and archaeologists accept that castles, as defined here, were introduced to England by the Normans. At first sight, there might seem to be plenty of evidence against this. There are pre-Conquest castles (known partly from documentary evidence) in Herefordshire (at Richard's Castle, Ewyas Harold, Hereford and possibly two other sites) and at Clavering (Essex): the *Anglo-Saxon Chronicle* in its coverage of the year 1051 lamented the 'injuries and insults … upon the king's men' inflicted by the occupants of one of these Herefordshire castles.[16] At Dover, the earliest earthworks have been held to date to 1064–65 because of chronicle references to the construction of a castle (*castrum, castellum*) here in connection with Harold Godwinson's oath to support William Duke of Normandy's claim to the English throne. A much earlier fortified home has been found by archaeologists at Goltho (Lincolnshire), where an earthen bank and ditch surrounding a hall has been dated to the mid-ninth century. At Sulgrave (Northamptonshire) a stone hall with earthen rampart might also pre-date the Conquest. From a literary perspective, the Anglo-Saxon word *burh* frequently meant a communal fortification – a walled town or fort – but in some contexts could refer to a fortified dwelling such as those at Goltho and Sulgrave: sufficient indication that the concept of a well-defended homestead was a familiar one in the upper reaches of pre-Conquest society. But all this can be explained in a way which retains the idea that castles arrived in England with the Normans. The Herefordshire and Clavering examples appear to be the result of settlement by Norman favourites of Edward the Confessor, while the original earthworks at Dover are now seen as Iron Age defences adapted for communal refuge by the Anglo-Saxons, the choice of 'castle' words by the chroniclers to describe them being interpreted as loose usage. As for archaeological and literary evidence of domestic *burhs*, they cannot be ranked as 'castles' because there is no sign that they were ever intended as administrative centres for the government of the surrounding area.[17]

If this seems to be straining the evidence, and underplaying the elements of continuity from the fortified home of the Anglo-Saxon nobleman or thegn to that of the incoming Norman lord, the fact remains that the novelty of castles in England in the aftermath of the Conquest was recognized at the time. The *Anglo-Saxon Chronicle* saw the building of 'castles far and wide throughout the land', with accompanying distress which 'went ever from bad to worse' as one of the immediate and striking impacts of the Duke of Normandy's victory; they were 'a sore burden to the poor', a phrase which implies the existence of 'government over the surrounding area' to set them apart from the fortified residences which had gone before. Orderic Vitalis (though writing in the first half of the twelfth century) attributed that success largely to the fact that for the English 'castles ... were scarcely known' so 'in spite of their courage and love of fighting' they 'could put up only a weak resistance to their enemies': not a claim that castles were totally unknown before 1066, but certainly support for the *Anglo-Saxon Chronicle* in its assertion that they spread thereafter, out of all proportion to what had gone before.[18] Given that debate centres on what does or does not fit modern scholars' definitions of 'castles', there will continue to be arguments in favour of pre-Conquest structures which deserve the appellation. But the texts leave us in no doubt at all of a widespread change of perception following the Norman Conquest: the 'age of the castle' had arrived.

With due regard to uncertainties over definition, it is generally accepted that rather more than 1,000 castles were built in England and Wales between the mid-eleventh century and the end of the fifteenth. Of these, at least 500 were probably in existence by 1100, and although the building of new castles certainly continued thereafter, the number in active use at any time may not have exceeded 600.[19] So the 'first century of English feudalism'[20] after the Norman Conquest – especially its earlier phase – was the busiest of all castle-building eras, even if most of the structures of this period were of earth and timber and most of the sites were subsequently abandoned. It is this period, down to the early years of Henry II's reign, which is the focus of this section of the chapter.

Most 'Norman castles' conformed to one of two main types: the motte-and-bailey, where an earthen motte or mound was the principal defensible feature, albeit with an accompanying bailey or courtyard, and the ringwork, where a rampart and ditch surrounded and protected the occupants, without there being an obvious focal point. Castle Neroche (Somerset), where excavation has shown that what was originally a ringwork of the late 1060s became a motte-and-bailey around 1100 through the addition of a motte at one end, serves to warn us of the dangers of classification, but the distinction is helpful nonetheless. We can point, for example, to some evidence of regional fashion, since there seems to have been a preference for ringworks on either side of the Bristol Channel, possibly associated with the prominence in the area of the Conqueror's half-brother Robert Count of Mortain and his followers. As for mottes, they appear to have been very rare in Normandy and non-existent in England before 1066. So their proliferation thereafter – coming to outnumber ringworks in England and Wales by over three to one – would only have reinforced the chroniclers' impression that something important had been added to the landscape.[21] These alternative approaches to early castle design introduce us to an enduring theme: the dichotomy between those which emphasized a single dominant feature – motte or great tower – and those which invested heavily in the surrounding enclosure, leaving interior buildings virtually unprotected if that enclosure was breached. This is a simple way of looking at castles, one which begs questions about the real purpose of the 'dominant feature' and is liable to break down altogether where designers ensured that both approaches were adopted, but it is worth keeping in mind during the survey which follows.

The distribution map of mottes shows a high concentration in the Welsh marches and above-average frequency in the midlands, as well as areas of density in south-west Wales and the eastern side of Ireland which are clearly linked to Norman colonization of these regions. As already suggested, many sites near the Welsh border were probably fortified by barons to whom estates were parcelled out in this frontier zone in the generation following the Conquest; some of those in the midlands, and elsewhere across the country, may have originated amid the prevailing insecurity of Stephen's reign, especially during the 1140s. As for the size of mottes, no less than 49 have been shown to be 10 metres or more in height from the previous ground level, all of them associated with the king (among them Oxford,

Cambridge, Lincoln and York) or a major baron (such as Robert Count of Mortain's Launceston in Cornwall or William of Warenne's Lewes in Sussex). Most of these belonged to the 'conquest and early settlement' phase of Anglo-Norman history, before 1100. Conversely, over 450 examples have been found to be less than 5 metres high, including the one at Hastings which is shown under construction in the Bayeux Tapestry.[22] Even small mottes, however, would have required the clearance of a substantial area around them, not only because their diameter was normally over twice that of their height, and because there was also the bailey to accommodate, but also because of the need to have some open space to prevent a concealed approach. In the countryside this would doubtless have involved a certain amount of tree-felling (so providing the timber for the castle buildings) and in urban areas the demolition of houses: as alluded to already, Domesday Book records this as having happened at Cambridge, Canterbury, Gloucester, Huntingdon, Lincoln, Norwich, Stamford, Shrewsbury, Wallingford, Warwick and York.[23]

It is often difficult to visualize the appearance of a castle which survives today only as earthworks (Figure 32) and archaeological excavation has revealed much which is not obvious in the landscape today. Most mottes

Figure 32: Fotheringhay Castle (Northamptonshire). The castle, which stood at a crossing of the River Nene at one end of the village, was gradually demolished during the seventeenth century, leaving the original motte-and-bailey earthworks. The parish church beyond was largely rebuilt in the fifteenth century for use by a college of priests.

seem to have had some form of timber tower on top – as lookout and refuge – but its construction could vary: the 3.7 metres-square tower at Abinger (Surrey) has been interpreted as resting on stilts inserted into the motte, while that at South Mimms (Hertfordshire) was built on the pre-existing ground surface, with the motte being piled up around its base. Double palisades have been found around the motte (as at Abinger) or bailey (as at Tamworth and also Hen Domen (Montgomeryshire), implying the existence of a walkway and fighting platform between them. A wooden bridge between motte and bailey – as depicted for this type of castle in the Bayeux Tapestry – is also in evidence at Hen Domen. Investigations of ringworks have also yielded interesting results. Excavations at Barnard Castle (County Durham) have shown the earliest complex on the site, built around 1095, to have been a ringwork with gatehouse, enclosing a timber hall 14 metres by 10.5 metres along with ancillary buildings (possibly stables). A small ringwork at Lydford had timber revetments abutting onto the inside of the rampart and this is thought to have been replicated on the outside as well, so as to form a 'box-rampart' in the manner of many Iron Age hillforts: the enclosing defences, in other words, did not have their present appearance of sloping linear embankments but presented themselves as substantial wooden barriers reinforced by earth. This was probably a widespread phenomenon.[24]

Earthwork and timber castles were relatively quick and inexpensive to build. Orderic Vitalis and William of Poitiers both mention eight days in connection with the Conqueror's structures at York and Dover respectively but cannot have meant that the entire projects were completed within this time; most would probably have taken a few months in total.[25] As such, they were ideal either for kings and major barons in the initial conquest-and-settlement phase of the occupation of the country (when the prime sites had not necessarily been identified) or for lesser lords with a limited amount to spend who felt obliged to defend themselves and their households as best they could: the apparent proliferation of mottes during the civil war of Stephen's reign must have taken 'castle-building' below the ranks of the baronage. In a category of their own are 'siege-castles', designed to house troops engaged against an established castle nearby: some 31 have been identified in England and Wales, mostly between 180 and 280 metres distant from the enemy site. 'Pampudding Hill' and 'The Rings', ringworks built, respectively, by Henry I against Bridgnorth Castle (Shropshire) in 1102 and by Stephen against Corfe Castle (Dorset) in 1139, are good surviving examples; it is likely that these were put up in a matter of weeks, with rudimentary accommodation within them. However, as temporary structures without an administrative purpose, intended to house troops (often mercenaries without any local connection), it is questionable whether they should really be called 'castles', despite the common usage.[26]

We should certainly not think that timber buildings in castles were necessarily mean in appearance, or that they were always replaced in stone at the earliest opportunity. An open-backed timber-framed tower was built into the defences of the motte at Deddington (Oxfordshire) as late as the end of the twelfth century. The illustrations in the Bayeux Tapestry apparently showing decorated timber structures on the tops of mottes, and the description of one such building at Durham Castle, possibly in the 1140s, as 'glittering with splendid beauty ... each face ... girded by a beautiful gallery' suggest that there was already a concern for display which transcended purely military requirements. There continued to be a timber-building tradition within castles partly constructed in stone well into the fourteenth century. At York, this included the rebuilding in timber of the tower on top of the motte after the original had burned down in 1190 (only to be replaced by the present Clifford's Tower, in stone, in 1245). A 'great wooden tower' on the motte at Shrewsbury, around which a wooden palisade had been built in the 1220s, survived until 1270.[27]

Despite the longevity of timber as a favoured material, it was of course vulnerable to fire and rot, so stone featured as an alternative almost from the outset: for example at the White Tower (the great square tower of London Castle), possibly begun in 1078, where imported Caen stone was used as the ashlar; at Colchester, where an even larger square tower, again incorporating Caen stone, seems to have been erected late in the Conqueror's reign; and at Corfe, where the pre-1100 curtain walls of a motte-and-bailey castle on an elevated site utilized local stone as the most readily available material. Stone also featured in some late eleventh-century castles which lacked either a motte or a dominant great tower: in the curtain walls of baronial castles at Peak, Ludlow (Shropshire) and Richmond (Yorkshire) and in the gate towers of Ludlow, Richmond and William the Conqueror's Exeter, the latter surviving largely intact.[28]

So in the century which followed the Norman Conquest, we have castles built with an emphasis on a 'dominant feature' – either motte-and-baileys or those with great stone towers – and we have others which relied for defence mainly on their enclosing 'ringworks' or stone curtain walls. Timber was the most widespread building material, but a minority were already incorporating stone. There is no neat progression through time here, but a series of local adaptations to what was readily available, affordable and met the requirements of the site. As we move on to consider the story of castles in the landscape through the rest of the middle ages, this remains the case: we cannot adhere too closely to a chronological approach. That said, castles did not develop in isolation from their political context, and in this connection the conclusion of the civil war of Stephen's reign does have a claim to be of major importance. The Treaty of Winchester of November 1153, which brought an end to the war by promising the throne to Henry Duke of Normandy (the future Henry II) on the death of the incumbent king, Stephen, included provision for the destruction of 'newly built' castles, and it is clear that efforts were made, even while Stephen was alive, to put this into effect. A statement by Robert de Torigni that in excess of 1,115 were to be 'overthrown' is incredible, but it does suggest that the number of active castles dropped dramatically around this time. Recent estimates have suggested that only about 30 brand-new castles were built during the reign but even if deliberate destruction was confined to some of these, far more would have been considered unusable against the improved siege artillery coming into use by the middle of the twelfth century and certainly available to the incoming king. Overwhelmingly, it was the earthwork-and-timber castles which dropped out of use, as – in Charles Coulson's words – 'obsolescence, physical decay, tenurial change and the cost of rebuilding in masonry contracted the social range of castle-ownership'.[29] From the late twelfth to the early fifteenth century, the castle – as fortified residence from which authority was exercised over the surrounding area – was essentially a royal or baronial phenomenon where for reasons partly of status and partly of defensibility against the improved siege artillery of the day the more significant buildings had to be in stone. Lesser lords could not afford to keep up, and most contented themselves with moated manor houses from hereon.

Great towers

The construction in stone of one great tower which stood out as superior to the rest of a castle – as those at London and Colchester were already doing by the 1080s – was to be an enduring tradition throughout the medieval period, although there would be differences in design and purpose according to time and place. Most of them have traditionally been given the appellation 'keep', a term which by the sixteenth century conveyed the notion of a defensible structure which could hold out if the rest of the complex fell. Thus, in 1541, two military surveyors recommended to Henry VIII that 'within the cyrcuyte of the said castelle [Wark-on-Tweed, Northumberland] a strong towre or kepe [be] devysed and made for the savegarde of such mens lyves as were within the said castell when in extreme need shoulde chance'.[30] However, the word was not in common use in the medieval period and the extent to which great towers (or *donjons* to use a medieval term) served a serious defensive purpose remains a matter for debate. The thirteenth-century *donjon* at Barnard Castle (County Durham) had comfortable residential accommodation in the lower portion but a guardroom above, which had direct access to the curtain wall and could be shut off in the event of attack; this seems to have been intended both as residence and as 'defence of last resort' in a manner conventionally ascribed to medieval castle keeps.[31] But many of these towers seem to have been designed with other functions in mind. Those built for William the Conqueror at London (the White Tower) and at Chepstow (Monmouthshire) initially lacked any residential accommodation and seem to have been built primarily for formal occasions and as statements of authority to overawe the local populace; the Tower went on to be used mainly as a prison, as did the *donjon* at Lydford (Devon), begun in 1195.[32] Other early structures generally known as 'keeps' also seem to have been used mainly for ceremonies and formal receptions; they might be seen as their lord's 'official residence' and even incorporate some domestic living space, but most of the time he dwelt elsewhere within the castle. This seems to have been the case, for example, at Henry I's great rectangular tower at Norwich, which had only a small amount of private accommodation within it; at Hedingham (Essex), where the great tower, built around 1140 for Aubrey de Vere apparently to mark his elevation to the earldom of Oxford, originally lacked any private chambers or kitchens (Figure 33); and at Castle Rising (Norfolk), where the highly decorated rectangular tower begun at about the same time for William d'Aubigny – proud to have married Henry I's widow – remained unfinished for well over a century while the lords of the castle normally lived in the bailey below.[32] There are echoes here of the great halls of early manor houses, already discussed in Chapter 3, which until the twelfth century seem normally to have been freestanding structures for entertainment and administration, separate from the living quarters elsewhere in the manorial enclosure.[33]

By the late twelfth century, however, there are signs that these towers were being provided with more private rooms to serve as domestic accommodation. This has been identified, for example, where they were newly built for Henry II, as at Scarborough (Yorkshire) and Newcastle-upon-Tyne, and also where older structures were converted, such as the great tower at Norham, originally of the 1120s, where the first-floor reception area was divided up. Most great towers would retain a residential function from hereon – not necessarily for the lord of the castle – but the question of how far they were seen as defensible buildings remains. Several visually impressive examples fail to withstand close scrutiny from this point of view. At Dover, the great tower built for Henry II seems to have been intended above all to provide both power-statement and fitting accommodation for a king whose territories bestrode the English Channel, but a ground floor entrance which gave direct access to the storerooms left it vulnerable: it was the construction of inner and outer curtain walls at Dover, fully in place by the end of John's reign, which seems to have been the principal defensive device. William d'Aubigny's tower at Castle Rising has the appearance even to the most casual observer

Figure 33: Hedingham Castle (Essex). The great tower which dominates the castle's inner bailey was built in the 1140s, evidently not as defensible accommodation but for grand receptions celebrating its owner's elevation to an earldom. It was well-appointed internally, with two rows of narrow windows (the middle pair shown here) lighting the Upper Hall.

today of a residence rather than a fortress: a neatly proportioned building of greater breadth than height, with many large windows and decorative blank arcading to impress the approaching visitor.

Further issues are raised by some of the great towers built from the mid-twelfth century to designs which deliberately offered alternatives to the traditional square or rectangular layout – such as the polygonal towers erected for Henry II in the 1170s at both Orford (Suffolk), a new site, and at Tickhill (Yorkshire), a former baronial castle, and also the circular *donjon* added to the castle at Conisbrough (Yorkshire) probably for the king's half-brother in the 1180s. The corners of rectangular towers were susceptible to mining and created blind spots which defenders could not cover, but these rounded or polygonal keeps were scarcely an improvement from a defensive point of view: the supporting buttresses which projected from the external walls at Orford and Conisbrough, for example, were liable to restrict defenders' field of vision and increase the number of vulnerable corners. The concern for external decoration which is apparent at these towers – at Conisbrough finely dressed ashlar covered the entire external walling while at Orford different coloured stone was used – strongly suggests that a desire for ostentatious display was a principal motivation in their design.[34]

But should a military purpose to these great towers be ruled out altogether? In interpreting them, much depends on how much functionality is accorded to the elements of 'fortification'. Thick walls, often splayed at the base to add stability, can be interpreted as giving added insurance against battery and mining, but also as a commitment to both opulence and insulation. Machicolation – stone parapets set on corbels which projected from the tops of some keeps, with holes in the floor through which items could be dropped – had some military purpose as a way of assaulting an enemy immediately below the wall, but are equally convincing as a decorative finish at the summit of the structure. Excessive height minimized the risk that attackers could reach the battlemented roofs and facilitated visual command far and wide, but also allowed the castle to be seen – and its lord feared or revered – over the same extensive area. A single well-protected doorway, normally at first-floor level, made a frontal assault difficult but also obliged visitors to arrive by a processional route and to look up to those waiting to greet them. And, once arrow-loops were introduced to castles towards the end of the twelfth century, a balance had to be struck between wide window-openings for sunlight and narrow openings for these loops, the strategic positioning of which sometimes lacks conviction from a strictly defensive point of view. A debate over how far 'conspicuous defensive features ... were rather to conform to the conventions of a militaristic society than for serious use' [35] will continue, but it is surely wrong to see the different purposes as mutually exclusive. Orderic Vitalis was well aware that both considerations could come into play when he described the 'very well-fortified castle of ashlar blocks' at Montreuil in western Normandy, built by Henry I's former justice Richard Basset who 'swollen with the wealth of England had made a show of superiority to all his peers and fellow-countrymen by the magnificence of his building in the little fief he had inherited'; this castle successfully resisted two assaults by invading Angevin forces during 1136.[36] The weaknesses in the design of the great tower at Rochester – lacking facilities from which to snipe at the enemy and with right-angled corners susceptible to undermining – eventually led to its garrison having to surrender to King John at the end of November 1215; but while this can be interpreted as a typical twelfth-century structure with decorated entrance and magnificent second-floor hall intended primarily for display, ceremonial receptions and a certain amount of accommodation, it played its part in the castle's seven-week resistance to the king, with the defenders continuing to hold out behind a cross-wall even after the south-east corner had collapsed. It would almost certainly have been hailed as a 'successful' military building if the hoped-for French relieving army had turned up.[37] In troubled times it was certainly safer to be inside a tall stone *donjon* than in an poorly fortified outbuilding, and if the erection of such a structure afforded an opportunity to display wealth, power and aesthetic taste, while also giving some protection, the temptation was hard to resist. We have to see these great towers as serving a variety of purposes – ceremonial, residential, military, aesthetic and aggrandizing – for the rest of the medieval period, while also questioning in each particular case whether they can truly be regarded as independently defensible.

From hereon, there was certainly variety in design: those who commissioned *donjons*, and those who devised and built them, were clearly prepared to experiment and to compete. Around the middle of the thirteenth century, the Earl of Surrey built a rounded structure with four projecting semi-circular turrets at Sandal Castle (Yorkshire); the Earl of Cornwall had a round tower added to the top of the motte at Launceston (Cornwall); and the royal castle at York was provided with 'Clifford's Tower' as a crown for its motte, based on four circles which would have touched had they been extended to the centre. Further cylindrical towers were built on royal initiative during the 1280s at the castles of Cambridge and Hawarden. About 1310, Edward II rebuilt the great tower at Knaresborough to a distinctive design, which made it appear three-sided from outside but rectangular within; in 1348 the Earl of Stafford commissioned a new stone one with octagonal corner turrets for the top of the motte at Stafford Castle; and the Percy Earls of Northumberland followed at the beginning of the fifteenth century with a stone structure on the motte at Warkworth (itself a replacement for a thirteenth-century predecessor of similar design) essentially square but with a polygonal projection on each side. In addition, several thirteenth-century castles in Wales, including the Clare family's Caerphilly and Edward I's Harlech and Beaumaris, were built with elaborately constructed gatehouses defended both in front and behind which served effectively both as accommodation and as the principal fortified buildings; the idea was not widely adopted in England, but can be found at Tonbridge (Kent), another Clare property, about 1300, and at Dunstanburgh (Northumberland), where a strong gatehouse originally of around 1320 was similarly remodelled for John of Gaunt during the 1380s.

For all their ostentation, every one of these structures can be considered to have had a serious defensive purpose: that at Sandal for example had an elaborate barbican protecting its entrance, its counterpart at Stafford was described as a 'castle' in itself in the building contract of 1348, while Knaresborough was still being regarded in a sixteenth-century government survey as 'a marvelous hous of strength … strongly fortified with worke and man's ingyne to abide all assaults'. While siting on top of mottes can be interpreted as a statement of domination, it also rendered great towers such as those at Stafford and York less vulnerable to armed assault. The motte-top tower at Warkworth is a magnificent assertion of authority over the town below – and the Percies could not resist adorning the side which faced the town with their heraldic device – but they were in too turbulent a part of the country to ignore the need for such defensive measures as splayed bases to the walls and arrow-loops at ground-floor level (Figure 34).[38]

However, there were certainly many other great towers built in medieval English castles which, however formidable they might appear, lack credibility in military terms. These include the D-shaped 'east tower' in the curtain wall at Helmsley Castle (Yorkshire) of about 1200, which had two entrances and so undermined its own security; the freestanding rectangular tower built at Whittington (Shropshire) in the 1220s with an undefended ground-floor doorway; the great tower designed as a rectangle with four rounded corner turrets erected at Dudley Castle (Warwickshire) for Roger de Somery in the 1270s, also with an undefended entrance at ground level and of no more than two storeys in height; and Sir John de la Mare's Nunney Castle (Somerset) some 100 years later, where the tower has a very similar layout to Dudley and provides no defence to the ground-floor entrance other than a drawbridge over the moat. In fairness, all these towers display some concern for military protection, however compromised, but there is no room for argument with the brick-built towers at Tattershall (Lincolnshire) and Caister-by-Yarmouth (Norfolk), both of the 1430s and 1440s for Lord Cromwell and Sir John

Figure 34: Warkworth (Northumberland) from the Town Bridge. The late fourteenth-century bridge over the River Coquet leads via a fortified gate tower to a main street of the town, with the great tower of Warkworth Castle dominating the settlement below. This elaborately designed building, an early fifteenth-century remodelling of an earlier structure, occupies the motte of the original castle.

Falstolf respectively, nor with the gatehouses, also in brick and intended as their castles' most impressive structures, at Herstmonceux (Sussex) for Henry VI's treasurer Sir Roger Fiennes and Kirby Muxloe (Leicestershire) for Edward IV's chamberlain William lord Hastings. Neither these, nor stone-built towers of the period, such as that at Hastings's other Leicestershire castle at Ashby-de-la-Zouch, had a serious defensive intent: they had wide low-level windows, provided (at best) limited protection to their ground-floor entrances and were built on sites which – other than through the addition of moats in some cases – offered easy access rather than defensive advantage. In these instances, it is abundantly clear that – notwithstanding a display of some of the trappings of militarism – the essential purpose was that of fine residential status symbol.[39]

It remains to consider briefly the relationship between these great towers and the mottes which had featured in the immediate post-Conquest period, since both were characteristic of castles designed to focus on a single 'dominant feature'. There was logic in building a stone tower on top of a pre-existing motte, often as successor to a timber one in the same position, since this preserved the overall configuration of the castle while also taking advantage of the extra height afforded by the motte. Rectangular *donjons* at Norwich, Norham and Okehampton, of the late eleventh and twelfth centuries, and polygonal ones at Tickhill and Richard's Castle, late in the twelfth century, were among those built on top of the mottes of existing motte-and-bailey castles, and as we have seen the elaborate keeps at Clifford's Tower, York and at Warkworth continued the tradition thereafter.[40] However, not every motte was sufficiently stable for this to be attempted. One solution, considered to apply at Berkeley (Gloucestershire) and possibly also at Kenilworth (Warwickshire), both during the twelfth century, was to build a large rectangular tower from the natural ground surface so that it encased the motte within. Another was to erect the structure from the original ground level but into the slope on one side of the motte: this happened at Guildford (Surrey), also in the twelfth century, and at Clun (Shropshire) in the thirteenth.[41] Apart from this, many *donjons* were built within what previously would have been seen as ringworks, or in brand-new castles where mottes were never considered: the de Vere family's Hedingham and Henry II's Scarborough being examples of the former, William d'Aubigny's two castles in Norfolk at Rising and New Buckenham illustrating the latter.

An alternative means of enhancing the dominant point in a castle, without risking a heavy masonry structure on top of the motte, was to build a 'shell keep', an encircling ring of stone around its summit. During the first half of the twelfth century, these were added around several mottes, including those at Arundel, Lincoln and Windsor (Berkshire); examples at Pickering (Yorkshire) and Tamworth followed in later decades, and they continued to be built occasionally into the thirteenth century, as at both Restormel (Cornwall) and Totnes. The term (which was popularized in the late nineteenth century) is not wholly satisfactory, but some of these 'shell keeps' certainly protected residential buildings constructed within them, so in effect fulfilled the same functions as great towers traditionally known as 'keeps'. Indeed, the shell keeps at Windsor and Pickering both came to be known as 'towers' and the term 'keep' itself may originally have been used in medieval times to refer to this type of structure.[42]

Curtain walls and towers

'Shell keeps' were, in effect, renderings in stone of the timber palisades which had commonly protected the original buildings on top of a motte. They were curtain walls, like those which came to be built around baileys as well. Carisbrooke Castle (Isle of Wight), first built by William fitz Osbern soon after the Norman Conquest, had been entirely rebuilt in stone by 1136 and its curtain walls survive, enclosing the bailey and running up the sides of the motte to link with a shell keep. Much the same can be seen – even at speed from the West Coast main line – at Berkhamsted Castle, another early motte-and-bailey now encircled in stone.[43] We have already seen that timber palisades, such as those at Tamworth and Lydford, could be quite sophisticated structures,[44] but few castles in England still active by the close of the twelfth century had not by then replaced them by a stone curtain wall: Castle Rising was one, with stone tower and stone gatehouse but otherwise reliant on massive embankments rather than a wall, but that only takes us back to the question of how far this castle was intended as a serious fortification, especially once the civil war of Stephen's reign was over. Yet while stone curtain walls might be considered to present a greater obstacle to assailants than their timber predecessors, they provided very limited protection to any member of the castle garrison who wanted to stand on the wall-walk, dodge between battlements and snipe at the enemy outside. There is sometimes evidence of postholes in the upper reaches of walls for timber hoardings used as projecting parapets from which items might be fired or dropped on those attacking the castle, similar in purpose to stone machicolation.[45] But this must have been a precarious business. An answer to the problem of how castle defenders could go onto the attack – could take the offensive against besiegers rather than sit passively in a great tower or behind curtain walls hoping that relief would come – was found in the provision of arrow-loops, especially if these were positioned within projecting 'curtain towers'.

Rectilinear towers set at intervals along stone curtain walls had been a feature of the pre-1100 castles at Ludlow and Richmond (Yorkshire) and this tradition continued into the twelfth century, for example at Carisbrooke for the Redvers family, Windsor for Henry II and Framlingham (Suffolk) for the Bigods. There were, however, important differences between them since – unless there was once timber, now vanished, covering the rear – the towers at Ludlow, Carisbrooke and Framlingham were open-backed, essentially realignments of the walls to create elevated projections, while at the other two they were four-sided, providing accommodation as well as fighting platforms. With the greater favour shown towards curved surfaces from about 1200, rounded towers became popular features of thirteenth-century castles, normally elevated above the curtain walls into which they were set and offering a combination of living quarters (usually for servants or members of the garrison) and defensible fighting arenas. Helmsley Castle was rebuilt in stone by Robert de Roos II from the 1190s with a new curtain wall which featured a D-shaped 'great tower' on its eastern face, rounded towers projecting from three corners (though not perfect circles since they were straight-sided within), and a north gate flanked by two D-shaped towers. These ideas can be seen under development at castles such as the Earl of Chester's Bolingbroke (Lincolnshire), Chartley (Staffordshire) and Beeston in the 1220s, all with D-shaped towers in the curtain walls (some of them open-backed in the case of Chartley) and with gatehouses which resembled that at Helmsley, though here with greater depth to the entrance passage since the flanking towers reached into the bailey behind.[46] By this time, so-called 'drum towers', fully (or almost entirely) circular, were also coming into vogue, whether as a series on the outer circuit of Kenilworth for King John, or as individual 'great towers' set into the curtain walls such as at Whittington for Fulk fitz Warin; they were to become major features of the castles built for Edward I to secure his conquest of North Wales in the last quarter of the century.

It is the absence of a recognizable keep or single great tower in some of these castles, such as Framlingham, Beeston and Bolingbroke, which led to the idea widely held until the middle of the twentieth century that such structures were no longer favoured once strategic thinking shifted towards curtain towers intended for attack as well as defence. The argument was certainly pushed too far, given the examples of continued building of *donjons* noted above and – in particular – instances where they were erected contemporaneously with curtain towers; this happened, for example, at the Earl of Chester's Chartley, which had a new cylindrical tower built on top of the motte, and at Edward I's Flint, where the round *donjon* forms a separately defended fourth corner tower to the inner bailey. That said, the trust evidently being placed by the thirteenth century in curtain walls, curtain towers, and their accompanying gatehouses did lead some castle designers to dispense with a keep or great tower and build opulent halls and chambers inside the walls instead:

even Edward I's castles at Rhuddlan, Conwy and Caernarfon lack a single 'dominant feature' which stands out from others, although any one of their curtain towers, and especially their gatehouses, could have been defended independently for a while, in the hope that relief would come.

The thirteenth century, when rising population inflated the incomes to be derived from landed estates, is generally reckoned to be the time when castle architecture reached its apogee in England – whether this is interpreted in terms of military defensibility or of conspicuous grandeur and display. As we have seen, the underlying design principle in this century was to strengthen the defensive ring, but in the greatest castles this involved more than merely placing towers along the curtain walls. On the one hand, gatehouses were not only enhanced through the provision of several barriers within the entrance passage itself but they were also provided with barbicans (fortified approaches) for added protection. On the other, the inner wards or baileys of some castles were completely surrounded by secondary outer baileys, to create so-called 'concentric castles'. The late-thirteenth-century Edwardian castles of North Wales are usually cited in this context, but there are plenty of examples in England. We have already seen that Henry II's stone *donjon* at Dover Castle was soon surrounded by a double line of walled defences. When Beeston was built for the Earl of Chester in the 1220s, an outer curtain wall with open-backed D-shaped towers – less substantial than those of the inner curtain – was constructed so as to create an outer bailey on the more vulnerable south-eastern slope from which the castle would normally be approached. Helmsley Castle was provided with barbicans outside its north and south gates during the course of the thirteenth century, allowing visitors to be contained before admission, with that on the south side being remodelled in the first half of the fourteenth to incorporate further domestic accommodation. And at Goodrich (Herefordshire), either side of 1300, a castle which in the twelfth century had been dominated by a square great tower underwent major rebuilding for Henry III's half-brother William de Valence and his son Aymer. The result was an inner ward housing domestic ranges, with round towers at three of its corners and a round-towered gatehouse at the fourth; added defence was provided by an outer curtain wall and barbican on two sides and a massive rock-hewn ditch elsewhere (Figure 35). To enhance the security of this outer ring, the gatehouse – which served as a residential block with chapel and well-appointed living rooms but was potentially the most vulnerable part of the defensive circuit – was furnished with a drawbridge, two portcullises, heavy wooden doors and 'murder-holes' in the vault above the entrance passage.[47]

Goodrich still presents a spectacular image to those travelling along the River Wye, and in assessing any castle of the thirteenth and early fourteenth centuries it is impossible to ignore a concern for grandiose display. Beeston,

Figure 35: Goodrich Castle (Herefordshire). Goodrich Castle was intended to command the Wye valley, both militarily and as a building to be admired. With its twelfth-century square keep, thirteenth-century round corner towers and large fourteenth-century D-shaped barbican, overlooking and protecting fine domestic accommodation, it is an excellent illustration of developments in medieval military architecture. (English Heritage Photo Library.)

for example, sits on a rocky crag from which eight counties can be seen and has different coloured masonry banded across its main entrance in a manner reminiscent of Henry II's keep at Dover and Henry III's curtain walls at Windsor; it gives every appearance of having been intended to signal the partly independent authority enjoyed by the Earl of Chester. Helmsley's early fourteenth-century gate passage in its southern barbican was provided with decorative stonework which had no military purpose and can only have been intended to impress legitimate visitors. By then there was already a 'processional route' at Helmsley, whereby visitors approaching from the ford over the nearby River Rye were guided not direct through the south gate but all the way round the castle so that its features could be admired before they were admitted.[48] The access to Goodrich via the barbican achieves a similar effect. Yet while these castles were certainly status symbols, designed to impress from an aesthetic point of view, they were also formidable structures in purely military terms. Their occupants must have taken considerable comfort from that.

Castles in context

The story from hereon has usually been written as one of castle 'decline', as the economic realities of the late middle ages took their toll. As we have seen, brick – usually locally available and much cheaper than stone – was introduced as the principal building material in a number of new castles of the fifteenth century. In place of several towers reliance came to be placed once again on one: sometimes a 'great tower' as at Warkworth or Ashby-de-la-Zouch, sometimes the gatehouse, where the main access to the castle was enhanced to become not only a residential block but also the grandest feature of the entire complex. Tattershall Castle is often cited as typical of the period, with its great tower in brick, built in the 1430s and 1440s and replete with decorative features, overseeing an adjoining hall: these two adjacent buildings replaced a thirteenth-century stone castle presumed to have had curtain walls and corner towers.

Seen strictly as fortifications, most of these late-medieval castles were unimpressive. If there was any military case for preferring cylindrical or D-shaped towers in the thirteenth century (itself open to debate) there was none for reverting to rectangular ones in the fifteenth – and we have already seen that those at Tattershall (in brick) and Ashby-de-la-Zouch (stone) had fundamental weaknesses in their defensibility. At Kirby Muxloe, four masons were specially employed to create 'pictures in the walls' using dark bricks – hence the diaper patterns still visible today – but the openings from which to fire cannon were placed below the waterline of the moat and had to be blocked in. Much of the machicolation below the battlements of castles of this period was too narrow to have been of any practical use; anything dropped from that at Caesar's Tower, Warwick, built in the 1360s, would have hit its own massively splayed base. All this lends credence to the view that from the early fourteenth century onwards, most castles were essentially for 'display', using the motifs of militarism – gun ports and machicolation among them – as decoration rather than for any serious offensive or defensive purpose. After all, the same architectural details – great gatehouse, battlements, traces of machicolation – can be found in late fifteenth-century buildings which are not usually considered to be 'castles', such as the Bedingfield family's Oxburgh Hall (Norfolk) for which a 'licence to crenellate' was issued in 1482, and the Bishop of Lincoln's Buckden Palace (Huntingdonshire). And already, from the late fourteenth century onwards, some members of the nobility were choosing to build sumptuous courtyard-houses – which had a hall range opposite the gatehouse and accommodation wings ranged along the other two sides – without even a nod to defensibility, in preference to more traditional military-looking structures: Dartington Hall (Devon) of the 1380s and 1390s for the future Duke of Exeter, South Wingfield (Derbyshire) of the 1440s for Lord Treasurer Cromwell and Knole (Kent) of the 1450s to 1480s for the Archbishop of Canterbury are cases in point. Layer Marney Tower, built in the early 1520s for one of Henry VIII's leading councillors, would have been another example had the family not died out when only one side of the courtyard had been built; as it is, we are left with a decorative brick-built gatehouse taller than any of its Tudor predecessors, boasting four corner turrets but with no battlements in sight. Nothing could send the message more clearly that for the late-medieval nobility, priorities in domestic accommodation had changed (Figure 36).

But how far should the story of castles in the fourteenth and fifteenth centuries really be told as one of 'decline'? Okehampton Castle, for example, originally a motte-and-bailey for William the Conqueror's sheriff of Devon, was extensively rebuilt in the first half of the fourteenth century with barbican, gatehouse, hall, lodgings, kitchens, and a residential extension to the Norman great tower: but there was an obvious weakness in the defensibility of all this, since in many places the new domestic buildings reached a height above that of the surrounding curtain wall. As the English Heritage Guidebook puts it, 'the role of Okehampton Castle had shifted from that of secure military stronghold … towards a country retreat, where the family could enjoy hunting and …

Figure 36: Layer Marney Tower (Essex). The tall brick gatehouse of the early 1520s had no military function but was intended as an impressive entrance to the courtyard of a palatial country house. This was never built, so the area is now used by livestock and cars, which approach the feature from the 'wrong' side.

impress guests with their wealth'; the adjoining deer park was developed accordingly.[50] Elsewhere, Bodiam Castle (Sussex), which dates to the 1380s, has a broad water-filled moat and an elaborate gatehouse, but can be criticized from a military standpoint on any number of counts: among them the ease with which the bank retaining the moat could be breached, the impracticality of its arrow loops and gun ports, and the modest size of the battlements so that a man standing upright would not be fully protected. Bodiam is in reality a small-scale castle, with round corner towers which would be dwarfed by those in North Wales, made to look bigger by its reflection in the moat. Yet close analysis of its landscape context shows the care which was taken to reveal the structure in stages to an approaching guest, whose route would be controlled by a causeway and who would encounter the moat, the chapel, the symmetrical north front, the gatehouse and the inner courtyard as a series of progressive disclosures. Much the same could be said of the less well-known castle at Cooling (Kent), also of the 1380s, where high ground to the north overlooks the outer ramparts, and the rounded curtain towers have no backs, but where a visitor would be guided through to behold the reflections in the broad moat of one apparently round tower after another, as well as the latest fashion in gun ports.[51] All this could be dismissed as a 'sham', yet these castles are a visual delight, offering enjoyment to the visitor and gratification to the owner. The proliferation of formal gardens within castles can be seen in the same light. One of the first tasks undertaken at Kirby Muxloe in 1480, before any buildings were put up, was to clear woodland so a garden could be planted; the elaborate sunken depressions to be seen at both Stafford and Ashby-de-la-Zouch can also safely be interpreted as late-medieval garden features, from which excellent views could be enjoyed from the great towers nearby (Figure 37).[52] In terms of what was intended, all this is a long way from 'decline'.

In reality, what we are seeing, in castles throughout the medieval period, is a continuing theme concerned with a display of authority, power and grandeur. That display took different forms at different times. In the modest earthwork castles of the first century or so after the Norman Conquest, the emphasis was on economy, functionality and basic protection against surprise attack, but other considerations already came into play. Even a motte-and-bailey would dominate its surroundings psychologically as well as physically and its timber tower might be decorated for aesthetic effect, as the illustrations on the Bayeux Tapestry imply. As early as 1068, William the Conqueror chose to provide his new motte-and-bailey castle at Exeter with a stone gatehouse, the design of which seems to have been a deliberate echo of the gate tower style favoured for the entrances to the fortified residences of Anglo-Saxon nobles: in military terms not particularly strong, but symbolically a powerful statement of continuity from the previous regime. Choice of

Figure 37: Ashby de la Zouch Castle (Leicestershire). The great tower of the 1470s, to right, overlooked elaborate sunken gardens, which were part of a wider ornamental landscape including a deer park. The small brick tower on the extreme left is one of three (probably added in the 1530s) from which these features could be admired.

sites in this early period was also often dictated by a mixture of pragmatism and symbolism: it made good military sense to re-use former barrows as mottes and Iron Age or Romano-British enclosures for baileys, and also to construct castles by enhancing pre-Conquest fortified residences, but these decisions also provided the new structures with authority carried forward from the past.[53] Stone castles of the late eleventh to the late thirteenth century became increasingly expensive to build and to maintain – so cutting down the numbers and restricting ownership to a royal and lordly élite – and certainly progressed in terms of their defensibility, but this growing elaboration also served to impress from an aesthetic point of view. Thus, the twelfth-century castle at Castle Acre (Norfolk) has been interpreted as part of a 'conscious manipulation of the landscape in order to present an impressive tableau to the visitor', embracing priory and planned vill as part of the structured approach to the castle, over 200 years before similarly designed landscapes were being provided as settings for Bodiam and Cooling.[54] Similarly, the deliberate creation of extensive water features surrounding Kenilworth Castle, including the raising of the 'Great Mere' by over 3 metres, can be traced back to the reigns of John or Henry III; these lakes were intended not for defence but for enjoyment, as the name of the banqueting hall and chambers built for Henry V at one corner of the Great Mere in 1414 – the 'Pleasance in the Marsh' – makes abundantly clear.[55] When all this is said, however, we ought not to deny a change of focus with the passage of time. As the ultimate vulnerability of defences was accepted during the fourteenth and fifteenth centuries, at the same time as landed incomes fell, there were urgent questions to be asked about whether the cost of building increasingly elaborate fortifications was worthwhile. So the quest for symbolism, comfort and aesthetic delight became even more important than hitherto: the motifs of fortification persisted – they were indelibly associated with the dwellings of kings and great lords – but in a context in which the urge to impress visitors and observers, rather than repel them by force, was paramount.

This chapter began with a definition of a 'castle', associated with the status of its principal occupant, the extent of its fortification and its role as an administrative centre. It goes without saying that some medieval fortified buildings did not measure up to this full definition, and that others commonly called 'castle' scarcely deserve the appellation. The original structure at Castle Acre (Norfolk), built by one of William the Conqueror's Norman magnates William de Warenne in the 1070s was an unfortified two-storey stone residence surrounded by a low ringwork bank; the gatehouse was of stone but had a wide entrance passage and (in the opinion of the excavators in the 1970s) was 'for ostentation rather than to withstand prolonged military assault'. Not until the 1130s and 1140s was what these archaeologists called a 'country house' extensively rebuilt with great tower, stone curtain wall and remodelled gatehouse incorporating a narrower entrance.[56] Stokesay Castle (Shropshire) is better regarded as a fortified manor house, since the addition in the 1290s of a battlemented south tower, with moat and curtain wall, scarcely altered its nature or purpose. It is possible to argue a 'defensive' motivation here, given the location in the Welsh marches, but by the closing years of the thirteenth century Edward I had improved security as a result of his North Wales campaigns, and the principal driver was surely a wish to demonstrate affiliation to the aristocracy through the addition of some of the trappings of militarism (Figure 38). Similar considerations almost certainly lay behind the so-called 'fortification' of the manor house at Greys Court, Rotherfield Greys (Oxfordshire), where four small battlemented towers were built into a low wall surrounding the fourteenth-century house. On the other hand, Markenfield Hall, near Ripon (Yorkshire), where a gatehouse with portcullis controls access across a moat, may well have had a more serious defensive intent, since the licence to crenellate here dates to 1310, when the northern counties were especially vulnerable to Scottish raiding parties.

It would be similarly hard to dismiss a genuine concern for security in the various 'pele towers', rectangular stone towers at least three storeys high, built mostly in the northern shires during the fourteenth and fifteenth

Figure 38: Stokesay Castle (Shropshire). The fortified manor house was built for the wool merchant Laurence of Ludlow, who bought the lordship of Stokesay in 1281. The centre-piece, an open hall with private and service ends, had a battlemented south tower (to right) added following the grant of a 'licence to crenellate' in 1291.

centuries; they were evidently a response on the part of local lords and parish clergy to a perceived need to take occasional refuge from attack. The vicar's peles at Corbridge and Embleton (Northumberland) and the manorial Thistlewood Tower at Ivegill (Cumberland) are good surviving examples, as are Longthorpe Tower near Peterborough and the tower at Brimstage Hall (Cheshire), despite their distance from the northern frontier. The fortification of some church towers in the north of England, also noted at the beginning of this chapter and apparently intended to serve as refuges for the local population, is a further reminder not to dismiss the importance of 'defensibility' wherever there was a perception of danger. The argument that castles should be seen as status symbols and places of aesthetic delight has added immensely to our understanding of these structures, but as one of its leading exponents has made clear, it is 'important that the pendulum does not swing too far' so as to 'deny or misinterpret more utilitarian explanations'.[57] Castles have recently been described as 'at once … symbolic, magnificent, powerful and prestigious':[58] defensive security, status, aesthetics and a natural desire for as much residential comfort as possible all have their place in the interpretation of medieval castles. Every site deserves to be considered on its own merits rather than in accordance with preconceived theory.

Town defences

There was brief reference to urban defences in an earlier chapter and it is appropriate to discuss them in more detail here. Over 200 towns in medieval England are reckoned to have had some form of protective circuit, although as with castles it is possible to debate the extent to which these were seriously regarded as effective defensive barriers and there was certainly considerable variety in the strength of the fortifications. Even a few settlements which cannot be regarded as towns, such as Anstey (Hertfordshire) and Castle Acre, the latter with a large embankment and twin-towered stone gatehouse, were provided with earthworks to surround them, but it is hard to see these 'fortified villages' in military terms and the defences have the appearance of being 'vanity projects' for their lords.[59]

An authoritative survey has demonstrated the re-use of Roman masonry circuits at some 17 English towns including Carlisle, Chester, Exeter, Gloucester, Lincoln, London, Winchester and York; the continued use of Anglo-Saxon earthwork defences (doubtless with timber palisades) at towns such as Bridgnorth, Cambridge and Guildford (Surrey); the reinforcement of such defences by the addition of stone at Tamworth, Cricklade (Wiltshire), Wareham (Dorset), Wallingford and elsewhere; and considerable new building in the century or so following the Norman Conquest. In some cases, as at Carlisle, Gloucester, Nottingham and Oxford, this involved enlarging the existing circuit, with at least some part of the extensions being built in stone. In others, like Newcastle-upon-Tyne, Devizes and Taunton, entirely new enclosures were constructed, in stone in the first case, earth-and-timber in the others. The thirteenth century saw a peak in activity, with various campaigns to replace earthen defences with stone, new circuits being built (such as the earthen ramparts with stone gatehouses at Salisbury and Sandwich), and stone extensions being added to accommodate increasing population (as at Bridgnorth, Bristol, Norwich, Shrewsbury, Worcester and York).[60] By the fourteenth and fifteenth centuries, however, some towns were demolishing their walls or allowing them to fall into disrepair. This evidently happened at Lincoln, where the 'commonalty' petitioned Edward II in 1325 to the effect that the governing town council was embezzling money raised for the maintenance of the walls and allowing them to decay. It has also been identified at Shrewsbury, where excavation has shown new houses to have been built over the foundations of the old circuit about 1400. Even so, considerable sums continued to be spent on urban defences elsewhere, such as in Coventry, whose twelfth-century earthen circuit was rebuilt in stone in a long-drawn-out campaign between 1355 and 1534, and in Kent at Canterbury (Figure 40), Rochester and Sandwich, where the walls were strengthened presumably because of a heightened threat of French raiding in this part of the country. Hartlepool, which played a key role as a north-east port in provisioning troops engaged against the Scots, had new stone walls built during the fourteenth century (Figure 39). Not until the Tudor and Stuart periods was there widespread demolition of town walls, by then regarded as expensive and unnecessary barriers to urban expansion, leaving them to survive only where they were considered still to provide a useful purpose.[61]

Urban defences, whether masonry walls or earthen banks and ditches, had many functions. One they shared with more modest boundary-markers was to delineate the area within which borough jurisdiction and trading privileges applied. More prosaically, the ditches around the circuits could contain water to house fisheries or drive mills, while towers and gates could serve as lock-ups, meeting places and accommodation for town officials.[62] Most obviously, there was a role in protecting the inhabitants and possibly serving as a communal refuge for the surrounding countryside as well. This certainly applied to the circuits around pre-Conquest *burhs*: Domesday Book mentions arrangements for the maintenance of town walls which hint at this purpose, since at Chester 'for the repair of the city wall and bridge, the reeve used to call out one man to come from each hide in the county', while at Oxford

Figure 39: Hartlepool Town Wall (County Durham). Founded as a port in the late twelfth century, the town had walls added during the fourteenth-century conflict with the Scots. The Sandwell Gate, an insertion of the 1390s or later, was a postern giving fishermen direct access to the sea, and evidently reflects reduced fear of attack. (Photograph by kind permission of Castle UK.)

the obligation to repair the wall was attached to specific 'wall-dwellings' (*mansiones murales*) many of which were otherwise rent-free.[63] But it is hard to sustain an argument for a primarily defensive purpose thereafter. As we have seen, several urban defences put up in the twelfth and thirteenth centuries consisted of earthen ramparts (presumed to have had timber palisades), at a time when castles were increasingly being built or rebuilt in stone. The introduction of murage taxes from 1220 – levies on goods brought into the town, specifically to be spent on the upkeep of the walls – facilitated some great building campaigns from then onwards, but examination of surviving remains suggests that the stone walls which were built were intended to be more impressive from without than within. Southampton's fourteenth-century stone wall was less than a metre thick and both here and at Oxford surviving examples of curtain towers show them to have been little more than semi-circular projections in the line of the wall, undefended on the inside. Had town walls been seen as essential to defensibility, urban centres in the north – including Lancaster, which housed the castle from which the Duchy bearing its name was administered, Appleby, Darlington, Kendal and Hexham – would surely have sought to provide them, notwithstanding the pressure on limited corporate funds this would have entailed, and King John would have had them built around his new town of Liverpool after 1207. Instead, we find them being erected in more prosperous but less vulnerable parts of the country, and it is hard to resist the conclusion that they were being seen above all as a status symbol. The burgesses of Coventry would have been delighted to see their town depicted with walls on the Gough Map, especially since nearby Warwick was shown without any.[64]

The components of the defensive circuit which offered most opportunity to impress the approaching visitor were of course the gateways. Indeed, some towns classed as 'fortified', such as Oakham (Rutland) and Whitchurch (Shropshire) had no encircling ramparts, only protective gates. This was also the case at Warkworth, where the fortified tower controlling access from the river bridge still stands – the only example of a medieval bridge in England where fortification survives, even though this is known to have been a fairly widespread phenomenon (Figure 34).[65] In design terms, both in gate towers and in other mural towers arranged at intervals along the wall, there was a sequence not unlike that for the towers of castles. Rectangular designs were the norm in the twelfth century (as at Monk Bar and Bootham Bar, York), rounded versions prevailed for much of the thirteenth and fourteenth centuries (examples being the Strandgate, New Winchelsea, and the West Gate and mural towers at Canterbury) (Figure 40), but rectangular forms returned thereafter (as at the Bondgate, Alnwick and the South Gate, King's Lynn). While the presence of arrow-loops, portcullises and (occasionally as at Walmgate Bar, York and Beverley Gate, Hull) projecting barbicans suggest that the defensibility of gates was not entirely irrelevant, there was clearly a significant element of symbolism and display involved in their design, which tended to override purely military considerations. At York's Walmgate Bar, for example, the effectiveness of the second-floor gun ports would have been inhibited by the portcullis winding gear immediately behind them and by a severely restricted field of fire. Rather, there was a concern to show off heraldic devices, whether it was the Percy lion on the town gate at Alnwick (Northumberland) or (more usually) a combination of royal and civic coats of arms (as at York and Exeter). When the upper portions of the Tile Tower, Carlisle, were rebuilt in brick from 1483 to accommodate three new gun ports, the opportunity was taken in this border location to make a political point by displaying the white boar badge of the new king of England, Richard III. Statuettes of figures allegedly protecting the town might also appear on the gates (such as Brennus and Belinus on St John's Gate, Bristol) and there was occasional use of decorative chequerwork, as at Sandwich.[66]

Yet when all this has been said, there are dangers in dismissing a military-defensive role altogether. We have already noted the considerable investment during the fourteenth and fifteenth centuries in improving the defences of some towns in Kent, against the perceived threat of French raids, and shortly after our period, during the reign of Elizabeth I, Berwick-on-Tweed would be provided with a new stone circuit which incorporated the latest style of

Figure 40: Canterbury Town Wall. Canterbury's walls, which follow the Roman circuit, were rebuilt in the late fourteenth century, the best surviving stretch being here on the south-eastern side of the city. The open-backed D-shaped interval towers include some of the earliest examples in England of 'keyhole'-style gun ports, in place of conventional arrow-loops.

angled bastions, now accepted as the most effective defence against artillery despite their omission from the south coast forts designed under Henry VIII. Against the examples which can be cited of late-medieval gun ports which were clearly ineffective can be set those in the otherwise-meagre town walls of Southampton: first, gun ports inserted on the west side, evidently in response to French attacks on the Isle of Wight in the 1370s, which were cleverly angled so that the fields of fire from handguns overlapped, and second, the fifteenth-century Catchcold Tower, projecting further beyond the main circuit than others, which was soundly constructed to bear the weight of cannon.[67] As with castles, so with urban defences, any explanation which assumes a single purpose is almost certainly wrong.

7

The end of the medieval English landscape?

This book, like so many others, draws a line under the middle ages sometime in the first half of the sixteenth century. Here the terminal date is 1540 and if we have to stop somewhere this is as good a date as any. But why is this so? If this was a political history of England one could point to the upheavals of the 1530s which transformed the Crown's relations with the Church and enhanced the role of parliament in government. If it was a social and economic history, one might point to renewed growth in population, the breakdown of manorial ties, increasing problems of poverty and vagrancy and the burgeoning cloth trade. If it was a religious history, the Reformation would be reason enough, even if Henry VIII's 'break with Rome' (encapsulated in his styling as 'Supreme Head' without any qualifying phrase in 1534) did not of itself mean the triumph of Protestantism in England, certainly not in his own reign. In an intellectual and cultural history, one would cite the impact of the Renaissance on architectural styles and the secularisation of thought, in a military history the increasing effectiveness of gunpowder in rendering conventional fortifications obsolete. In fact, as a history of the landscape, the book takes account of all these developments, and much else besides. The forces for change with which we began – the impact of population pressure upon resources, individual and collective power to shape one's surroundings, the effects of technological advance – were all here at work, and together they would bring profound and lasting changes to the appearance of the country.

The early Tudor kings, Henry VII and Henry VIII, were successful in ending the period of rebellion and civil war dubbed the 'Wars of the Roses' and in channelling aggression towards military adventures across the Channel instead. Although claims to the French throne must have seemed increasingly unrealistic as the decades passed since Henry V's triumphs had been reversed under Henry VI, they still gave an excuse for the two Tudor Henries to invade France several times between them. At the same time, castles rapidly disappeared in large numbers as functioning features of the English landscape, partly because of changing aristocratic tastes, partly because of their indefensibility against gunpowder, and partly because many passed from private to royal hands as a result of forfeiture or failure of the line and were left thereafter to decay. By the closing years of Henry VIII's reign, John Leland was repeatedly lamenting the ruinous state of one after another. Only a limited number in the possession of the crown, whether by inheritance from previous kings or by recent acquisition, had money spent on them during the course of the sixteenth century, the rare exceptions including the Tower of London, Carisbrooke and Wark because of their strategic importance; and such as Windsor, Pontefract, Kenilworth and Fotheringhay as royal residences. By 1609, an exchequer list of over 60 castles in England and Wales described virtually all of them as 'very ruinous' or 'utterly decayed', the only ones still with a claim on the king's finances being Windsor (a residential palace), Dover and the Tower of London (key defensible structures), Chester and Ludlow (centres of local and regional government), Tutbury (a hunting lodge and stud farm) and Pontefract ('to prevent the ruin of a monument of such antiquity and goodly building').[1]

The demise of the castle was accompanied by increased activity among the nobility in the building of country houses instead, a development which meant that 'the division between a [lordly] dwelling and fortification was complete … as much an indication of the end of the middle ages as the Dissolution of the Monasteries'.[2] We have seen that some late-medieval noble residences were already more like palaces than castles, but the popularity of this type of grand house spread, with a clear emphasis on comfort and ostentatious display and no regard for fortification except occasionally as a decorative motif. From Compton Wynyates (Warwickshire) completed for Sir William Compton in 1520, through Burghley House (Northamptonshire) built for William Cecil Lord Burghley between 1577 and 1587, to Hardwick Hall (Derbyshire) begun in 1576 for Elizabeth Countess of Shrewsbury and still incomplete when she died in 1607, there is a splendid series, through which can be traced an evolution from the medieval layout of a great hall flanked by living quarters at one end and service rooms at the other towards the very different concept of a house constructed entirely as two-storey and double-pile (embracing front and back rooms), with increasing evidence of the impact of Renaissance ideas of symmetry and formal decoration.[3] Below this élite level, too, among country gentry and substantial freeholders, open halls with one or more ends increasingly gave way to dwellings which were virtually of two storeys throughout. Behind all this lay a major change in outlook, a preference for living in privacy rather than sharing the communal experience of the open hall, which was typically reduced to a single bay; the hall took on the role it still plays in twenty-first century houses as a reception area for visitors. Behind this, too, was a wish to escape the atmosphere of the hall with open hearth from which smoke meandered up to the roof, seen in the insertion of specially constructed bays or chimneys to confine the smoke, which preceded or accompanied the conversions of open halls to two storeys. Such imperatives were less pressing in the north of England, where fire hoods were already established as means to control smoke from hearths, and this must have been a factor in prolonging the importance of the central hall and delaying two-storey conversions or new build into the early seventeenth century.[4] But the essential point remains that a domestic style shared by a wide sector of society, marked by the prominence of a communal room open to the roof, was coming to an end for those who could afford it as the sixteenth century wore on.

These changes in domestic architecture came at a time when – in many respects – the nobility and gentry wielded less power over the residents on their estates than their forebears two centuries earlier. By the mid-sixteenth century, unfree peasant tenure was a memory which very occasionally provoked resentment or was seized upon as a rare financial perquisite by an opportunistic lord, but could be described by contemporary commentators as virtually extinct: and with its passing went much of the incentive to a lord to maintain an effective manorial administration. Such was the decline of the manor as a unit of local control that successive sixteenth-century parliaments entrusted increasing local government responsibilities to the parish instead, with provision for the election of officers such as surveyors of the highways and overseers of the poor.[5] The weakening of manorial ties facilitated the depopulation of weaker rural settlements – as peasants readily departed and lords were sometimes prepared to remove those who remained – a matter which by the early sixteenth century had come to be seen as a major social problem. This perception was almost certainly associated with rising population, which contributed to falling living standards and an increase in poverty and vagrancy, although a sustained increase in numbers after the downturn of the late middle ages can only be claimed with confidence once epidemic disease became far less frequent from the middle of the sixteenth century.[6] With that population increase came a greater concentration in towns than had been the case hitherto. While England's population roughly doubled between the middle of the sixteenth and the middle of the seventeenth centuries, the proportion resident in towns with populations above 10,000 more than tripled: a consequence largely of the rapid growth of London, to a lesser extent the enhanced prosperity of certain cloth-making centres such as Norwich and Exeter and a phenomenon which was to have profound effects on the countryside where the production of food for urban markets inevitably intensified, through enclosure and the adoption of new crops and methods.[7]

These developments were played out against a background of religious conflict which, to a greater or lesser extent, affected the whole of sixteenth-century Europe. But of greater long-term impact on society than the differences between Protestantism and Catholicism was the growing secularisation in outlook among artists, intellectuals and patrons, ultimately derived from late-medieval humanism. This shift has been traced in patterns of philanthropic expenditure[8] and in landscape terms is reflected in the focus of building endeavour. Major construction work on churches, old or new, fell dramatically after 1530. Langley Chapel (Shropshire) which carries dates of 1564 externally and 1601 on a roof beam and is still furnished within as befitted the Anglicanism of the 1559 prayer book, is a very rare example of a complete newly-built place of worship for the Established Church in the period between the Reformation and the Restoration of Charles II. With the dissolution of the chantries in 1547, the chapels with which they were associated also ceased to be added to existing structures, most effort going instead on remodelling the interiors of churches to meet the changing demands of successive religious settlements. While dissolved monasteries fell into ruin or were converted to dwellings or other secular purposes, post-Reformation England witnessed the erection of new town halls, new almshouses and new schools and colleges, none of which had been absent from the philanthropy of the medieval period but which now came to the fore.[9] England was still of course a religious country, and one where the impulse towards collective endeavour which had infused the middle ages was still very much alive: but religious and communal duty could now be expressed more broadly, increasingly to fund buildings which served this world as well as the next.

For all this, it is easy to forget that the sixteenth century was a time of significant continuity as well as of change. Despite the reversal of the downward trend of the post-Black Death era, the national population level remained well below that of the early fourteenth century. This meant that those rural settlements which survived, and many of the smaller urban centres too, would easily have been recognizable in terms of their street pattern and the size of the built-up area to a resident of 1300 revisiting as a time traveller three, or even four, centuries later. Despite the ink spilt about depopulating enclosure, large-scale open field arable farming persisted into the eighteenth and early nineteenth centuries over much of the midlands, and to a lesser extent in the north east and south, so that some 21% of the land surface of England, and over 50% of that of Oxfordshire, Cambridgeshire,

Northamptonshire and Huntingdonshire, still had to undergo expensive parliamentary enclosure to enable owners to get rid of what in origin was an early medieval land-sharing arrangement.[10] The almost complete absence of church building in the century after 1540 meant that towns and villages retained their medieval parish churches, which despite some rearrangement internally were scarcely altered in terms of the external appearance they presented as part of the landscape. Medieval parishes survived and were given a new lease of life as units of local secular administration, medieval roads and bridges persisted even though new arrangements had to be made for their upkeep. How far a youthful traveller through England in 1540, retracing his steps in old age in 1600, would have perceived there to be have been far-reaching changes in the English landscape during his lifetime would have depended on the route which he took: sooner or later he would have encountered ruined monasteries, decaying castles, newly built country houses, and the changing face of towns, but it would have been quite possible to journey through one village after another which retained their accustomed layouts, their old field systems and their old parish churches, features which must have appeared immutable.

Yet there was one traveller through England in the 1530s and 1540s whom we have often had occasion to quote and who was in no doubt that he was living through dramatically changing times. When John Leland composed his 'New Year's Gift' to Henry VIII towards the end of 1545, commenting on his efforts to rescue collections from monastic libraries and promising a series of books based on all he had learned on his travels around the country, he clearly saw himself as contributing to the dawn of a new age. A store of knowledge, long buried in the monasteries, would be 'brought owte of deadely darkenes to lyvely lighte', partly through Leland's own endeavours and partly through the new medium of 'enprinting'. This would refute 'the usurpid autorite of the Bishop of Rome and his complices', rid the country of 'al maner of superstition and craftely coloured doctrine of a rowte of the Romaine bishopes' and demonstrate that nowhere 'may justely be more extollid … for trewe nobilite and vertues' than the Tudor kingdom. And such had been his travels that 'there is almoste nother cape, nor bay … river or confluence of rivers … forestes, wooddes, cities, burges, castelles, principale manor placis, monasteries, and colleges but I have seene them'. He hoped to provide some historical background to the places he had visited: 'I truste so to open this wyndow, that the lighte shall be seen … and the olde glory of your renowmid Britaine to reflorisch thorough the worlde'. Time and again, as he endeavoured to explain the growth and decline of towns and the condition of castles, churches and bridges, he succeeded in his mission of enlightenment. Following his mental breakdown in 1547, he never did write up the notes he took on his journeys in the manner intended, but his observations survive and we have had occasion to be grateful for them many times in this book. With his eye for detail, coupled with a concern to explain what he saw in historical terms, John Leland was justly proud of the 'description ... of your reaulme yn writing' he had worked so hard to prepare. It gives him a fair claim to be called 'the father of English landscape history', in whose footsteps the rest of us follow.[11]

Notes

Chapter One

1 For a succinct discussion of theories surrounding this frontier, see Rowley (2001), 77–9.

2 Carpenter (2004), 13–14.

3 Hoskins (1978), 115.

4 Knowles (1950), 702–3; Knowles and Hadcock (1971), 52–82, 253–69.

5 E.g. Britnell (1997), 1, 254; but cf. Walsham (2011b), esp. 99–105, for contemporary appreciation of the Reformation era as a time of dramatic change.

6 Darby (1977), 303; Nightingale (1996), 105; Smith (2002), 181.

7 Carpenter (2004), 3–11.

8 Stringer (1993), 36–7.

9 Plucknett (1949), 5–86; Elton (1960), 2–12, 331–4, 355–6.

10 On all this, see, for example, Walton (1991), 331–2; Roe and Marx (1994); Hatcher and Bailey (2001); Langdon and Maaschaele (2006), 35–81.

11 Harke (2002), 167–68; Maddicott (1997), 7–54.

12 Darby (1977), 89, 303–9, 336–45, 364–8; all the shepherds were in Sussex, all men with gardens in Oxfordshire, all mill keepers in Derbyshire and Herefordshire.

13 *EHD*, II, 884–92; Darby (1977), 85–6; Harke (2002), 162–3.

14 Smith (2002), 177–81.

15 Postan and Titow (1958–59).

16 *EHD*, III, 265–6; Kershaw (1973); Bolton (1980), 58.

17 Bailey (1991); Mate (1991); Smith (1991).

18 Schofield and Vince (2003), 27.

19 Ormrod and Lindley (1996), 4, 22–4; Horrox (1994), 5–11.

20 Bridbury (1973); Hatcher (1994); Fox (2001), 145–67; Wrigley and Schofield (1989), 528; Smith (2002), 181–201; Schofield and Vince (2003), 232; Dodds (2008), 136–41.

21 *VCH: Leicestershire*, II, 15; Bolton (1980), 221–4; Platt (1981), 90–1.

22 *Chronicle of Battle Abbey* (1980), 8, 50–3.

23 Knowles (1950), 702; Mellows (1947), xviii–xx, xxxv.

24 See especially Creighton (2009).

25 *Records of the Templars in England in the Twelfth Century* (1935), 131, 135; Langdon, (1994), 9, fn. 23; Derry and Williams (1960), 95–6, 174–5.

26 *Walter of Henley and other Treatises on Estate Management and Accounting* (1971), 319; Langdon (1982); Langdon (1984); Harrison (1992); Cooper (2006), 22–4.

27 Campbell (1983); Thirsk (1997), 17.

28 Muir (2000), xv; Muir (2007), xi.

29 Cantor (1982), 219.

Chapter Two

1 *Henry of Huntingdon, Historia Anglorum* (1996), 10–11.

2 Higham (2004), 68.

3 Carpenter (2004), 410–11; cf. Phythian-Adams (1992), which traces the evolution of W. G. Hoskins's thinking on the significance of the 'yeoman' class of substantial free peasants.

4 *Aelfric's Colloquy* (1978), 20–1; the translation of this late tenth- or early eleventh-century representation of a 'ploughman's voice' is by A. E. Watkins.

5 Gray (1915), 64; Campbell (1981), 112. Convenient summaries of the main features of the 'midland system' are to be found in e.g. Fox (1981), Rowley (1982), Astill (1988) and Hall (1995), 8–35.

6 Roberts and Wrathmell (2002), 123–4, where it is also argued that three-field systems were a later development, in evidence only from the late twelfth century onwards. This is consistent with the findings of Hall (1995), 53–63, where no examples of three-field arrangements are cited earlier than the thirteenth century.

7 Roberts and Wrathmell (2003); Rippon (2008), 3.

8 *Description of England by William Harrison* (1968), 199, 217. For John Leland's use of the term 'champion' to point up the contrast with enclosed land, see e.g. *Itinerary of Leland*, I, 151, 156 (on Somerset), IV, 17–19 (on Nottinghamshire). However, Homans (1942), 13, 419, traces the term 'champion' in this sense to a Derbyshire court-roll of 1310.

9 Oosthuizen (2011); cf. Rippon (2008), 23–6, 147, 194 on Somerset and Norfolk.

10 Baker and Butlin (1973), 328, 332, 362, 404, 423–4; Rippon (2008), 153–64.

11 Baker and Butlin (1973), 393–419; Roberts and Wrathmell, (2002), 158–9. Roberts and Wrathmell (2003) *passim* emphasize that some form of farming in open strips – often in association with farming in enclosed fields – was to be found in virtually all the local regions into which the country can be subdivided.

12 *EHD*, I, 403, 405, 436.

13 Roberts and Wrathmell (2002), 95–6, 103–4, 111.

14 Rippon (2002); Oosthuizen (2005).

15 Astill (1988), 77–8; Taylor and Fowler (1978), 159–62; Harrison (2002); Oosthuizen (2003); Gerrard and Aston (2007), 44–55, 973–4.

16 Rippon (2008), 153–67.

17 Hall (1982), 42–55; Hall (1995), 131–6; Harvey (1983); Roberts and Wrathmell, (2003), 53; Roberts (2008), 99–101. For a warning against concluding that shorter strips were invariably preceded by longer ones, see Jones and Page (2006), 94.

18 For the geographical distribution of partible inheritance customs, see Roberts and Wrathmell (2002), 178, Fig. 7.1.

19 Roberts and Wrathmell, (2002), 143; Campbell (1981), 113–17.

20 Rippon, Fyfe and Brown (2006).

21 Fox (1981), esp. 98–102; Lewis, Mitchell-Fox and Dyer (1997), 90–5; Bassett (1997); Rippon (2008), 15, 138–200.

22 Fox (1991), 303–23; Fyfe (2004); Herring (2006), 62, 69, 96–7; Rippon (2008), 130–5.

23 Rippon (2008), 136–7, 198–200, 255–60.

24 Rippon (2008), 64–95; Higham (2004), 66; Gerrard and Aston (2007), 979.

25 Maitland (1889), 161–4, 172; Wake (1922); Lewis, Mitchell-Fox and Dyer (1997), 177–9; Harvey (1989); Carpenter (2004), 413–14.

26 Hilton (1975), 66–7.

27 Roberts and Wrathmell (2002), 128–33, 139; Roberts (1987), 84, 172–5, 212–13; Stewart-Brown (1916); Higham, (2004), 63–4; Booth (1981), 127–8.

28 Evans (1956), based on oral evidence from Blaxhall, Suffolk.

29 Fox (1981), 89; Gerrard and Aston (2007), 74–101, 972–4; Oosthuizen (2010).

30 Bishop (1954), esp. 30–2; Baker and Butlin (1973), 41–92, 337; Hall (1982); Muir and Muir (1989), 41–2; Sylvester (1958).

31 Campbell (1983); Baker and Butlin (1973), 261; Beckett (1989), 22; quotation from Oosthuizen (2011), 22.

32 Page (1934), 162; Fox (1981), 94–8; Lewis, Mitchell-Fox and Dyer (1997), 148, 178.

33 *VCH Oxfordshire*, II, 171; Gray (1915), 80; Hall (1995), 55–62.

34 Baker and Butlin (1973), 260.

35 *Registrum Antiquissimum of the Cathedral Church of Lincoln*, IV (1937), 266. On regular distributions of strips, see e.g. Roberts (2008), 81–7, 248–50.

36 Ault (1972), 83, 88; Dale (1950), 46–7.

37 Kosminsky (1956), 197–255.

38 Cambridge University Library: EDR/G/3/27, f. 60.

39 Dyer (1988), 19; Lennard (1959), 393; Reeves and Williamson (2000); Taylor (2000a); Hey (2000); Everitt (2000).

40 Dyer (2006); White (2012).

41 Hall (2005), 12, 22–3.

42 Ault (1972), 106–7, 131, 136; Cheshire Record Office: DLE 47.

43 Baum (1963), 28.

44 Beresford (1948); Taylor (1975), 78–88; Hooke (1991); Hall (1995), 36–9; Williamson, (2003), 148–55. For a variant reverse-J course to ridges in Cornwall, and the implications of this for the design of the plough, see Herring (2006), 69.

45 Palin (1844) 62–3; Kerridge (1951); Williams (1997).

46 On the significance of extensive ridge and furrow in an area of dispersed settlement, see Croft and Mynard (1993), 131–41.

47 Beresford and St Joseph (1979), 133–4; Muir and Muir (1989), 50–3, 79–81; White (1995); cf. Herring (2006), 60.

48 Taylor (1973), 96–8 and plate 6; Beresford (1979), 150–2 by P. F. Brandon; Taylor (1974), 30, 61, 67, 77; Herring (2006), 50.

49 Cameron, Delano-Smith and Wood (1980); Wheeler and Wood (1987); Beckett (1989), esp. 273–4, 316–23.

50 Rackham (1986), 337.

51 Darby (1977), 149–59; Rackham (1986), 335–6.

52 Galbraith (1974), 37–9; Darby (1977), 137–48; *Little Domesday: Norfolk* (2000), I, fos. 110v–111v.

53 *Domesday Book: Cheshire*, (1978), 264c; White (1988), 11–12. There was communal grazing on this meadow, with cattle being allowed in on the Monday after the second Sunday in August, until the 1960s.

54 Darby (1971), 239–40.

55 Darby and Terrett (1954), 90–1, 140, 294–6; Darby (1971), 129–30, 183–4; cf. Rackham (1986), 334–5.

56 Darby (1977), 142–6.

57 Greig (1988), 120; Muir and Muir (1989), 187; *Eynsham Cartulary* (1908), 5; Rodwell and Rodwell (1985), 182–3.

58 Rackham (1986), 334–7.

59 *Chronicle of Battle Abbey* (1980), 86–7; Searle (1974), 38–9.

60 Hall (1995), 96–9, 294.

61 Dyer (2006), 25–9; on the date of the Assize of *Novel Disseisin*, see White (2000), 205–12, 216–18.

62 Bailey (1989); Turner (2006), 188.

63 Rackham (1986), 316; Hey (2000), 196.

64 Winchester (1987), 20, 92–5, 117; on the word *skali*, cf. below, Chapter 3, p. 78.

65 Winchester (1987), 6, 139–43; Hey (2000), 196; Winchester (2003).

66 *Accounts of the Manor and Hundred of Macclesfield, Cheshire, Michaelmas 1361 to Michaelmas 1362* (2003), xxiv–lxiv.

67 Hey (2000), 194–6.

68 Beresford and St Joseph (1979), 159; Platt, (1969), 67–8, 98.

69 Hey (2000), 198; Winchester (1987), 51.

70 Darby (1940), 128–40.

71 Cracknell (1959); Rackham (1986), 380–1; Reeves and Williamson (2000); Barber and Priestley-Bell (2008), 19.

72 Rackham (1986), 375–82; Taylor (2000a), 175.

73 Ravensdale (1974), 14–16, 100–1; Taylor (1973), 147.

74 Godwin (1978), 145–63; Darby (1940), 22–37; Page (1934), 416.

75 Ravensdale (1974), 48–51, 151–2.

76 Williamson (1997); Taylor (2000a), 174–8.

77 Thirsk, (1953), with quotation from Arthur Young in 1799 on p. 19.

78 Stone (2005), 43–5.

79 Darby (1940), 149–68; Darby (1956), 1–5.

80 Hallam (1965), 4–17, 40–51, 71–85; Darby (1940), 24–6, 152, 159–60, 167–8; Rackham (1986), 392–3; Darby (1956), 227–31 and plate 31.

81 Rackham (1986), 75–8; Short (2000), 133.

82 *Dialogus de Scaccario* (1983), 56–61.

83 Darby (1977), 189; *PR 2 Hen.II*, 27, 30; *PR 9 Hen.II*, 36, etc.

84 Short (2000), 133; Rackham (1990), 55; Peterken (1996), 326–7.

85 Pollard, Hooper and Moore (1974), 28–31, 86–95; Peterken (1996), 17–18; Rackham (1990), 113, 132, 192.

86 Peterken (1993), 12, 44, 51–5, 310–15; Marren (1992), 10–22, 137; Rackham (1980), 1–2, though his definition of the threshold for 'ancient woodland' as 1700 (rather than 1600) is not now generally followed.

87 Rackham (1990), 70–5; Rackham (1975), esp. 5–168. The cutting down of trees for coppicing or pollarding should not be confused with the 'wasting' of woods at fn. 82, above.

88 Peterken (1993), 12–17; Peterken (1996), 784–8; Rackham (1980), 175–6.

89 Peterken (1993), 12–17.

90 Rackham (1980), 175–80.

91 *ASC E* 1086 (for 1087) in *Anglo-Saxon Chronicle* (1953), 221; Liddiard (2003), 5–6.

92 *EHD*, II, 418–20.

93 Holt (1965), 52–5, 328–9, 359–62; Rowley (1986), 121–3.

94 *VCH Cheshire*, II, 178 (for the enclosure of Delamere Forest from 1813); Foot (2010), 30–1.

95 Bond (1997), 37–41.

96 Liddiard (2003a); Darby (1977), 201–7.

97 Cantor (1983), 123; Mileson (2009), 76.

98 Sykes (2007); Birrell (1992). *Henry of Huntingdon, Historia Anglorum* (1996), 20–1, describes Salisbury (close to the New Forest and also the new royal park of Clarendon) as noted for 'wild game', which supports Birrell's claim that poaching was rife.

99 Bond (1997); Roberts (1997), 9–10; Bond (1994), 139; Birrell (1992), 123–4; Creighton (2009), 127–8; Rowe (2007), 133–4; Beresford (1957), 97–8, 231–5.

100 Bettey (2000), 37; Hoppitt (2007), 153.

101 Beresford (1957), 195–7; Moorhouse (2007), 108 (cf. Fig. 65, although this enclosure is of 1560–61).

102 Richardson (2007), 30–7; Winchester (2007), 175; Rackham (1986), 125–7, where it is estimated that about 50% of all parks were compartmentalized for management purposes.

103 Moorhouse (2007), 123–4; Faull and Moorhouse (1981), III, 780.

104 *Chronicle of Jocelin of Brakelond* (1949), 28; Mileson (2009), 28–32; Creighton (2009), 152–3; Sykes (2007), 52–5.

105 *Henry of Huntingdon, Historia Anglorum* (1996), 470–1; *William of Malmesbury, Gesta Regum Anglorum* (1998–99) I, 740, II, 372–3; Green (2005), 5.

106 Richardson (2007); Beaumont-James and Gerrard (2007); Richardson (2005), 130–2; Taylor (2000b), 42; Mileson (2009), 86–91.

107 *Dialogus de Scaccario* (1983), 60; *PR 2 Hen.II*, 36, 56–7 (£15 spent on the 'king's houses' at Woodstock; £5. 6s. 8d and £4. 7s. 0d. spent on those at Clarendon).

108 *Register of Edward the Black Prince, Part Three: Palatinate of Chester, 1351–65* (1932), 273; Austin, Daggett and Walker (1980); cf. Bond (1997), 31.

109 Derbyshire (2010).

110 Williamson, (2006), 6–13; the earliest documentary reference to coneys in England dates to 1135.

111 Bailey (1988); Dyer (1989), 155–56; *EHD*, V, 203.

112 Bailey (1988), 7–8; Williamson (2006), 14–66; Linehan (1966).

113 Langdon (1994), 31, fn. 81.

114 Miller and Hatcher (1978), 12–13; Darby (1977), 270–5; Langdon (1994); *VCH Cambridgeshire*, I, 357–9; *Glanvill, Tractatus de Legibus* (1965), 168–9.

115 *Geoffrey Chaucer: The Canterbury Tales, a Verse Translation* (2008), 15.

116 *Book of Margery Kempe* (1940), 9–11; Watts (2002), 116; Holt (1988), 166–70.

117 Holt (1988), 133–7.

118 Hoskins (1963), 126, with suggested reinterpretation in Everson and Brown (2010), 55.

119 Watts (2002), 84–9.

120 Langdon (1994), 10–11.

121 *Chronicle of Jocelin of Brakelond* (1949), 59–60; Holt (1988), 171–5.

122 Salmon (1941), 88–99.

123 Taylor (1974), 57, 119.

124 Salmon (1941), 100 and plate xiii; Salmon (1966); Watts (2002), 111–13.

125 Holt (1988), 77–8, 86–7.

Chapter Three

1 *Description of England by William Harrison* (1968), 217.

2 Jones and Page, (2006), 1–2; cf. Lewis, Mitchell-Fox and Dyer (1997), 5, which has 'most' villages falling 'between … 60 and 6 households', with hamlets below that minimum; Jones (2010).

3 Jones and Page (2006), 3–5; Rippon (2008), 3; Roberts and Wrathmell (2003), 3, 11–12. For the controversy generated by the *Atlas* and its companion volume, *Region and Place*, see e.g. Taylor (2007) and Williamson (2007).

4 Oosthuizen (2010).

5 Astill (1988), 37; cf. Taylor (1983), 125.

6 Taylor (1983), 116–22; Lewis, Mitchell-Fox and Dyer (1997), 79–81.

7 Fox (1981), 89; Lewis, Mitchell-Fox and Dyer (1997), 82; Jones and Page (2006), 87–8; Taylor (1977); Williams and White (1988), 195.

8 Williamson (2003), 118–22, 160–196; Roberts and Wrathmell (2003), 55–6, 64.

9 Jones and Page (2006), 95–6; Rippon (2008), 198.

10 Brown and Foard (1998); Lewis, Mitchell-Fox and Dyer (1997), 83–95.

11 Blair (2005), 395, 411–17; Hooke (1985), 70–1.

12 Turner (2006), 98.

13 Darby (1977), 90–132, 338; Roberts and Wrathmell (2003), 56.

14 Rippon (2008), 250–68.

15 Hoskins (1988), 164–5; Barnwell and Giles (1997), 146–54.

16 Beresford (1975), 7–9, 19–23; Beresford (1987); Taylor (1983), 122–3; Brown and Foard (1998); Mortimer (2000).

17 Gerrard and Aston (2007), 72–5, 974–8; cf. Beresford (2009), 57–8, 229–30 and Oosthuizen (2010), 118–19.

18 *Chronicle of Battle Abbey* (1980), 48–67, 128–9 (quotations from pp. 63–5); Searle (1974), 23–4, 36–8; above, Chapter 2, p. 22.

19 Taylor (1983), 126–8; Jones and Page (2006), 94–5; above, Chapter 2, p. 20; quotation from Oosthuizen (2010), 131.

20 Roberts and Wrathmell (2003), 10; Brown and Taylor (1989); Roberts and Wrathmell, 86–9.

21 Jones and Page (2006), 85–9; *VCH Buckinghamshire*, I, 238, 250, 259.

22 Wade-Martins (1980); Taylor (2003), 128–9; Williamson (2003), 160–79; Rippon (2008), 182–9 (quotation on p.188); cf. for Suffolk, Warner (1987), e.g. 13–18, 44–5.

23 Bird (2007), 114–40; White (1995); Phillips and Phillips (2002), 52–3; Higham (2004), 135.

24 Sheppard (1974); Sheppard (1976); Roberts (1987), 172–3; Taylor (1983), 133–8; Roberts and Wrathmell (2002), 86–7, 112–14.

25 Winchester (1993), 12–17; Blair (1991), 58–9.

26 Roberts and Wrathmell (2002), 101–3, 108–11, where other examples are cited; Wade-Martins (1980), 49–52.

27 Auduoy and Chapman (2009), 28–30, 52–4; quotation from Taylor (1983), 146–7.

28 Roberts and Wrathmell (2002), 86–7.

29 Mortimer (2000), 6, 20–1; Taylor (1983), 151–9; Ravensdale (1974), 121–3; Rowley and Wood (1982), 15; cf. for reverse-S house-plots at Caldecote (Hertfordshire) Beresford (2009), 57–8, 279–80.

30 Taylor (1983), 175–83; Williamson (1986); Rippon (2008), 122–4, 149–79.

31 Rodwell and Rodwell (1985, 1993), I, 183–5, II, 176.

32 Rippon (2008), 124–31, 179–81.

33 Hallam (1981), 32–3, where elements including *cot, feld, thorp, wald, wic, wordig* and *wudu* are cited; cf. Miller and Hatcher (1978), 35.

34 Harley (1958); Roberts (1968); Dyer (1991), esp. 27–51.

35 Hallam (1965), 12–14, 31–2; Taylor (1983), 184–5.

36 *Earldom of Gloucester Charters* (1973), 65–6; Hoskins and Finberg (1952), 78–82; Beresford and St Joseph (1979), 95–6; Linehan (1966), 119, 133–4; *Registrum Antiquissimum of the Cathedral Church of Lincoln* II (1933), 79–82.

37 Gardiner (1997), 64–7.

38 Darby (1977), 263–5; Dyer (2003), 168–70; Hodgkinson (2008), 52–3; Blanchard (1972); Blanchard (1974); Hatcher (1974); Stanier (2000), 83.

39 Beresford and St Joseph (1979), 262–5; Hallam (1965), 5–6, 40–1, 77–8; Fielding and Fielding (2006), 13–16.

40 Stanier (2000), 63–7, 76–84; Beresford and St Joseph (1979), 146–7, 254–5; Rowley (1978), 114.

41 The extensive literature on this subject, with indications of sites which may be visited, includes Galloway (1992), 1–27; Beresford and St Joseph (1979), 256–7; Hayman (2005), e.g. 11–17, 20–1; Hodgkinson (2008), e.g. 54, 136–7; Faull and Moorhouse (1981), III, 775–86; Meredith (2006), 61–8; Gerrard (2000), e.g. 47–55, 130, 140–8, with grid references to major sites; Newman (1998); Newman, (2006); Hatcher (1970), e.g. 188; Preston-Jones and Rose (1986); Shaw (2009), e.g. 232.

42 *VCH Durham*, I, 341; Gerrard (2000), 47–9 and plates 2, 3; Rippon, Claughton and Smart (2009), 49.

43 Hodgkinson (2008), 97; Faull and Moorhouse, (1981), III, 776; Geddes (1991), 169; Winchester (2000), 13.

44 Bolton (1980), 155–6; Netherton and Owen-Crocker (2005), 102.

45 Keene (1990), 203–8; Walton (1991); *Records of the Templars* (1935), 50; Carus-Wilson (1954); Bolton (1980), 157–8.

46 Hilton (1957), 102; Watts (2002), 115; *VCH Berkshire*, IV, 219–20.

47 Hatcher (1994), 16–18, 29–30.

48 Schofield (1965); White (2008).

49 Hurst (2005), 54, 108; Watson (1932), 265, 295, 323; Carus-Wilson (1962), 151– 67; Beresford and St Joseph (1979), 266–9; *VCH Suffolk*, II, 254–70.

50 Winchester (1987), 18, 120–1; Meredith (2006), 61–8. Danby had 50 people assessed to the lay subsidy of 1301, compared to 96 at Whitby: Waites, (1997), 50.

51 *Domesday Book: Cheshire* (1978), 268a–268b; Darby (1977), 260–5; Fielding and Fielding (2006), 6–7, 21–2.

52 Blanchard (1974), esp. 63, 73–4.

53 Blanchard (2001), II, 583–620, 673–81; *RRAN* III, no. 258; Robert de Torigni in *Chronicles of the Reigns of Stephen, Henry II and Richard I*, IV (1889), 123; Blanchard (1996). Robert de Torigni assigns significant new discoveries to the year 1133, but the silver mines of Carlisle were already yielding £45 per annum to the crown in 1130 (*PR 31 Hen.I*, 142).

54 Pearce (1995), 1–7; Shaw (2009), 17–18.

55 Rippon, Claughton and Smart (2009), 48–50, 53–63, 75–84, 109–20, 141–59 (quotation on p. 158).

56 Beresford (1988), 405–6; *Cornwall Industrial Settlements Initiative: Looe* (2002), 9, 30–31.

57 Fox (2001), 12, 122–38.

58 Taylor (1983), 187–91; Fox (2001), 145–9, 177–83; cf. above, Chapter 2, p. 34.

59 Aberg (1978), 1–4, 21–8, 46–55; Le Patourel (1973), esp. 1–22.

60 Astill (1988), 44–7; quotation from Fox (2001), 134.

61 Astill (1988), 39–50; Barber and Priestley-Bell (2008), 302.

62 Astill (1988), 39–58. For descriptions of some of these features, see e.g. Beresford (1975), 14–15, 22, 25, 28, 30, 35, 44, and plate Va (water pits); Beresford (2009), 88 (pits remaining from the digging of gault clay from which to make cob walls); Browning and Higgins (2003), 72 (cobbled standing area).

63 Beresford (1977); Grenville (1997) 95–8; Gardiner (2000).

64 *Bede: A History of the English Church and People* (1968), 127; *Langland, Piers Plowman* (1959), 153; see also Girouard (1978), 30; Grenville (1997), 66, 107.

65 Mercer (1975), 19–20.

66 Beresford and Hurst (1976), esp. 122–6, 141–4; Beresford and Hurst (1990), 44–51.

67 Jones and Page (2006), 180–5.

68 Beresford (1987), 10–12, 29–84; Blair (1993); Grenville (1997), 66–88, 95; Jones and Smith (1958).

69 Cherry (1989); Wood (1965), 41, 71–5, 133; Gardiner (2000), 170–4.

70 Giles (1986), 195, 212; Beresford (1974); Jones (1975–76).

71 Beresford and Hurst (1971), 104–25.

72 Beresford and Hurst (1990), 39–41; Wrathmell (1989); Smith (2010), 77–80.

73 Higham (2000), 98; Higham (2004), 136–7; Ivens, Busby and Shepard (1995).

74 Dyer (1986); Wrathmell (1989), 253–7

75 Higham (2000), 101; Higham (2004), 133–7.

76 Dyer (1986), 23–4, 27–34; Phelps-Brown and Hopkins (1962), 177.

77 Mercer (1975), 8–22; Grenville (1997), 151–6; Gerrard and Aston (2007), 291–3.

78 Beresford (1975), 13–18; Gardiner (2000), 164–7.

79 Beresford (1975), 26, 28; Mercer (1975), 14–16, 28–44; cf. below, Chapter 7.

80 Evans and Jarrett (1987); Evans, Jarrett and Wrathmell (1988); Hinton (2010); Williamson (2010).

81 Batey (1968); Broad (2010).

82 Beresford (1957), 116–23; Hutchings (1989). But see also Everson and Brown (2010) for the possibility that some features on deserted settlement sites may be post-medieval.

83 Roberts and Wrathmell (2003), 28; Dyer (1982); Jones (2010), 19–23.

84 Aston (1989), 114; Miles and Rowley (1976); Dyer (1982), 23; Beresford and St Joseph (1979), 119–21.

85 Mew (2000); Hallam (1965), 127; Jones, (2010), 21.

86 Mileson (2009), 162–3.

87 *Walter Map, De Nugis Curialium* (1983), xliii–xliv, 92–5; Donkin (1978), 39–51.

88 Rous (1745), 122–4; *EHD*, IV, 1014–16.

89 *EHD*, V, 926, 933.

90 *Utopia by Sir Thomas More, translated by Ralph Robynson 1556* (1999), 101.

91 Dyer (2000); Dyer (2010), 43–4.

92 Dyer (1982), 33; Dyer (2010), 38–42.

93 Dyer (1982), 24–5; Hilton and Rahtz (1966).

94 Dyer (2010), 32–7.

95 Hoskins (1963), 115–30; *EHD*, V, 933.

96 Roberts and Wrathmell (2002), 8, 11; Rowley and Wood (1982), 7, 52; Jones, (2010), 16–18.

97 Dyer (1989), 56–7.

98 Thorpe (1962), 55–9; *EHD*, V, 933–5; Beresford and Hurst (1971), 57.

Chapter Four

1 Rigby (2010).

2 Schofield and Vince (2003), 152–3; Griffiths (2007), 220–5.

3 Holt and Rosser (1990), 3–6.

4 Goddard (2011), 6–8.

5 Reynolds (1977), ix–x; Palliser (2000), 5; Dyer (2003), 98, 102–4.

6 Darby (1977), 289–309, 318–19, 364–70 (the total of 112 boroughs includes Rhuddlan in North Wales); Laughton and Dyer (1999), 25.

7 Darby (1977), 293, 302–09, 364–8.

8 Miller and Hatcher (1995), 257–8.

9 Darby (1977), 293–5; *Lincolnshire Domesday and Lindsey Survey* (1924), 7, 364–8; below, Chapter 6, p. 190.

10 Haslam (2010), 52–4.

11 Haslam (2010), 13–18.

12 Reynolds (1977), 16–42; Miller and Hatcher (1995), 18–25; Haslam (2010), 19–52; Fleming (2011), 241–68.

13 In the 1156 pipe roll, London is shown against an assessment for *auxilium* of £120, Lincoln £60, York £40, Norwich £33, 6s. 8d., the others at sums between £20 and £15 (*PR 2 Hen.II, passim*), although the crown also extracted further payments from the leading towns, apparently regarding the assessments as outdated; cf. White (2000), 153–4. For the rankings of towns in various assessments of the twelfth to sixteenth centuries, see Palliser (2000), 752–70 (by A. Dyer).

14 Reynolds (1977), 56–62; White (2000), 131.

15 *Henry of Huntingdon, Historia Anglorum* (1996), 20–1; *Gesta Stephani* (1976), 58–9; *EHD*, III, 881–4.

16 Dyer (2003), 88; Miller and Hatcher (1995), 145–55; Dyer (2002).

17 *RRAN*, III, nos. 172, 293, 384–5, 456; cf. no. 597 from Empress Matilda.

18 Schofield and Vince (2003), 26–7; Britnell (1996), 81–2, 158–60; Coates (1965).

19 *Bracton: De Legibus et Consuetudinibus Angliae* III (1940), 198–9; Gardiner (1997), 71.

20 Farmer (2000), 353; Dyer (1996); *English Lawsuits from William I to Richard I* (1990– 91), II, 382–4.

21 Britnell (1981), 212; *Register of Edward the Black Prince, Part Three* (1932), 133; *Registrum Simonis Langham* (1956), 193–4; Dymond (1999).

22 *RRAN*, III, nos. 914, 952.

23 Gurnham (2009), 65; *Charters of the Anglo-Norman Earls of Chester* (1988), 23, 33–4; Jones, Stocker and Vince (2003), 227.

24 *Liber Memorandorum Ecclesie de Bernewelle* (1907), xxvii, 87; *VCH Cambridgeshire*, III, 11; *English Lawsuits from William I to Richard I* (1990–91), II, 647–8.

25 Lilley, Lloyd and Campbell (2009), 18.

26 Masschaele (1993); Edwards and Hindle (1991); Schofield and Vince (2003), 35.

27 Laughton and Dyer (1999), 39; Oosthuizen (1993); *VCH Cambridgeshire*, X, 420–7; Hatcher and Bailey (2001), 146–7.

28 *Henry of Huntingdon, Historia Anglorum* (1996), 22–5; Cooper (2000).

29 Harrison (2004), 47–8; Hindle (1998), 31–5; Millea (2007); Lilley, Lloyd and Campbell (2009).

30 Taylor (1979), 120–5; Bird (2007), 200–11.

31 Harrison (2004), 47–8.

32 Walsham (2011a), 77.

33 Cooper (2006), 145–6; Harrison (2004), 44–9, 57, 223; Hindle (1998), esp. 20; Morriss, (2005), esp. 35–42; Albert (1972), 202; Farmer (2000), 352–7.

34 *Itinerary of Leland*, I, 11, 261; Harrison (2004), 94, 97.

35 Cooper (2006), 10–23, 46–59.

36 Cooper (2006), 95; Harrison (2004), 110–12; Harrison, McKeague and Watson (2011), 45–6.

37 *EHD*, IV, 724–5.

38 *VCH Surrey*, III, 420.

39 Salter (1920), 154, 177; Cooper (2006), 51–2; Harrison (2004), 201– 2.

40 Webb and Webb (1913), 87–9.

41 Cook (1998), 15–17; Harrison (2004), 86, 102–9, 136–8; Schofield and Vince (2003), 35.

42 Harrison (2004), 110–45 and plate 22 for quotation; Cook (1998), 31–5.

43 *EHD*, II, 1031–2, 1042–3.

44 Reynolds (1977), 98–139, 171–81; Palliser, Slater and Dennison (2000), 178.

45 West (1983), 103–17; Swanson (1999), 67–96; *VCH Leicestershire*, IV, 1–30; Dyer (2003), 104.

46 Beresford (1988), v–vii (Falmouth omitted from Beresford's total because founded in 1613), 637–41; Butler (1976), 32.

47 Reynolds (1977), 52–6.

48 Britnell (1996), 58; Dyer (2003), 91–2.

49 Davison (1967); Clarke, Pearson, Mate and Parfitt (2010), 23–5.

50 Conzen (1968), 122–7; Goddard (2011), 31; quotation from Roberts (2008), 121.

51 Beresford (1988), 466, 517.

52 Beresford (1988), 429, 476, 502, 505; Roberts (2008), 119.

53 *Itinerary of Leland*, II, 88; Aston and Bond (1976), 79–81; Goddard (2011); Beresford (1988), 479; Varey (2008), 33–4.

54 *Chronicle of Battle Abbey* (1980), 7–8, 50–9; Beresford (1988), 394, 452–3, 462–5, 504.

55 Beresford (1988), 447–9, 457–9, 461, 496–8, 511–12, 515–16; Stewart-Brown (1916), 25–30; *Chronicon Monasterii de Melsa*, II (1867), 192.

56 Aston and Bond (1976), 86–97; Beresford (1988), 441, 456, 468–9, 477–8, 500; Palliser, Slater and Dennison (2000), 167–9; Rodwell (1975), 85–92, 147–54.

57 *English Lawsuits from William I to Richard I* (1990–91), II, 662–4.

58 Stenton (1934), 28; Platt, (1976a), 45–8.

59 *William Worcestre: the Topography of Medieval Bristol* (2000), viii, 83 (for conversion of steps to feet), 11, 21, 33, 79, 81, etc.; Platt (1976b), 53; Platt (1976a), 45, 50.

60 Inderwick (1882), 153–219; Beresford (1988), 14–28, 497–8; Butler (1976), 35.

61 Beresford (1988), 150–1, 433, 479; Butler (1976), 32–8 (accepting Butler's reservations about two cases in Beresford's list, originally published in 1967).

62 Beresford (1988), 157; *ASC E*, 1137, in *Anglo-Saxon Chronicle* (1953), 265. Speed's early seventeenth-century street plan of Peterborough, showing a rectilinear market place with streets parallel and at right-angles to it immediately outside the west gate of the cathedral (formerly abbey) precincts is reproduced in Mellows (1939), frontispiece.

63 Butler (1976), 40, 45.

64 Beresford (1988), 435, 452–3, 457–9 (quotation, p. 458), 466–7, 473–4, 490, 492, 523–6; Butler (1976), 37, 39–45; *Itinerary of Leland*, II, 113–14 (where the fact that the parish church lies a mile outside the town is rightly taken to indicate that Uxbridge 'is no very olde towne').

65 Slater (1981); Baker (2010), 170.

66 Rodwell (1975), 19; Quiney (2003), 87; Aston and Bond (1976), 98–9; Slater (1981).

67 Jones, Stocker and Vince (2003), 204; Clarke, Pearson, Mate and Parfitt (2010), 41, 50–1.

68 Schofield and Vince (2003), 68–72.

69 Jones, Stocker and Vince (2003), 186, 226, 242–5, 262; Baker (2002), 15–18, 206–26; Keene (1976).

70 Schofield and Vince (2003), 67, 92–4.

71 *London Assize of Nuisance* (1973), ix–xxxiv, 45; Pallister, Slater and Dennison (2000), 178, for the provision of this 'necessary house' on Queenhithe at royal expense as early as the twelfth century.

72 Quiney (2003), 90, 372, 386; Palliser, Slater and Dennison (2000), 184.

73 Quiney (2003), 161–63, 190–8.

74 Quiney (2003), 177–80; Platt (1976a), 54–9. The Norman House in Lincoln was formerly known as 'Aaron the Jew's House' but this prominent resident is now known to have lived elsewhere; however the Jew's House has been shown to have been occupied by a Jewess called Balaset in the late thirteenth century.

75 Quiney (2003), 185–6, 199–241; Grenville (1997), 179. The Bromsgrove house has been re-erected at Avoncroft Museum, Stoke Prior.

76 Quiney (2003), 192, 201–2, 207–8, 231; Bott (1993), 16–20.

77 Platt (1976a), 59–64; Grenville (1997), 181–9; Quiney (2003), 235–54; Brown (1999), esp. 164, 183–4; Baker (2010),173–4.

78 Schofield and Stell (2000), 371.

79 Brown (1999), esp. 1–13, 55–62; Grenville (1997), 180–1; Baker (2010), 76–80, 170.

80 Grenville (1997), 190–2; Schofield (2003), 55; Quiney (2003), 265–6.

81 Platt (1976a), 68–9; Dalwood and Edwards (2004), 68–73; Schofield (2003), 46, 53; Clarke, Pearson, Mate and Parfitt (2010), 180.

82 Aston and Bond (1976), 106–7; Platt (1976a), 148–56; Beresford (1988), 463–4, 479; *Itinerary of Leland*, II, 88.

83 Schofield and Vince (2003), 63–4; Parker (1971), 143–5; Newman and Pevsner (2006), 383–4; Cherry and Pevsner (2002), 401–2, 423; Pevsner and Neave (2005), 48, 194–5, 210, 216–19, 228–9.

84 Britnell (1997), 160; *Itinerary of Leland*, I, 172, V, 44; Lee (2010), 24.

85 Palliser (2000), 758–63 (by A. Dyer), based on multipliers of 1.9 for 1377 and 7.0 for 1524–25, although as is pointed out some figures may be defective.

86 *Itinerary of Leland*, I, 47, IV, 114.

87 Schofield and Stell (2000), 372, 393; Dobson (2000), 277.

88 Phythian-Adams (1979), esp. 35–6, 63, 198, 283; *Itinerary of Leland*, II, 108; *Records of the City of Norwich* (1906–10), II, 105, 122.

89 Palliser (2000), 758–63, where (using A. Dyer's maximum suggested multipliers of 7 and 1.9, an increase for Canterbury of c. 4890 to c. 5490 is implied; Britnell (1986), 202, 266.

90 Hare (2009); Dyer (2003), 111; Baker (2010), 161.

91 Beresford (1988), 290–315, 463–5, 475, 513–14; *Chronicon Monasterii de Melsa*, III (1868), 16, 79.

92 Dobson (2000), 318, 332; Palliser (2000), 755–67; for Lavenham's protest in 1525, see e.g. Phythian-Adams (1979), 63.

93 *Itinerary of Leland*, I, 129, IV, 16, V, 41; Lee (2010), 12–14, 24.

94 Bailey (1993).

95 Schofield and Stell (2000), 377; Palliser, Slater and Dennison (2000), 178; *VCH Staffordshire*, XIV, 15; Dyer (2003), 113; Phythian-Adams (1979), 61–2.

Chapter Five

1 E.g. Barlow (1983), 110–18 (on William Rufus's attitude to Christianity) and Blair (2005), 476–89, Walsham (2011), 18–79 (on popular blendings of folklore with religious observance).

2 Lawrence (1989), 1–11; Devlin (1984).

3 Warren (1985), 8, 37, where a distinction is drawn between hermits who 'were free to move about' and anchorites who 'took vows of permanent stability'; McEvoy (2011).

4 *The Rule of St Benedict* (1984), 44, 66, 84.

5 Knowles and Hadcock (1971), 52–8, 253–5.

6 Knowles (1950), 31–56; Knowles and Hadcock (1971), 52–82, 251–69.

7 Bond (2001), 88–136.

8 Knowles (1950), 105–32; Knowles and Hadcock (1971), 57–9, 76, 258; Butler and Given-Wilson (1979), 37.

9 Knowles and Hadcock (1971), 53–4, 489, 493.

10 Fernie (2002), 19–26, 153–4.

11 Verey and Brooks (2002), 403–6, 713–18; Fernie (2002), 148–52, 160–5.

12 *Monastic Constitutions of Lanfranc* (2002).

13 Knowles and Hadcock (1971), 96–103; Burton (1994), 36–9; Pinnell (2009), 12–13.

14 *EHD*, II, 738–42.

15 Knowles (1959), 220–1.

16 Robinson (2002); Thompson (2001), 51–5.

17 *Orderic Vitalis: Ecclesiastical History*, IV (1973), 326–7.

18 Knowles (1979), 35–7; Coppack (1993), 74; Greene (1994), 104; Hoey (1995); Fergusson, Coppack and Harrison (2006).

19 Knowles and Hadcock (1971), 133–6; Coppack and Aston (2002).

20 Blair (2005), 361.

21 Burton (1994), 45–56; Dickinson (1950), 98–108.

22 Fernie (2002), 188; Pevsner and Hyde (2010), 222–6.

23 Greene (1989), esp. 1–22, 73–157.

24 Knowles and Hadcock (1971), 137–82, 489–90.

25 Pevsner and Neave (2002), 342–6; Rogan (2000), 15–51; Clifton-Taylor (1986), 271–3.

26 *EHD*, III, 651–2.

27 Greene (1992), 28–9; Knowles and Hadcock (1971), 183–93; Platt (1984), 60, 188–91; Hartwell and Pevsner (2009), 249–51; Higham (2004), 210.

28 Barber and Bate (2002), 1–23; Aston (2000), 121–2; Knowles and Hadcock (1971), 290–309.

29 Knowles and Hadcock (1971), 493.

30 Greene (1992), 29–30; Aston (2000), 94–5; Golding (1995), esp. 191–262.

31 Scott (2001), 150–60; Gilchrist (1994), 114, 121–7; Fernie (2002), 172–8.

32 Platt (1969), 16–75; Coppack (2000), 95–121; Aston (2000), 128–31.

33 Platt (1969), esp. 16–75, 138–245; Butler and Given-Wilson (1979), 37; Coppack (2000), 95–121; Aston (2000), 128–31, 144–9.

34 Hatcher and Bailey (2001), 29–30.

35 Binski (1995), 10–51.

36 Carpenter (2010), 32–3.

37 Knowles and Hadcock (1971), 212–50 (short-lived foundations have been omitted from the calculations); *EHD*, IV, 995–7.

38 *VCH: Cambridgeshire*, II, 275.

39 *Geoffrey Chaucer: The Canterbury Tales, a Verse Translation* (2008), 263.

40 Knowles and Hadcock (1971), 230–1; Knowles (1948), 78–84; Knowles (1959), 206–11.

41 *Visitations of Religious Houses*, II (1918), 16, 33, 54–60, 150. The reference to the regrowth of stumps is an indication of the woodland management practice of coppicing, on which see Chapter 2, pp. 42–3.

42 Knowles (1955), 309–30; Welander, (1991), esp. 164–281; Crook (1993); Gem (1997), 123; Snape (1980), 31–2; Collinson, Ramsay and Sparks (1995), 69–153; Luxford (2005), 202; Knowles (1959), 21–4.

43 *Visitations of Religious Houses*, II (1918), 175–6; Walcott (1869).

44 Rubin (1987), 246–9; Walsham (2011a), 56; Bernard (2011), 394.

45 Lehmberg (2005), 82–4.

46 *New Testament 1526, translated by William Tyndale* (2000), 548 ('Revelation', ch. 21, vv. 2, 3); Wilson (1992), 8.

47 Wilson (1992), 22–3, 160–78; Kidson (1994), where at 25–6 contemporary chroniclers' claims that the collapse at Lincoln was caused by an earthquake are dismissed for lack of corroborating evidence elsewhere in the town.

48 Wilson (1992), 185–212.

49 *Gervase of Canterbury, Opera Historica*, I (1879), 6–7; Kidson (1994), 27–30; Wilson (1992), 84–6, 117, 160–1.

50 Wilson (1992), 160–3, 174, 207, 212–16.

51 Maddison (1993), 76–80; Snape (1980), 31–2.

52 Kidson (1994), 37–8; Wilson (1992), 168, 175.

53 See, especially, Blair (2005), 368–504.

54 *William of Malmesbury: Gesta Regum Anglorum* (1998–99) I, 460–1; *Orderic Vitalis: Ecclesiastical History*, II (1968), 256–7; Lennard (1959), 292–4; Sawyer (1976), 2–3; Darby (1977), 52–6; Fernie (2002), 208–32.

55 Blair (2005), 355–9.

56 Blair (2005), 402–22; Lennard (1959), 319–23; Barlow (1979), 51–3; Platt (1981), 1–12; above, Chapter 4, p. 137.

57 Rodwell (1981), 142; Blair (2005), 374–83, 476–88; Walsham (2011a), 29–36; Rackham (1986), 229–30.

58 Walsham (2011a), 55–64.

59 Morris (1989), 248–53 (where alternative explanations for the proximity of church and motte in particular cases – such as the building of an earthwork next to the church in time of war – are also noted); Blair (2005), 387–90.

60 Morris (1989), 272–3; Blair (1991), 58–60; Blair (2005), 394–5; cf. above, Chapter 3, p. 63.

61 Beresford and Hurst (1971), 184.

62 Rodwell (1981), 63, 110; Beresford and Hurst (1976), 132.

63 Petts and Turner (2009).

64 Fernie (2002), 219–25.

65 Fernie (2002), 225–32; Morris (1989), 289–95; Roffey (2007), 101–3 (where the annual installation of an Easter sepulchre on the north side of the church is cited). The church at Wharram Percy was unusual in having its south aisle built first.

66 Platt (1981), 11–12, 72–8; Davies (1968), 52–94; Blair (2005), 458; tithe was notionally one-tenth of produce set aside for the support of the parish priest.

67 Rodwell (1981), 111–12; cf. Rodwell (1989), 31.

68 Morris (1989), 335–6.

69 *Lincolnshire Domesday and Lindsey Survey* (1924), liv–lv.

70 Smith, Hutton and Cook (1976), 118.

71 Platt (1981), 127.

72 Duffy (1992), 131–54; Roffey (2007), esp. 89–103, 132–9, 168–9, 176–7; Bettley and Pevsner (2007), 529–30.

73 *Visitations of the Diocese of Lincoln, 1517–1531* (1940), xxviii–xxix, 24, 71, 137–40; Bowker (1968), 126–30; Morris (1989), 323–4.

74 Verey and Brooks (2002), 59, 246–51.

75 Morris (1989), 279, 307–9, 371–3; Platt (1981), 92–3.

76 Harper-Bill (1988); Swanson (1989), 252–308; Duffy (1992), 9–376; Britnell (1997), 148–66; Walsham (2011a), 49–79.

Chapter Six

1 Brown (1989), 2.

2 Taylor (1958).

3 E.g. Platt (1982), Thompson (1987), Muir (1990), Thompson (1991), McNeill (1992).

4 Mathieu (1999); Gilchrist (1999), 109–42; Johnson (2002), esp. 116–18.

5 Liddiard (2003b), 2.

6 Coulson (1996); Creighton (2002), 35–52.

7 Platt (2007), quotations on p. 83 and (from Coulson) p. 85; Creighton and Liddiard (2008), quotation on p. 167.

8 Wheatley (2004), 19–43.

9 Haskins (1918), 277–82; Brown (1976), 49. The text went on to assert the duke's right to take castles into his own hand.

10 *William of Malmesbury, Historia Novella* (1998), 82–3; Harrison (2007), 67–9; Wheatley (2004), 99–102. For machicolation, see below, p. 196.

11 Pounds (1990), 260–3; Coulson (1993); Coulson (1994a); Coulson (1994b); Coulson's general argument is that the issue of licences was essentially symbolic.

12 Reynolds and White (1995); Reynolds and White (1997-98); Creighton (2002), 52–3, 59–60; Renn (1968), 50–3; Higham (2004), 141–4; cf. Morgan (1988), 32–3.

13 Creighton (2002), 36–7, 91, 133–6. On the issue of a 'master-plan', cf. Beeler (1956); Hollister (1965), 161–6.

14 Strickland (1992).

15 Creighton (2002), 43–4, 51; Colvin (1982), 367–83 (quotation on p. 377).

16 *ASC E* 1048 (for 1051) in *Anglo-Saxon Chronicle* (1953), 173–4; Wardle (2009), 138–46.

17 Taylor (1958), 99; Beresford (1987), 8–14 and 29–60 (first of a sequence of three such fortified houses which preceded the Norman motte-and-bailey castle on the site, though on the dating see Creighton (2002), 21–4; Davison (1977); Williams (2003); Coad (1997), 19–20.

18 *Ecclesiastical History of Orderic Vitalis*, II (1968), 218–19; *ASC D* 1066, *ASC E* 1086 (for 1087) in *Anglo-Saxon Chronicle* (1953), 200, 220.

19 Various estimates are summarized and synthesized in Eales (2003).

20 The phrase was coined by Sir Frank Stenton, whose 1929 Ford lectures were published in 1932 as *The First Century of English Feudalism, 1066–1166*.

21 King and Alcock (1969); Renn (1968), 252; Higham and Barker (1992), 198–200. Although most mottes had additional baileys and most ringworks did not, there were exceptions which still give rise to several problems of interpretation.

22 King and Alcock (1972); Kenyon (1990), 21, 33–4.

23 Darby (1977), 295, 364–8; Creighton (2002), 139–40; above, Chapter 4, p. 102.

24 Higham and Barker (1992), 277–80, 293–6, 303–4, 308–10, 331–3.

25 E.g. *Ecclesiastical History of Orderic Vitalis*, II (1968), 222–3: 'the king remained a further eight days in the city [York], built a second castle, and left Earl William fitz Osbern as castellan there'; *Gesta Guillelmi of William of Poitiers* (1998), 144–5: 'after the surrender of the castle [at Dover], he spent eight days in fortifying it where it was weakest' (with an editorial note suggesting that reference to a pre-Norman 'castle' is the product of loose usage); McNeill (1992), 40, where there is an estimate of between 40 and 120 working days.

26 Creighton (2002), 56–7.

27 Gravett (2009), 24; Higham and Barker (1992), 118–20, 138–9, 147–56, 171–93; Hope-Taylor (1957), 242–3 and plates xli, xlii (though the author suggests a military function for the exterior patterning).

28 Brown (1976), 62–6; Thompson (1991), 63, 74–6, 87; Higham and Barker (1992), 350, for measures to contain the threat from fire.

29 Coulson (1994), 69–70; Eales (2003); White (2000), 7, 69–72.

30 King (1988), 189.

31 Marshall (2002), 27.

32 Coulson (1994), 81–3; Dixon (1998); Dixon (2002), 11; Hulme (2007–8), 210.

33 Above, Chapter 3, pp. 83–4.

34 Brown (1976), 78–87; Thompson (1991), 82–3; Coulson (2001), 69–75, 80–1; Dixon (2002), 11.

35 Marshall (2002), 28–9.

36 *Ecclesiastical History of Orderic Vitalis*, VI (1978), 466–9; Hulme (2007–8); Liddiard (2005), 46–54.

37 Port (1987), 3–13, 22–4; Thompson (1991), 79; McNeill (1992), 91–4. On the siege, which ended with the collapse of the south-east corner of the great tower after a mine had been dug beneath it, see e.g. Painter (1949), 363–4.

38 Brown (1976), 78, 122; King (1988), 118–20; Hislop (2010), 216–29; Creighton (2002), 71–2; Colvin, Brown and Taylor (1963), I, 329–30, II, 690; Darlington (2001), 48; Pevsner and Richmond (2002), 617–18.

39 Brown (1976), 146; King (1988), 188–9; Thompson (1987), 73–4, 83–96.

40 Brown, (1976), 57–61; Thompson (1991), 54; Higham and Barker (1992), 244–325; Goodall (2011a), 107–37.

41 King (1988), 48, 73; Thompson (1991), 60; Goodall (2011a), 129.

42 Brown (1976), 86; King (1988), 64; Dixon (2002), 9; Goodall (2011a), 238–9.

43 Brown (1976), 84–5; Higham and Barker (1992), 189.

44 See also Addyman (1973); Higham and Barker (1992), 190, 274–7, 289–93, 326–47; Soden (2007), 24–9.

45 Higham and Barker (1992), 181.

46 McGuicken (2010).

47 Goodall (2011a), 208–11.

48 Goodall (2011a), 141, 178; McGuicken (2010), 65, 76–9; Clark (2004), 5–6, 21, 24–5. Ellis (1993), 101–2, notes evidence of limewashing of the masonry.

49 Goodall, (2011b), 23; Goodall (2011a), 378; Thompson (1987), 52–9, 64–6, 97–102.

50 Endacott (2003), 28.

51 Johnson (2002), xiii–xix, 19–33.

52 Goodall (2011a), 377; Darlington (2001), 89-91; Goodall (2011b) 13–16.

53 Creighton (2002), 69–70; Coulson (2001).

54 Liddiard (2005), 134–9.

55 Creighton (2002), 76–8.

56 Coad and Streeton (1982), quotation on p. 164.

57 Creighton (2002), 88.

58 Goodall (2011a), 3.

59 Bond (1987), 92, 103; Creighton and Higham (2005), 218, 249; Kenyon (1990), 184.

60 Bond (1987), 94, 100–2; Kenyon (1990), 185; Schofield and Vince (2003), 40.

61 Creighton and Higham (2005), 85–7, 110–14, 221–7; Kenyon (1990), 184–5; Daniels (1986); Gurnham (2009), 41.

62 Schofield and Vince (2003), 51.

63 *Domesday Book: Cheshire* (1978), 262c, 262d; *Domesday Book: Oxfordshire* (1978), 154a, 154b.

64 Kenyon (1990), 187; Bond (1987), 104; Lilley, Lloyd and Campbell (2009), 9; White (2003), 115–16.

65 Bond (1987), 104; Harrison, McKeague and Watson (2011), 47–9, for evidence of 39 fortified bridges in medieval England and Wales identified to date.

66 Kenyon (1990), 183–99; Creighton and Higham (2005), 114, 137–49.

67 Creighton and Higham (2005), 111–13; Colvin (1982), 648.

Chapter Seven

1 *Itinerary of Leland*, I, 162, 166, 173, 177; V, 64, 82, 87; Colvin (1968); cf. Colvin (1975), 180, 225–2, where there is reference to a decision by a group of Elizabeth I's councillors in 1562 to keep the castle at Tutbury because it was 'an old and statly Castle' with 'forests, parks and chases', and also that at Tickhill as 'an ancient monument'.

2 Thompson (1987), 112.

3 Hoskins (1988), 130–3.

4 Mercer (1975), 11–31.

5 Hilton (1975), 66–7; Hilton (1983), 54–8; Webb and Webb (1906), 125–32.

6 Smith (2002), 198.

7 Clark and Slack (1976), 161–2; Wrigley (1986); Corfield (1990); Dyer (1991a), esp. 52.

8 Jordan (1964), 368.

9 Howard (2007), esp. 13–93.

10 Turner (1980), 34–5, 180–1.

11 *Itinerary of Leland*, I, xxxvii – xliii; Leland was described by the television presenter Nicholas Crane as 'the father of English topography' in a BBC 2 programme in a series on *Great British Journeys* in September 2007.

Bibliography

Aberg, F. A. (1978) *Medieval Moated Sites*, London: Council for British Archaeology.

Accounts of the Chamberlains and their Officers of the County of Chester, 1301–1360 (1910) R. Stewart-Brown ed., Record Society of Lancashire and Cheshire, 59.

Accounts of the Manor and Hundred of Macclesfield, Cheshire, Michaelmas 1361 to Michaelmas 1362 (2003) P. H. W. Booth ed., Record Society of Lancashire and Cheshire, 138.

Addyman, P. V. (1973) 'Excavations at Ludgershall Castle, Wiltshire, England, 1964–72', *Chateau Gaillard*, 6, 7–13.

Aelfric's Colloquy (1978) G. N. Garmonsway ed., Exeter: University of Exeter Press.

Albert, W. (1972) *The Turnpike Road System in England and Wales, 1663–1840*, Cambridge: Cambridge University Press.

Anglo-Saxon Chronicle (1953) G. N. Garmonsway ed., London: Dent.

Astill, G. (1988a) 'Rural settlement: the toft and the croft' in G. Astill and A. Grant (eds), *The Countryside of Medieval England*, Oxford: Blackwell, pp. 36–61.

—(1988b) 'Fields' in G. Astill and A. Grant (eds), *The Countryside of Medieval England*, Oxford: Blackwell, pp. 62–85.

Aston, M. (1989) 'A regional study of deserted settlements in the west of England', in M. Aston, D. Austin and C. Dyer (eds), *The Rural Settlements of Medieval England*, Oxford: Blackwell, pp. 105–28.

—(2000) *Monasteries in the Landscape*, Stroud: Tempus.

Aston, M. and Bond, J. (1976) *The Landscape of Towns*, London: Dent.

Auduoy, M. and Chapman, A. (eds) (2009) *Raunds: the Origin and Growth of a Midland Village, AD 450 – 1500*, Oxford, Oxbow.

Ault, W. O. (1972) *Open-field Farming in Mediaeval England: Study of Village Bye-laws*, London: Allen and Unwin.

Austin, D., Daggett, R. H. and Walker, M. J. C. (1980) 'Farms and fields in Okehampton Park, Devon: the problems of studying medieval landscape', *Landscape History*, 2, 39–57.

Bailey, M. (1988) 'The rabbit and the medieval East Anglian economy', *Ag. Hist. Rev.*, 36, 1–20.

—(1989) 'The concept of the margin in the medieval English economy,' *Ec. Hist. Rev.*, 42, 1–17.

—(1991) '*Per impetum maris*: natural disaster and economic decline in eastern England, 1275–1350', in B. M. S. Campbell ed., *Before the Black Death*, Manchester: Manchester University Press, pp. 184–208.

—(1993) 'A tale of two towns: Buntingford and Standon in the later middle ages', *Journal of Medieval History*, 19, 351–71.

Baker, A. R. H. and Butlin, R. A. (eds) (1973) *Studies of Field Systems in the British Isles*, Cambridge: Cambridge University Press.

Baker, N. ed., (2002) *Shrewsbury Abbey*, Shrewsbury: Shropshire Archaeological and Historical Society.

—(2010) *Shrewsbury: an Archaeological Assessment of an English Border Town*, Oxford: Oxbow.

Barber, L. and Priestley-Bell, G. (2008) *Medieval Adaptation, Settlement and Economy in a Coastal Wetland: The Evidence from around Lydd, Romney Marsh, Kent*, Oxford: Oxbow.

Barber, M. and Bate, K. (2002) *The Templars*, Manchester: Manchester University Press.

Barlow, F. (1979) *The English Church, 1066–1154*, London: Longman.

—(1983) *William Rufus*, London: Methuen.

Barnwell, P. S. and Giles, C. (1997) *English Farmsteads, 1750–1914*, Swindon: Royal Commission on Historical Monuments, England.

Bassett, S. (1997) 'Continuity and fission in the Anglo-Saxon landscape: the origins of the Rodings (Essex)', *Landscape History*, 19, 25–42.

Batey, M (1968) 'Nuneham Courtenay: an eighteenth-century deserted village', *Oxoniensia*, 33, 108–25.

Baum, P. F. (1963) *Anglo-Saxon Riddles in the Exeter Book*, Durham, North Carolina: Duke University Press.

Beaumont-James, T. and Gerrard, C. (2007) *Clarendon: Landscape of Kings*, Macclesfield: Windgather.

Beckett, J. V. (1989) *A History of Laxton*, Oxford: Blackwell.

Bede: A History of the English Church and People (1968) L. Shirley-Price and R. E. Latham (eds), Harmondsworth: Penguin.

Beeler, J. H. (1956) 'Castles and strategy in Norman and early Angevin England', *Speculum*, 26, 581–601.

Beresford, G. (1974) 'The medieval manor of Penhallam, Jacobstow, Cornwall', *Medieval Archaeology* 18, 90–145.

—(1975) *The Medieval Clay Land Village: excavations at Goltho and Barton Blount*, London: Society for Medieval Archaeology.

—(1977) 'Excavation of a moated site at Wintringham in Huntingdonshire', *Archaeological Journal*, 134, 194–286.

—(1979) 'Three deserted medieval settlements on Dartmoor: a report on the late E. Marie Minter's excavations', *Medieval Archaeology*, 23, 98–158.

—(1987) *Goltho: the Development of an Early Medieval Manor, c.850–1150*, London: English Heritage.

—(2009) *Caldecote: The Development and Desertion of a Hertfordshire Village*, Leeds: Society for Medieval Archaeology.

Beresford, M. W. (1948) 'Ridge and furrow and the open fields' (1948) *Ec. Hist. Rev.*, 2, 34–45.

—(1957) *History on the Ground*, London: Lutterworth Press.

—(1988) *New Towns of the Middle Ages*, Gloucester, Alan Sutton.

Beresford, M. W. and Hurst, J. G. (1971) *Deserted Medieval Villages*, London: Lutterworth Press.

—(1976) 'Wharram Percy: a case study in microtopography', in P. H. Sawyer ed., *Medieval Settlement: Continuity and Change*, London, Edward Arnold, pp. 114–44.

—(1990) *Wharram Percy: Deserted Medieval Village*, London: English Heritage.

Beresford, M. W. and St Joseph, J. K. S. (1979) *Medieval England, An Aerial Survey*, 2nd edn., Cambridge: Cambridge University Press.

Bernard, G. W. (2011) 'The dissolution of the monasteries', *History*, 96, 390–409.

Bettey, J. (2000) 'Downlands' in Thirsk (2000) pp. 27–49.

Bettley, J. and Pevsner, N. (2007) *The Buildings of Essex*, New Haven: Yale University Press.

Binski, P. (1995) *Westminster Abbey and the Plantagenets: Kingship and the Representation of Power, 1200–1400*, New Haven: Yale University Press.

Bird, P. (2007) 'Landownership and settlement change in south-west Cheshire from 1750 to 2000', unpublished PhD., University of Liverpool.

Birrell, J. (1992) 'Deer and deer farming in medieval England', *Ag. Hist. Rev.*, 40, 112–26.

Bishop, T. A. M. (1954) 'Assarting and the growth of the open fields', in E. M. Carus-Wilson ed., *Essays in Economic History*, London: Edward Arnold, I, pp. 26–40.

Blair, J. (1991) *Early Medieval Surrey: Landholding, Church and Settlement before 1300*, Stroud: Alan Sutton.

—(1993) 'Hall and chamber: English domestic planning 1000–1250' in G. Meirion-Jones and M. Jones (eds), *Manorial Domestic Buildings in England and Northern France*, London: Society of Antiquaries, pp. 1–21.

—(2005) *The Church in Anglo-Saxon Society*, Oxford: Oxford University Press.

Blanchard, I. (1972) 'The miner and the agricultural community in late medieval England', *Ag. Hist. Rev.*, 20, 93–106.

—(1974) 'Rejoinder: stannator fabulosus', *Ag. Hist. Rev.*, 22, 62–74.

—(1996) 'Lothian and beyond: the economy of the English empire of David I' in R. H. Britnell and J. Hatcher (eds), *Progress and Problems in Medieval England*, Cambridge: Cambridge University Press, pp. 23–43.

—(2001) *Mining, Metallurgy and Minting in the Middle Ages*, Stuttgart: Franz Steiner.

Bolton, J. L. (1980) *Medieval English Economy, 1150–1500*, London: Dent.

Bond, C. J. (1987) 'Anglo-Saxon and medieval defences' in J. Schofield and R. Leech (eds), *Urban Archaeology in Britain*, London: Council for British Archaeology, pp. 92–116.

Bond, J. (1994) 'Forests, chases, warrens and parks in medieval Wessex' in M. Aston and C. Lewis, *The Medieval Landscape of Wessex*, Oxford: Oxbow, pp. 115–58.

—(1997) 'Woodstock park in the middle ages', 'Woodstock Park in the sixteenth and seventeenth centuries' in J. Bond and K. Tiller (eds), *Blenheim, Landscape for a Palace*, 2nd edn., Stroud: Sutton, pp. 22–66.

—(2001) 'Monastic water management in Great Britain: a review', in G. Keevil, M. Aston and T. Hall (eds), Monastic Archaeology, Oxford: Oxbow.

Book of Margery Kempe (1940) S. B. Meech and H. E. Allen (eds), London: Early English Text Society.

Booth, P. H. W. (1981) *The Financial Administration of the Lordship and County of Cheshire, 1272–1377*, Manchester: Chetham Society.

Bott, A. (1993) *Merton College: A Short History of the Buildings*, Oxford: Merton College.

Bowker, M (1968) *The Secular Clergy in the Diocese of Lincoln, 1495–1520*, Cambridge: Cambridge University Press.

Bracton: De Legibus et Consuetudinibus Angliae, III (1940) G. E. Woodbine ed., New Haven: Yale University Press.

Bridbury, A. R. (1973) 'The Black Death', *Ec. Hist. Rev.*, 26, 577–92.

Britnell, R. H. (1981) 'The proliferation of markets in England, 1200–1349', *Ec. Hist. Rev.*, 34, 209–21.

—(1986) *Growth and Decline in Colchester, 1300–1525*, Cambridge: Cambridge University Press.

—(1996a), *The Commercialisation of English Society, 1000–1500*, 2nd edn., Manchester: Manchester University Press.

—(1996b), 'Boroughs, markets and trade in northern England, 1000–1216', in R. H. Britnell and J. Hatcher (eds), *Progress and Problems in Medieval England*, Cambridge: Cambridge University Press, pp. 46–67.

—(1997) *The Closing of the Middle Ages? England, 1471–1529*, Oxford: Blackwell.

Broad, J. (2010) 'Understanding village desertion in the seventeenth and eighteenth centuries' in Dyer and Jones (2010) pp. 121–39.

Brown, A. ed. (1999) *The Rows of Chester*, London: English Heritage.

Brown, A. G. and Foard, G. (1998) 'The Saxon landscape: a regional perspective' in P. Everson and T. Williamson (eds), *The Archaeology of Landscape*, Manchester: Manchester University Press, pp. 67–94.

Brown, A. G. and Taylor, C. (1989) 'The origins of dispersed settlement: some results from fieldwork in Bedfordshire, *Landscape History*, 11, 61–91.

Brown, R. A. (1976) *English Castles*, 3rd edn., London: Batsford.

—(1989) *Castles from the Air*, Cambridge: Cambridge University Press.

Browning, J. and Higgins, T. (2003) 'Excavations of a medieval toft and croft at Cropston Road, Anstey, Leicestershire', *Transactions of the Leicestershire Archaeological and Historical Society*, 77, 65–81.

Burton, J. (1994) *Monastic and Religious Orders in Britain, 1000–1300*, Cambridge: Cambridge University Press.

Butler, L. (1976) 'The evolution of towns: planned towns after 1066' in M. W. Barley ed., *The Plans and Topography of Medieval Towns in England and Wales*, London: Council for British Archaeology, pp. 32–48.

Butler, L. and Given-Wilson, C. (1979) *Medieval Monasteries of Great Britain*, London: Michael Joseph.

Cambridge University Library: EDR/G/3/27 (Ely Coucher Book).

Cameron, A., Delano-Smith, C. and Wood, B. A. (1980) 'Laxton before 1635', 'Laxton in 1635' and 'Laxton in the twentieth century', *East Midland Geographer*, 7, 6, 219–237.

Campbell, B. M. S. (1981) 'Commonfield origins – the regional dimension' in T. Rowley ed., *The Origins of Open Field Agriculture*, London: Croom Helm, pp. 112–29.

—(1983) 'Agricultural progress in medieval England: some evidence from eastern Norfolk', *Ec. Hist. Rev.*, 36, 24–46.

Cantor, L. (1982) 'Introduction' to L. Cantor ed., *The English Medieval Landscape*, London: Croom Helm, pp. 17–24.

—(1983) *The Medieval Parks of England: a Gazetteer*, Loughborough: Loughborough University of Technology.

Carpenter, D. A. (2004) *The Struggle for Mastery: The Penguin History of Britain 1066–1284* London: Penguin.

—(2010) 'King Henry III and the chapter house of Westminster Abbey' in W. Rodwell and R. Mortimer (eds), *Westminster Abbey Chapter House*, London: Society of Antiquaries of London, pp. 32–9.

Carus-Wilson, E. M. (1954) 'An industrial revolution of the thirteenth century' in E. M. Carus-Wilson ed., *Essays in Economic History*, I, London: Edward Arnold, pp. 41–60.

—(1962) 'Evidences of industrial growth on some fifteenth-century manors' in E. M. Carus-Wilson ed., *Essays in Economic History*, II, London: Edward Arnold, pp. 151–67.

Charters of the Anglo-Norman Earls of Chester, c.1071–1237 (1998) G. Barraclough ed., Gloucester: Alan Sutton.

Cherry, B. and Pevsner, N. (2002) *The Buildings of England: Devon*, New Haven: Yale University Press.

Cherry, M. (1989) 'Nurstead Court, Kent: a re-appraisal', *Archaeological Journal*, 146, 451–64.

Cheshire Record Office: DLE 47 (Leche family deeds).

Chronicle of Battle Abbey (1980) E. Searle ed., Oxford: Clarendon Press.

Chronicle of Jocelin of Brakelond (1949) H. E. Salter ed., London: Nelson.

Chronicon Monasterii de Melsa, II (1867) III (1868) E. A. Bond ed., London: Rolls Series.

Clark, J. (2004) *Helmsley Castle*, London: English Heritage.

Clark, P. and Slack, P. (1976) *English Towns in Transition, 1500–1700*, Oxford: Oxford University Press.

Clarke, H., Pearson, S., Mate, M. and Parfitt, K. (2010) *Sandwich: a Study of the Town and Port from its Origins to 1600*, Oxford: Oxbow.

Clifton-Taylor, A. (1986) *The Cathedrals of England*, London: Thames and Hudson.

Coad, J. G. (1997) *Dover Castle*, London: English Heritage.

Coad, J. G. and Streeton, A. D. F. (1982) 'Excavations at Castle Acre castle, Norfolk, 1972–1977: country house and castle of the Norman Earls of Surrey', *Archaeological Journal*, 139, 138–301.

Coates, B. E. (1965) 'The origin and distribution of markets and fairs in medieval Derbyshire', *Derbyshire Archaeological Journal*, 85, 92–111.

Collinson, P., Ramsay, N. and Sparks, M. (eds) (1995) *A History of Canterbury Cathedral*, Oxford: Oxford University Press.

Colvin, H. M. (1968) 'Castles and government in Tudor England', *English Historical Review*, 83, 225–34.

Colvin, H. M., Brown, R. A. and Taylor, A. J. (eds) (1963) *History of the King's Works*, I, II, London: H. M. S. O.

Colvin, H. M., Ransome, D. R. and Summerson, J. (eds) (1975) *History of the King's Works*, III, London: H. M. S. O.

Colvin, H. M., Summerson, J., Biddle, M. and Hale, J. R. (eds) (1982) *History of the King's Works, IV*, London: H. M. S. O.

Conzen, M. R. G. (1968) 'The use of town plans in the study of urban history' in H. J. Dyos ed., *The Study of Urban History*, London: Edward Arnold, pp. 113–30.

Cook, M. (1998) *Medieval Bridges*, Princes Risborough: Shire.

Cooper, A. (2000) 'The king's four highways: legal fiction meets fictional law', *Journal of Medieval History*, 26, 351–70.

—(2006) *Bridges, Law and Power in Medieval England, 700–1400*, Woodbridge: Boydell Press.

Coppack, G. (1993) *Fountains Abbey*, London: English Heritage.

—(2000) *The White Monks: the Cistercians in Britain, 1128–1540*, Stroud: Tempus.

Coppack, G. and Aston, M. (2002) *Christ's Poor Men: the Carthusians in England*, Stroud: Tempus.

Corfield, P. (1990) 'Urban development in England and Wales in the sixteenth and seventeenth centuries' in J. Barry ed., *The Tudor and Stuart Town, 1530–1688*, London: Longman, pp. 35–62.

Cornwall Industrial Settlements Initiative: Looe (2002) Cahill Partnership and Cornwall Archaeological Unit.

Coulson, C. (1993) 'Specimens of freedom to crenellate by licence', *Fortress* 18, 3–15.

—(1994a) 'The castles of the Anarchy' in E. J. King ed., *The Anarchy of King Stephen's Reign*, Oxford: Oxford University Press, pp. 67–92.

—(1994b) 'Freedom to crenellate by licence: an historiographical revision', *Nottingham Medieval Studies*, 38, 86–137.

—(1996) 'Cultural realities and reappraisals in English castle-study', *Journal of Medieval History*, 22, 171–207.

—(2001) 'Peaceable power in English castles', *Anglo-Norman Studies*, 23, 69–95.

Cracknell, B. E. (1959) *Canvey Island: the History of a Marshland Community*, Leicester: Leicester University Press.

Creighton, O. H. (2002) *Castles and Landscapes: Power, Community and Fortification in Medieval England*, London: Continuum.

—(2009) *Designs upon the Land: Elite Landscapes of the Middle Ages*, Woodbridge: Boydell and Brewer.

Creighton, O. H. and Higham, R. (2005) *Medieval Town Walls*, Stroud: Tempus.

Creighton, O. H. and Liddiard, R. (2008) 'Fighting yesterday's battle: beyond war or status in castle studies', *Medieval Archaeology*, 52, 161–70.

Croft, R. A. and Mynard, D. C. (1993) *The Changing Landscape of Milton Keynes*, Aylesbury: Buckinghamshire Archaeological Society.

Crook, J. ed. (1993) *Winchester Cathedral: Nine Hundred Years, 1093–1993*, Chichester: Phillimore.

Dale, M. K. ed. (1950) 'Court Roll of Chalgrave Manor, 1278–1313', *Bedfordshire Historical Record Society*, 28, 46–7.

Dalwood, H. and Edwards, R. (2004) *Excavations at Deansway, Worcester, 1988–89: Romano-British Small Town to Late Medieval City*, York: Council for British Archaeology.

Daniels, R. (1986) 'The medieval defences of Hartlepool, Cleveland: the results of excavation and survey', *Durham Archaeological Journal*, 2, 63–72.

Darby, H. C. (1940) *The Medieval Fenland*, Cambridge: Cambridge University Press.

—(1956) *The Draining of the Fens*, Cambridge: Cambridge University Press,

—(1971) *Domesday Geography of Eastern England*, 3rd edn., Cambridge: Cambridge University Press.

—(1977) *Domesday England*, Cambridge: Cambridge University Press.

Darby, H. C. and Terrett, I. B. (eds) (1954) *Domesday Geography of Midland England*, Cambridge: Cambridge University Press.

Darlington, J. ed. (2001) *Stafford Castle*, I, Stafford, Stafford Borough Council.

Davies, J. G. (1968) *The Secular Use of Church Buildings*, London: S. C. M. Press.

Davison, B. K. (1967) 'The late Saxon town of Thetford', *Medieval Archaeology*, 11, 189–95.

—(1977) 'Excavations at Sulgrave, Northamptonshire, an interim report', *Archaeological Journal*, 134, 105–14.

Derbyshire, M. (2010) 'Old-style deer leaps', *Rural History Today*, 19, 4–5.

Derry, T. K. and Williams, T. I. (1960) *A Short History of Technology*, Oxford: Oxford University Press.

Description of England by William Harrison (1968) G. Edelen ed., Ithaca, New York: Cornell University Press.

Devlin, D. (1984) 'Feminine lay piety in the high middle ages: the Beguines' in J. A. Nichols and L. T. Shank (eds), *Medieval Religious Women vol. i: Distant Echoes,* Kalamazoo, Michigan: Cistercian Publications, pp. 183–96.

Dialogus de Scaccario (1983) C. Johnson, F. E. L. Carter and D. E. Greenway (eds), Oxford: Clarendon Press.

Dickinson, J. C. (1950) *The Origins of the Austin Canons and their Introduction into England*, London: S. P. C. K.

Dixon, P. (1998) 'Design in castle-building: the control of access to the lord', *Chateau-Gaillard*, 18, 47–57.

—(2002) 'The myth of the keep' in G. Meirion-Jones, E. Impey and M. Jones (eds), *The Seigneurial Residence in Western Europe, AD c.800–1600*, Oxford: Archaeopress, pp. 9–13.

Dobson, R. B. (2000) 'General survey, 1300–1540' in D. M. Palliser ed., *The Cambridge Urban History of Britain, I, 600–1540*, Cambridge: Cambridge University Press, pp. 273–90.

Domesday Book: Cheshire (1978) P. Morgan ed., Chichester: Phillimore.

Domesday Book: Oxfordshire (1978) J. Morris ed., Chichester: Phillimore.

Donkin, R. A. (1978) *The Cistercians: Studies in the Geography of Medieval England and Wales*, Toronto: Pontifical Institute of Medieval Studies.

Duffy, E. (1992) *The Stripping of the Altars; Traditional Religion in England, 1400–1580*, New Haven: Yale University Press.

Dyer, A. (1991) *Decline and Growth in English Towns, 1400–1640*, London: Macmillan.

Dyer, C. (1982) 'Deserted medieval villages in the west midlands', *Ec. Hist. Rev.*, 35, 19–34.

—(1986) 'English peasant buildings in the later middle ages (1200–1500)', *Medieval Archaeology*, 30, 19–45.

—(1988) 'Documentary evidence: problems and enquiries' in G. Astill and A. Grant (eds), *The Countryside of Medieval England*, Oxford: Blackwell, pp. 12–35.

—(1989a) *Standards of Living in the Later Middle Ages: Social Change in England, c.1200–1520*, Cambridge: Cambridge University Press.

—(1989b) 'The retreat from marginal land? The growth and decline of medieval rural settlements' in M. Aston, D. Austin and C. Dyer (eds), *The Rural Settlements of Medieval England*, Oxford: Blackwell, pp. 45–57.

—(1991) *Hanbury: Settlement and Society in a Woodland Landscape*, Leicester: Leicester University Press.

—(1996) 'Market towns and the countryside in late medieval England', *Canadian Journal of History*, 31, 17–35.

—(2000) 'Compton Verney: landscape and people in the middle ages' in R. Bearman ed., *Compton Verney: a history of the house and its owners*, Stratford-upon-Avon: Shakespeare Birthplace Trust, pp. 49–94.

—(2002) 'Small towns with large consequences: the importance of small towns in England, 1000–1540', *Historical Research*, 75, 1–24.

—(2003a) *Making a Living in the Middle Ages*, London: Penguin.

—(2003b) 'The archaeology of medieval small towns', *Medieval Archaeology*, 47, 85–114.

—(2006) 'Conflict in the landscape: the enclosure movement in England, 1220–1349', *Landscape History*, 28, 21–33.

—(2010) 'Villages in crisis: social dislocation and desertion, 1370–1520' in Dyer and Jones (2010) pp. 28–45.

Dyer, C. and Jones, R. (eds) (2010) *Deserted Villages Revisited*, Hatfield: University of Hertfordshire Press.

Dymond, D. (1999) 'God's disputed acre', *Journal of Ecclesiastical History*, 39, 464–97.

Eales, R. G. (2003) 'Royal power and castles in Norman England' in R. Liddiard ed., *Anglo-Norman Castles*, Woodbridge: Boydell Press, pp. 41–67.

Earldom of Gloucester Charters (1973) R. B. Patterson ed., Oxford: Clarendon Press.

Ecclesiastical History of Orderic Vitalis, II (1968) IV (1973) VI (1978) M. Chibnall ed., Oxford: Clarendon Press.

Edwards, J. F. and Hindle, B. P. (1991) 'The transportation system of medieval England and Wales', *Journal of Historical Geography*, 17, 123–34.

Ellis, P. (1993) *Beeston Castle, Cheshire: Excavations by Laurence Keen & Peter Hough, 1968–85*, London: English Heritage.

Elton, G. R. (1960) *The Tudor Constitution*, Cambridge: Cambridge University Press.

Endacott, A. (2003) *Okehampton Castle*, London: English Heritage.

English Historical Documents [I, c.500–1042 (1979) D. Whitelock ed., 2nd edn., London: Eyre Methuen; II, 1042–1189 (1981) D. C. Douglas and G. W. Greenway (eds.), 2nd edn., London: Eyre Methuen; III, 1189–1327 (1975) H. Rothwell ed., London: Eyre and Spottiswoode; IV, 1327–1485 (1969) A. R. Myers ed., London: Eyre and Spottiswoode; V, 1485–1558 (1967) C. H. Williams ed., London: Eyre and Spottiswoode].

English Lawsuits from William I to Richard I, (1990–1) R. C. van Caenegem ed., London: Selden Society.

Evans, D. H. and Jarrett, M. G. (1987) 'The deserted village of West Whelpington, Northumberland, third report, part one', *Archaeologia Aeliana* 5th series 15, 199–308.

Evans, D. H., Jarrett, M. G. and Wrathmell, S. (1988) 'The deserted village of West Whelpington, Northumberland, third report, part two', *Archaeologia Aeliana* 5th series 16, 139–92.

Evans, G. E. (1956) *Ask the Fellows who Cut the Hay*, London: Faber and Faber.

Everitt, A. (2000) 'Common Land' in Thirsk (2000) pp. 210–35.

Everson, P. and Brown, G. (2010) 'Dr Hoskins I presume! Field visits in the footsteps of a pioneer' in Dyer and Jones (2010) pp. 46–63.

Eynsham Cartulary, II (1908) H. E. Salter ed., Oxford: Oxford Historical Society.

Farmer, D. L. (1991) 'Markets, fairs and transport' in E. Miller ed., *Agrarian History of England and Wales*, III, 1348–1500, Cambridge: Cambridge University Press, pp. 327–58.

Faull, M. L. and Moorhouse, S. A. (eds) (1981) *West Yorkshire, an Archaeological Survey*, Wakefield: West Yorkshire Metropolitan County Council.

Fergusson, P., Coppack, G. and Harrison, S. (2006) *Rievaulx Abbey*, London: English Heritage.

Fernie, E. (2002) *The Architecture of Norman England*, Oxford: Oxford University Press.

Fielding, A. and Fielding, A. (2006) *The Salt Industry*, Princes Risborough: Shire.

Fleming, R. (2011) *Britain After Rome: the Fall and Rise, 400 to 1070*, London: Penguin.

Foot, D. (2010) *Woods and Forests*, Stroud: History Press.

Fox, H. S. A. (1981) 'Approaches to the adoption of the Midland system' in T. Rowley ed. (1981) *The Origins of Open Field Agriculture*, London: Croom Helm, pp. 64–111.

—(1991) 'Farming practice and techniques, Devon and Cornwall' in E. Miller ed., *Agrarian History of England and Wales*, III, 1348–1500, Cambridge: Cambridge University Press, pp. 303–23.

—(2001) *The Evolution of the Fishing Village: Landscape and Society along the South Devon Coast, 1086–1550*, Oxford: Leopard's Head Press.

Fyfe, R. M. (2004) 'Characterising the late prehistoric, 'Romano-British' and medieval landscape, and dating the emergence of a regionally distinct agricultural system in south west Britain', *Journal of Archaeological Science*, 31, 1699–1714.

Galbraith, V. H. (1974) *Domesday Book, its Place in Administrative History*, Oxford: Clarendon Press.

Galloway, R. L. (1882) *A History of Coal Mining in Great Britain*, London: Macmillan.

Gardiner, M. (1997) 'Trade, rural industry and the origins of villages: some evidence from south-east England' in G. de Boe and F. Verhaeghe (eds), *Rural Settlements in Medieval Europe*, Zellik: Instituut voor het Archeologisch Patrimonium.

—(2000) 'Vernacular buildings and the development of the later medieval plan', *Medieval Archaeology*, 44, 159–79.

Geddes, J. (1991) 'Iron' in J. Blair and N. Ramsay (eds), *English Medieval Industries: Craftsmen, Techniques, Products*, London: Hambledon, pp. 167–88.

Gem, R. ed. (1997) *English Heritage Book of St Augustine's Abbey, Canterbury*, London: Batsford.

Geoffrey Chaucer: The Canterbury Tales, a Verse Translation (2008) D. Wright ed., Oxford: Oxford University Press.

Gerrard, C. and Aston, M. (2007) *The Shapwick Project, Somerset: A Rural Landscape Explored*, Leeds: Society for Medieval Archaeology.

Gerrard, S. (2000) *The Early British Tin Industry*, Stroud: Tempus.

Gervase of Canterbury, Opera Historica, I (1879) W. Stubbs ed., London: Rolls Series.

Gesta Guillelmi of William of Poitiers (1998) R. H. C. Davis and M. Chibnall (eds.), Oxford: Clarendon Press.

Gesta Stephani (1976) K. R. Potter and R. H. C. Davis (eds), Oxford: Clarendon Press.

Gilchrist, R. (1994) *Gender and Material Culture: the Archaeology of Religious Women*, London: Routledge.

—(1999) *Gender and Archaeology, Contesting the Past*, London: Routledge.

Giles, C. (1986) *Rural Houses of West Yorkshire, 1400–1830*, London, Royal Commission on Historical Monuments, England.

Girouard, M. (1978) *Life in the English Country House: A Social and Architectural History* New Haven: Yale University Press.

Glanvill, Tractatus de Legibus (1965) G. D. G. Hall ed., London: Nelson.

Goddard, R. (2011) 'Small boroughs and the manorial economy: enterprise zones or urban failures?', *Past and Present*, 210, 3–31,

Godwin, H. (1978) *Fenland: its Ancient Past and Uncertain Future*, Cambridge: Cambridge University Press.

Golding, B. (1995) *Gilbert of Sempringham and the Gilbertine Order, c.1130–c.1300*, Oxford: Clarendon Press.

Goodall, J. (2011a) *The English Castle, 1066–1650*, New Haven, Yale University Press.

—(2011b) *Ashby de la Zouch Castle and Kirby Muxloe Castle*, revised edn., London: English Heritage.

Gravett, C. (2009) *English Castles, 1200–1300*, Oxford: Osprey.

Gray, H. L. (1915) *The English Field Systems*, Harvard: Harvard University Press.

Green, J. A. (2005) *Henry I, King of England and Duke of Normandy*, Cambridge: Cambridge University Press.

Greene, J. P. (1989) *Norton Priory: the Archaeology of a Medieval Religious House*, Cambridge: Cambridge University Press.

—(1994) *Medieval Monasteries*, London: Leicester University Press.

Greig, J. (1988) 'Plant resources' in G. Astill and A. Grant (eds), *The Countryside of Medieval England*, Oxford: Blackwell, pp. 108–27.

Grenville, J. (1997) *Medieval Housing*, London: Leicester University Press.

Griffiths, R. A. (2007) 'Crossing the frontiers of the English realm in the fifteenth century' in H. Pryce and J. Watts (eds), *Power and Identity in the Middle Ages*, Oxford: Oxford University Press, 2007, pp. 211–25.

Gurnham, R. (2009) *A History of Lincoln*, Chichester: Phillimore.

Hall, D. (1982) *Medieval Fields* Princes Risborough: Shire.

—(1995) *The Open Fields of Northamptonshire*, Northampton: Northants. Record Society.

Hallam, H. E. (1965) *Settlement and Society: a Study of the Early Agrarian History of South Lincolnshire*, Cambridge: Cambridge University Press.

—(1981) *Rural England, 1066–1348*, London: Fontana.

Hare, J. (2009) 'Salisbury: the economy of a fifteenth-century provincial capital', *Southern History*, 31, 1–26.

Harke, H. (2002) 'Kings and warriors: population and landscape from post-Roman to Norman Britain' in P. Slack and R. Ward (eds), *The Peopling of Britain: the Shaping of a Human Landscape*, Oxford: Oxford University Press, pp. 145–75.

Harley, J. B. (1958) 'Population trends and agricultural developments from the Warwickshire Hundred Rolls of 1279', *Ec. Hist. Rev.*, 11, 8–18.

Harper-Bill, C. (1988) 'Dean Colet's convocation sermon and the pre-Reformation church in England', *History*, 73, 191–210.

Harrison, D. (1992) 'Bridges and economic development, 1300–1800', *Ec. Hist. Rev.*, 45, 240–61.

—(2004) *The Bridges of Medieval England: Transport and Society, 400–1800*, Oxford: Oxford University Press.

Harrison, D., McKeague, P. and Watson, B. (2011) 'England's fortified medieval bridges and bridge chapels: a new survey', *Medieval Settlement Research*, 25 [for 2010], 45–51.

Harrison, P. (2007) *Castles of God: Fortified Religious Buildings of the World*, Woodbridge: Boydell Press.

Harrison, S. (2002) 'Open fields and earlier landscapes: six parishes in south-east Cambridgeshire', *Landscapes*, 3 i, 35–54.

Hartwell, C. and Pevsner, N. (2009) *Lancashire: North*, New Haven, Yale University Press.

Harvey, M. (1983) 'Planned field systems in east Yorkshire: some thoughts on their origin', *Ag. Hist. Rev.*, 31, 91–103.

Harvey, P. D. A. (1989) 'Initiative and authority in settlement change' in M. Aston, D. Austin and C. Dyer (eds), *The Rural Settlements of Medieval England*, Oxford: Blackwell, pp. 31–43.

Haskins, C. H. (1918) *Norman Institutions*, New York: Harvard University Press.

Haslam, J. (2010) *Early Medieval Towns in Britain*, Oxford: Shire.

Hatcher, J. (1970) *Rural Economy and Society in the Duchy of Cornwall, 1300–1500*, Cambridge: Cambridge University Press.

—(1974) 'Myths, miners and agricultural communities', *Ag. Hist Rev.*, 22, 54–61.

—(1994) 'England in the aftermath of the Black Death', *Past and Present*, 144, 3–35.

Hatcher, J. and Bailey, M. (2001) *Modelling the Middle Ages*, Oxford: Oxford University Press.

Hayman, R. (2005) *Ironmaking: History and Archaeology of the Iron industry*, Stroud: Tempus.

Henry of Huntingdon, Historia Anglorum (1996) D. Greenway ed., Oxford, Clarendon Press.

Herring, P. (2006) 'Cornish strip fields' and 'Medieval fields at Brown Willy, Bodmin Moor' in S. Turner ed., *Medieval Devon and Cornwall, Shaping an Ancient Countryside*, Macclesfield: Windgather, pp. 44–77, 78–103.

Hey, D. (2000) 'Moorlands' in Thirsk (2000) pp. 188–209.

Higham, N. J. (2000) 'The Tatton Park project, part 2', *Journal of the Chester Archaeological Society*, 75 [for 1998–99], 61–133.

—(2004) *A Frontier Landscape: the North West in the Middle Ages*, Macclesfield: Windgather.

Higham, R. and Barker, P. (1992) *Timber Castles*, London: Batsford.

Hilton, R. H. (1957) 'Winchcombe Abbey' in H. P. R. Finberg, *Gloucestershire Studies*, Leicester: Leicester University Press.

—(1975) *The English Peasantry in the Later Middle Ages*, Oxford: Clarendon Press.

—(1983) *The Decline of Serfdom in Medieval England*, 2nd edn., London: Macmillan.

Hilton, R. H. and Rahtz, P. H. (1966) 'Upton, Gloucestershire, 1959–1964', *Transactions of the Bristol and Gloucestershire Archaeological Society*, 85, 70–146.

Hindle, B. P. (1998) *Medieval Roads and Tracks*, Princes Risborough: Shire.

Hinton, D. A. (2010) 'Deserted medieval villages and the objects found from them' in Dyer and Jones (2010) pp. 85–108.

Hislop, M. (2010) 'A missing link: a reappraisal of the date, architectural context and significance of the great tower of Dudley Castle', *Antiquaries Journal*, 90, 211–33.

Hodgkinson, J. (2008) *The Wealden Iron Industry*, Stroud: Tempus.

Hoey, L. R. (1995) 'The thirteenth-century choir and transepts of Rievaulx Abbey' in L. R. Hoey ed., *Yorkshire Monasticism: Archaeology, Art and Architecture*, Leeds: British Archaeological Association, pp. 97–116.

Hollister, C. W. (1965) *The Military Organization of Norman England*, Oxford: Clarendon Press.

Holt, J. C. (1965) *Magna Carta*, Cambridge: Cambridge University Press.

Holt, R. (1988) *The Mills of Medieval England*, Oxford: Blackwell.

Holt, R. and Rosser, G. (1990) *The Medieval Town, A Reader in English Urban History, 1200–1540*, London: Longman.

Homans, G. C. (1942) *English Villagers of the Thirteenth Century*, Cambridge, Mass.: Harvard University Press.

Hooke, D. (1985) *The Anglo-Saxon Landscape: the kingdom of the Hwicce*, Manchester: Manchester University Press.

—(1991) 'The relationship between ridge and furrow and mapped strip holdings', *Landscape History*, 13, 69–71.

—(1998) *The Landscape of Anglo-Saxon England*, London: Leicester University Press.

Hope-Taylor, B. (1957) 'The Norman motte at Abinger, Surrey, and its wooden castle' in R. L. S. Bruce-Mitford ed., *Recent Archaeological Excavations in Britain*, London, Routledge and Kegan Paul.

Hoppitt, R. (2007) 'Hunting Suffolk's parks: towards a reliable chronology' in Liddiard (2007) pp. 146–64.

Horrox, R. ed., (1994) *The Black Death*, Manchester: Manchester University Press.

Hoskins, W. G. (1963) *Provincial England,* London: Macmillan.

—(1978) *One Man's England*, London: BBC.

—(1988) *The Making of the English Landscape* (revised ed. by C. Taylor), London: Hodder and Stoughton.

Hoskins, W. G. and Finberg, H. P. R. (1952) *Devonshire Studies*, London: Cape.

Howard, M. (2007) *The Building of Elizabethan and Jacobean England*, New Haven: Yale University Press.

Hulme, R. (2007–8) 'Twelfth century great towers: the case for the defence' in *The Castle Studies Group Journal*, 21, 210–29.

Hurst, D. (2005) *Sheep in the Cotswolds*, Stroud: Tempus.

Hutchings, N. (1989) 'The plan of Whatborough: a study of the 16th century map of enclosure', *Landscape History*, 11, 83–92.

Inderwick, F. A. (1882) *The Story of King Edward and New Winchelsea*, London.

Ivens, R., Busby, P. and Shepard, N. (1995) *Tattenhoe and Westbury: two medieval settlements in Milton Keynes, Buckinghamshire*, Aylesbury: Buckinghamshire Archaeological Society.

Johnson, M. H. (2002) *Behind the Castle Gate: from Medieval to Renaissance*, London: Routledge.

Jones, M. J., Stocker, D. and Vince, A. (2003) *The City by the Pool*, Oxford: Oxbow.

Jones, R. (2010) 'Contrasting patterns of village and hamlet desertion in England' in Dyer and Jones (2010) pp. 8–27.

Jones, R. and Page, M. (2006) *Medieval Villages in an English Landscape: Beginnings and Ends*, Macclesfield: Windgather.

Jones, S. R. (1975–6) 'West Bromwich manor-house', *South Staffordshire Archaeological and Historical Society*, 17, 1–63.

Jones, S. R. and Smith, J. T. (1958) 'Manor house, Wasperton: an early 14th century timber-framed house', *Transactions of the Birmingham Archaeological Society*, 76, 19–28.

Jordan, W. K. (1964) *Philanthropy in England, 1480–1660: A Study of the Changing Pattern of English Social Aspirations*, London: Geo. Allen and Unwin.

Keene, D. (1990) 'The textile industry' in M. Biddle, *Object and Economy in Medieval Winchester*, Oxford: Oxford University Press, pp. 203–8.

Keene, M. (1976) 'Suburban growth' in M. W. Barley ed., *Plans and Topography of Medieval Towns*, London: Council for British Archaeology, pp. 71–82.

Kenyon, J. R. (1990) *Medieval Fortifications*, Leicester: Leicester University Press.

Kerridge, E. (1951) 'Ridge and furrow and agrarian history', *Ec. Hist. Rev.*, 4, 14–36.

Kershaw, I. (1973) 'The great famine and agrarian crisis in England, 1315–1322', *Past and Present*, 58, 3–50.

Kidson, P. (1994) 'Architectural history' in D. M. Owen ed., *A History of Lincoln Minster*, Cambridge: Cambridge University Press, pp. 14–46.

King, D. J. C. (1988) *The Castle in England and Wales: an Interpretative History*, London: Croom Helm.

King, D. J. C. and Alcock, L. (1969) 'Ringworks of England and Wales', *Chateau-Gaillard*, 3, 90–127.

—(1972) 'The field archaeology of mottes in England and Wales', *Chateau-Gaillard*, 5, 101–12.

Knowles, D. M. (1948) *Religious Orders in England*, I, Cambridge: Cambridge University Press.

—(1950) *The Monastic Order in England*, Cambridge: Cambridge University Press.

—(1955) *Religious Orders in England*, II, Cambridge: Cambridge University Press.

—(1979) *Religious Orders in England*, III, Cambridge: Cambridge University Press.

Knowles, D. M. and Hadcock, R. N. (1971) *Medieval Religious Houses of England and Wales*, London: Longman.

Kosminsky, E. A. (1956) *Studies in the Agrarian History of England in the Thirteenth Century*, R. H. Hilton ed., Oxford: Blackwell.

Langdon, J. (1982) 'The economics of horses and oxen in medieval England', *Ag. Hist. Rev.*, 30, 31–40.

—(1984) 'Horse hauling: a revolution in vehicle transport in twelfth- and thirteenth-century England?', *Past and Present*, 103, 37–66.

—(1994) 'Lordship and peasant consumerism in the milling industry of early fourteenth century England', *Past and Present*, 145, 3–46.

Langdon, J. and Maaschaele, J. (2006) 'Commercial activity and population growth in medieval England', *Past and Present*, 190, 35–81.

Langland, Piers Plowman (1959) J. F. Goodridge, ed. Harmondsworth: Penguin.

Laughton, J. and Dyer, C. (1999) 'Small towns in the east and west midlands in the later middle ages: a comparison', *Midland History*, 24, 24–52.

Lawrence, C. H. (1989) *Medieval Monasticism*, 2nd edn., London: Longman.

Le Patourel, H. E. J. (1973) *The Moated Sites of Yorkshire*, London: Society for Medieval Archaeology.

Lee, J. S. (2010) 'The functions and fortunes of English small towns at the close of the middle ages: evidence from John Leland's *Itinerary*', *Urban History*, 37, 3–25.

Lehmberg, S. E. (2005) *English Cathedrals, a History*, London: Hambledon and London.

Leland's Itinerary in England and Wales (1907) L. Toulmin-Smith ed., London: Bell.

Lennard, R. (1959) *Rural England, 1086–1135*, Oxford: Clarendon Press.

Lewis, C., Mitchell-Fox, P. and Dyer, C. (1997) *Village, Hamlet and Field: Changing Medieval Settlements in Central England*, Manchester: Manchester University Press.

Liber Memorandorum Ecclesie de Bernewelle (1907) J. W. Clark ed., Cambridge: Cambridge University Press.

Liddiard, R. (2003a) 'The deer parks of Domesday Book', *Landscapes*, 4.1, 4–23.

—(2003b) 'Introduction' to R. Liddiard ed., *Anglo-Norman Castles*, Woodbridge: Boydell Press.

—(2005) *Castles in Context: Power, Symbolism and Landscape, 1066 to 1500*, Macclesfield: Windgather.

—ed. (2007) *The Medieval Park, New Perspectives*, Macclesfield: Windgather.

Lilley, K. D., Lloyd, C. D. and Campbell, B. M. S. (2009) 'Mapping the realm: a new look at the Gough Map of Britain (c.1360)', *Imago Mundi: The International Journal for the History of Cartography*, 61, 1–28.

Lincolnshire Domesday and Lindsey Survey (1924) C. W. Foster and T. Longley (eds), Lincoln Record Society.

Linehan, C. D. (1966) 'Deserted sites and rabbit warrens on Dartmoor, Devon', *Medieval Archaeology*, 10, 113–39.

Little Domesday: Norfolk (2000) London: Alecto Historical Editions, I.

London Assize of Nuisance, 1301–1431: A Calendar (1973) H. M. Chew and W. Kellaway (eds) Leicester: London Record Society.

Luxford, J. M. (2005) *The Art and Architecture of Benedictine Monasteries, 1300–1540: A Patronage History*, Woodbridge: Boydell Press.

Maddicott, J. T. (1997) 'Plague in seventh century England', *Past and Present*, 156, 7–54.

Maddison, J. (1993) 'Building at Lichfield Cathedral during the episcopate of Walter Langton (1296–1321)' in J. Maddison ed., *Medieval Archaeology and Architecture at Lichfield*, London, British Archaeological Association, pp. 65–84.

Maitland, F. W. (1889) *Select Pleas in Manorial and other Seigneurial Courts*, I, London: Selden Society.

Marren, P. (1992) *The Wild Woods*, Newton Abbot: David and Charles.

Marshall, P. (2002) 'The great tower as residence' in G. Meirion-Jones, E. Impey and M. Jones (eds), *The Seigneurial Residence in Western Europe, AD c.800–1600*, Oxford: Archaeopress, pp. 27–44.

Masschaele, J. (1993) 'Transport costs in medieval England', *Ec. Hist. Rev.*, 46, 266–79.

Mate, M. (1991) 'The agrarian economy of south-east England before the Black Death: depressed or buoyant?' in B. M. S. Campbell ed., *Before the Black Death*, Manchester: Manchester University Press, pp. 79–109.

Mathieu, J. R. (1999) 'New methods on old castles: generating new ways of seeing', *Medieval Archaeology*, 43, 115–42.

McEvoy, L. H. (2011) 'Liminal spaces and the anchorite life in medieval Chester' in C. A. M. Clarke ed., *Mapping the Medieval City: Space, Place and Identity in Chester, c.1200–1600*, Cardiff: University of Wales Press, pp. 99–113.

McGuicken, R. (2010) 'Castle in context? Redefining the significance of Beeston Castle, Cheshire', *Journal of the Chester Archaeological Society*, 81, 65–82.

McNeill, T. (1992) *English Heritage Book of Castles*, London: Batsford.

Mellows, W. T. (1939) *Peterborough Local Administration: Churchwardens' Accounts 1467–1573 with Supplementary Documents 1107–1488*, Kettering: Northants. Record Society.

—(1947) *The Last Days of Peterborough Monastery*, Northampton, Northants. Record Society.

Mercer, E. (1975) *English Vernacular Houses*, London: Royal Commission on Historical Monuments, England.

Meredith, J. (2006) *The Iron industry of the Forest of Dean*, Stroud: Tempus.

Mew, K. (2000) 'The dynamics of lordship and landscape as revealed in a Domesday study of the *Nova Foresta*', *Anglo-Norman Studies*, 23, 155–66.

Miles, D. and Rowley, T. (1976) 'Tusmore deserted village', *Oxoniensia*, 41, 309–15.

Mileson, S. A. (2009) *Parks in Medieval England*, Oxford: Oxford University Press.

Millea, N. (2007) *The Gough Map: the earliest road map of Great Britain?*, Oxford: Bodleian Library.

Miller, E. and Hatcher, J. (1978) *Medieval England: Rural Society and Economic Change, 1086–1348*, London: Longman.

—(1995) *Medieval England: Towns, Commerce and Crafts, 1086–1348*, Harlow: Longman.

Monastic Constitutions of Lanfranc, D. Knowles (ed. and trans.) (2002) revised edn. by C. N. L. Brooke, Oxford: Oxford University Press.

Moorhouse, S. (2007) 'The medieval parks of Yorkshire: function, contents and chronology' in Liddiard (2007) pp. 99–127.

Morgan, P. (1988) *Domesday Book and the Local Historian*, London: Historical Association.

Morris, R. (1989) *Churches in the Landscape*, London: Dent.

Morriss, R. K. (2005) *Roads: Archaeology and Architecture*, Stroud: Tempus.

Mortimer, R. (2000) 'Village development and ceramic sequence: the middle to late Saxon village of Lordship Lane, Cottenham, Cambridgeshire', *Proceedings of the Cambridge Antiquarian Society*, 39, 5–33.

Muir, R. (1990) *Castles and Strongholds*, London: Macmillan.

—(2000) *The New Reading the Landscape: Fieldwork in Landscape History*, Exeter: University of Exeter Press.

—(2007) *Be Your Own Landscape Detective*, Stroud: Sutton.

Muir, R. and Muir, N. (1989) *Fields*, London: Macmillan.

Netherton, R. and Owen-Crocker, G. R. (eds) (2005) *Medieval Clothing and Textiles*, Woodbridge: Boydell Press.

New Testament 1526, William Tyndale (trans.) (2000) W. R. Cooper ed., British Library: Oxford.

Newman, J. and Pevsner, N. (2006) *The Buildings of England: Shropshire*, New Haven: Yale University Press.

Newman, P. (1998) *The Dartmoor Tin Industry: A Field Guide*, Newton Abbot: Chercombe.

—(2006) 'Tin working and the landscape of medieval Devon, c.1150–1700' in S. Turner ed., *Medieval Devon and Cornwall*, Macclesfield: Windgather, pp. 123–43.

Nightingale, P. (1996) 'The growth of London in the medieval English economy' in R. H. Britnell and J. Hatcher (eds), *Progress and Problems in Medieval England*, Cambridge: Cambridge University Press, pp. 89–106.

Oosthuizen, S. (1993) 'Isleham, a medieval inland port', *Landscape History*, 15, 29–36.

—(2003) 'The roots of the common fields: linking prehistoric and medieval field systems in west Cambridgeshire', *Landscapes*, 4 i, 40–64.

—(2005) 'New light on the origins of open field farming?', *Medieval Archaeology*, 49, 165–93.

—(2010) 'Medieval field systems and settlement nucleation: common or separate origins?' in N. J. Higham and M. J. Ryan (eds), *Landscape Archaeology of Anglo-Saxon England*, Woodbridge: Boydell Press, 107–31.

—(2011) 'The distribution of two- and three-field systems in south Cambridgeshire before about 1350', *Medieval Settlement Research*, 25 [for 2010], 21–31.

Ormrod, W. M. and Lindley, P. G. (eds) (1996) *The Black Death in England*, Stamford: Paul Watkins Publishing.

Page, F. M. (1934) *The Estates of Crowland Abbey*, Cambridge: Cambridge University Press.

Painter, S. (1949) *The Reign of King John*, Baltimore: Johns Hopkins Press.

Palin, W. (1844) 'Cheshire Farming: a report on the agriculture of Cheshire', *Journal of the Royal Agricultural Society of England*, 5.

Palliser, D. M. (2000) 'Introduction' in D. M. Palliser ed., *The Cambridge Urban History of Britain, I, 600–1540*, Cambridge: Cambridge University Press, pp. 3–15.

Palliser, D. M., Slater, T. R. and Dennison, E. P. (2000) 'The topography of towns, 600–1300' in D. M. Palliser ed., *The Cambridge Urban History of Britain, I, 600–1540*, Cambridge: Cambridge University Press, pp. 155–86.

Parker, V. (1971) *The Making of Kings Lynn*, Chichester: Phillimore.

Pearce, A. ed. (1995) *Mining in Shropshire*, Shrewsbury: Shropshire Books.

Peterken, G. F. (1993) *Woodland Conservation and Management*, 2nd edn. London: Chapman and Hall.

—(1996) *Natural Woodland: Ecology and Conservation in Northern Temperate Regions*, Cambridge: Cambridge University Press.

Petts, D. and Turner, S. (2009) 'Early medieval church groups in Wales and western England' in N. Edwards ed., *The Archaeology of the Early Medieval Celtic Churches*, Leeds: Maney, pp. 281–99.

Pevsner, N. and Hyde, M. (2010) *Buildings of England: Cumbria: Cumberland, Westmorland and Furness*, New Haven: Yale University Press.

Pevsner, N. and Neave, D. (2005) *The Buildings of Yorkshire: York and the East Riding*, New Haven: Yale University Press.

Pevsner, N. and Richmond, I (2002) *Buildings of Northumberland*, revised edn., New Haven: Yale University Press.

Phelps-Brown, E. H. and Hopkins, S. V. (1962a) 'Seven centuries of building wages', in E. M. Carus-Wilson ed., *Essays in Economic History*, II, London: Edward Arnold, pp. 168–78.

—(1962b) 'Seven centuries of the prices of consumables, compared with builders' wage rates', in E. M. Carus-Wilson ed., *Essays in Economic History*, London: Edward Arnold, II, pp. 179–96.

Phillips, A. D. M. and Phillips, C. B. (2002) *A New Historical Atlas of Cheshire*, Chester: Cheshire County Council and Cheshire Community Council Publications Trust.

Phythian-Adams, C. (1979) *Desolation of a City: Coventry and the Urban Crisis of the Late Middle Ages*, Cambridge: Cambridge University Press.

—(1992) 'Hoskins's England: a local historian of genius and the realisation of his theme', *Trans. Leics. Archaeol and Hist Soc.*, 66, 143–59.

Pinnell, J. (2009) *Wenlock Priory*, revised edn., London: English Heritage.

Pipe Rolls [31 Hen. I (1833) J. Hunter ed., Record Commission; 2–4 Hen. II (1844) J. Hunter ed., Record Commission; 5 Hen. II onwards (from 1884) Pipe Roll Society].

Platt, C. (1969) *The Monastic Grange in Medieval England: A Reassessment*, London: Macmillan.

—(1976a) *The English Medieval Town*, London: Secker and Warburg.

—(1976b) 'The evolution of towns: natural growth' in M. W. Barley ed., *Plans and Topography of Medieval Towns*, London: Council for British Archaeology, pp. 48–56.

—(1981) *The Parish Churches of Medieval England*, London: Secker and Warburg.

—(1982) *The Castle in Medieval England and Wales*, London: Secker and Warburg.

—(1984) *The Abbeys and Priories of Medieval England*, London: Secker and Warburg.

—(2007) 'Revisionism in castle studies: a caution', *Medieval Archaeology*, 51, 83–102.

Plucknett, T. F. T. (1949) *Legislation of Edward I*, Oxford: Oxford University Press.

Pollard, E., Hooper, M. D. and Moore, N. W. (1974) *Hedges*, London: Collins.

Port, G. (1987) *Rochester Castle*, London: English Heritage.

Postan, M. M. and Titow, J. Z. (1958–9) 'Heriots and prices on Winchester manors', *Ec. Hist. Rev.*, 11, 392–417.

Pounds, N. J. G. (1990) *The Medieval Castle in England and Wales: A Social and Political History*, Cambridge, Cambridge University Press.

Preston-Jones, A. and Rose, P. (1986) 'Medieval Cornwall', *Cornish Archaeology*, 25, 135–85.

Quiney, A. (2003) *Town Houses of Medieval Britain*, New Haven: Yale University Press.

Rackham, O. (1975) *Hayley Wood: its History and Ecology*, Cambridge: Cambridgeshire and Isle of Ely Naturalists' Trust.

—(1980) *Ancient Woodland: its History, Vegetation and Uses in England*, London: Edward Arnold.

—(1986) *The History of the Countryside*, London: Dent.

—(1990) *Trees and Woodland in the British Landscape*, revised edn., London: Dent.

Ramsay, N. (1991) 'Introduction' to J. Blair and N. Ramsay (eds), *English Medieval Industries: Craftsmen, Techniques, Products*, London: Hambledon, pp. xv–xxxiv.

Ravensdale, J. (1974) *Liable to Floods: Village Landscape on the Edge of the Fens* Cambridge: Cambridge University Press.

Records of the City of Norwich (1906–10) W. Hudson and J. C. Tingey (eds), Norwich and London: Jarrold and Sons.

Records of the Templars in England in the Twelfth Century (1935) B. A. Lees ed., London: British Academy.

Reeves, A. and Williamson, T. (2000) 'Marshes' in Thirsk (2000) pp. 150–66.

Regesta Regum Anglo-Normannorum, III (1968–69) H. A. Cronne and R. H. C. Davis (eds), Oxford: Clarendon Press.

Register of Edward the Black Prince, Part Three: Palatinate of Chester (1932) London: H. M. S. O.

Registrum Antiquissimum of the Cathedral Church of Lincoln II (1933) C. W. Foster ed., Lincoln Record Society, 28.

Registrum Antiquissimum of the Cathedral Church of Lincoln IV, (1937) C. W. Foster and K. Major ed., Lincoln Record Society, 32.

Registrum Simonis Langham (1956) A. C. Wood ed., Oxford: Oxford University Press.

Renn, D. F. (1968) *Norman Castles in Britain*, London: Baker.

Reynolds, S. (1977) *An Introduction to the History of English Medieval Towns*, Oxford: Clarendon Press.

Reynolds, S. and White, G. (1995) 'A survey of Aldford castle', *Cheshire Past*, 4, 14–15.

—(1997–8) 'A survey of Pulford castle', *Cheshire History*, 37, 23–5.

Richardson, A. (2005) *The Medieval Forest, Park and Palace of Clarendon, Wiltshire c.1200–c.1650: Reconstructing an Actual, Conceptual and Documented Wiltshire Landscape*, Oxford: Archaeopress.

—(2007) 'The King's chief delights: A landscape approach to the royal parks of post-Conquest England' in Liddiard (2007) pp. 27–48.

Rigby, S. H. (2010) 'Urban population in late-medieval England: the evidence of the lay subsidies', *Ec. Hist. Rev.*, 63, 393–417.

Rippon, S. (2002) 'Infield and outfield: the early stages of marshland colonisation and the evolution of medieval field systems' in T. Lane and J. Coles (eds), *Through Wet and Dry: essays in honour of David Hill*, Sleaford: Heritage Trust of Lincolnshire, pp. 54–70.

—(2008) *Beyond the Medieval Village: the Diversification of Landscape Character in Southern Britain*, Oxford: Oxford University Press.

Rippon, S., Claughton, P. and Smart, C. (2009) *Mining in a Medieval Landscape*, Exeter: University of Exeter Press.

Rippon, S., Fyfe, R. M. and Brown, A. G. (2006) 'Beyond villages and open fields: the origins and development of a historic landscape characterised by dispersed settlement in south-west England', *Medieval Archaeology*, 50, 31–70.

Robert de Torigni in *Chronicles of the Reigns of Stephen, Henry II and Richard I*, IV (1889) R. Howlett ed., London: Rolls Series.

Roberts, B. K. (1968) 'A study of medieval colonisation in the forest of Arden, Warwickshire', *Ag. Hist. Rev.*, 16, 101–16.

—(1987) *The Making of the English Village*, Harlow: Longman.

—(2008) *Landscapes, Documents and Maps: Villages in Northern England and Beyond, A.D. 900–1250*, Oxford: Oxbow.

Roberts, B. K. and Wrathmell, S. (2002) *Region and Place: a Study of English Rural Settlement*, London: English Heritage.

—(2003) *An Atlas of Rural Settlement in England*, revised edn., London: English Heritage.

Roberts, J. (1997) *Royal Landscape: The Gardens and Parks of Windsor*, New Haven, Yale University Press.

Robinson, D. M. (2002) *Buildwas Abbey*, London: English Heritage.

Rodwell, K. ed. (1975) *Historic Towns in Oxfordshire*, Oxford: Oxford Archaeological Unit.

Rodwell, W. (1981) *The Archaeology of the English Church*, London: Batsford.

—(1989) *English Heritage Book of Church Archaeology*, revised edn., London: Batsford.

Rodwell, W. and Rodwell, K. (1985, 1993) *Rivenhall: Investigation of a Villa, Church and Village, 1950–1977*, London: Council for British Archaeology.

Roe, M. and Marx, L., (eds) (1994) *Does Technology Drive History?: The Dilemma of Technological Determinism*, Cambridge, Mass.: MIT Press.

Roffey, S. (2007) *The Medieval Chantry Chapel: an Archaeology*, Woodbridge: Boydell Press.

Rogan, J. ed. (2000) *Bristol Cathedral: History and Architecture*, Stroud: Tempus.

Rous, J. (1745) *Historia Regum Angliae*, Oxford.

Rowe, A. (2007) 'The distribution of parks in Hertfordshire' in Liddiard (2007) pp. 128–45.

Rowley, T. (1978) *Villages in the Landscape*, London: Dent.

—(1982) 'Medieval field systems' in L. Cantor ed., *The English Medieval Landscape* London: Croom Helm, pp. 25–55.

—(1986) *The High Middle Ages, 1200–1550*, London: Routledge and Kegan Paul.

—(2001) *The Welsh Border: Archaeology, History and Landscape*, Stroud: The History Press.

Rowley, T. and Wood, J. (1982) *Deserted Villages*, Princes Risborough: Shire.

Rubin, M. (1987) *Charity and Community in Medieval Cambridge*, Cambridge: Cambridge University Press.

Rule of St Benedict (1984) D. Parry ed., London: Darton, Longman and Todd.

Salmon, J. (1941) 'The windmill in English medieval art', *Journal of British Archaeological Association*, 3rd series, 6, 88–102.

—(1966) 'A note on early tower windmills', *Journal of the British Archaeological Association*, 29, 75.

Salter, H. E. (1920) *Munimenta Civitatis Oxonie*, Devizes: Oxford Historical Society.

Schofield, J. (2003) *Medieval London Houses*, New Haven: Yale University Press.

Schofield, J. and Stell, G. (2000) 'The built environment, 1300–1540' in D. M. Palliser ed., *The Cambridge Urban History of Britain, I, 600–1540*, Cambridge: Cambridge University Press, pp. 371–93.

Schofield, J. and Vince, A. G. (2003) *Medieval Towns: the Archaeology of British Towns in their European Setting*, 2nd edn., London: Equinox Publishing.

Schofield, R. S. (1965) 'The geographical distribution of wealth in England, 1334–1649', *Ec. Hist. Rev.*, 18, 483–510.

Scott, I. R. (2001) 'Romsey abbey: Benedictine nunnery and parish church' in
    G. Keevil, M. Aston and T. Hall (eds), *Monastic Archaeology*, Oxford: Oxbow.
Searle, E. (1974) *Lordship and Community: Battle Abbey and its Banlieu,*
    1066–1538, Toronto: Pontifical Institute of Medieval Studies.
Shaw, M. (2009) *The Lead, Copper and Barytes Mines of Shropshire,* Woonton
    Almeley: Logaston.
Sheppard, J. A. (1974) 'Metrological analysis of regular village plans in Yorkshire',
    Ag. Hist. Rev., 22, 119–35.
—(1976) 'Medieval village planning in northern England: some evidence from
    Yorkshire', *Journal of Historical Geography,* 2, 3–20.
Short, B. (2000) 'Forests and wood-pasture in lowland England' in Thirsk (2000)
    pp. 122–49.
Slater, T. R. (1981) 'The analysis of burgage patterns in medieval towns', *Area* 13
    (3), 211–16.
Smith, E., Hutton, G. and Cook, O. (1976) *English Parish Churches,* London:
    Thames and Hudson.
Smith, R. M. (1991) 'Demographic developments in rural England, 1300–48:
    a survey', in B. M.S. Campbell ed., *Before the Black Death,* Manchester:
    Manchester University Press, pp. 25–77.
—(2002) 'Plagues and peoples: the long demographic cycle, 1250–1670' in P.
    Slack and R. Ward (eds), *The Peopling of Britain: the Shaping of a Human*
    Landscape, Oxford: Oxford University Press, pp. 177–210.
Smith, S. V. (2010) 'Houses and communities: archaeological evidence for
    variation in medieval peasant experience' in Dyer and Jones (2010) pp. 64–84.
Snape, M. G. (1980) 'Documentary evidence for the building of Durham
    Cathedral and its monastic buildings' in N. Coldstream and P. Draper
    (eds), *Medieval Art and Architecture at Durham Cathedral,* London: British
    Archaeological Association pp. 20–36.
Soden, I. ed. (2007) *Stafford Castle,* II, Stafford: Stafford Borough Council.
Stanier, P. (2000) *Stone Quarrying Landscapes: the Industrial Archaeology of*
    Quarrying, Stroud: Tempus.
Stenton, F. M. (1934) *Norman London,* London: Historical Association.
Stewart-Brown, R. (1916) 'The townfield of Liverpool, 1207–1807', *Trans. Hist.*
    Soc. Lancs. and Ches., 67, 1–51.
Stone, D. (2005) *Decision Making in Medieval Agriculture,* Oxford: Oxford
    University Press.
Strickland, M. (1992) 'Securing the north: invasion and the strategy of defence
    in twelfth-century Anglo-Scottish warfare' in M. Strickland ed., *Anglo-Norman*
    Warfare: Studies in Late Anglo-Saxon and Anglo-Norman Military Organization
    and Warfare, Woodbridge: Boydell, pp. 208–29.
Stringer, K. J. (1993) *The Reign of Stephen,* London: Routledge.
Swanson, H. (1999) *Medieval British Towns,* Basingstoke: Macmillan.
Swanson, R. N. (1989) *Church and Society in Late Medieval England,* Oxford:
    Blackwell.
Sykes, N. (2007) 'Animal bones and animal parks' in Liddiard (2007) pp. 49–62.
Sylvester, D. (1958) 'A note on three-course arable systems in Cheshire', *Trans.*
    Hist. Soc. Lancs and Ches., 110, 183–6.
Taylor, A. J. (1958) 'Military architecture' in Poole, A. L. ed., *Medieval England,*
    Oxford: Clarendon Press, I, 98–125.

Taylor, C. (1973) *The Cambridgeshire Landscape*, London: Hodder and Stoughton.

—(1974) *Fieldwork in Medieval Archaeology*, London: Batsford.

—(1975) *Fields in the English Landscape*, London: Dent.

—(1977) 'Polyfocal settlement and the English village', *Medieval Archaeology*, 21, 189–93.

—(1979) *Roads and Tracks of Britain*, London: Dent.

—(1983) *Village and Farmstead: a History of Rural Settlement in England*, London: George Philip.

—(2000) 'Medieval ornamental landscapes', *Landscapes*, I, 38–55.

—(2007) 'Reason misplaced', *Medieval Settlement Research Group Annual Report*, 21 [for 2006], 7–9.

Taylor, C. and Fowler, P. J. (1978) 'Roman fields into medieval furlongs?' in H. C. Bowen and P. J. Fowler, *Early Land Allotment*, Oxford: British Archaeological Reports, pp. 159–62.

Thirsk, J. (1953) 'The Isle of Axholme before Vermuyden', *Ag. Hist. Rev.*, 1, 16–28.

—(1997) *Alternative Agriculture: A History from the Black Death to the Present Day*, Oxford: Oxford University Press.

—(2000) *Rural England: an Illustrated History of the Landscape*, Oxford: Oxford University Press.

Thompson, M. W. (1987) *The Decline of the Castle*, Cambridge: Cambridge University Press.

—(1991) *The Rise of the Castle*, Cambridge: Cambridge University Press.

—(2001) *Cloister, Abbot and Precinct in Medieval Monasteries*, Stroud: Tempus.

Thorpe, H. (1962) 'The lord and the landscape' *Transactions of the Birmingham Archaeological Society*, 80, 38–77.

Turner, M. (1980) *English Parliamentary Enclosure: its Historical Geography and Economic History*, Folkestone: Dawson.

Turner, S. (2006) *Making a Christian Landscape: the Countryside in Early Medieval Cornwall, Devon and Wessex*, Exeter: University of Exeter Press.

Utopia by Sir Thomas More, translated by Ralph Robynson 1556 (1999) D. H. Sacks ed., Boston, Mass.: Bedford/St Martin's.

Varey, S. M. (2008) 'Society and the Land – the Changing Landscape of Baschurch, north Shropshire, c.1550–2000', unpublished Ph.D., University of Liverpool.

Verey, D. and Brooks, A. (2002) *Gloucestershire I: the Cotswolds*, New Haven: Yale University Press.

Victoria History of the Counties of England (1900–, in progress), several editors and publishers.

Visitations of the Diocese of Lincoln, 1517–1531 (1940) A. Hamilton Thompson ed., Lincoln Record Society.

Visitations of Religious Houses II (1918) A. Hamilton Thompson ed., Lincoln Record Society.

Wade-Martins, P. (1980) *Fieldwork and Excavation on Village Sites in Launditch Hundred, Norfolk*, Dereham: East Anglian Archaeology, 10.

Waites, B. (1997) *Monasteries and the Landscape in North-East England*, Rutland: Multum in Parvo Press.

Wake, J. (1922) 'Communitas villae', *English Historical Review*, 37, 406–13.

Walcott, M. E. (1869) 'Inventories and Valuations of Religious Houses at the time of the Dissolution', *Archaeologia*, 43, 207–11.

Walsham, A. (2011a) *The Reformation of the Landscape: Religion, Identity and Memory in Early Modern Britain and Ireland*, Oxford: Oxford University Press.

—(2011b) 'The Reformation of the generations: youth, age and religious change in England, c.1500–1700', *Transactions of the Royal Historical Society*, 6th series 21, 93–121.

Walter Map, De Nugis Curialium (1983) M. R. James, C. N. L. Brooke and R. A. B. Mynors (eds), Oxford: Clarendon Press.

Walter of Henley and other Treatises on Estate Management and Accounting, D. Oschinsky ed. (1971) Oxford: Clarendon Press.

Walton, R. (1991) 'Textiles' in J. Blair and N. Ramsay (eds), *English Medieval Industries: Craftsmen, Techniques, Products*, London: Hambledon, pp. 319–54.

Wardle, T. (2009) *England's First Castle*, Stroud: History Press.

Warner, P. (1987) *Greens, Commons and Clayland Colonisation: the Origins and Development of Greenside Settlement in East Suffolk*, Leicester: Leicester University Press.

Warren, A. K. (1985) *Anchorites and their Patrons in Medieval England*, Berkeley: University of California Press.

Watson, C. E. ed. (1932) 'Minchinhampton Custumal' in *Transactions of the Bristol and Gloucestershire Archaeolical Society*, 54, 203–384.

Watts, M. (2002) *The Archaeology of Mills and Milling*, Stroud: Tempus.

Webb, S. and Webb, B. (1906) *The Parish and the County*, London: Longmans.

—(1913) *The Story of the King's Highway*, London: Longmans Green.

Welander, D. (1991) *The History, Art and Architecture of Gloucester Cathedral*, Stroud: Alan Sutton.

West, J. (1983) *Town Records*, Chichester: Phillimore.

Wheatley, A. (2004) *The Idea of the Castle in Medieval England*, Woodbridge: York Medieval Press/Boydell Press.

Wheeler, P. T. and Wood, B. A. (1987) 'The reorganisation of the open fields at Laxton, Nottinghamshire, 1900–1910', *Trent Geographer*, 11, 2–15.

White, A. (2003) *Lancaster: A History*, Chichester: Phillimore.

White, G. J. (1988) 'Glimpses of the open field landscape', *Cheshire History*, 21, 6–20.

—(1995) 'Open fields and rural settlement in medieval west Cheshire' in T. Scott and P. Starkey, *The Middle Ages in the North West*, Oxford: Leopard's Head Press, pp. 15–35.

—(2000) *Restoration and Reform: Recovery from Civil War in England, 1153–1165*, Cambridge: Cambridge University Press.

—(2008) 'Royal income and regional trends' in P. Dalton and G. J. White (eds), *King Stephen's Reign*, Woodbridge: Boydell Press, pp. 27–43.

—(2012) 'The enclosure of west Cheshire: keeping ahead of "Champion England"' in S. M. Varey and G. J. White (eds), *Landscape History Discoveries in the North West*, Chester: University of Chester Press.

William of Malmesbury, Gesta Regum Anglorum (1998–99) R. A. B. Mynors, R. M. Thomson and M. Winterbottom (eds), Oxford: Clarendon Press.

William of Malmesbury, Historia Novella (1998) E. J. King and K. R. Potter (eds), Oxford: Clarendon Press.

William Worcestre: the Topography of Medieval Bristol (2000) F. Neale ed., Bristol: Bristol Record Society.

Williams, A. (2003) 'A Bell-house and a burh-geat: lordly residences in England before the Norman Conquest' in R. Liddiard ed., *Anglo-Norman Castles*, Woodbridge: Boydell Press, pp. 23–40.

Williams, S. R. (1997) *West Cheshire from the Air: an Archaeological Anthology*, Chester: Chester City Council.

Williams, V. and White, G. J. (1988) *Adult Education and Social Purpose: A History of the WEA Eastern District, 1913–1988*, Cambridge: WEA Eastern District.

Williamson, T. (1986) 'The development of settlement in N.W. Essex: the results of a recent field survey', *Essex Archaeology and History*, 17, 120–32.

—(1997) *The Norfolk Broads: A Landscape History*, Manchester: Manchester University Press.

—(2003) *Shaping Medieval Landscapes*, Macclesfield: Windgather.

—(2006) *The Archaeology of Rabbit Warrens*, Princes Risborough: Shire.

—(2007) '*Region and Place*: some queries', *Medieval Settlement Research Group Annual Report*, 21 [for 2006], 18–19.

—(2010) 'At pleasure's lordly call: the archaeology of emparked settlements', in Dyer and Jones (2010) pp. 162–81.

Wilson, C. (1992) *The Gothic Cathedral: the Architecture of the Great Church, 1130–1530*, London: Thames and Hudson.

Winchester, A. J. L. (1987) *Landscape and Society in Medieval Cumbria*, Edinburgh: Donald.

—(1993) 'Field, wood and forest – landscapes of medieval Lancashire' in A. G. Crosby ed., *Lancashire Local Studies*, Preston: Carnegie Publishing, pp. 7–27.

—(2000) *The Harvest of the Hills*, Edinburgh: Edinburgh University Press.

—(2003) 'Demesne livestock farming in the Lake District: the vaccary at Gatesgarth, Buttermere, in the later thirteenth century', *Transactions of the Cumberland & Westmorland Antiquarian & Archaeology Society*, 3, 109–18.

—(2007) 'Baronial and manorial parks in Medieval Cumbria', in Liddiard (2007) pp. 165–84.

Wood, M. (1965) *The English Medieval House*, London: Dent.

Wrathmell, S. (1989a) 'Peasant houses, farmsteads and villages on north-east England' in M. Aston, D. Austin and C. Dyer (eds), *The Rural Settlements of Medieval England*, Oxford: Blackwell, pp. 247–67.

—(1989b) *Domestic Settlement 2: Medieval Peasant Farmsteads*, York: University of York.

Wrigley, E. A. (1986) 'Urban growth and agricultural change: England and the continent in the early modern period' in R. I. Rotberg and T. K. Rabb (eds), *Population and Economy: Population and History from the Traditional to the Modern World*, Cambridge: Cambridge University Press, pp. 123–68.

Wrigley, E. A. and Schofield, R. S. (1989) The *Population History of England*, 2nd edn., Cambridge: Cambridge University Press.

Index

Page references to illustrations are in bold italics